1997

Arenas of Conflict

Arenas of Conflict

Milton and the Unfettered Mind

Edited by
Kristin Pruitt McColgan
and Charles W. Durham

SUP

Selinsgrove: Susquehanna University Press
London: Associated University Presses

Associated University Presses
440 Forsgate Drive
Cranbury, NJ 08512

Associated University Presses
16 Barter Street
London WC1A 2AH, England

Associated University Presses
P.O. Box 338, Port Credit
Mississauga, Ontario
Canada L5G 4L8

The paper used in this publication meets the requirements of the American National Standard for Permanence of Paper for Printed Library Materials Z39.48–1984.

Library of Congress Cataloging-in-Publication Data

Arenas of conflict : Milton and the unfettered mind / edited by
Kristin Pruitt McColgan and Charles W. Durham.
  p.   cm.
Includes index.
ISBN 0-945636-93-8 (alk. paper)
1. Milton, John, 1608–1674—Criticism and interpretation.
2. Milton, John, 1608–1674—Knowledge and learning.   3. Great
Britain—Intellectual life—17th century.   I. McColgan, Kristin
Pruitt.   II. Durham, Charles W.
PR3588.A74   1997
821'.4—dc20
                                                          96-31256
                                                          CIP

PRINTED IN THE UNITED STATES OF AMERICA

To *William B. Hunter and Joseph Wittreich,*
who have visited the "Heav'nly Muse,"
with gratitude for sharing their
"Light from above" with us.

Contents

Acknowledgments

WE are grateful to the Middle Tennessee State University Faculty Research Committee for a grant that facilitated the editing of this volume; to Kevin J. Donovan for continuing to work with us on the many aspects of conference planning; to John T. Shawcross for his total support of everything we attempt; to Donald P. McDonough and a host of lively participants and panelists for helping to ensure the success of the Second Southeastern Conference on John Milton; to the Virginia Peck Foundation Trust Fund Committee for a grant that made that conference a reality; to our colleagues at Christian Brothers University and Middle Tennessee State University for supporting our projects and encouraging our efforts; to our families for readily granting us the Miltonic freedom to complete this volume; to Lucy and Paul Dampier for providing bed and board on numerous occasions and a trip to Keeneland on one very special one; and especially to our contributors for being generous with their time and timely with their essays and for demonstrating what Wittreich, later in these pages, calls "the enduring value of discussion, debate, dispute, dissent."

Introduction

"I cannot praise a fugitive and cloistered virtue, unexercised and un-breathed, that never sallies out and sees her adversary, but slinks out of the race where the immortal garland is to be run for, not without dust and heat" (728).[1] So wrote John Milton in *Areopagitica,* one of many testaments to his willingness to engage in "wars of Truth" (796) and to champion mental and spiritual freedom, often exercised amidst the "dust and heat" of public controversy. That Milton courted controversy, that he sought out "arenas of conflict" where, with his unfettered mind, he might "try the matter by dint of argument" (746) and purify the argument by "trial . . . by what is contrary" (728) is evidenced in prose tracts that he wrote with varied purposes. For example, in an early academic exercise delivered at Cambridge (*Prolusion 1*), the young orator envisioned an environment charged with contention, with "the quarrels that the competitive spirit en-genders in colleges among those who are interested in different subjects and even among those who pursue the same subjects with different conceptions of them" and voiced his appreciation of the "friendly" few, whose "ap-proval" meant far more "than that of countless legions of ignorant fellows who have no mind" (595). Much later, in the *Christian Doctrine* (itself a field of argument, as William B. Hunter's researches into its authorship suggest), undertaken to redress the theological abuses of "indolent credu-lity," Milton begs "lovers of truth not to cry out that the Church is thrown into confusion by that freedom of discussion and inquiry that is granted to the schools" (901).

Similarly, Milton the poet presented characters whose reason and faith are tested in hostile circumstances. In *Comus,* the Lady challenges her would-be seducer:

> Thou canst not touch the freedom of my mind
> With all thy charms, although this corporal rind
> Thou hast immanacl'd.
>
> (663–65)

Adam and Eve, exiled from Paradise "To the subjected Plain" (*Paradise Lost,* 12.640), enter a world of "dust and heat" where patriarchs like Noah will stand "Against allurement, custom, and a World / Offended; fearless

11

of reproach and scorn" (12.810–11), anticipating the Son in *Paradise Regained*, who resists Satan's temptation to "Be famous then / By wisdom; as thy Empire must extend, / So let extend thy mind o'er all the world" (4.221–23), by countering that "he who receives / Light from above, from the fountain of light, / No other doctrine needs" (288–90). And Samson, blind and captive, responds to the Philistine command to appear at the festival of Dagon: "Commands are no constraints. If I obey them, / I do it freely" (1372–73).

In the opening essay in this collection, Joseph Wittreich examines seventeenth-century interpretations of Genesis, from commentators like William Whately, who promoted patriarchal, misogynistic views of women, to more egalitarian views of the sexes promulgated by men like Henry Ainsworth and John Salkeld, in order to establish the context for Milton's portrayal of Eve in *Paradise Lost*. Wittreich argues that "what we have been thinking of as a *tradition* needs to be reconceived in a way that allows for contending perspectives" and that "In [Milton's] poetry no less than in his prose writings, a hermeneutics of certainty is gradually displaced by a hermeneutics of suspicion and interrogation." *Paradise Lost*, then, embodies the "arenas of conflict" implicit in Milton's day, and, as "a battleground for its culture's contending viewpoints and ideologies, testifies to the enduring value of discussion, debate, dispute, dissent."

In line with Wittreich's suggestion that readers' assumptions regarding politics, theology, and gender enter into their interpretations of Scripture and of Miltonic texts, William B. Hunter maintains that the assumption that Milton authored the *Christian Doctrine* (*De Doctrina Christiana*, also referred to as *DDC*) has contributed to critical distortions of the canonical works and to the attribution of "some eccentric religious doctrines now generally accepted as Milton's but that find sole or major support from *DDC* alone." Hunter brings Wittreich's "spirit of contradiction" and interrogation to an examination of the evidence supporting a Continental source for the *Christian Doctrine* and maintains that scholars should use caution in "basing the discussion of their ideas upon *DDC* alone without concurrent support from the canonical works."

Whereas Wittreich investigates male perspectives of women revealed in seventeenth-century scriptural commentaries, David Boocker researches the attitudes of such nineteenth-century American feminists as Sarah Grimké and Elizabeth Cady Stanton toward Milton as "'the man who did so much to popularize the idea of woman's subordination to man.'" Boocker demonstrates that *Paradise Lost* was often used as propaganda to support women's subordination and their prescribed gender roles and concludes that "attacking [Milton] was necessary . . . because attaining equal status in an extreme patriarchal society depended on it."

In another essay examining the historical contexts of Milton's work,

Blake Greenway contends that Milton's portrayal of "the one just man, the one who will stand against the many" in his *History of Britain* was inspired by the author's own resistance to "the domineering and liberty-reducing elements" of the Puritan Parliament. Identifying differences between Milton and earlier historians, Greenway believes that "Although Milton's hero might admittedly serve some type of larger partisan end, the pattern of his heroism always moves from the individual spark within one figure and then disperses outwardly toward the larger mass."

In the first of the essays with a concentrated focus on Milton's poetry, Jay Russell Curlin sees, in the "fusion of academic declamation with drama" in *Comus*, evidence of Milton's successful experimentation with genre. The "friendly 'disagreement' between brothers" represents "a vision of what disputation could be," of what Wittreich identifies as "the enduring value of discussion, debate, dispute, dissent"; according to Curlin, the elder and younger brothers engage "in a mutual quest for truth," and "Their debate . . . seems in retrospect to be more like discussion than disputation."

Hope A. Parisi's examination of the Lady's ability to "[stand] strong in reason" in *Comus* combines two concerns of previous essays: gender roles and individual autonomy. Viewing Lady Alice as a model of "a genderless intellect" in which "Reason was a potential democratizer," Parisi asserts that Milton's portrayal of Alice "anticipates later feminists' efforts to abstract reason from among the differences between genders in order to support women's claim for education."

Steven Jablonski unearths another of Wittreich's "contending perspectives" in considering a seeming contradiction in *Paradise Lost:* "How," he questions, "could Milton, an Arminian, be both a professed enemy of earthly kings and a proponent of liberty and yet represent God in his greatest work as a king and Satan as a proponent of liberty?" Responding to this paradox, Jablonski surveys seventeenth-century views of the relation between free will and political liberty, analyzes Milton's depiction of Heaven in *Paradise Lost,* and concludes that "because the problem for Milton was not simply that earthly monarchs seldom behaved like God but that earthly subjects seldom behaved like angels, he eventually decided that only a well-designed and carefully limited republic would serve through its institutions the sovereignty of reason that he could not otherwise take for granted."

Robert Thomas Fallon pursues a similar theme in suggesting that "when Satan sounds like Oliver Cromwell, the champion of the English Revolution, and God Almighty for all the world like the King of England, one is hard-pressed to know where to place the poet within the spectrum of allegiances of his day." However, he argues that "the political structures of *Paradise Lost* do not reflect the poet's political allegiances," that the various governments in the poem reflect a "politics of love" or its antithesis, and that, finally, it is foolish to attempt to reconcile ideology with art, political position with poetic achievement.

Whereas Fallon asserts that "God's love is confirmed, and defined, by its opposite," Alice M. Mathews considers God's justice in *Paradise Lost* from the perspective of Michel Foucault's work on penal systems and Elizabeth Fuller's study of motion in *Paradise Lost*. In viewing judgment as an announcement of guilt and punishment as an application of "natural principles," Mathews counters critical interpretations of Milton's God as punitive and authoritarian, outlining instead "a system based on harmony as an essential good in God's creation and on motion as a means of dealing with sin." In his poem, Milton formulates a divine plan that works "toward the preservation or restoration of purity" through the "ejection of impurity followed by a recoiling of impurity upon itself."

Mary F. Norton, in relating the observations of contemporary scientific chaos theorists to Milton's depiction of Chaos, Eden, and Earth in *Paradise Lost*, also sees patterns in the poet's generation of "increasingly complex moral systems," and she identifies movement, or "the inevitability of change," as a distinctive feature of the "nonlinear" world of the poem, in which "no system is static." Challenging critical assumptions that Chaos is "degenerative or evil" or a principle reflecting "the mere antithesis of order," Norton asserts that "Milton's treatment of Chaos anticipates the primary claim of chaos theory, that chaos is 'order's precursor or partner rather than its opposite'" and, as "the beginning of a continuum of creation," it "must be evaluated as an intrinsic, inexorable force in the poem's physical and moral universe."

Also rejecting views of Milton's Chaos as evil or, at best, neutral in light of modern chaos theory that the poet brilliantly anticipated in *Paradise Lost*, Catherine Gimelli Martin suggests that the source of "problematic responses" to Milton's allegorical representation are Chaos's "ambiguous ontological status" and "an apparent hostility to his putatively divine origin." Nonetheless, her analysis uncovers a "monistic continuity of epic processes wholly in harmony with Milton's philosophical materialism," a fusion of scientific principles and the "*ex deo* form of creation." Because "*in potentia* its universal physical properties remain essentially on the side of life rather than the death principle," because Milton associates its "vacuities with those of divine freedom," Martin concludes that "Milton makes his reformed Chaos far more positive than negative, a medium of regeneration as well as choice."

Angelic and human natures, not allegorical figures, are the focus of Janna Thacher Farris's investigation of the apocryphal Book of Tobit as "Milton's source for Raphael's intervention into Adam and Eve's prelapsarian world in *Paradise Lost*." Her comparison supports the claim that "Milton intentionally reduces the hierarchical distance between Raphael and the prelapsarian humans in order to stress the perfection of paradisal existence." In having Raphael associate with Adam and Eve as friend and companion rather than as a superior being, the role Raphael assumes in the story of Tobias, "Milton successfully illustrates yet another significant loss to humankind as a result of the Fall."

Anna K. Nardo, examining Milton's angelology from a broader perspective, also considers the relationship between angels and human beings, their common "potential to fail," and what angels can learn as a result of their interactions with Adam and Eve. Milton's "subplot of angelic education" in *Paradise Lost* demonstrates that through seemingly futile tasks, such as "guarding Eden and Heaven, the good angels learn their own limitations, experience and manifest the truth of their intuitions about God's love, and discover the vulnerability of the human charges they must learn to love. Through their relations with humankind, they confront what they could never have known intuitively—the poignancy of human time, the love of man and woman, the misery of fallen humanity, and their future roles in salvation history."

"[T]he misery of fallen humanity" is aptly illuminated in Louis Schwartz's discussion of seventeenth-century obstetrics and Milton's allegorical presentation of Sin in book 2 of *Paradise Lost*, in which the key images are those of "violent, incestuous sexuality and painful, disfiguring, and dangerous childbirth." As Schwartz documents, in Milton's time "the childbed was a place in which men and women regularly confronted some of the most difficult aspects of the human condition," and the poet was surprisingly sensitive to "the emotional and spiritual problems presented by . . . catastrophic circumstances." An understanding of these circumstances gives to "Sin's pitiable and extravagant account of her own experience . . . a referential concreteness not wholly accounted for by an allegorical reading" and supports Milton's definition of "common sin" in the *Christian Doctrine*.

In another investigation of bodily distress as a result of sin, Peter M. McCluskey demonstrates that Milton "consistently emblematizes folly with flatulence in his prose and poetry, particularly in *Paradise Lost*, where folly and flatulence figure prominently." In tracing this imagery from *Prolusion* 6 through *Paradise Lost*, McCluskey argues for the Miltonic emphasis on "temperance in diet and learning to nourish us both in this world and in the next." Without it, McCluskey and Milton conclude, "we will inherit the wind."

A more positive approach to the theme of nourishment and temperance is advanced by W. Gardner Campbell, who focuses on the unfallen world and bodily satisfaction. His analysis of Milton's treatment of paradisal appetite demonstrates that it "is strikingly similar to certain aspects of the philosophy of Nicholas of Cusa," who "imagines a perfect food which satisfies hunger and quickens appetite simultaneously." According to Campbell, in Milton's Paradise "you can eat all you want, secure in knowing that you'll always be full, and always want more, and always be able to eat more"; there, Campbell contends, "The ontological provocation of life . . . is much too much—and thus just enough."

Gender as an "arena of conflict" in Milton's poetry is the subject of the final three essays in the collection. Joan S. Bennett examines the "pivotal" roles of Eve in Paradise Lost and Dalila in Samson Agonistes, roles larger than those of their biblical counterparts. After the Fall, Eve pulls Adam out of his "deadly isolation" through her "commitment to their particular relationship." Dalila's encounter with Samson, "her insistence on relationship, pulls a despairing Samson back into history." In both these "androcentric" works, woman's "attractiveness and attraction figure the divine pull of humans into relationships with one another, both domestic and political. Her insistence both on being her own 'other' self and on holding onto relationship is an insistence on the praxis that requires phronesis, or right reason, which is both private and public." Like Wittreich, Bennett argues that "all the serious questions in Milton's poetry are raised not so much to be 'answered' as to be 'deepened' or 'opened out,'" and her consideration of Milton's "sense of 'woman'" deepens and opens out "within the framework of Milton's radical Christian humanism."

From the vantage point of Boccaccio's de casibus tradition and portrayals of Delilah in Chaucer, Lydgate, and seventeenth-century misogynists, Lee A. Jacobus investigates the confrontation between Samson and Dalila, finding it "one of the most distinctively gendered agons in all western literature." Because of the misogynistic tradition, Jacobus believes that the poet's "treatment of Dalila is one of the ultimate tests of his attitude toward misogyny," and that, in his revisionist drama, he "avoids condemning Dalila as a woman even though he condemns her as a person." Despite Milton's use of the serpentine imagery associated with misogynistic depictions, Dalila is, according to Jacobus, "sympathetic to most readers upon initial contact," and he concludes that "her crime against Samson is not specifically a woman's crime. It is, instead, an act of betrayal painfully gendered by the circumstances of being married to Samson."

Stella Revard, like Bennett, regards the scriptural presentations of Eve and Delilah as "only half the story for Samson Agonistes and Paradise Lost." In examining Milton's adaptation of, and additions to, biblical sources, Revard contends that Delilah's temptation of Samson in the Bible prepares "us for the second tempting in Samson Agonistes, and the scene of Eve's morning interview with her husband prepares us for Milton's biblically based account of her encounter with the Serpent. Knowing what the biblical Delilah said before or the biblical Eve later affects our view of Milton's dramatic confrontations in his drama and epic." On the one hand, his construction of the meeting between Samson and Dalila replicates the biblical temptation, but "in having her deny the one motive the Bible assigns to her, Milton makes us seriously reexamine the motives of this biblical temptress." On the other hand, Eve's colloquy with Adam shows "that [she] could have used her reason . . . to engage in fruitful debate and to carry her own arguments against the Serpent by applying the same skills she had in debate with her husband." Revard argues that "Both Miltonic Man *and* Miltonic Woman can stand alone. This is perhaps Milton's most important addition to the Genesis text."

The contents of this collection were originally presented in shorter forms at the Second Southeastern Conference on John Milton at Middle Tennessee State University, Murfreesboro, Tennessee, 21–23 October 1993. In their sometimes complementary, sometimes contradictory, and consistently interrogative views of Milton and his work, these essays offer an arena of debate for future studies. For, as Wittreich asserts, "By dislodging commonplaces and effecting dislocations, contradictions open seemingly closed systems, or enlarge those needlessly constructed, and, admitting to the possibility of coexisting meanings and rival interpretations, stimulate the pursuit of truth even as they keep all notions of truth contingent, perspectival." Or, as Milton himself claimed in *Areopagitica*, "Where there is much desire to learn, there of necessity will be much arguing, much writing, many opinions; for opinion in good men is but knowledge in the making" (743). According to Wittreich, "Criticism of the highest order unfetters—it does not constrain—the mind." Of course, so, too, does literature of the highest order.

Notes

1. John Milton, *Areopagitica*, in *John Milton: Complete Poems and Major Prose*, ed. Merritt Y. Hughes (New York: Odyssey, 1957). All references to Milton's poetry and prose are to this edition and are noted parenthetically in the text.

Arenas of Conflict

"He Ever Was A Dissenter": Milton's Transgressive Maneuvers in *Paradise Lost*

Joseph Wittreich

Mr. *Busire* having dropt in, was avised to ask Mr. *Milton* why, having had an university Education, he had not entered the Church. He replied, drylie enough, because he woulde not subscribe himselfe *Slave* to anie Formularies of Men's making.

Anne Manning

Over the centuries, many Miltonists have supposed that, while in touch with heterodox, esoteric, and peripheral traditions, Milton eschews them in his poetry, which, evading what is marginal in the poet's culture, embraces only its central truths, many of which are scriptural and most of them the common glosses of theologians. The notion that "there is something more ultimate than the scriptures in terms of which the scriptures need to be explained" would be an anathema to Milton's contemporaries for whom, says one critic, "the scriptures would have been used to explain everything else. The Renaissance, whatever else it may have done, had done nothing to question this tradition" of scriptural authority and interpretive "complacency."[1] Implicit in this assumption are two equations: Milton's thinking *equals* the thinking of his contemporaries; and their thinking, broadly speaking, *equals* Renaissance thought, which itself, again implicitly, observes the very traditions that it fulfills and, rather than challenging, confirms. Whether these formulae elucidate the Renaissance mind is for others to decide. At issue in this essay is whether they pertain to Milton for whom the matter is simple: the Scriptures still need and regularly receive explanations authorized by ongoing revelation. In his poetry no less than in his prose writings, a hermeneutics of certainty is gradually displaced by a hermeneutics of suspicion and interrogation.

Milton's habits of thought need studying in their own right and, with respect to scriptural interpretation, force the acknowledgment of an essential difference between biblical and literary hermeneutics where in the first

21

instance, questions are designed to evoke existing answers but where in the latter enterprise, questions uproot the usual answers, putting in their place new interpretive possibilities. Such acknowledgment of Milton's agenda comes quickly from Sir Allen Apsley who, once he has indicted poets for roving and wandering in "defective Traditions," creates a counter-poem called *Order and Disorder*, presumably with *Paradise Lost* in mind, as fortification against its transgressive maneuvers and their possibly corrupting influence. In doing so, he affords the reminder that the more conservative of Milton's commentators often move against his poetic procedures.[2] Such critics uproot the ambiguities he implants in his poems, and remove the contradictions therein, thus turning *Paradise Lost* into a series of predictable answers to the perplexing questions it poses.

If the Bible typically produces a hermeneutics of confirmation, Milton's poetry yields a hermeneutics of inquiry. If the biblical exegete says, this is how to read the text, this is what it means, the literary hermeneut (like Milton) wonders with Odo Marquard: "Can this text not be understood differently—and in case that is not enough—still differently, and then differently once again?"[3] Although Milton's poems may emerge from sometimes monolithic biblical traditions and enunciate their interpretive commonplaces, they also belong within the orbit of literary hermeneutics and dialogic discourse, thus promoting open rather than closed readings at a time when received interpretations of scriptural texts are themselves becoming riddled with contradictions. Even if it were not always so, it was certainly true in the seventeenth century that the Christian tradition of scriptural interpretation, in the words of James Grantham Turner, was becoming "profoundly and incurably restless, condemned perpetually to shuttle between dichotomies that it must raise but cannot solve" so that, in *Paradise Lost*, "multiple responses [to the Book of Genesis] are brought to a head."[4] The inconsistency, diversity, indeed multiplicity of interpretations that now come to mark the Genesis hermeneutics find their counterpart in the sometimes fissured text and frequent psychic friction of *Paradise Lost*.

> *Scripture* speaketh not a word of Inequality. . . . [A]ll the Objections . . . drawn there-from, are but Sophisms of Prejudice.
>
> François Poullain de La Barre

What to make of Milton's representations and transgressions of scriptural tradition can be determined best by examining the nature and extent of the transgressions themselves and by granting, as a working premise, that what is still the crucial interpretive issue is suggested by the dedicatory poems accompanying the second edition of *Paradise Lost:* is this a poem that propounds or perplexes traditional explanations? is it a poem of declaration or disclosure? In a recent attempt to grapple with just these questions, one critic has concluded that evidence for Milton's conformity to, and complicity in, Christian cliché and cultural commonplace is to be found in his failure to hold open—or to open still further—the space being created by his contemporaries in their interpretations of the Genesis myth and in their dissertations on the relationship between the sexes.[5] Yet when we examine the evidence, and sort out the different Genesis hermeneutics, the facts seem otherwise.

Clearly, the same options are available to male and female writers: they can either submit to and promote male myths or use those myths against themselves to expose their falsehood. *Paradise Lost* is not just another packaging of the Genesis story by still another masculinist interpreter; rather, it marks the creation of a new myth, a countermyth, through which conventional interpretation can be questioned, through which the meaning concealed in the old myth can be disclosed. Milton is a resistant, not quiescent, reader of the myths his poems inscribe, and he invites the same kind of reading for the poems he writes. Offering not just a clustering but an intensification of the tensions within the Genesis tradition, Milton's poem stands out from previous imaginative treatments of the Genesis story precisely because, as Turner remarks, Milton has here "hatched the contradictions in the text and the tradition that elsewhere lie dormant" and, doing so, uses crypsis and contradiction calculatedly—as a "way of stimulating the pursuit of truth."[6]

It is revealing to pair Milton's last poems with their biblical counterparts and then to examine the hermeneutics accruing to each of their stories. If hermeneutic tradition produces a monologic discourse that would fix interpretation, Milton's poetry yields a dialogic discourse of floating interpretations. Though the notion may be generally true that hermeneutical traditions do strike a monologic relationship with texts in contrast to the tendency of literary works, which relate dialectically to their pre-texts and often antithetically to existing interpretations, it is a truth, or complex of truths, actively complicated by the unsettling of received interpretation during the seventeenth century. The hermeneutical project of Milton's age is given chiseled definition by many of his contemporary commentators whose agenda is to challenge, not confirm, venerable interpretations of key biblical stories—with the consequence that, as Milton's century progresses, interpretation becomes increasingly conflicted. There is no single Samson hermeneutics and, correspondingly, no *one* hermeneutics either for the Creation/Fall story or for the tale of Jesus tempted in the wilderness.[7] Any poem of Milton's century at all faithful to hermeneutic tradition in its seventeenth-century phase will necessarily array competing interpretations of a given story or myth and (to the extent that the poem captures the intricacy of either) will produce a subtle mapping of rival discourses, marking contradictions both within and between them, even perhaps marbleizing inherited contradictions within newly invented ones.

Whether the point of reference is Milton *or* the Bible then, the same observation holds true: "a revisionist dynamic inheres in the whole project"; or, as Herbert Schneidau also says, the intellectual processes at work here "are . . . mythoclastic . . . because they are critical, dissolvent, and revisionist."[8] Milton's project is *biblical* in the strictest sense—is to interrogate, often with the intention of tearing down, the cherished commonplaces of his culture, and to do so by using his stories not to elaborate or dramatize fixed "truths," nor to expose them as simply lies, but to reveal them instead as concepts at once partial and sometimes stultifying. In its transgression of biblical stories and their timeworn interpretations, in the interpolations it provides for the one and in the revisions it forces upon the other, Milton's narrative cuts across the grain of those orthodoxies long associated with patriarchal thinking. My recognition of this fact is meant to harbor the reminder that, in *Paradise Lost*, in the different faces worn by Eve, we witness proliferating representations of women and see, in those very representations, a gradual and steady shifting away from the extremes of negativity.

At that negative extreme are the views of William Whately writing in 1640, and they are a fitting starting point for a review of Genesis interpretation inasmuch as they represent the kinds of attitudes that some feminist criticism has attributed to Milton. As Milton is sometimes said to do, Whately takes his interpretive cues from St. Paul: "man was made in the first place and woman after him, to shew that man is superiour in nature, woman was made for man and not man from woman, therefore was man made first and woman after, and so doth the Apostle reason in two places where he handles the difference of Sexes, I *Cor.* 11. 8, 9. I *Tim.* 2. 13." Holding unswervingly to Paul's interpretation, Whately privileges Genesis 2: Eve is created after and for Adam in order to instruct them both that "shee should acknowledge her subjection unto him."[9]

If his interpretive cues are Pauline, Whately's interpretive tradition is rabbinical, enabling him to out-Paul Paul, wrapping patriarchy in misogyny, as he explains that Genesis gives Adam's death date, but not Eve's, in order "to humble womankinde" for being the first to bring death into the world and thus to show women not deserving "to have the continuance of their lives [or their deaths] recorded by Gods pen." God chooses, according to Whately, for history to be his story, not hers, although just enough of her story is told in Genesis to impress upon women the lesson of subjection: "it is sure *Evah* was before her fall at least, and probable after too [her husband's subject], for we reade of no braules betwixt them."[10] Within the context of Whately's commentary, what is remarkable is the extent to which Milton has supplemented Eve's story even to the point of including a scene in which Adam and Eve do bicker ("Thus they in mutual accusation spent / The fruitless hours . . . / And of thir vain contest appeer'd no end" [9.1187–89])[11]—an episode preceded by a displacement of the "first-is-best" with the "last-is-best" formula. Milton has not silenced women but, especially in his last poems, has actually given them a voice (an *interpretive* one) that is compelling, often astute, in its various utterances.

What seem to be simply innovative details acquire interpretive significance and force when correlated with this or that hermeneutics. If *not* bickering is a sign of female subjection, doing so may encode an alternative proposition. If *her* silence is evidence of *his* rightful domination, her having the first and last words in the dialogue with Michael may, in fact, show man and woman moving toward and not away from equal society, as seems fitting in a world where woman falls first but man falls further. Nor should it be supposed that Milton is alone among Renaissance commentators in challenging Paul's authority.

Calvin led the way when he asked "why Paul denieth a woman to be the image of God: whereas Moses giueth this honour generally to both kindes," having just explained that "the chiefe seate of Gods image, was in the minde and in the heart, where it had the preeminence: notwithstanding there was no parte wherein some sparckes did not appeare." In acknowledging that some regard the Genesis 2 account of Eve's creation as "a fable" and think of man (in the generic sense) as "A little worlde," Calvin will also propose without ever promoting the idea that, in Eve's creation, mankind, "like unto a building . . . not finished," is "perfected."[12] What is expressed here in easily missed parentheses gets highlighted in *Paradise Lost* as Milton translates the topos of an unfinished creation into the hint that Adam is a rough draft in comparison with Eve who, in the last books of the poem, emerges as a second edition. Moreover, in juxtaposing Raphael's and Adam's discrepant accounts of Creation and thereupon aligning them, respectively, with Genesis 1 and 2, Milton suggests why he will privilege the priestly over the Jahwist account: one is fact, the other fiction; one is history, the other *fable*.[13]

Subsequent to Calvin, various commentators proceed to soften the hard lines of Pauline interpretation, which, at least initially, Calvin had himself begun to ameliorate. Andrew Willet (1605), Henry Ainsworth (1616), John Salkeld (1617), and a commentary by various hands, produced in association with the Westminster Assembly (1645), provide the salient examples. More rigid in certain of his formulations than Calvin, Willet nonetheless contends that God's image belongs to man and woman alike; but he asserts that the image is in the soul, not the body, with the consequence that neither man nor woman is a visible image of God. Willet also holds to Calvin's notion of woman's secondariness as he attempts to reconcile contending interpretations concerning God's decree concerning the apple: some think it was

"giuen both to *Adam* and *Eve:* some think it was delivered onely to Adam."
Willet thinks "it more probable, that God gaue this charge vnto them both
together" inasmuch as, in their shared dominion, Adam is their "common
name," even as he allows that man "was the more principall, and . . . had
charge of the woman."[14]

However, from Willet's standpoint, male authority is no certification for
female bondage: woman is no "seruant to attend vpon him: for shee is
appointed to be his fellow helper, not his seruant"; nor is woman's creation
from man's side warrant for her subjection to him: "shee is called a helpe
like to man . . . because shee was made like vnto man, as well as in proportion of bodie, as in the qualities of the mind, beeing created according to
the image of God." If Genesis 3.16 requires that woman, after the Fall, at
times "against her will . . . often endureth the hard yoke of an unequall
commander," it also makes clear that subjection is neither woman's "naturall
desire" nor her first condition. Like Calvin, Willet reads Genesis 2 as a
"recapitulation" of Genesis 1, its story "rehearsed more at large in the
second chap[ter]."[15]

The style of Creation in Genesis 2 is, for Willet, "a surer bond of loue":
"woman is born not from man's head, to illustrate she is proud, and not
from his feet, to evidence she is mans vassell," but from his side, "to shew
the loue and coniunction betweene them" and certainly not, as some sup-
pose, to signify woman's "subiection" or "her hard and intollerable nature."
"[M]ost of all," says Willet, woman is thus "ioyned to man, because of the
promised seede of the woman, of whome came our Saviour Christ." No
less than man, Willet contends, "shee had her soule from God immediately
as Adam had, because they were both created according to Gods image";
and in naming her, says Willet, Adam utters a one-word prophecy, declaring
Eve to be the mother of all the living: "the name was giuen . . . here he
calleth her Hevah, as by her proper name; so that these words, *because
shee was the mother of all liuing,* were not the words of Adam, who yet
by prophesie did foresee that it should be so."[16]

However, Willet's most intriguing observations, given Milton's peculiar
rendering of the Creation and Fall story, may come in the following observations. First, during Eve's creation "Adam was in an *ecstasis* . . . beeing
illuminated of God," and hence comes by his knowledge of her creation
through "deuine reuelation." Milton develops a parallel moment for Eve in
book 11, lines 367–69:

> let Eve . . .
> Here sleep . . .
> As once thou slepst, while Shee to life was formd.

By allowing Eve to achieve knowledge of future history in a similar *ecstasis*,
Milton exalts her, as Willet does Adam, as "illuminated of God," as a bearer

of "deuine reuelation," and as a female prophet. Second, in suggesting that while some thought "Adam and the woman were ignorant of the fall of the Angels . . . yet it seemd to be otherwise," Willet paves the way not only for Milton's paralleling of their respective falls but for his account analogizing their fall with Satan's, hence for introducing to *Paradise Lost* the whole story of the celestial battle. Third, given Milton's deployment of the Samson story in book 9, lines 1059–66, Willet's use of the same legend in his commentary affords an apt perspective on Milton's: "Adam did not onely incline vnto her . . . of a loving minde . . . entised as Sampson was by Dalilah . . . but . . . he was seduced by the same flattering and false perswasions, whereby she was first beguiled, being carried away with an ambitious desire, in knowledge, not to be equalized."[17] In *Paradise Lost*, the same analogy presses the point that both Adam and Eve are (like "Sampson") deceived, Milton's poem thereby challenging the proposition of its sometimes Pauline narrator that Eve alone is deceived. In their aspirations, Adam and Eve each fall up rather than down.

Willet's annotations open interpretive space that those of Ainsworth and Salkeld will widen. Ainsworth's strategy is to invoke the Pauline argument for "womans subjection"—that Eve, a second half, is created *of* man—in order to interrogate and eventually dismiss Paul's argument. "A little world," Ainsworth argues, man, like God, is a pluralization in the Genesis story; that is, just as God comprehends the Trinity, so Adam is "the name of the woman also . . . and so of all mankind," all of whom "resembled God." Originally, according to this argument, there is equality between the sexes: man and woman, *one flesh*, are both given the name of Adam, and likewise each is given the interdiction. Accepting these premises, Ainsworth then conjectures: "Howbeit in the dominion and glorie of man & woman," except by falling, could there be "*in*equality" between the sexes?[18]

Less reticent than Willet in equalizing the relationship between the sexes, Ainsworth and Salkeld sharpen the lines of difference with Calvin. Calvin may have thought it improper to comprehend Adam and Eve as one before their marriage; but reading backward from Genesis 5 where Adam is their common name, Ainsworth and Salkeld are emphatic: Adam and Eve are one in their creation, sharing *equally* in the divine image and together assuming dominion over the rest of creation, which they rule "as a master . . . over servants"; as one (Adam being the name of the woman as well) they receive the interdiction and, according to Ainsworth, name the creatures.[19] Not only do Ainsworth and Salkeld open space for revisionist readings of Genesis by allowing Adam and Eve to share in the interdiction and in the wisdom that the naming of creation implies—(space that in *Paradise Lost* Milton will confiscate); but again in anticipation of Milton, Ainsworth certainly, attending to *her* name, will effect the exaltation of Eve.

Without ignoring St. Paul's interpretation, Ainsworth overrules it:

"Adam first called her *Woman* . . . God called her *Adam* . . . and now man calleth her *Eve, Life.*" That is, Eve, whose name means "*strength* and valour," takes on these attributes in both Ainsworth's reading and Milton's poem where the point is made insistently that, "*the* mother of all the *living*" and "the *Mother* of the faithfull," she gives birth not to Jesus only but to all of God's children: "Christ, all Christians . . . are Eves seed" with Christ (Eve's chief seed, "the one special seed") overthrowing Satan and all his destruction and delivering us from a death sentence. Indeed, if Adam and Eve have parity before the Fall, the advantage is given to her afterward as can be seen in the fact that "Adams confession is mixed with excuses, and further evils," including "charging the woman, and God himself, with the cause of his fall." There is poetic justice, then, in Ainsworth's conclusion that Adam's name is used for "base men" and Eve's, for "noble men,"[20] with Ainsworth, in turn, along with Salkeld, providing powerful precedent for various of Milton's transgressive maneuvers in *Paradise Lost,* including the exaltation of Eve in books 11 and 12. On the other hand, Ainsworth, like Salkeld, defines certain limits that Milton, through his rhetoric as well as through his insinuations of equality and his blurring of hierarchies, will transcend. Because in making "mankinde" God did *not* make "male and female together" and because he made the woman "*of the man,*" according to Ainsworth, God allowed for "womans subjection."

More egalitarian, perhaps, is John Salkeld's reading of the Creation story wherein satanic analogies are displaced by a typology paralleling, first, Christ's similitude with the Father and Adam's as well as Eve's similitude with the Son and, second, Eve's creation with that of the Church: "as *Eue* was framed out of the first *Adams* ribbe, so was the Church out of the side of the second." Salkeld dismisses as "improper signification" the notion that man was made in the image of God and Eve in the likeness of Adam. Rather, Salkeld argues, "as man was made to the image of God, so likewise was the woman made to the same"; and then, as if to dispel altogether the implication that woman is less than man, Salkeld contends that woman's coming from man's rib is evidence not of her subordination and subjection but only of their "perfect loue" and "mysticall vnion"; that "it hapneth often-times, that some women are more adorned with these supernaturall graces, and gifts, and consequently are more like vnto God then many men." Adam and Eve alike are the similitude and likeness of the Son who, in turn, is the similitude and likeness of his Father; together they are "the type and image of the diuine nature and being."[21]

For Salkeld, humankind's likeness to God is the best evidence we have that "man should not haue . . . power ouer man," that "all were to bee equall in power and dominion" and hence that the conditions of bondage, slavery and subjection, rooted in sin, proceed from fallen human nature. "[B]ase bondage, uile slauerie, and ignominious subiection proceedeth of sinne"—in other words, they are of the Fall and not of the Creation, with the latter story making "no mention of the power of man ouer man, because all men were equally made to the image of God." Every detail, including that of the interdiction, supports an egalitarian view of Creation—"all were equally . . . born both in perfection . . . and . . . grace . . . all . . . equall in power and dominion"—although, Salkeld concedes, the interdiction is given "principally" to Adam only because upon him "posterities happinesse did solely depend, not vpon *Eues.*" Like Salkeld, Milton will draw attention to Adam's blame-shifting after the Fall and use this detail to advantage Eve. Moreover, one analogy in Salkeld's account of the Creation story—the conjecture that man was taken into paradise after the Creation rather as "the Angell *Raphael* . . . lead *Tobias*"—may explain Raphael's prominent presence in the prelapsarian books of *Paradise Lost.*[22]

But then, as if to rein in the egalitarian spirit of this interpretation, Salkeld hedges on three occasions: first, even if Paradise is created for "the whole man," both corporeal and spiritual, the divine image belongs only to the spiritual portion of the human condition; second, though Eve is perfect in her creation, Adam is "the most perfect"; from which a third point follows, namely that there are orders and degrees within a hierarchy freely selected rather than imperiously imposed, "not by . . . absolute authoritie, but by a voluntarie and sweet subiection flowing from nature, and confirmed by grace." If there are orders and degrees in Heaven, then "euen in the state of innocencie" there must have been a hierarchy, hence some provision for "subordination":

> The wife should haue beene subiect to her husband, the children to their parents, the youth to their elders, and finally all inferiours to their superiours.
> But how then . . . was the subiection of the wife vnto her husband inflicted as a punishment due vnto her sinne. . . .
> I answere briefly, that there is a twofold subiection of the wife to her husband; the one voluntary, the other involuntary; the one of nature, the other of sinne.[23]

Whereas contradictions are foreign to Salkeld's system (two kinds of considerations do not "imply contradiction"[24]), in Milton's system such contradictions are a conspicuous and crucial feature. The forced, sometimes grating, harmonies of Salkeld's interpretation sit within Milton's poem as contradictions to be addressed. Moreover, Milton's inclination is to moderate or altogether eliminate hedgings like those found in Salkeld's interpretation. In *Paradise Lost,* the divine image belongs to body and soul alike. The rhetoric of "perfect" and "most perfect" is moderated into a rhetoric of *equal* and *more equal;* and the principle (enunciated by Satan) that "Orders and Degrees / Jarr not with liberty" (5.792–93) is but one proposition within an intricately conceived and insistently problematized notion of hierarchy. In a deft move, Satan, often represented as the opponent and defiler of hierarchy,[25] here figures as its proponent and champion. The sharp boundaries of hierarchy maintained in Satan's universe blur in both God's world and man's, and the elected subordination of wife to husband in Salkeld's system gets modified in Milton's where, by implication, subjection and subordination, superiority and inferiority, are elements in the world that require purging before the millennium can establish itself in history.[26]

The 1645 *Annotations,* prepared by John Downame and others in association with the Westminster Assembly, follow certain inflections that were established by Willet's interpretation and deepened by Ainsworth's and Salkeld's: in naming Eve, Adam utters "a Prophecie [of what] . . . she should be"; and what she is, according to some annotators, is not only "the authour of a better life" but also the image of God equally communicated to them both, within a sequence where "by degrees" creation moves "from good to better, and best of all" and where there is "no mention of Dominion among mankind over one another, but only over the other creatures." To say that woman is created out of man is to say no more than that "Womans original was not so high as the head, nor so low as the foote, because she neither was to be her husbands Mistresse nor his Slave, but betwixt both."[27] The force of such interpretation is so considerable that by 1670 it can be said by a respected authority that woman like man is "made in the Image of God, and *so it is commonly interpreted,*" with the accompanying explanation that the image of God refers to "the Intellective Spirit of Man . . . the true Spiritual Image of God in the Soul."[28]

By fastening attention to the circumstances of Eve's creation and placing a more positive construction upon them, Willet, Ainsworth, Salkeld, and the 1645 annotators pave the way for the more exalted conceptions of Eve that emerge from the writings of John Trapp (1650) and Robert Norwood (1653). Pursuing the same line of generous interpretation that we have witnessed in the writings of some of the aforementioned commentators, Trapp is equally exalting of womankind who, if man is called "A little world," should themselves be "stiled . . . *the second Edition of the Epitome of the whole world.*"[29] Trapp's conceit is doubly interesting; for it is perhaps evidence that the debate over the sexes fueled by Joseph Swetnam's misogynous attack upon women is here making an incursion into biblical commentary as later it will assume a presence in Milton's epics.

The pseudonymous Constantia Munda, for example, while calling Swetnam's misogyny the devil's device, claims that woman is "the crowne, perfection, & the meanes / Of all mens being." The capstone to her argument that woman is God's "second Tome," "the most absolute worke composed by the worlds great Architect" and that to chastise woman as "imperfect, froward, crooked and peruerse" is blasphemy, is a representation, virtually the same as Trapp's later one, of "Woman [as] the second edition of the

Epitome of the whole world."[30] What this early seventeenth-century tract makes clear is that if men are going to enlist poets like Juvenal and Euripides as authoritative voices in this debate, women will follow suit by appropriating the superior authority of epic poets like Homer and Virgil or, as will be the case in the immediate aftermath of *Paradise Lost*, like Milton himself. And *Paradise Lost*, it should be remembered before returning to Trapp, is itself a study in how a second edition relates to a first—disguising not voiding balances and symmetries but also affording focalization for that which is of defining importance—and a study in how a second edition may improve upon a first without devaluing the former.

Like Milton, Trapp seems to be saying that man and woman alike are created in God's image, but his attention then fixes on woman who as helpmeet is "an *Alter-ego*, a second-self"—"a great help . . . in points of learning . . . as busie in his study, as about her huswifery." Woman can be good or evil, making of the house "either a heaven, or a hell"; yet in this she is like the man, not "preferred" before him but not "set behind man" either. If matter in the beginning of time was taken from the man, "in the fulness of time, [it] was taken from a woman to make a man, even the man *Christ Jesus*." (So Satan reminds his legions in *Paradise Regained*: Jesus is "Man by Mothers side at least" [2.136]). A realization of woman's position similar to Satan's allows Trapp to argue that, even if woman is subject to the curse of the Fall, man should rule her "not with rigor" but "make her yoke as easie as may be."[31]

In representing woman as being "grac't / The sourse of life" (11.168–69), Milton is, in the last books of *Paradise Lost*, at least as generous as Trapp in his observation and sentiment. Moreover, when we remember that during the 1650s some like Sir Robert Filmer, who are also critical of Milton as a subverter of patriarchy, used the story of Adam and Eve to subtend patriarchy and uphold monarchy, we may begin to wonder about the all-too-common tendency to confuse his sexual politics with theirs. If anti-patriarchalism had been detected in Milton's prose writings, furnishing the grounds for Filmer's critique of Milton, one can easily imagine the sort of attack that Filmer might have mounted against *Paradise Lost*, especially in view of his arguments that "the greatest liberty in the world . . . is for people to live under a monarch"; that the first government in the world is a monarchy with absolute power bestowed upon Adam alone; that being "sole monarch of the world" he is, as natural magistrate, lord over all others (including Eve) who are his natural subjects. Also to be remembered is Filmer's chastizing of those "who magnify liberty as if the height of human felicity were only to be found in it, never remembering that the desire of liberty was the first Cause of the Fall of *Adam*."[32]

When Filmer finally turns to Milton, it is by way of arguing that kings are anointed not chosen, appointed not elected. "[N]ot so diverse," says

Filmer, father and king "may be all one" and, instead of being associated with bondage and slavery, should rather be seen as champions of liberty which, for Filmer, resides in the freedom to choose not government but religion. The supposed freedom to choose government is rather an abrogation of liberty and, because it is "the cause of endless sedition," it is also the worst "mischief" imaginable in the world. No less than Milton's prose works to which Filmer refers, *Paradise Lost* suggests otherwise even though, as if to pique the likes of Filmer, Milton presents his poem as an "imagining [of] aristocracy and democracy in heaven, as on earth."[33] Even more, he uses his poem to mount a critique of the patriarchy to which his prose writings, most notably the divorce tracts, once subscribed, especially as he becomes increasingly aware, in part through Royalist propaganda precisely like Filmer's, of the essential incompatibility between his own governmental and sexual politics.

Just such a critique (without reference to Milton) had already been mounted by Robert Norwood. Allowing that mankind is created "after the image of God," having already identified as a "grand aberration" the attribution of government to the head, which is, in fact, "the cause of all mis-governments," Norwood urges foregoing the head in favor of the heart, "the Center from whence the whole Circumference may be ruled, guided, and governed." God is said to have given "the full impress, image, or character of . . . [Him]self" to "the Whole Creation" and to have given to this creation dominion and rule over the rest of creation as Norwood, citing Genesis, urges that God never gave man lordship or kingship over another man: it is "a grand and gross mistake . . . to attribute rule and government unto the Head," rather than the heart, "it being the center of the body, the seat and center of light and life in the body: the government of the head, which . . . it hath usurped over the heart, is that which hath and doth disorder and undo us."[34]

Theology here invades politics, indeed sexual politics, with Norwood implying that as the Father and the Son are one, so man and woman are one, or should be—his ideal being "one entire unity . . . no more division . . . but . . . One, One, One; a most absolute, intire, and perfect One."[35] To return to the Father's house (or law) is to return to the mother's house (or love), which is the heart not the head. In this context, we should remember not only Milton's exaltation of Eve in the last books of *Paradise Lost*, but the representation of Jesus in the last lines of *Paradise Regained:* "hee unobserv'd / Home to his Mothers house private return'd" (4.638–39). And we should remember, too, that prelapsarian existence in *Paradise Lost* is founded upon the premise that Adam and Eve are "one Flesh, one Heart, one Soul" (8.499); in addition, Adam's insistence concerning "Those thousand decencies," which flow daily from all Eve's words, "declare . . . / Union of Mind, or ˌ us both one Soul" (8.601–4), goes unchallenged until after the Fall, the challenge then coming from Eve as she argues that if this be so, then "One Heart, one Soul" will now find their parallel in "one Guilt, one Crime" (9.964–71). In Eve's perverse logic, Adam's proposition finds its proof. And within the context of Norwood's tract, it seems right to say that both *Paradise Lost* and *Paradise Regained* are poems of the heart and that in keeping with much of the commentary here cited, Milton's poems are more admiring of womankind than is sometimes thought.

Take as an example, because of their apparent recognition of Milton's position, the popular annotations composed by followers of Matthew Poole and obviously indebted to Milton, where God's image is made to include male and female alike: "It shines forth even in the Body, in the Majesty of mans Countenance, yet principally consists and most eminently appears in man's Soul." Indeed, for Poole's followers the plurality of beings in God is paralleled by the plurality of beings in man: "man was the last, so the most perfect" in a tale wherein male and female are "both comprehended in the word, *Man*," where "Image and likeness are two words noting the same thing, even exact likeness," where the interdiction is given to woman as well as man, and where the name Adam, as it is used in Genesis 5, is "given . . . both to Man and the Woman, who are called by one name, to shew their intimate Union and Communion in all things."[36] In two crucial lines, Milton lays to rest the long-standing belief that mankind's resemblance to God is spiritual only: God

> on thee
> Abundantly his gifts hath . . . pour'd
> Inward and outward both, his image fair.
>
> (8.219–21)

Interestingly, Poole is one of the few biblical commentators of the seventeenth century cited by Milton's eminent bibliographer, who does so in the following manner: "Influence and language from *Paradise Lost* in annotations to Genesis, without acknowledgment."[37] When Poole's followers refer (presumably to Milton) as "A late ingenious and learned Writer,"[38] they go on to notice the poet's seeming departures from tradition and implicitly praise him for providing them with a means for accommodating rival hermeneutics. No poet of commonplaces, Milton achieves authority here as a transgressor of received tradition and as a mediator of rival interpretations, with *Paradise Lost* now authorizing an uncommonly generous Genesis hermeneutics.

Such is the authority of Milton that, in the initial phase of Milton criticism, men like Sir Allen Apsley will protest and women like Jane Lead will embrace. And Milton's poem is of essentially the same moment as—indeed its publication is framed on either side by—the appearance of Margaret Fell

Fox's *Womens Speaking Justified, Proved, and Allowed of by the Scriptures* (1666) and François Poullain de La Barre's *De l'égalité des deux sexes* (1673), which formulates a caveat as pertinent to its own argument as to Milton's *Paradise Lost:* "both Sexes are equal; that is to say that *Women* are as noble, as perfect, as capable as men. This cannot be established, but by refuting two sets of adversaries; the vulgar, and almost all the learned."[39]

Much in—and about—*Paradise Lost* has gone unacknowledged, including certain forms of its influence. *Paradise Lost* inscribes patriarchy, misogyny, and feminist sentiment—provides an early mapping of these discourses—in a way that submits each category of thought, each attitude of mind, to analysis and that through its analyses achieves unexpected accents. Moreover, when Milton's poem is situated within such a context, it becomes apparent that what we have been thinking of as a *tradition* needs to be reconceived in a way that allows for contending perspectives and that encompasses evolutions of mind in the seventeenth century.

Within a tradition of evolution, Milton is perhaps more representative, less transgressive, than some might have supposed. Yet within *Paradise Lost,* he foregrounds not what is conventional but what is innovative in biblical commentary, while elaborating upon some and taking to logical conclusion other of its strikingly new features: the idea of an androgynous creation wherein, created together, man and woman are jointly responsible for the Fall; man's losing his preeminence with the consequence that the sexes, leveled into equality, both exhibit virtues customarily associated with the other; a re-formation of the usual conceptions of masculinity and femininity accompanied by the suggestion that none of the virtues is sex- or gender-specific; the elaboration of woman's history and the centering of her in the historical process with the attendant implication that woman's spiritual equality, evinced in her full participation in the drama of salvation, may give her claim to social and political equality as well; that a hierarchal order, if it persists, will be purged of structures founded upon sex and gender differences.

Very simply, *Paradise Lost* figures majorly in the formation of a feminist consciousness, through its acts of critique and reinterpretation exploring woman's relationship to the divine and quietly subverting patriarchal paradigms.[40] Moreover, when read as poetic commentary, its central books may be seen, according to Hans Robert Jauss, as filling in the gaps that become visible once Milton poses the "impudent question as to what Adam and Eve actually did and how they related to one another before they forfeited their paradise," with Milton in the process deconstructing in book 8 "the traditional superiority of the male, a superiority that even Milton had maintained in Book IV."[41] And in book 4, there is the irony compounded of the facts that, in important details, Adam subscribes to the Genesis 1 (or feminist) account of Creation (4.413–15, 428–32), while Eve observes the Gene-sis 2 and Pauline (or masculinist) version of the same story (4.440–48, 471–75, 481–91).

The most important lessons to be learned from any study of *Paradise Lost* in relation to the Bible and its hermeneutic traditions, especially in their seventeenth-century phase, are, first, that Milton (in the recent and very simple formulation of Christopher Hill) is "not an orthodox reader"[42]—or interpreter—of Scripture, his project involving less the repro-duction of biblical tales than the reimagining of their myths in the light of current politics and contemporary history. Second, not only *Paradise Lost* but its scriptural subtexts (and add here *Samson Agonistes* and its scriptural sources) are inspired with contradictions so unsettling that the typical ten-dency in criticism, as well as the enterprise of both poet-imitators and book illustrators, is to contradict both texts (biblical no less than Miltonic) out of their contradictions.

Third, and finally, rather than fogging over the meaning(s) of *Paradise Lost*, the spirit of contradiction in Milton's poem, the clashing perspectives in the poem, and its different arenas of conflict are the transmitters of meanings—not easy but subtle and sophisticated, often stinging conscious-ness onto a new level of awareness. Itself a field of contending forces and competing paradigms, Milton's poem contains—but is not contained by—frustrating tensions and ambiguities that, a goad to truth, are also the poem's most distinctive defining features. If, as Gerald Graff contends, "the most influential tradition in today's politically oriented academic criticism is to see works of art not as simple ideological statements but as swords of ideological and psychological conflict,"[43] then *Paradise Lost*, a battleground for its culture's contending viewpoints and ideologies, testifies to the endur-ing value of discussion, debate, dispute, dissent. To move from Milton's prose writings to his last poems is not to move from politics to poetry but from the writings of a feisty polemicist to those of a wily politician who knows that inscribing contradictions leads to debating alternatives—a de-bate, in turn, that, putting the mind on the stretch, witnesses to the positive potentiality of controversy.

Milton's poetry is marked, not marred, by its contradictions; they inhabit its very center where competing hermeneutics vie with one another: which should be privileged, the Genesis account of the Fall or Paul's interpretation of it? which takes precedence, Genesis 1 or 2? and when these versions conflict with one another, which of them should prevail? Who leads the angels in battle—Michael or Christ? and is the battle itself actual or imagi-nary, carnal or spiritual? And at the poem's center are contending images of Christ the tiger and Christ the lamb, as well as contrary cosmologies—Ptolemaic and Copernican—that find their counterparts in conflicting the-ologies. The contradictions within Milton's poems, that is, find their parallels in conflicts both within the scriptural texts and hermeneutic traditions on which they are based and within the critical tradition they initiated.

Transported from Milton's sources, some of these conflicts inhabit *Paradise Lost* as vexing complexities, but others exist in the poem as glaring contradictions—a point worth insisting upon just because Milton criticism, especially of late, has been paralyzed, indeed impoverished, by the suppression of such conflicts or just plain avoidance of them. To set the critical understanding free again, we may have to reclaim *Paradise Lost* as a poem of proliferating contradictions, restore a conflict model to its criticism, and then remember this poem for what, historically, it has always been: the battleground for competing intellectual paradigms and clashing critical methodologies. More than signaling a move against existing traditions and interpretations, contradictions are a means of complicating and reconstituting both. By dislodging commonplaces and effecting dislocations, contradictions open seemingly closed systems or enlarge those that are needlessly constricted, and, admitting to the possibility of coexisting meanings and rival interpretations, stimulate the pursuit of truth even as they keep all notions of truth contingent, perspectival.

As with Milton's poetry, so with Milton criticism generally, and so with Milton in the culture wars today: the temptation is always to choose sides when the wiser recourse, on occasion, may be to choose not to choose, thus locating significance in the conflict and wresting meaning from the contradiction. That may also be the wiser course for a new Milton criticism, which, instead of confronting opposing points of view in order to silence one of them, might be empowered and emboldened by competing interpretations to produce finer honings of its own (not always fully nuanced) readings. Criticism of the highest order unfetters—it does not constrain— the mind; it may correct but does not coerce. When it cries up liberty, it means liberty, testing the values it posits, tolerating unavoidable ambiguities as well as differences of opinion, and, as a matter of course, hosting conflicting systems of thought. Such criticism, rather like Milton's poetry, makes space for thinking the unthinkable, for speaking the unspeakable, and for challenging what for too long has gone unchallenged. Like A. Bartlett Giamatti's ideal university, *Paradise Lost* is a place where competing systems of thought collide; where they are "tested, debated . . . freely, openly,"[44] and, even if hotly, usually civilly.

While *Paradise Lost* may not settle, it nonetheless brings and keeps under scrutiny the nagging questions, the thorny issues of theology and politics, reminding us through its sexual politics and gender trouble of the enormous barriers to changing entrenched structures and ideas as well as of the imminent dangers in remaining sexually and culturally blind. As much about what unites as about what divides us; acutely sensitive to the interconnectedness of science and religion, of history, politics, and poetry—their interdependency and mutuality; in its global reach uniquely poised for global challenges and in its vast learning seemingly addressed to knowledge-based societies still in the future; here threatened by the right and there scorned by the left: in all these ways, *Paradise Lost* is at once a harbinger of cultural transformations and a preparation for them. From its perspectives of history, *Paradise Lost* itself forms a perspective on history—on the politics as well as the poetry of a history seething with contradictions, yet rife with possibilities. A poet of the seventeenth century, Milton, with his future gaze, may prove to be (singularly among the triumvirate of Chaucer, Shakespeare, and Milton) the poet *for* the new millennium—the poet *for* the twenty-first century.

The eye altering alters all: at the dawn of this century Milton seemed indubitably the poet of the past—"a monument to dead ideas."[45] Yet in the still dark hours before the dawn of the next century it appears as if Milton might be the poet for the future of which his last poems are an embodiment. But let it not be said of the new age as Margaret Fuller said of the last, that "the Father is still far beyond the understanding of his child."[46] Instead, let it continue to be said that, still a champion of its freedoms and an exponent of its ethics and ideas, Milton continues to agitate the world from sleep; that by Milton the dark clouds of ignorance are again being rolled into the distance.

Notes

This essay was completed with generous assistance from the PSC-CUNY Research Foundation. The title for the essay comes from Jonathan Richardson, "The Life of the Author," in *Explanatory Notes and Remarks on Milton's "Paradise Lost"* (London, 1734), xxxix; and the epigraph is from Anne Manning's *The Maiden and Married Life of Mary Powell . . . And the Sequel Thereto Deborah's Diary* (1849–50, 1860; reprint with an introduction by W. H. Hutton, London: John C. Nimmo, 1898), 35. The two quotations framing the main body of the essay are from François Poullain de La Barre, *The Woman As Good as the Man Or, the Equality of Both Sexes*, trans. A. L., ed. Gerald M. MacLean (1677; reprint, Detroit: Wayne State University Press, 1988), 151. A. L. translates *De l'égalité des deux sexes* originally published in 1673.

The larger concerns of this essay—some of which have been addressed in various publications by Diane McColley, Dayton Haskin, and James Grantham Turner—are the subject of my book-in-progress, *Wars of Truths: Milton and the New Criticisms*.

1. Balachandra Rajan, *"Paradise Lost" and the Seventeenth Century Reader* (London: Chatto and Windus, 1947).

2. See Sir Allen Apsley, *Order and Disorder: Or; The World Made and Undone. Being Meditations Upon The Creation and the Fall; As it is Recorded in the beginning of GENESIS* (London, 1679), [A1]. For discussion of the Apsley imitation, see Joseph Wittreich, "Milton's Transgressive Maneuvers: Receptions, Repressions, and the Sexual Politics of *Paradise Lost*," in *Heretical Milton*, currently being assembled by John Peter Rumrich.

3. Odo Marquard, as quoted by Hans Robert Jauss, *Question and Answer: Forms of Dialogic Understanding*, ed. and trans. Michael Hays (Minneapolis: University of Minnesota Press, 1989), 54.

4. James Grantham Turner, *One Flesh: Paradisal Marriage and Sexual Relations in the Age of Milton* (Oxford: Clarendon, 1987), 7–8. And further:

> In Milton's own lifetime . . . interpretations and applications of Genesis multiply at an astonishing rate. . . . Milton himself responded to this crisis of interpretation in ways that reflect the divisions within his own mind: . . . he welcomed the energetic polyphony of opinion and shared in several of these revisionist tendencies, sometimes directly, sometimes by a kind of osmosis or interior dialogue with them. His synthesis of the disintegrating Genesis-tradition shows a striking commitment to imaginative boldness and personal vision. . . . Milton is both a comprehensive figure of his age, and an isolated individual . . . who converts all interpretations to his own private mythology. (175)

On Milton as exegete, see Michael Lieb who argues that "Nothing gets settled; everything just gets more complicated. It is out of this complex of exegetical positions and negotiations . . . that . . . Milton's own epic comes into being" (see "'Two of Far Nobler Shape': Reading the Paradisal Text," in *Literary Milton: Text, Pretext, Context*, ed. Diana Treviño Benet and Michael Lieb [Pittsburgh: Duquesne University Press, 1994], 131).

5. See, for example, Mary Nyquist, "The Genesis of Gendered Subjectivity in the Divorce Tracts and in *Paradise Lost*," in *Re-membering Milton: Essays on the Texts and Traditions*, ed. Mary Nyquist and Margaret W. Ferguson (New York: Methuen, 1987), 107–11.

6. Turner, *One Flesh*, 27, 285, but see also 3, 8, 12, 32.

7. My own concerns are shared by Dayton Haskin, *Milton's Burden of Interpretation* (Philadelphia: University of Pennsylvania Press, 1994).

8. See Herbert Schneidau, "Biblical Narrative and Modern Consciousness," in *The Bible and the Narrative Tradition*, ed. Frank McConnell (New York: Oxford University Press, 1986), 148–49.

9. William Whately, *Prototypes, Or, The Primary Precedent Ovt of the Booke of Genesis* (London, 1640), 3–4.

10. Ibid., 7, 9.

11. John Milton, *Paradise Lost*, in *The Complete Poetry of John Milton*, ed. John T. Shawcross, rev. ed. (New York: Doubleday, 1971). All references to Milton's poetry are to this edition and are cited parenthetically in the text.

12. John Calvin, *A Commentarie . . . vpon the first booke of Moses called Genesis*, trans. Thomas Tymme (London, 1578), 42, 44, 45, 75, 76.

13. For opposing views on which account Milton privileges, see Nyquist, "The Genesis," 99–127, and Joseph Wittreich, "'Inspir'd with Contradiction': Mapping Gender Discourses in *Paradise Lost*," in *Literary Milton*, ed. Benet and Lieb, 133–60.

14. Andrew Willet, *Hexapla in Genesin: That Is, A Sixfold Commentarie Vpon Genesis* (Cambridge, 1605), 33.

15. Ibid., 35–36, 51–52.

16. Ibid., 37–38, 52–53.

17. Ibid., 35, 37–38, 47.

18. Henry Ainsworth, *Annotations Upon the first book of Moses, called Genesis* (London, 1616), Bv.

19. Ibid., Bv; see also C–Cv, F. Says Ainsworth: "this law was given both to the man and woman, (which were both called Adam)" (C–Cv).

20. Ibid., Cv, C2, [C4v], D, [D2v]. "*Adam* is used for base men, born of *adamah, the earth:* so *ish,* is used for noble men. . . . Also *ish,* is used, both for *man & husband:* and *ishah,* both for *woman* and *wife.*" Yet the very argument used here seemingly to exalt Eve is abandoned in the realization that her being created "*out of*" Adam "is a third reason for womans subjection" (C2).

21. John Salkeld, *A Treatise of Paradise. And The Principall contents thereof* (London, 1617), 104–6, 119, 172, and see also 107–20. Salkeld is not inventing a new typology. Rather, he is drawing upon a typology that, however conventional, is positive rather than negative in its analogies for women. Salkeld is insistent that, in the Genesis text, "*image* doth equally signifie, and may be equally attributed both to man, and woman" (105).

22. Ibid., 126–27, 142, 147.

23. Ibid., 6–7, 127–29, 182. On 182, Salkeld contends that had "there . . . beene more men, then women . . . we [would] have persisted in the state of innocencie," and he even implies that women are created not for their intelligence but "for the naturall propagation of mankinde."

24. Ibid., 177.

25. See, for example, Jacob Boehme, *Mysterium Magnum, Or An Exposition of the First Book of Moses called Genesis* (1654), 2 vols., trans. C. J. B[arker] (London: John M. Watkins, 1924), 1:75.

26. For elaboration, see Joseph Wittreich, "'John, John, I Blush for Thee!': Mapping Gender Discourses in *Paradise Lost,*" in *Out of Bounds: Male Writers and Gender(ed) Criticism,* ed. Laura Claridge and Elizabeth Langland (Amherst: University of Massachusetts Press, 1990), 22–54.

27. John Downame et al., *Annotations Upon all the Books Of The Old and New Testament,* 3d ed. (1645; London, 1657), annotations to Genesis 3.20, 1.26, 2.22; see also the annotation to 9.2. In seeming contradiction to the usually generous spirit of this commentary, in the gloss for Genesis 3.16 the annotator concedes that "The subjection of the woman to her husband, was not repugnant to the state of Innocencie." Again, see the annotation to 9.2.

28. Samuel Gott, *The Divine History Of The Genesis Of The World Explicated & Illustrated* (London, 1670), 462, 466 (emphasis mine).

29. John Trapp, *A Clavis to the Bible. Or A New Comment Upon The Pentateuch* (London, 1650), 18. Genesis 2.23 ("bone of my bone"), says Trapp, presents "the first Prophecie that was ever uttered in the world" (28); and also, according to Trapp, man becomes, after the Fall, "frail, sorry . . . a map of mortality, a masse of misery" (26).

30. Constantia Munda, *The Worming of a mad Dogge: Or, A Soppe for Cerbervs the Iaylor of Hell* (London, 1617), [A2v], 2–3, and see also 9–15 on poets as authoritative voices in this debate.

31. Trapp, *A Clavis to the Bible,* 25–27, 40.

32. Sir Robert Filmer, *Patriarcha; Or The Natural Power of Kings* (1680), *Patriarcha and Other Political Writings,* ed. Peter Laslett (Oxford: Basil Blackwood, 1949), 53, 55, 58, 72, 75.

33. Ibid., 256, 260.

34. Robert Norwood, *A Pathway unto England's Perfect Settlement; and Its Centre and Foundation of Rest and Peace* (London, 1653), title page and 9, 10, 11.

35. Ibid., 29.

36. Matthew Poole, *Annotations upon the Holy Bible,* 2 vols. (London, 1683, 1685), 1: annotations to Genesis 1.26, 2.21, 3.16; see also the annotation to 5.2. I make a point of saying "Poole's followers" both here and later because the proposers

of this edition are quick to explain: "we do not pretend . . . to translate Mr. Poole's Synopsis Criticorum. . . . [W]e have only hinted the Senses which in our Judgment seemed fairest, and least constrained . . . [and] shewed the Consonancy of them to other Scriptures" (A2v). The reference is to Poole's *Synopsis Criticorum: Aliorumque S. Scripturae Interpretum,* 3 vols. (London, 1669–76), which is missing the apparent allusion to Milton: "A late ingenious and learned Writer."

37. See John T. Shawcross, *Milton: A Bibliography for the Years 1624–1700* (Binghamton, N. Y.: Medieval and Renaissance Texts and Studies, 1984), 274, no. 948. While there may be no grounds for claiming Milton's influence on a seventeenth-century writer like Pierre Allix, there are two points of contact between their respective readings of the Genesis story of Creation. If Milton's Eve names the flowers, Allix's Eve names her progeny—specifically Cain and Seth; and if, by way of arguing for his perfection, Allix denies that the mind of first man was "tainted with Popular Errors," Milton shows both Adam and Eve, still perfect, in possession of the interpretive commonplaces of Ptolemaic theory and patriarchal thinking that his own poem reviews without explicitly refuting. See Allix's *Reflexions,* 2 vols. (London, 1688), especially 1:49, 56. Much of the material in this essay confirms Roland Muschat Frye in his quip to me: the essay that needs writing is "Milton's Influence on the Bible."

38. Poole, *Annotations upon the Holy Bible,* 1: annotation to Genesis 3.1.

39. See Apsley, *Order and Disorder;* Lead, *A Fountain of Gardens* (3 vols.; London, 1696–1701), especially the poem "Solomon's Porch" at the beginning of volume 1 where Lead pleads with Milton to join his voice to hers in singing in the millennium ([F4v]); Fox, *Womens Speaking Justified* (London, 1666), and for the quotation from François Poullain de La Barre, see the unnumbered headnote above.

40. Gerda Lerner's new book provides an important perspective on feminist acts; see *The Creation of Feminist Consciousness: From the Middle Ages to Eighteen-Seventy* (New York: Oxford University Press, 1993), 138 (see also 274).

41. See Jauss, *Question and Answer,* 102, 104.

42. Christopher Hill, *The English Bible and the Seventeenth-Century Revolution* (London: Penguin, 1993), 373.

43. Gerald Graff, *Beyond the Culture Wars: How Teaching the Conflicts Can Revitalize American Education* (New York: W. W. Norton, 1990), 159.

44. A. Bartlett Giamatti, *A Free and Ordered Space: The Real World of the University* (New York: W. W. Norton, 1990), 29–30.

45. Walter Raleigh, *Milton* (1900; reprint, New York: Benjamin Blom, 1967), 85.

46. Margaret Fuller, "The Prose Works of Milton," in *Papers on Literature and Art* (New York, 1846), 39.

Ramblings in Elucidation of the Authorship of the *Christian Doctrine*

William B. Hunter

The *Christian Doctrine* (in Latin *De Doctrina Christiana;* henceforth *DDC*), has been attributed to John Milton ever since its discovery in 1823. Despite the many varied and fundamental ways in which, as I have shown,[1] ideas in the Milton canon differ from those of this heterodox religious treatise, some scholars are hesitant to commit themselves to full dismissal of his authorship of it. This is easily understandable: so many of our interpretations of his works have been based on the assumption that he wrote it and in so many details it is congruent with his genuine writings that acceptance of my thesis now would lead to future embarrassment should the book turn out after all to be his. I am quite well aware that my argument has not yet yielded final proof, though I see no reason to avoid using the treatise to interpret Milton's thought as one does with any other pertinent seventeenth-century source. Scholars should be wary only of basing the discussions of their ideas upon *DDC* alone without concurrent support from the canonical works.

Stylistic differences could be conclusive, but, lacking the means and the ability to compare the Latin of *DDC* with that of a canonical work like *Literae Pseudo-Senatus Anglicani,*[2] I have grounded my arguments primarily upon the disjunction of ideas between treatise and canon. Examples that I have already demonstrated include the differing interpretations of the Incarnation, of Sabbath observance, of the salvation of pagans, of whether Christ died in both his divine and human natures or only in the human, of whether one may invoke the Holy Spirit, of justification by faith and/or works, of adult baptism, and of consubstantiation. The concepts of *unio* (union) underlying marriage are quite different in the divorce tracts and the treatise, though this fact may be explained by different dates of composition. The three invocations in books 1, 3, and 7 of *Paradise Lost* are Trinitarian[3] as *DDC* emphatically is not.

Because a number of scholars have relied heavily upon *DDC* to make their points and because to argue that agreement exists, they may have somewhat distorted statements in the canonical works to which they apply them, I think that reconsideration and possible modification should be given to some eccentric religious doctrines now generally accepted as Milton's but that find sole or major support from *DDC* alone. Examples (explanations of which often have added new words to our vocabularies) include chiliasm, monophysitism, mystical theopantism, the theopaschite heresy, and the theopathetic tradition.[4]

My second argument against Milton's authoring of *DDC* is its clear orientation to a continental context for the authorities it cites, not an English one. Such evidence strongly favors an origin in the Low Countries, from where it could have passed into his possession as in time it certainly did. Milton was engaged with the Dutch in government negotiations in the early 1650s. His *Doctrine and Discipline of Divorce* was translated into Dutch there in 1655, and the evidence of *DDC* supports its having had some influence on his ideas about divorce.

A third area that can be shown to distance Milton from the treatise is the differing citations of proof texts typically made by Calvinists, who always argued their doctrines from supportive biblical passages. For a single example, a major aspect of Milton's opposition to forced tithing, which he expressed in his pamphlet *Hirelings* (1659), is his extended interpretation (7:284–90)[5] of Genesis 14.18–20, where Abram, returning victorious from a military campaign, gives a tenth of his plunder to a priest, Melchizedek. In the New Testament, Hebrews 7.1–10 interprets this as support for the priesthood of Christ. Because Milton's opponents in this pamphlet, Henry Spelman and William Prynne, employed these same texts to support tithing, they are fundamental to the arguments in his tract too. But neither Old nor New Testament passage is cited in the discussion of tithing in *DDC* (6:595–600), which barely mentions Melchizedek once in another context (6:517). I have traced several other ideas in *Hirelings* and in the companion pamphlet *Civil Power* (also 1659) which Milton supports with one set of proof texts, the author of *DDC* with quite another—not at all likely for a single author working at the same time on both.

A final fact distancing Milton from *DDC* that must not be forgotten is the improbability of a blind man being able to control its complex arguments, based as they are upon quotation of over eight thousand texts from the Bible.

1

With this summary of my previous investigations, I will go on to other comparisons of canon and treatise. First, continuing that of the insights derived from comparison of proof texts, it seems clear, as I have said, that there is no substantive relation between those in *DDC* and those in Milton's two pamphlets published in 1659, when he apparently did not have access to the manuscript. Fourteen years later, in 1673, the evidence provided by the proof texts cited in *Of True Religion* is quite different, for it exhibits a direct correspondence between that pamphlet and the treatise. For example, on the subject of the rejection of other religious traditions, in *Of True Religion* (8:479) Milton quotes three proof texts: Galatians 1.8, Deuteronomy 4.2, and Revelation 22.18–19. All three appear among the nine texts on the same subject in *DDC* (6:591). It is worth mentioning that an unidentified amanuensis has added the reference to Deuteronomy 4.2 to the original text,[6] perhaps at Milton's own direction if in 1673 he were consulting the proofs offered for this subject in the treatise. Again, on the topic of idol worship not being instructive for Christians, *Of True Religion* (8:433) relies on two texts, Jeremiah 10.8 and Habakkuk 2.18, both of which are included among four in the treatise on this subject (6:693). Further, in arguing that one should know Scripture well enough to evaluate its teachers, *Of True Religion* (8:435) employs three proof texts, Ephesians (wrongly identified as "Eccles.") 4.14, Acts 17.11, and Revelation 2.2, which all appear among about a dozen on this topic in the treatise (6:601). Kelley's textual note (6:830) to the manuscript's pages 414 and 415 observes that an anonymous amanuensis has made changes in this section too. From these convergences I conclude that in 1673 Milton probably had access to the Picard text of the treatise,[7] which he used as a convenient concordance for citations and perhaps for ideas. He certainly had the work in his possession when he died the next year, for it turned up among his effects. But the diverging evidence of the tracts published in 1659 suggests that it was not available to him that early.

2

I move now to some new insights from the manuscript of *DDC* itself. On many pages there are additions, corrections, and redactions, which run into the hundreds. Maurice Kelley has minutely examined and classified them.[8] From their characteristic writing patterns he has identified seven different hands and thinks that there may be more.[9] The obvious implication of this information is that only a blind or otherwise handicapped person would have to rely on so many assistants for work on his text, and Milton of course was blind. But let us examine this evidence in detail.

There is general agreement that a known amanuensis, Jeremie Picard, copied from a now lost original the entire text of *DDC*. This text was then subjected to the emendations already mentioned. Wherever their order of entry can be determined, it seems clear that Picard himself made all the earliest changes and was then followed by the various anonymous hands.

Sometime later, perhaps after Milton's death in 1674 when the manuscript came into his possession, a second known scribe, Daniel Skinner, recopied a number of pages. I shall ignore his work at this point because it occurs too late to be significant for my discussion of this issue.

Limiting myself then to the Picard pages with their earliest emendations in his hand and the addenda of the several other amanuenses, I conclude from Kelley's enumeration that about 560 can be traced to Picard.[10] In particular, he amplified dogma forty-two times and rewrote five pages.[11] In addition to such major alterations, he also made the following somewhat less important ones:[12]

added letters or words	37 examples
deleted letters or words	43
separated words or numbers	34
corrected words	17
corrected citations	72
changed diction	26
changed word order	8
made restatements	21
amplified points	51
added cross references	4
changed order of paragraphs	2
rearranged proof texts	18
added proof texts	90
shortened or extended proof texts	21
emended proof texts	74

None of the anonymous amanuenses approach such numbers or such significance for their contents. Kelley's amanuensis A, the most important, recopied 549 to 52; introduced changes at the end of book 1, chapter 17, that required some adaptations early in chapter 18; and made 19 minor revisions.[13] The changes by other amanuenses are also insignificant in Kelley's survey and all together, including those of A, total about 100. In comparison, Picard's occur far more frequently and are often of a more substantive nature, going beyond routine revisions to imply that he was associated in some direct way with the genesis of the work. And, to repeat, his entries antedate all others whenever it is possible to place them in order.

With some reservation, then, I very tentatively suggest that Picard himself wrote *DDC*. He certainly was directly involved as the original hand in the surviving copy. His alterations may be more the work of an active author than of a passive copyist. The trouble is that we really know nothing about him except that he was in England in 1655 and was associated with Milton between 1658 and 1660, when he disappears from the record. (Efforts reported by William R. Parker to discover anything more about him failed.[14]) We may know so little because the search has been undertaken in the wrong place—in England rather than Holland, which I have suggested as the probable origin of the work.

I have made inquiries into the surviving records of universities then established in the Low Countries. A Gwualtherus Piccardus was registered in theology on 10 September 1624 at Groningen University, and a Joannes Picard was there in August 1647.[15] A Johannes Piccardus, aged twenty, from Germany, was registered in theology in October 1622 at Leiden and another of the same name in medicine in June 1628. In April 1644 Claudius Picardus, aged forty-five, from France, was enrolled there in theology.[16] Dr. Marian Schulder, curator of the Universiteitsmuseum at the University of Amsterdam, has written me (November 15, 1993) that there was a Joannus Piccardus on the faculty at Franeker in 1620, but she reports that no Picard appears in the records of other universities. She adds that there seem to be no lists of students surviving from the Remonstrant Seminary in Amsterdam (founded in 1634). This is especially regrettable because of the clear relations to the Remonstrant movement that *DDC* demonstrates.

Nugatory though investigation of university records of the earlier seventeenth century in the Netherlands has proved, Dr. Schulder also suggested that I check the records in the Municipal Archives of the city of Amsterdam. In them Dr. W. Chr. Pieterse, director of these archives, has indeed identified for me a Jeremie Picard (Jeronimus Pietersen Pickart), a painter from Rotterdam who in October 1646 married a woman six years his senior, Annetie Jans. He was then eighteen years old. Dr. Pieterse also referred me to the Thieme-Becker *Künstler-Lexicon*, which records this Jeronimus Pickaert (the name is spelled variously) as a landscape painter, born about 1628 and pupil of Jan Fyt. He was in Middelburg, where he belonged to the St. Luke Guild, in 1649; in Leiden in 1655; in Rotterdam in 1659, and in Amsterdam in 1674. But, as Dr. Pieterse concludes, "There appears to be no English connection of this painter."[17]

Although this Jeremie Picard should not be ruled out as Milton's associate in the late 1650s and as the possible author of DDC, his age at the time (his early thirties) and his occupation as painter may make him a questionable candidate for a work like the treatise. He seems to have left some identifiable (that is, signed) paintings, but Marijke C. de Kinkelde of the Rijksbureau voor Kunsthistorische Documentatie's-Gravenhage has written me (May 26, 1994) that its files contain no readable signatures from his work. She suggested that I inquire about Picard's witnessing signature to a document of September 9, 1655, concerning custody of the children of a fellow painter, Adam Pick, in the archives of the city of Leiden, and that to another document concerning some pictures in the archives of the city of Amsterdam dated 15/18 November 1670. Thanks to officials of both cities I have copies of these signatures. They do not give examples of many letters, however, and one reproduction is dark. Comparison of them with a Picard signature made in England in 1658,[18] when the composition of DDC was supposedly being actively undertaken, is not helpful in that the English example is printed. Besides, as Dr. Gordon Campbell has remarked to me in a letter of February 5, 1994, "It is always difficult to be confident about handwriting, especially when signatures are involved, as signatures often reflect the immature hand of an otherwise mature writer." Certainly these signatures themselves show no relationship. In conclusion, the limited evidence of the Dutch signatures does not support the identity of the Dutch Picka(e)rt with the English Picard.

3

Dr. Robert Fallon has raised an issue that I have not hitherto addressed, the relationship of the DDC manuscript to another surviving one, that of the State Papers (henceforth SP).[19] The latter is entirely in the hand of Daniel Skinner, as are many pages of the former. Skinner certainly possessed both after Milton's death and tried unsuccessfully to publish them. Through the agency of his father they finally came into the hands of Sir Joseph Williamson, secretary of state, who deposited them in the State Paper Office.[20] Robert Lemon recovered both in 1823 but would publish only DDC. Such early and close association of the two manuscripts could suggest a common authorship although, of course, Milton did not control the subject matter of SP.

Let us consider the evidence. The SP exist in several early forms:

1. Columbia University's manuscript copy, made probably just before the Restoration in 1660. Because of the early date I can disregard it here.

2. *Literae Pseudo-Senatus Anglicani,* published by two different presses on the Continent in 1676. Its compiler has not been identified.

3. The surviving Skinner manuscript, *SP.*[21] Everyone has assumed that he copied it from Milton's originals well before the latter's death and at his direction, to appear as part of the book now entitled *Epistolarum Familiarium,* published in 1674.[22] When the censor refused permission to print its political documents, Milton inserted instead his early "Prolusions" to fill out the volume. The conclusion drawn is that Skinner "retained the [rejected] manuscript that he had made"[23] and tried to publish both it and the manuscript of *DDC* abroad but failed with both; meanwhile, someone else did manage to publish there another and independent transcription of the State Papers as *Literae* (number 2 above), to Skinner's considerable vexation. My concern is that if Skinner had worked so early on *SP* to prepare its contents for publication in 1674, he should have known Milton well enough to be aware of whether he had also authored *DDC* as its new owner would claim.

The conclusion that Skinner was the faithful young amanuensis of Milton's last years owes entirely to modern biographers, especially Parker. Skinner finds mention among contemporary biographies only in John Aubrey's notes, which read, "His familiar learned Acquaintance were Mr. Andrew Marvell, Mr. Skinner, Dr. Paget M.D. [and] Mr. . . . Skinner, who was his disciple." This last is further identified a few pages later as possessor of what is almost certainly the *DDC* manuscript.[24] The "Acquaintance" named Skinner has been generally and plausibly identified with Milton's friend and former pupil Cyriack; the other Skinner, the "disciple," with Daniel. But his discipleship has been worked pretty hard. Without a shred of evidence Parker fictionalizes Milton as having tutored him and even helped him to be admitted to Trinity College, Cambridge. Although Parker, of course, knew all about the shady activities of this young man, which I have summarized in "Provenance,"[25] he leaves Daniel pretty much exonerated and urges that we let him "rest in peace,"[26] something I am willing to do only if Daniel, not being at all a close associate of Milton as has been assumed, believed in ignorance that the anonymous manuscript of *DDC* that he got his hands on was really by him.

The evidence supporting such close association of Skinner with Milton lies in the assumed history of Skinner's *SP* manuscript. As Dr. Fallon observes, "most scholars agree that [this manuscript] is the one originally prepared for the volume" *Epistolarum,*[27] a dogma that no one has hitherto challenged. But that Skinner's manuscript was not the one prepared for that work seems probable from one important fact: he could not date several letters (numbers 112–22 of *SP*) that *Literae* does place in nearly correct order.[28] Thus I suggest that another (anonymous) amanuensis who could get these approximate dates from Milton prepared the material of the *SP* for the 1674 volume. When English censorship forbade its publication, this amanuensis managed to publish it abroad as *Literae*. Even the irritated Skinner reports that the editor of *Literae* had his material directly from Milton—if "surreptitiously."[29] Skinner, an ambitious young outsider, managed to get permission to copy those letters that now constitute *SP* just as did the transcribers of the texts that would become the publications of Leti and Lünig noted above. Dr. Shawcross dates Skinner's copy tentatively in 1675, after Milton's death,[30] about the same time I should judge that he was working on his pages of *DDC*. Skinner then tried fruitlessly to publish both manuscripts abroad. In my original argument of 1992, I suggested that he loudly noised in London the fact that he had this religious work that he thought was Milton's, a rumor picked up by the early biographers only at a distance, as can be deduced from the fact that they lacked some significant facts—the title, for example, or for that matter Skinner's first name (though the Anonymous Biographer also heard about its heresies that kept Daniel from publishing it in Holland).[31] The evidence, in short, cannot support attribution of *DDC* to Milton and only its possession to Skinner, who seems in ignorance honestly to have assigned the work to him. We may indeed let Daniel rest in peace.

4

In summary, *DDC* originated from a continental, most likely a Dutch, context. A copy in the handwriting of Jeremie Picard came into Milton's possession sometime in the late 1650s but before 1673, when he may have used some of its contents and dictated some minor changes to various anonymous amanuenses. This Picard may have been responsible for the work. There was a contemporary Dutch landscape painter with this name who cannot be certainly identified with him. At or shortly before Milton's death, that manuscript as well as the materials constituting *SP* passed to Milton's youthful but not intimate acquaintance, Daniel Skinner, who copied all the latter and a good many pages of the former. In ignorance he attributed the work to Milton.

Notes

1. William B. Hunter, "The Provenance of the *Christian Doctrine*," *SEL* 32 (1992): 129–42, 163–66; "The Provenance of the *Christian Doctrine:* Addenda from

the Bishop of Salisbury," *SEL* 33 (1993): 191–207; and "Animadversions upon the Remonstrants' Attacks upon Burgess and Hunter," *SEL* 34 (1994): 195–203.

2. Computer-driven stylistic comparisons are currently being undertaken by Gordon Campbell of the University of Leicester, Thomas Corns of the University College of North Wales, and John Hale of the University of Otago in New Zealand.

3. See William B. Hunter, *Descent of Urania: Studies in Milton, 1946–1988* (Lewisburg, Pa.: Bucknell University Press, 1989), 31–45.

4. For chiliasm, see Michael Fixler, *Milton and the Kingdoms of God* (Evanston, Ill.: Northwestern University Press, 1964); for monophysitism, Barbara Lewalski, *Milton's Brief Epic: The Genre, Meaning, and Art of "Paradise Regained"* (Providence: Brown University Press, 1966), 155–56; for mystical theopantism, Walter Clyde Curry, *Milton's Ontology, Cosmogony, and Physics* (Lexington: University Press of Kentucky, 1957), 43; for the theopaschite heresy, William B. Hunter, "Milton on the Incarnation," in *Bright Essence: Studies in Milton's Theology* (Salt Lake City: University of Utah Press, 1971), 144; for the theopathetic tradition, Michael Lieb, "Milton and the Anthropopathetic Tradition," *Milton Studies* 25 (1989): 213–43. I have briefly considered this last concept in the appendix to "Milton on the Passions," *Milton Studies* 31 (1995): 87–88. Note also Dennis Danielson's unease over the disparity of the conceptions of theodicy between *DDC* and the rest of the canon in his stimulating book, *Milton's Good God: A Study in Literary Theodicy* (Cambridge: Cambridge University Press, 1982), especially 157.

5. John Milton, *Complete Prose Works of John Milton*, 8 vols., ed. Don M. Wolfe et al. (New Haven: Yale University Press, 1953–82). All references to Milton's prose are to this edition and are cited parenthetically in the text.

6. See Maurice Kelley's textual note to the manuscript's page 399, in his edition of *DDC* in *Complete Prose Works* (6:829).

7. On the other hand, the general directions to read Scripture diligently (8:433–35) include six proof texts that do not appear in a cluster in *DDC,* nor does the passage on "hainous Transgressions" (8:440), supported by three proof texts, have parallels in it. But the treatise does not specifically address either of these issues, another distancing of it from a canonical work.

8. Maurice Kelley, *This Great Argument* (Princeton: Princeton University Press, 1941).

9. Ibid., 41.

10. Ibid., 42–56, 227–51.

11. Ibid., 300–4.

12. Ibid., 227–51.

13. Ibid., 42–56.

14. William Riley Parker, *Milton: A Biography*, 2 vols. (Oxford: Clarendon, 1968), 2:1008 n. 256.

15. Albert Beuse, head of Searchroom, Rijksarchief, Groningen, letter to author, October 19, 1993.

16. H. E. Korenromp, admissions officer, Rijks Universiteit, Leiden, letter to author, September 13, 1993.

17. W. Chr. Pieterse, Gemeentearchief, Amsterdam, letter to author, October 18, 1993.

18. James Holly Hanford, "The Rosenbach Milton Manuscripts," *PMLA* 38 (1923): 290–96.

19. For the information that follows see Robert Thomas Fallon's fine recent book, *Milton in Government* (University Park: Pennsylvania State University Press, 1993), especially Appendix B dealing with "The Seventeenth-Century Manuscripts,"

220–28. I follow his descriptions, not having myself been able to examine the original documents.

20. Details of the history of the *State Papers* and Skinner's activities, recovered from his correspondence, are available in David Masson, *The Life of John Milton*, 7 vols. (1859–94; reprint, Gloucester: Peter Smith, 1965), 6:720–21 and 790–806; Parker, *Milton: A Biography*, 1:601–12, 637, and notes; John T. Shawcross, "A Survey of Milton's Prose Works," in *Achievements of the Left Hand: Essays on the Prose of John Milton*, ed. Michael Lieb and John T. Shawcross (Amherst: University of Massachusetts Press, 1974), 347–54; and John T. Shawcross, *Milton: A Bibliography for the Years 1624–1700* (Binghampton: Medieval and Renaissance Texts and Studies, 1984), items 716, 720 (2), and 749.

21. Dr. Shawcross has made convincing cases for two other transcriptions, now lost but represented in two different publications. Gregorio Leti's *Historia* (Amsterdam, 1692) has forty-nine state letters that differ sufficiently in details from the other transcriptions to prove independence of them; and John Lünig's *Literae Procerum Europae* (Leipzig, 1712) has 165 letters whose variants prove also an independent source. See Shawcross, "Survey," 354–58; his information about the latter derives from Leo Miller's discovery reported in *Notes & Queries* 17 (1970): 412–14.

22. Fallon, *Milton in Government*, 226, as well as all others who discuss the matter.

23. Parker, *Milton: A Biography*, 1:611–12.

24. Helen Darbishire, ed., *The Early Lives of Milton* (London: Constable, 1932), 7, 9–10.

25. Hunter, "Provenance," 136–37.

26. Parker, *Milton: A Biography*, 1:610.

27. Fallon, *Milton in Government*, 226.

28. Ibid., 221 n. 3, 225.

29. Masson, *Life*, 6:794.

30. Shawcross, *Milton: A Bibliography*, 87.

31. Darbishire, *Early Lives*, 29, 31.

"Women Are Indebted to Milton": Milton and Woman's Rights in the Nineteenth Century

DAVID BOOCKER

> Milton's "Paradise Lost" is responsible for many existing views in regard to woman. After the Reformation, as women began to waken to literature, came Milton, a patriot of patriots—as patriots were held in those days, a man who talked of liberty for men—but who held man to stand in God's place toward woman. . . . Between Milton and his wives, we know there was tyranny upon one side and hatred on the other. He could not gain the love of either wife or daughter, and yet he is the man who did so much to popularize the idea of woman's subordination to man. "He, for God; she, for God in him"—as taught in the famous line: "God thy law, thou mine."
>
> (*History of Woman Suffrage*, 1881)

IN 1838 Sarah Grimké published her *Letters on the Equality of the Sexes* in response to charges by a group of Massachusetts ministers that her own and her sister's activities in the abolitionist movement were unwomanly. Appearing six years before Margaret Fuller's *Woman in the Nineteenth Century* and ten years before Elizabeth Cady Stanton and Lucretia Mott organized the first woman's rights convention, this series of fifteen "letters" represents an important and influential work in the history of the woman's rights movement. Indeed, they were the first full-length philosophical statement on "the woman question" written by an American woman.[1] Like other early feminists, Grimké placed emphasis on education and law as the means by which women were to gain freedom and equality. And, like other feminists, she believed the institution of marriage represented for women an unequal place in society and forced them to sacrifice their independence and individuality.

For readers of Milton, what truly distinguishes Grimké's *Letters* is that they represent a uniquely feminist way of reading both Genesis and *Paradise Lost* and indicate a notable shift in women's attitudes toward the author of

51

Paradise Lost. According to Joseph Wittreich, "In the eighteenth century, when there was perhaps a deeper gulf between the sexes but not so great a distance between the popular culture and the intellectual elite, Milton's name was a strong presence in both cultures, but it was a name revered particularly by women."[2] Wittreich demonstrates how eighteenth-century women were encouraged to read *Paradise Lost* with the idea "that for women to know their history was for them to know their Milton."[3] He reviews "women's observations on Milton" from about 1700 to 1830 and concludes that "in Milton studies, women have a history and have had an influence of their own—and perhaps more unexpected, that Milton was not just an ally of feminists but their early sponsor."[4]

If we extend the scope of Wittreich's study to include American women from the 1830s on, what appears is a much different kind of response to Milton and *Paradise Lost.* Women such as Grimké, Elizabeth Wilson, and Elizabeth Cady Stanton speak out against the unequal status of women in society and accuse Milton of being "the man who did so much to popularize the idea of woman's subordination to man."[5] Milton's "bogey" seems to have appeared to these women long before it appeared to Virginia Woolf.[6] For these women, Milton was as guilty as Paul of providing generations of antifeminists with the fodder they needed to develop elaborate arguments against equal rights for women. Milton was an obvious target. Late eighteenth- and early nineteenth-century moralist leaders used the Bible and Milton's representation of prelapsarian Adam and Eve to "educate" women about their proper duties as wives. It is not surprising, then, that Grimké and other outspoken woman's rights activists attempted to provide a biblical justification for the liberty and equality of women as moral beings. But what is, perhaps, a little surprising is the effort they made to attack the one man they believed most responsible for confirming woman's unequal status in society: Milton.

Much of Grimké's argument in the *Letters* centers on providing a scriptural basis for the equality of the sexes. The main arguments of her reading of Genesis found in her *Letters* were that God created men and women in his image, which means there is no difference between them; God gave dominion to both over other creatures but not over each other; God created woman as a helpmeet, a helper *like unto himself,* for man, which implies woman's moral and intellectual equality; and Adam sinned equally with Eve because he ate the fruit. If Adam had tried to make Eve repent instead of sharing her guilt, Grimké says she would allow man the moral superiority he claims. For readers of Milton, what is of particular interest is her reading of Genesis that gives Adam as much guilt for sinning as Eve.

Grimké claimed in her first letter on "The Original Equality of Woman" that her discussion would "depend solely on the Bible to designate the sphere of women." Yet, in this letter she describes Eve Miltonically "wandering alone amid the bowers of Paradise" to encounter Satan,[7] and near the end of the letter she includes the following lines of poetry:

> Authority usurped from God, not given,
> He gave him only over beast, flesh, fowl,
> Dominion absolute: that right he holds
> By God's donation: but man o'er woman
> He made not Lord, such title to himself
> Reserving, human left from human free.[8]

No doubt Grimké expected her readers to recognize these lines from book 12 of *Paradise Lost*, which she adapted to her argument. In the poem these are Adam's lines; he is "fatherly displeas'd" as he comments on the story of Nimrod and the Tower of Babel. But with the alterations—"fish" to "flesh," "that right we hold" to "that right he holds," and "Man over men" to "man o'er woman"—Grimké, "womanly displeas'd," appropriates Milton to deny man's despotic rule over woman—that is, to make the point that God gave humankind dominion over all other creatures, but not over each other.[9] Man and woman were created equal, and neither one was intended to be subservient to the other. In the letter she maintains that Genesis 3.16, "Thou wilt be subject to thy husband, and he will rule over thee," is simply prophecy, not a manifest command by God to woman.[10]

The appropriation is important because it is clear that Grimké understood the role that *Paradise Lost* played in the creation of the image of the submissive woman in American society. Indeed, the poem was nothing less than a poetic icon, used by conservative patriarchal writers to argue that women should be held in submission. One way to counter these conservative writers was to appropriate their text, to read it aright, and, if necessary, to rewrite it. But another way to counter Milton was to blast Milton, and in a subsequent letter Grimké turned iconoclast and blamed Milton for woman's unequal status in society:

> If man is constituted the governor of woman, he must be her God; and the sentiment expressed to me lately, by a married man, is perfectly correct: "In my opinion," said he, "the greatest excellence to which a married woman can attain, is to worship her husband." He was a professor of religion—his wife a lovely and intelligent woman. He only spoke out what thousands think and act. Women are indebted to Milton for giving to this false notion, "confirmation strong as proof of holy writ." His Eve is embellished with every personal grace, to gratify the eye of her husband; but he seems to have furnished the mother of mankind with just intelligence enough to comprehend her supposed inferiority to Adam, and to yield unresisting submission to her lord and master. Milton puts into Eve's mouth the following address to Adam:
>
> > My author and disposer, what thou bidst,
> > Unargued I obey; so God ordains—

God is thy law, thou mine: to know no more,
Is woman's happiest knowledge and her praise.

This much admired sentimental nonsense is fraught with absurdity and
wickedness. If it were true, the commandment of Jehovah should have run thus:
Man shall have no other gods before me, and woman shall have no other gods
before man.[11]

Grimké compares Milton to Iago. Whereas Iago planted a "napkin" for
Cassio to find, explaining that "Trifles light as air / Are to the jealous
confirmations strong / As proofs of holy writ" (*Othello*, 3.3.324–26), Milton planted a "false notion" about woman, creating his Eve inferior to
Adam, for subsequent generations of readers to find. Thus, for Grimké,
Eve is the prototype of the inferior and submissive woman held up before
the women of Grimké's day as their model. Grimké suggests that if Milton
had been correct in his depiction of Adam and Eve, then Jehovah's second
commandment would have been something closer to what Milton writes in
Paradise Lost, "Hee for God only, shee for God in him" (4.299).

Sarah Grimké paved the way for other women to follow. In 1849 Elizabeth Wilson of Cadiz, Ohio, published her *Scriptural View of Woman's
Rights and Duties* "to demonstrate the equality of the sexes" using the
Bible.[12] In chapter 1, "The Equality of the Sexes at the Creation and Since
the Fall," Wilson interprets Genesis to prove that God created man and
woman equal from the beginning. Because she was created of the same
substance as Adam, Eve is "equal."[13] Like Grimké, Wilson suggests that
the serpent selected Eve because she was alone in the garden, not because
she was weaker, and she argues that Genesis 3.16 was prophecy. For Wilson,
the source of man's claim of superiority over woman is not Genesis, but
the "testimony of the idiocy of Eve compared with Adam" as represented
by theologians and poets like Milton:[14]

Milton represents Adam and Eve's appearance in the garden as follows:

"though both,
Not equal, as their sex not equal seem [*sic*];
For contemplation, he, and valour formed;
For softness, she, and sweet attractive grace;
He for God only, she for God in him:
His fair large front and eye sublime declared
Absolute rule. She for God in him!"

Idolatrous nonsense! which cannot be surpassed by his holiness the Pope.[15]

For Wilson, Milton and his Adam are as idolatrous as the pope himself
because they exalt themselves as God's agent or "secondary God."[16] Wilson

sees Eve placed in an inferior position not because of her own deficiencies, but because Adam is exalted above his proper station:

> Thus she must serve the creature instead of the Creator. Man usurps the throne of God. Milton's character of Eve is much admired, and our theological ethics correspond with it, with few exceptions.
>
> Milton represents Eve to be liberally endowed with the spirit of her station. She is well aware that ignorance must be a prominent constituent part of her character. She says, "to know no more is woman's happiest knowledge and her praise."[17]

For both Grimké and Wilson, Milton's Eve was created not equal, but stupid. Not surprisingly, both women compare the condition of woman in the mid-nineteenth century to that of the slave who was kept ignorant because knowledge was either the source of unhappiness or liberty. For example, Wilson complains that a woman was "not to search the scriptures daily for herself," but to submit to her husband the control of her mind:

> Not only is she to give her husband the control of her physical operations, but, in a special manner, he is to control her mind; as an absolute rule, she is to be "taught by her husband at home"—she is not to search the scriptures daily for herself, to see whether those things she is taught are so; but say to her husband, as Milton represents Eve to say to Adam—
>
> > "God is thy law, thou mine: to know no more,
> > Is woman's happiest knowledge, and her praise."
>
> No matter though your husband is wallowing with his fellow-creature in the gutter, and does not know the first letter in the alphabet, still it is his *official duty* to be your teacher.[18]

Thus, woman is always the learner, never the teacher, and always content with her inferior station in life. And since the husband teaches his wife about God, it follows that a woman worships God through her husband: "shee for God in him." For Wilson, this worship of man was nothing less than idolatry.[19]

Thus, Milton's poetry was used time and again by early woman's rights activists to illustrate the root cause of woman's unequal status in society. Yet from the perspective of the late twentieth century, it is unclear whether it was Milton's poetry or the commentator on woman's role in society who used Milton's poetry who was most responsible for the inferior position suggested for nineteenth-century women. Late eighteenth- and early nineteenth-century moralist readers and interpreters of Milton's *Paradise Lost,* in their attempt to counter the image of the "masculine" woman presented by Mary Wollstonecraft and to "educate" women using Milton's representation of prelapsarian Adam and Eve, seem as responsible as Milton himself for the antifeminist views that led to charges against the poet. But as John T. Shawcross explains, to blame Milton for society's notions of "male superiority" is off target; instead, blame is more properly cast on "those who misread, who would find like gender-attitudes elsewhere, and who were probably raised with the same unconscionable belief[s]."[20]

The fact is, the beginning of the nineteenth century was not a good time to be a feminist or a woman. In her study, *Changing Ideas About Women in the United States, 1776–1825*, Janet James explains that around 1800 there emerged in both England and America a great religious revival concerned with the "manners and morals" of women.[21] According to these "reformers," courtship and marriage were to be the central concerns of ladies, and any dereliction of household duty was roundly condemned. Thus, the focus of a girl's education was how to make herself pleasing to men, and the average young lady of the period was not delivered unto her husband without a generous portion of advice on the conduct of being a wife, and all too often this advice was supported with lines from *Paradise Lost*. Therefore, to fully understand the attacks by Grimké and Wilson, among others, it is necessary to examine how women were "educated" using Milton's *Paradise Lost*. By looking at advice given to them in *The Lady's Monitor* and other periodicals and writings of the late eighteenth and early nineteenth centuries, I want to demonstrate how lines from Milton's *Paradise Lost* were often used to support advice given to women about being good wives, and that this advice often involved deliberate misreading of Milton's poem.

The Lady's Monitor was published in New York in 1801–2 to keep women "up to date on the latest London fashions, new country dances and literary news."[22] Despite its short run, I believe that what it had to say about Milton is representative of what women were being taught in the early nineteenth century about reading *Paradise Lost*. Most articles focus on some technical aspect of Milton's poetry. One article suggests, for instance, that Milton's genius was "too impetuous and sublime to be curbed by the mechanism of rhyme" and that "The language . . . of Milton's blank verse was not studied, but the natural application of his own tongue to deliver his own ideas."[23] Another article compares James Thomson's use of blank verse in his *Seasons* with Milton's in *Paradise Lost,* and another discusses the beauty and sublimity found in Milton's poem.[24] There is one article, however, that considers how thorough Milton's knowledge of the "human heart" was:

> Although Milton cannot very justly be famed for his knowledge of the human heart, there are some passages in his works which evince him to have been acquainted with the general emotions of our nature. Indeed the poem of Paradise Lost has, as Dr. Johnson observes, "this inconvenience that it comprises neither human actions nor human manners. And such is the original formation of this

poem, as it admits no manners till the fall, it can give little assistance to human conduct." Yet limited as it is to this constitutional defect, in utility, it is far from being deficient in instruction. Where there is play for our passions, they are exhibited.[25]

This writer cites Samuel Johnson to argue that *Paradise Lost* is incapable of teaching its women readers about "human conduct." But if the poem is "far from being deficient in instruction," what can it teach its female audience? According to the reviewer in *The Lady's Monitor*, when he applies the poem to "the experiences of real life," it teaches him about the "inveterate antipathy which appears to rankle in a great part of those who are entitled Old Maids, towards the youthful exercises of love." To prove this point, the writer quotes the lines from *Paradise Lost* that show Satan jealously observing the love between Adam and Eve (4.496–504). These lines, he writes, always cause him to think about the "envious disposition of the old," and to consider that "one cannot fail to suspect that, having poisoned their own springs of enjoyment, they are become [like Satan in *Paradise Lost*] haters of all pleasure in another."[26]

What is most revealing about all this discussion of *Paradise Lost* is how the issues of gender that so concerned Grimké and Wilson are absent. And when gender issues are raised, they are done so in order to give conservative advice about the need for marrying so as to avoid the dangers of becoming an old maid. Yet, I believe both the absence of gender discussions and the presence of gender to offer conservative advice have the same purpose: to promote and uphold the patriarchy. James Machor argues that those who wrote reviews of fiction for women readers "conceived of themselves as caretakers of culture."[27] He demonstrates how "reviewers, editors, and fellow columnists, most of whom were male, acted as avatars of the dominant culture, which included traditional ideas about women's status, interests, and reading abilities as well as the assumption that the purpose of reading was to obtain knowledge that facilitated one's ability to contribute to the prevailing social order."[28] Thus, Machor writes, these reviewers "sought to exercise their self-appointed roles as cultural custodians by directing and refining response patterns of the public to bring them in line with a standard of reading epitomized by the reviewers themselves."[29] According to Machor, these reviewers did not write

to create new strategies for interpreting texts that challenged old assumptions. Instead, it was to be a form of self-validation and confirmation of the already known. Through a strategy of informed reading that was essentially conservationist and ultimately narcissistic, reviewers sought to multiply their own images, as cultural incarnations, in modified and well-controlled female replicas that could reinforce patriarchal hegemony.[30]

Machor draws his conclusions from reviews of antebellum fiction, yet I believe what he concludes about the self-perceived role of these reviewers and editors applies to what is seen in *The Lady's Monitor*. It is no coincidence that the weekly column that sometimes included discussions of Milton's poetry was called "The Reflector." That most of the focus in these articles is on the same technical issues—language, blank verse, sublimity— that male readers had been discussing for a hundred years indicates that *The Lady's Monitor* was attempting to teach women to read "like men" and to divert attention away from gender issues. The last thing the editors of this magazine wanted was for women to approach *Paradise Lost*, or any other reading, from a female perspective. Thus, women were discouraged from reading self-reflexively; to do so might generate responses like those of Grimké and Wilson. On the other hand, the advice to marry, to avoid the dangers of becoming an old maid, was an attempt to "facilitate [women's] ability to contribute to the prevailing social order" by insuring that they fulfill their traditional roles as wife and mother.

What we see in *The Lady's Monitor* typifies the kind of advice given to women of the period and how Milton was used to support such advice. As George Sensabaugh illustrates, "Americans found Milton instructive on manners and morals in a number of ways, but what they responded to most, or what they repeatedly recalled, was the picture of marital bliss Milton had painted in . . . *Paradise Lost*."[31] This point cannot be emphasized enough; Americans framed Milton's picture of marital bliss, and writers of the period used the picture to teach women proper "manners and morals." For example, in his *Sermons to Young Women*, first published in England in 1766, and published in America well into the nineteenth century, James Fordyce offered to his young women readers a picture of Milton's Eve "as a model of a woman most amiably feminine" and the best example of "female reserve" and "meekness."[32] Similarly, in an essay called "On the Female Accomplishments most agreeable to a Husband," Elizabeth Griffith suggested that as a wife, Eve possessed "all the real elegant reserve of conduct which Milton makes the characteristic of woman; which he calls, 'Not obvious, not obtrusive, / but retir'd.'"[33] The Reverend John Bennett's *Letters to a Young Lady*, published first in England and then several times between 1790 and 1810 in the American periodicals, presented Eve and the Edenic marriage to ladies as patterns of emulation:

> The immortal poem of Paradise Lost should not only be in the hands, but graven on the hearts of every woman, because Milton, above all other authors, describes the distinguishing graces of the sex, and, in his Eve, has exhibited an exquisite pattern of female perfection. . . . Milton, like other great men, was fully sensible of the blessings we derive from the society of women, and how cheerless the face of nature would have been without them. He, therefore, labours to make

the mother of Paradise every thing that could charm and every thing that could alleviate the infelicities of life.[34]

That nature had a "cheerless" face until Eve's appearance was reiterated time and again. An essay appearing in *The Hive* suggested that Adam was in "rapture" when he "received this last best gift of heaven, *Woman!* And indeed his heart might well dance with joy at obtaining such a prize; for, according to the vivid painting of the immortal Milton, 'Grace was all in her steps, heaven in her eye, / In all her actions dignity and love.'" This essay goes on to explain that "fair Eve" was precisely "the thing" that Adam wanted.[35]

It is clear from these examples that a woman with every "charm" and "grace . . . in her steps" was man's "prize" and that her role in life was to make man's life complete. Again and again Eve is presented to young ladies, by both men and women, as the model woman. This model woman, of course, attended to domestic affairs. In *The Boarding School* (1798), a novel by Mrs. Hannah Foster, the preceptress instructs her young girls by approvingly quoting Milton's "nothing lovelier can be found / In woman, than to study household good."[36] In an essay appearing in Oliver Oldschool's *Port Folio*, John Hall told women that if they "consult" the portraits of "Eve of Milton, the Imogen of Shakspeare [*sic*], the Belphaebe of Spencer [*sic*], the Armida of Tasso," and "lay aside their pride and affectation . . . [t]he spear of Ithuriel will touch lightly, and not display a single stain on the white robe of their purity." Hall began his essay with the same lines from book 9 invoked by the teacher in Mrs. Foster's novel, and then quoted lines 285–311 of book 4, where Milton described "the *excellent form* and *happy state* of our *general* ancestors, as they were first seen by Satan." These lines, Hall said, "cannot be too often quoted," because they clearly illustrate the differences in Adam and Eve: his authority and her submission.[37] And James Wilson, a professor of law, in a discussion of whether women might be capable of participating in government or of receiving a law education, used the same descriptions of Adam and Eve in book 4 to show what nature from the beginning said about men and women. His conclusion was that although women can influence public affairs, woman is formed for "domestic society," and can most influence public affairs by educating her children.[38] Clearly, these examples illustrate the belief that God created man and woman with distinct natures, and to create harmony in nature, both man and woman must live according to the roles they were created to play.

Perhaps the most oft-quoted passage of Milton appearing in early periodicals is the marriage hymn, lines 450–70 of book 4. Here was the "picture of marital bliss." A number of essayists suggested that marriage is the social institution upon which rests the entire fabric of human society, and they quoted the marriage hymn to illustrate the "blissful state," or to hearken

back to a time when "conjugal infidelity" was not a problem.[39] Happy
matrimony, then, depends on the kind of "reciprocal love" seen in the
relationship between Adam and Eve in book 4. In the marriage in which
"two conjugal souls are united," the man is "all truth" and the woman
"all tenderness":

> he possessed of cheerful solidity, she of rational gaiety; acknowledging his supe-
> rior judgment, she complies with all his reasonable desires, whilst he, charmed
> with such repeated instances of superior love, endeavours to suit his requests to
> her inclinations; his home is his heaven upon earth, and she his good genius,
> ever ready to receive him with open arms and a heart dilated with joy.[40]

The Weekly Visitor, or, Ladies Miscellany sometimes used lines from the
marriage hymn as a heading above the wedding announcements of prominent people.[41]

No doubt the most unusual use of the hymn occurred in an essay called
"Instructions to a Lady how to preserve the lasting Affections of her Husband." Here the young lady is told what to do if she experiences "(. . .
Heaven forbid) any emotions of jealousy." She is not to try to find out if
her jealousy is grounded in truth, but if she discovers his guilt, she is not
to be "ashamed of what he has been guilty of," and if she intends to reclaim
him, she is neither to reproach him nor to complain:

> the one would *harden* him in his crime; the other; by *wearying* him, afford some
> pretence for returning where he can be more at rest, and in some measure destroy
> the effect of that regret, which I believe all men of sense must feel, sooner or
> later, for having been guilty of an injustice of this nature, and which, of itself, if
> left to operate, would bring them back to virtue, and make them say with *Milton*,
> in his admirable description of Marriage, 'Hail, wedded love! . . .'[42]

This use of the marriage hymn reveals more about nineteenth-century
attitudes about the role of women and marriage than it does about Milton's
opinions. Whatever Milton's views toward women and their role in marriage might have been—whether misogynist or subordinationist or not—
surely he did not intend his marriage hymn to be read in support of adul-
tery, which Milton did consider grounds for divorce.

Thus *Paradise Lost* was handed down to a generation of women readers.
It is no wonder that many women were outraged: the fact that Milton was
used in support of such advice no doubt contributed to the kinds of charges
against him made by Sarah Grimké and Elizabeth Wilson. Obviously,
Grimké and Wilson were not the first women to recognize the extent to
which "women are indebted to Milton" for their place in society. On the
one hand, as Joseph Wittreich says, in the eighteenth century, "as now,
some women were schooled into submission to patriarchal culture, even

sometimes through the agency of *Paradise Lost*."[43] On the other hand, while it is true that Milton's poetry was "abused" by a patriarchal culture, many nineteenth-century readers, such as Margaret Fuller and Mrs. Hugo Reid, admired Milton and offered the poet as a man worthy of hero worship to both women and men and his works as examples of genius.[44] Fuller avoided gender issues as they touched upon Milton's work. According to Kevin Van Anglen, what is "most striking" about Fuller's feelings about Milton "is her avoidance of a radical response to Milton on the question of gender authority (despite the fact that his 'Divorce Tract' and treatment of Adam and Eve in *Paradise Lost* provided her with ample excuse to do so."[45] Van Anglen writes that Fuller "repressed both the patent confliction in his epic and the darker side of his contemporary attitude toward women, in order to favor a position more typical of her class."[46]

What distinguished Grimké and Wilson was their "radical response to Milton on the question of gender authority." This response was based largely on an attempt to reverse years of interpretation of the Bible and Milton's *Paradise Lost*. Unlike Mary Wollstonecraft who, in her "Vindication of the Rights of Woman," denied the literal truth of the biblical creation of Eve from one of Adam's ribs because it subjugated woman,[47] both Grimké and Wilson accepted God's word, but denied the tradition of interpretation, of which Milton was an integral part, that made Eve inferior to Adam. Instead, they worked to create a new feminist reading.

Others followed. In 1850, Elizabeth Jones, in an address to the Ohio Women's Convention, used Grimké's appropriation of Milton—"but man o'er woman / He made not Lord"—to argue that God, not man, "defined" woman's appropriate sphere.[48] And in her *Woman's Bible*, published much later in 1895, Elizabeth Cady Stanton reveals the influence of both Grimké and Wilson in her reading of Genesis.[49] And lest we think that the issues raised by nineteenth-century woman's rights activists in regards to Milton are somehow dead, we need only look at recent scholarship by Joan Webber, Marcia Landy, Barbara Lewalski, Diane McColley, Christina Froula, Edward Pechter, Julia M. Walker, William Shullenberger, and James Grantham Turner,[50] to name only a few, to realize that questions such as "Is Eve subordinate to Adam?" and "Does subordination mean inferiority?" are still hotly debated.

If there are differences in the approach to the answers, perhaps it is, in part, because women such as Grimké and Wilson were themselves victims of the patriarchal attitudes they attempted to fight. Grimké learned very early what it meant to have something denied to her because of her sex; her father told her that she "would have made the greatest jurist in the land—had she not been a woman."[51] Thus, for these woman's rights activists, Milton was for their patriarchal society a spokesman whose word was as good as "holy writ," and attacking him was necessary not just to establish a feminist reading of a great literary work, but because attaining equal status in an extreme patriarchal society depended on it.

Notes

I would like to thank John Shawcross, Joseph Wittreich, and Stephen Buhler for their help and encouragement. The epigraph is from Elizabeth Cady Stanton, Susan B. Anthony, and Matilda Joslyn Gage, eds., *History of Woman Suffrage*. 5 vols. (New York: Fowler and Wells, 1881), 1:779–80.

1. Elizabeth Ann Bartlett, ed., *Sarah Grimké: Letters on the Equality of the Sexes and Other Essays* (New Haven: Yale University Press, 1988), 1, hereafter cited as *Sarah Grimké: Letters*.

2. Joseph Wittreich, *Feminist Milton* (Ithaca: Cornell University Press, 1987), 2.

3. Ibid., 4.

4. Ibid., ix.

5. Stanton, Anthony, and Gage, *History*, 1:780.

6. See Sandra Gilbert, "Patriarchal Poetry and Women Readers: Reflections on Milton's Bogey," *PMLA* 93 (1978): 360–82.

7. Sarah M. Grimké to Mary S. Parker, 11 July 1837, in *Sarah Grimké: Letters*, 32. The letter appeared in *The Liberator* 8, no. 1 (5 January 1838): 4.

8. Ibid., 33.

9. See John Milton, *Paradise Lost*, in *The Complete Poetry of John Milton*, ed. John T. Shawcross, rev. ed. (New York: Doubleday, 1971), 12.66–71. All references to Milton's poetry are to this edition and are cited parenthetically in the text.

10. Sarah M. Grimké to Mary S. Parker, 11 July 1837, in *Sarah Grimké: Letters*, 33.

11. Sarah M. Grimké to Mary S. Parker, September 1837, in *Sarah Grimké: Letters*, 80–81. The letter appeared in *The Liberator* 8, no. 5 (2 February 1838): 20.

12. Elizabeth Wilson, *A Scriptural View of Woman's Rights and Duties, In All the Important Relations of Life* (Philadelphia: Wm. S. Young, 1849), 1.

13. Ibid., 17.

14. Ibid., 21.

15. Ibid., 22–23.

16. Ibid., 22.

17. Ibid., 51.

18. Ibid., 225.

19. Elizabeth Wilson, "Elizabeth Wilson to Woman's Rights Convention at Worcester," 27 September 1850, *The Liberator* 20, no. 46 (15 November 1850): 181.

20. John T. Shawcross, *John Milton: The Self and the World* (Lexington: University Press of Kentucky, 1993), 197–98.

21. Janet James, *Changing Ideas About Women in the United States, 1776–1825* (New York: Garland, 1981), 124.

22. Jean Hoornstra and Trudy Heath, eds., *American Periodicals, 1741–1900* (University Microfilms International, 1979), 117.

23. "Milton," *The Lady's Monitor*, 1, no. 25 (7 February 1802): 197–98.

24. "The Reflector. No. XV. Thomson's Seasons," *The Lady's Monitor* 1, no. 27 (20 February 1802): 212–13; "The Reflector. No. XIV. On Milton's Paradise Lost," *The Lady's Monitor*, 1, no. 26 (13 February 1802): 204–6.

25. "The Reflector. No. X," *The Lady's Monitor* 1, no. 21 (9 January 1802): 163–64.

26. Ibid., 164.

27. James Machor, "Historical Hermeneutics and Antebellum Fiction," in *Readers in History: Nineteenth-Century American Literature and the Contexts of Response*, ed. James Machor (Baltimore: Johns Hopkins University Press, 1993), 74.

28. Ibid., 65.

29. Ibid.

30. Ibid., 74–75.

31. George Sensabaugh, *Milton in Early America* (Princeton: Princeton University Press, 1964), 195.

32. James Fordyce, D. D., *Sermons to Young Women*, 3d American ed. 2 vols. (Philadelphia: M. Carey, 1809), 1:48–49, 2:111.

33. [Elizabeth Griffith], "On the Female Accomplishments most agreeable to a Husband," *The Massachusetts Magazine or Monthly Museum of Knowledge and Rational Entertainment*, 1, no. 26 (January 1794): 37–40.

34. John Bennett, "On Poetry: Collected from Bennet's [sic] Letters to a Young Lady," *The Literary Tablet*, 12 March 1806: 50. See also *The American Museum or Universal Magazine*, January 1792: 9–11; February 1792: 70–72; April 1792: 139–42.

35. Philo. Biblos, "Traits of Women, from Sacred History. Eve," *The Hive*, 27 February 1805: 145.

36. Quoted in James, *Changing Ideas About Women*, 149.

37. Sedley [John Hall], "The American Lounger. No. 177," *The Port Folio*, n. s., 4 October 1806, 193–95. Oliver Oldschool was the pen name for Joseph Dennie, editor.

38. "Extract From the Introductory Lecture of the hon. James Wilson, L.L.D. professor of law in the College of Philadelphia.—Published by T. Dobson, price three eights of a dollar," *The American Museum or Universal Magazine*, January 1791, 21–24.

39. See "On Matrimonial Happiness," *The Weekly Magazine*, 3 March 1798, 153–54; "Epistles, Odes and Other Poems, by Thomas Moore, Esq.," *The Monthly Register*, February 1807, 166–67; "Men and Women. A Moral Tale by the Wanderer," *The Monthly Register*, November 1807, 356–69.

40. "On Matrimonial Happiness," *The Weekly Magazine*, 3 March 1798, 153–54.

41. *The Weekly Visitor, or, Ladies Miscellany*, 15 February 1806, 26; 21 June 1806, 271.

42. Mira, "Instructions to a Lady how to preserve the lasting Affection of her Husband," *The New York Magazine: or Literary Repository*, June 1795, 358–61.

43. Wittreich, *Feminist Milton*, xiii.

44. Margaret Fuller, *Papers on Literature and Art*. 2 vols. (London: Wiley & Putnam, 1846), 1:33–42; Mrs. Hugo Reid, *Woman, Her Education and Influence* (New York: Fowler and Wells, 1847), 162.

45. Kevin P. Van Anglen, *The New England Milton: Literary Reception and Cultural Authority in the Early Republic* (University Park: Pennsylvania State University Press, 1993), 180.

46. Ibid.

47. Mary Wollstonecraft, "A Vindication of the Rights of Woman," *The Works of Mary Wollstonecraft*, ed., Janet Todd and Marilyn Butler. 7 vols. (New York: New York University Press, 1989), 5:95.

48. J. Elizabeth Jones, "An Address Delivered Before the Ohio Women's Convention, At Salem, April 19, 1850," *The Liberator* 20.23 (7 June 1850), 92.

49. Elizabeth Cady Stanton, *The Woman's Bible* (New York: European Publishing Company, 1895), 14–27.

50. Joan Mallory Webber, "The Politics of Poetry: Feminism and *Paradise Lost*," *Milton Studies* 14 (1980): 3–24; Marcia Landy, "Kinship and the Role of Women in *Paradise Lost*," *Milton Studies* 4 (1972): 3–18; Barbara K. Lewalski, "Milton on Women—Yet Once More," *Milton Studies* 6 (1974): 4–20; Diane McColley, *Milton's Eve* (Urbana: University of Illinois Press, 1983); Christina Froula, "When Eve Reads Milton: Undoing the Canonical Economy," *Critical Enquiry* 10 (1983): 321–47; Edward Pechter, "When Pechter Reads Froula Pretending She's Eve Reading Milton; or, New Feminist Is But Old Priest Writ Large," *Critical Enquiry* 11 (1984): 163–70; Julia M. Walker, ed., *Milton and the Idea of Woman* (Urbana: University of Illinois Press, 1988); William Shullenberger, "Wrestling with the Angel: *Paradise Lost* and Feminist Criticism," *Milton Quarterly* 20 (1986): 69–85; James Grantham Turner, *One Flesh: Paradisal Marriage and Sexual Relations in the Age of Milton* (Oxford: Clarendon, 1987).

51. Bartlett, *Sarah Grimké: Letters*, 15.

Milton's *History of Britain* and the One Just Man

BLAKE GREENWAY

BEGINNING with his early years of political involvement in the 1630s, Milton denounced the "corrupted Clergy, then in their height,"[1] associating them with vestiges of Roman Catholicism from which he wished to purify the English Church. For Milton, Archbishop William Laud had epitomized this type of self-seeking clergyman, and his execution in 1646 had seemed the landmark event that would usher in the revolution the Puritans had sought. Furthermore, the popishly inclined Stuart monarchy seemed all but impotent. Years before the execution of Charles I, as early as Cromwell's decisive victories at Marston Moor in 1644 and at Naseby in 1645, the king had become nothing more than a figurehead. Parliament now ran the country. The rule of the saints on earth seemed near.

But during the late 1640s, Milton's attitude changed remarkably toward this government he had fought so hard to install, as he watched the members of the Long Parliament begin to become more self-seeking than the government they had replaced. In "The Character of the Long Parliament," a section of his 1648 *History of Britain,* Milton reserves his harshest diatribe for the members of his own party. Rather than living up to their original idealistic aims, "every one betooke himself, setting the common-wealth behinde and his private ends before, to doe as his owne profit or ambition led him" (5:443).[2] Milton presents the unlikely analogy upon which he will build the *History of Britain:* a comparison between England in the 1640s after the Royalist government was removed and England in the fifth century after the Romans withdrew. Concerning both sets of political circumstances, Milton believes that the removal of the existing government opened the door to lawlessness and a Hobbesian pre-government state of rapine and plunder. It seems odd that he would credit Royalists this way, but Milton appears convinced that the analogy is too apparent to ignore, "since god afte[r] 12 ages and more had drawne so neare a parallel betweene their state and ours in the late commotions" (5:441).

Seventeenth-century war tracts such as Cromwell's *The Honour of the English Soldiery* drew attention to the problem of post-battle plunder. Both armies "like the Locuss, devoured what the Palmerworm had left, utterly drained them of their wealth and provisions, [and] cleared both man and beast (driving all away) to the impoverishing and starving of many thousands."[3] Cromwell had exhorted New Model Army soldiers not to plunder the countryside before and after a battle, and his words had had some effect. Even partisan Royalist observers were forced to admit that New Model Army soldiers did not plunder the English countryside as they themselves did. When the war was over, however, Milton watched as the real post-battle plunder went on in the two houses of Parliament. Exasperated by what he perceives as the doom of the Interregnum government, he laments, "Thir votes and ordinances which men look'd should have contain'd the repealing of bad laws & the immediate constitution of better, resounded with nothing els but new impositions, taxes, excises, yearlie, monthlie, weeklie[,] not to reck'n the offices, gifts, and preferments bestow'd and shar'd among themselves" (5 : 445). Thus, in the *History of Britain* we learn something seminal to Milton's developing political thought—the realization that it is as necessary to stand alone against the domineering and liberty-reducing elements of his own Puritan party as it had been to resist the centralizing force of Laudian Anglicanism.

Against this backdrop of a self-seeking parliament that is impoverishing the country and a self-seeking ecclesiastical bureaucracy that had controlled the church, the *History of Britain* begins to shape a heroic paradigm, the figure of the one just man, the one who will stand against the many, that will realize its mature definition in *Paradise Lost*'s Enoch, Noah, and Abdiel. Wyman Herendeen has called this pattern in the *History of Britain* "a vision of the rebel able to resist the tyranny of an immoral age."[4] Although Milton's hero might admittedly serve some type of larger partisan end, the pattern of his heroism always moves from the individual spark within one figure and thence disperses outwardly toward the larger mass. Never does Milton's heroism originate from within a larger organizational framework and trickle down into the hearts of individual warriors or worshippers.

In his account of Cassius Scaeva, a first-century soldier serving under Julius Caesar, Milton introduces a tension between military discipline and rashness, and in what seems an unlikely position for him,[5] Milton places the greater value on military rashness. From four sources—Valerius Maximus's *Memorable Deeds and Sayings,* Thomas North's translation of Plutarch's *Lives,* William Camden's *Britannia,* and John Speed's *Historie*—Milton distills his own version of the Scaeva episode: "In this confused fight Scaeva *a Roman Souldier,* having press'd too farr among the Britans, and besett round, after incredible valour shewn, single against a multitude, swom back safe to his General; and in the place that rung with his praises, earnestly besought pardon for his rash adventure against Discipline" (5 : 45–46).

Milton's treatment of his source material reveals something about his turn of mind in 1648. Plutarch lists Scaeva merely as one in a long list of examples that demonstrate Caesar's good leadership, attributing these acts of valor specifically to Caesar's generous war gifts. Caesar has laid up a trust fund for just such purposes: "All he received was but a public fund laid by for the reward and encouragement of valor."[6] But, ignoring the gist of Plutarch's version of the Scaeva episode, Milton fashions instead a lone figure motivated by the heroic seed within him, rather than by some larger organizational framework. This impulse also prompts Milton to ignore the argument of Valerius's version, which attributes Scaeva's heroism to Caesar's military discipline. Valerius describes Scaeva as "great in fight, but greater in the remembrance of Military Discipline,"[7] whereas Milton calls Scaeva's deed a "rash adventure against Discipline." In any case, Milton never liked Julius Caesar, and in book 2 of the *History of Britain* he aligns himself clearly on the side of Cassius and the antidespot faction (5:61). Besides, Milton seems to wish not to emphasize group heroism, but to call attention rather to the small germ of valor. Thus, his Scaeva is more of an impetuous warrior than we find in William Camden's account.[8] While Camden's Scaeva fights in the midst of things for a time and is then deserted by his fellows, in Milton's version Scaeva gets carried away, "press'd too farr among the *Britans*," and was then "besett round."[9] Milton's Scaeva places himself in a position that, had he been prudent, he would not have chosen. Venturing too far out among the enemy suggests more of Scaeva's sense of irrational judgment than his being merely deserted by his fellows in the midst of battle, as Camden presents. Milton seems at every point willing to forgive a lack of rational discipline if in its place there is the spirit of inflamed heroism, no matter how unbridled and rash.

After the Romans withdrew, the fifth-century Britons were undoubtedly a slothful and uninspired lot, a group who needed somehow to be made more heroic. But although Milton thinks military discipline might be able to work some sort of cursory, cosmetic changes upon them, he seems convinced that no amount of discipline can instill in them the spark of heroic zeal. The only thing that can do that is the catalyst of one single heroic heart standing against a consensus. Given this heroic spark, it is a relatively easy matter to institutionalize it into some kind of military usefulness. But it is the inflamed spark that is for Milton indispensable. This insight is crucial to understanding why Milton so attracted the Romantic poets. It is that revolutionary sublime toward which William Blake was so magnetized in *The Marriage of Heaven and Hell*. Even before Milton's "major works" appear, we recognize a characteristic inflamed madness expressing itself in the revolutionary heroic.

Like Scaeva, Milton's Godwin also acts heroically apart from the organizational structure of the larger army. In a rash moment Godwin steals out of camp the night before Canute plans to attack the Swedes and defeats them himself, before the general's plans can be carried out: "*Godwin* stealing out of the Camp with his English (the night before), assaulted the *Swedes,* and had got the Victory ere *Canute* in the morning knew of any fight. For which bold enterprise, though against Discipline, he had the English in more esteem ever after" (5:362). As in the Scaeva episode, Milton here values the inspired spontaneous over the dutifully restrained. He even troubles to add the editorialization "against Discipline," for it is not in his Henry of Huntingdon source.[10] Clearly, Godwin acts apart from the sanction of Canute's larger organization. There is in Godwin's "stealing" out of the camp the sense both that he is trying not to wake everyone and that if he had he would have been asked to wait on the official orders of his general. This tension between individual spontaneity and group discipline is missing from Huntingdon's account. Godwin's impulse to function autonomously from larger controlling structures in Milton's version resembles a similar impulse in the John Milton of "Elegy I," who was rusticated for not functioning within the organizational framework of Cambridge. The passage, moreover, assumes that Canute and the representatives of his organization are either unable or have no wish to fault Godwin for his rashness. The necessity for inspired heroism is of such moment in times of immediate warfare that rash behavior can be overlooked.

Later in book 6, as the Danish army ravages northern England, Milton relates the story of one single man's heroism in the face of invasion. Milton goes well beyond his sources in emphasizing how the Danes ravage the beautiful pastoral countryside.[11] Again Milton uses the image of one man standing against the many: "and [to] the Villages therabout they turn'd thir fury, slaying all they met save one man, who getting up into a Steeple, is said to have de-fended himself against the whole *Danish* Army" (5:345). Milton frames his hero against a particularly controversial seventeenth-century issue, an army plundering a countryside, with its villages and landscape. The Danish soldiers become symbols of beastly appetite, who, after they have plundered the countryside, "like wild Beasts glutted, return to thir Caves" (5:345). The image is central to the analogy around which Milton has built the *History of Britain.* Humankind's appetite, which expresses itself by pillaging the English countryside, mirrors the plundering of England's resources by the taxation of a self-seeking Parliament. The Danes eventually give up on the man in the steeple and return to their ships. The lone warrior's moral victory represents the potency of one just man in the face of a consensus.

In a later section that Milton could easily have used to discuss the evils of pride and boastfulness, he instead shapes William of Malmesbury's account of a lone Norwegian soldier into his own version of the rash, inspired warrior: "One man of the Norwegians is not to be forgott'n, who with incredible valour keeping the Bridge a long hour against the whole English

Army, with his single resistance delai'd thir Victorie; and scorning offerd life, till in the end no man dareing to graple with him, either dreaded as too strong, or contemn'd as one desperate, he was at length shot dead with an Arrow" (5:397–98). There was negative language in Malmesbury's account, had Milton wanted to use it. Malmesbury's Norwegian soldier is "boastfully flourishing about . . . too incautious from his security," and Malmesbury concludes that the warrior's defeat was somehow brought on by his own incaution.[12] Milton could have demonstrated here how soldiers should be disciplined, how they should not boast, and how pride leads to a fall, but he is willing instead to see the soldier's rashness as positive. For Milton it is important that the soldier has gone through the mental process of having decided to die rather than to live under the conditions that will be imposed on him should he surrender. Having thus given up any chance of survival, "contemn'd as one desperate," reckless disregard for his own life ironically makes the Norwegian soldier safer on the battlefield. Lieutenant Robert Ward in *Animadversions of Warre* (1639) argued that "Valour hath double oddes of a fearefull Cowards heart, so that he hath no ability left to offend his enemy, or defend himselfe; This makes victory so easily gaind, for the spirits of a Coward are so retired . . . that there is hardly strength left to make the least resistance."[13] Men who are afraid are forced to leave their normal battle plan and are thus less dangerous.

Milton makes his Norwegian soldier into a more solitary figure than he finds in his sources. Huntingdon's account presents a band of soldiers who have already fought heroically even before the one Norwegian takes the stage. Huntingdon paints a colorful group picture of the Norwegians "driven back across the river, with the living crossing over on the dead," adding that "they offered a courageous resistance."[14] Milton deletes this picture of the soldiers' collective heroism. Huntingdon adds, moreover, that, although the group of Norwegians were in fact forced to give ground, they did not flee. Milton omits these kinds of editorializations that would make the soldier seem merely one of a group of heroes.

Huntingdon tells us that the Norwegian soldier's weapon is a battle-ax, an especially telling weapon because one can fight with it only at close range. That nobody wants to get close to the Norwegian emphasizes his fierceness. The English here rely on their greater numbers as a kind of nebulous advantage they hope will overawe the Norwegians, something like the technique used by the French soldiers at Agincourt in Shakespeare's *Henry V*. But on a bridge, before the discovery of gunpowder, it little matters how many thousands of soldiers wait somewhere back in the field. The English cannot cross the bridge until somebody gets close enough to kill this one desperate Norwegian. Pre-gunpowder warfare makes possible an exaggerated kind of heroism. It is entirely conceivable that one man could fend off a group of soldiers, for whoever finally kills him must necessarily bring himself into close physical proximity with him and at some point match his own single skill against the hero's. The obvious exception to this dilemma would be some means of warfare that does not require the warriors to come into close physical proximity, namely the bow and arrow, which in its ability to fire long-range has a similar effect to gunpowder in that it takes away one warrior's ability to engage an entire squadron. This is in fact how the English are finally forced to kill the Norwegian. Milton omits Huntingdon's more obviously symbolic unmanning of the soldier— the enemy soldier stabs the Norwegian through the *celanda* (Latin for "private parts")—which would necessarily bring the soldiers into close physical proximity, albeit through the side pillars of the bridge.

Book 3 defines even more explicitly how one germ of valor is able to multiply. Germanus represents the spiritually inflamed in the face of consensus lethargy. The British army prevails because of the zeal of this one man, whose language becomes a pattern of Milton's heroic principle. Germanus's battle plans position the Britons in a valley surrounded by hills where they will ambush the Anglo-Saxons. In choosing this battle site, Germanus thinks not of swords and spears, but of echoes and acoustics. It is a plan of warfare that exaggerates the multiplication of language. The spoken word, "*Halleluia*," is taken up by the rest of the army, and eventually "redoubled" by "the Hills and Valleys" (5:137). This multiplication of language unnerves the opposing army, causing them to flee. Milton's principle of the small germ of valor multiplying into an eventual consensus is thus enacted in terms of language. Such a passage as this may have suggested to Milton the Sonnet 18 image in which a just cause, verbalized in the form of the Waldensians' groans, multiplies via echo into something greater than it initially appeared: the Waldensian massacre becomes one small incident in the larger progression of the kingdom of God. Moreover, from the account of the Germanus episode in Bede's *Ecclesiastical History*, Milton alters the language to emphasize even more explicitly the idea of one man, one word. Milton changes Bede's plural "bishops," who initially speak the word "halleluia," to the singular, "Germanus," thus emphasizing his heroic pattern more explicitly.[15]

Milton further politicizes this argument of military autonomy in his contrast between Ambrosius and Vortigern. From Geoffrey of Monmouth, Milton got the idea to connect Ambrosius with a crisis in freedom of religion. Not only are the Britons before the coming of Ambrosius enslaved to another people, they are also enslaved specifically away from freedom of religion. As Geoffrey of Monmouth put it, the Angles and Picts have "well-nigh done away all Christianity from sea to sea."[16] In this context, Vortigern becomes Milton's "Other" figure, the negative representation against which he will define the principle of spiritual autonomy in Ambrosius. Because Vortigern will not stand alone, he must rely on another nation's political strength. Vortigern had invited the Anglo-Saxons to protect Britain from the Irish and the Picts, but their real intention was to subdue the country. When the Angles eventually ally with the Picts, the Britons find themselves at the mercy of another nation. For Milton, Vortigern becomes a microcosm of British lack of backbone, and he dies enclosed within a tower because of cowardice rather than valor: an inversion of the soldier in the steeple who resisted the pillaging of his country.

The analogy underlying the *History of Britain*, both in "The Character of the Long Parliament" and in the political sections at the beginning of book 3, suggests that without heroic figures like Ambrosius, seventeenth-century Englishmen will once again find themselves enslaved to their enemies. David Loewenstein calls the prominence of this analogy in the *History of Britain* "Milton's sense of a cyclical pattern of history."[17] If the English are unwilling to stand as autonomous political beings, their slothfulness will eventually bring them into subjection to a foreign yoke.[18] Milton warns English citizens in the *Second Defense* that "If you plunge into the same depravity, if you imitate their excesses and hanker after the same vanities, you will become royalists as well as they, and liable to be subdued by the same enemies."[19] Like fifth-century Britain, Milton's England needs a heroic spark, which Milton is convinced can come only from the catalyst of one just man.

Herendeen calls this Miltonic principle "the potency of the individual to break from history."[20] Like the Norwegian soldier who knows he must be enslaved if he surrenders or the soldier in the steeple whose pastoral world has been invaded, and like Milton's Cromwell, Ambrosius is one man among a spineless nation who retains the spirit of Roman hardness. Milton calls him "a vertuous and modest man, the last heer of *Roman* stock" (5:154–55).

Admiration for both Ambrosius and Cromwell originates from the same impulse in Milton's mind. The Cromwell he develops in both prose and rhyme (in *Observations Upon the Articles of Peace*, "A Postscript," Sonnet 16, and the *Second Defense*) moves from a Royalist England to the New Model Army to the Interregnum and, in the process, from one group who would subsume him into its ideology to another. Presenting Cromwell as the one just man who must stand in the face of an unrighteous consensus, Milton remarks in the *Second Defense*, "In this state of desolation to which we were reduced you, O Cromwell, alone remained to conduct the government, and to save the country."[21]

While the threat posed by the Angles and the Picts in the Ambrosius section was of the extinction of the church—they had "well-nigh done away all Christianity from sea to sea"—in book 4 of the *History of Britain* Milton deals with the threat of too much church. He focuses on the spiritual wisdom of one solitary Christian Hermit in the face of a swelling, ecclesiastical bureaucracy. The contrast carries with it a tacit analogy between Augustine of Canterbury's seventh-century England and Milton's seventeenth-century England, as Augustine's compulsive attempt to "unify" the English church becomes a prefiguration of Archbishop Laud's uniformity movement.[22] Both seek a national uniformity in what would seem to be trivial matters of church procedure. Against this homogenizing force, Milton poses the righteous humility of one Christian Hermit.

Milton describes Augustine's visit to England, on papal injunction, in hopes of resolving the Easter crisis. Seized by a kind of holy compulsive binge, Augustine compels all English churches to observe Easter on exactly the same day. From his treatment of source material, it becomes clear both how Milton views Augustine's reform programs and how he wishes his reader to view them. Though Bede was predictably supportive of Catholic church authority, Milton shapes the Augustine incident into a diatribe against ecclesiastical pride. He seems to want his seventeenth-century readership to recognize in Augustine's mission the same papist smell that he detected in Archbishop Laud's programs, and he makes explicit that this leviathan impulse of the larger institution to subsume all smaller branches into itself has its origin in the church at Rome. Augustine requires all English churches "to conform with him in the same day of celebrating *Easter*, and many other points wherein they differ'd from the rites of *Rome*" (5:192). From the list of Catholic paraphernalia that Augustine brings with him on his mission to England, Milton has no trouble inferring that these men are evil Romanists, "who what they were, may be guess't by the stuff which they brought with them, vessels and vestments for the Altar, Coaps, reliques, and for the Archbishop *Austin* a Pall to say Mass in" (5:190). The catalog resembles the list of Catholic paraphernalia clung to by those souls headed for the "Paradise of Fools" in *Paradise Lost* (3.496) and indicates a similar Miltonic disgust for religious iconography. Milton summarizes his account of Augustine's mission with the comment, "to such a rank superstition that Age was grown" (5:190), which seems to carry with it the tacit analogy, and so has ours.

As in the earlier Germanus episode, Milton is in the awkward position of having to concede the tremendous role that Catholic missionaries played in the Christianization of England, but not wishing to venerate Roman Catholicism any more than he has to. To be academically credible, his language must retain a surface fidelity to its source. But Milton cites Bede sarcastically, when, for example, he refers to "the great work of converting" (5:190) that Augustine is doing. Augustine is involved in no epic mission to bring Christianity into a new part of the world, but is rather assuring his own compulsive sensibility that a few already converted priests get their ecclesiastical days right, which "mission" Milton sees as a gross bureaucratic misdirection of time and energy. "*Austin* laboured well among Infidels,"

Milton notices, "but not with like commendation soon after among Christians" (5:192).

Milton wrote the *History of Britain* just two years after William Laud was beheaded and one year before Charles was beheaded. These were the two figures most responsible for the Anglican "uniformity" movement. Fears had been deep among seventeenth-century Protestants that Laud would attempt to reintroduce Catholic practices into the Anglican church. Charles allowed his Catholic wife Henrietta Maria and foreign ambassadors staying in London to hold Catholic masses at his court, and Charles himself was in the habit of receiving visitors from the pope. Archbishop Laud increasingly favored a type of church service that "appeared to many Protestants to be as near to Catholicism as to make no difference."[23] His attempts "to promote the sacramental and ceremonial aspects of church services at the expense of sermons" was regarded by most Puritans as an attempt to undo, rather than to further, the Reformation.[24]

Milton had witnessed, for example, Laud's reforming zeal in his campaign to make all English and Scottish churches place the communion table at the east end of the quire. Referring to precedents set by the Archbishops of Bath and Salisbury, Laud insisted that "there is nothing done either by violence or command to take off the refferency of the standing of the Holy Table either way, but only laying fairely before men, how fitt it is, there should be order and unanimity."[25] Aware that his reforms would be perceived by most Englishmen as Catholic, Laud in his uniformity tracts shows a constant sensitivity to his Puritan adversaries. "I would faine know," he complains, "how any discreet moderate man dares say, that the placing of the Holy Table Alter-wise (since they will needs call it so) is done either to advance or usher in Popery."[26] Another of Laud's favorite arguments is that Queen Elizabeth herself was known for banishing popery, and yet *even she* kept the communion table at the east end of the quire.[27]

Both sets of issues resonate with bureaucratic triviality. But in ages of religious controversy like the fifth and the seventeenth centuries, trivial matters become a metonymy for larger struggles of ideology and class that are by no means trivial. Though Laud's compulsive love of regularity may appear to be a kind of ecclesiastical eccentricity, the deeper spirit of his reforms comes suspiciously close to the Catholic doctrine of the "Real Presence." Moreover, Laud's insistence on the location of the communion table resonates with social class distinction. Laud insists, innocently enough, on more reverence during communion, arguing that "bowing towards a Table, a stoole, a stone, a Wall, a House, a church, a dore, an Altar, or any thing else that is before a man when he cometh for divine worship, doth not thereby become Idolatry, but bowing towards any thing with relation to it, as of greater Holiness."[28] But by "more reverence" Laud really means prohibiting unsavory characters from loitering around the

communion table, which they will do if it is in the middle of the church.
Lower-class rustics, particularly in some of the outlying smaller and more
crowded churches, were in fact in the habit of laying their hats and coats
on the communion table, and some of Laud's High Church officials even
alleged that in the smaller country parishes, cockfighting went on in the
front of the church.[29] Laud reveals some of his social class disgust when he
complains that "the common people, when they go into the church, doth
no more reverence to God then a Tincker and his Bitch when they come
into an alehouse."[30] Laud's reforms carry with them an implicit social
agenda that would mystify church furnishings, thus giving the Anglican
church administration a more sure hold on the behavior of the masses,
much as Augustine had fortified his own ecclesiastical authority with impressive iconography.

Milton established the haughtiness of Augustine's Catholic bureaucracy
in order to contrast it to the righteous humility of one just man. In the
midst of his account of Augustine's Easter crusade, Milton presents the
story of one solitary Hermit who, through years of private dedication to
God, has developed a humble wisdom that enables him to stand firm in the
face of religious bureaucracy. As in earlier passages like the Germanus episode, Milton revises his sources to emphasize more clearly the idea of one
man standing out from the many. While others trooped off to see Augustine,
"One man there was who staid behind, a Hermit by the life he led, who
by his wisdom effected more then all the rest who went" (5:192). Though
the appearance of a politically powerful conclave having arrived from the
immediate presence of the pope would offer just the kind of networking
any aspiring clergyman might wish for, Milton's Hermit refuses to be caught
up in the visit of church officials. His refusal to attend the meeting registers
a passive resistance to the Catholic bureaucratic system that would control him.

Ironically, it is the very fact that the Hermit cares so little about gaining
political power within the church that empowers him. It is specifically because of the Hermit's custom of retiring daily by himself in private devotion
that, as Milton tells us, his advice is sought out by his fellow English
Christians: "they held him as an Oracle," Milton says, and for that reason
they demand of him his divinely inspired counsel (5:192). Because of his
habit of looking past the surface of things into the real indicators of spirituality, the Hermit can advise his fellow Christians that body language is a
truer indicator of one's spiritual state than verbal language. He sees that
the essential problem with which he and his fellow English Christians must
deal is Augustine's spiritual pride: "Austin [was] thus exalted to Archiepis-
copal authority," and in this state of hubris "so quickly they step't up into
fellowship of pomp with Kings" (5:190). Milton's Hermit warns his fellow
Christians to observe Augustine for signs of pride, particularly in the Arch-

bishop's body language: "if they found him meek and humble, they should be taught by him, for it was likeliest to be the yoke of Christ . . . but if he bore himself proudly, that they should not regard him, for he was then certainly not of God" (5:192). Due to the advice of the Hermit concerning Augustine's body language, the English Christians do not harken to the visitors, since "*Austin* being already there before them, neither arose to meet, nor receiv'd in any brotherly sort, but sat all the while pontifically in his Chair" (5:192).

In his resistance to bureaucratic control, Milton's Hermit's behavior embodies the revolutionary ethos of all of Milton's heroes which is to follow the biblical injunction, "We ought to obey God rather than men" (Acts 5.29).[31] This was an attitude characteristic of seventeenth-century Protestant figures like William Prynne, who was publically shorn of his ears for standing up to Archbishop Laud. Ironically, Milton's heroes usually define themselves in terms of a rebellious orthodoxy in the face of a consensus of anarchy, one man standing in the face of slothfulness, anarchy, Catholicism, religious bureaucracy. Like the Puritan cause itself, this resistance is never mere rebellion for its own sake, but rather rebellious orthodoxy against corruption within the system, a type of rebellious purity. For Milton, this moral single-mindedness is all that can save a doomed Interregnum government.

Notes

1. John Milton, "Headnote" to *Lycidas,* in *John Milton: Complete Poems and Major Prose,* ed. Merritt Y. Hughes (New York: Odyssey, 1957), 120. All references to Milton's poetry are to this edition and are cited parenthetically in the text.

2. John Milton, "The Character of the Long Parliament," in *Complete Prose Works of John Milton,* 8 vols., ed. Don M. Wolfe et al. (New Haven: Yale University Press, 1953–82). All references to Milton's *History of Britain* and "The Character" are to this edition and are cited parenthetically in the text.

3. Oliver Cromwell, *The Honour of the English Soldiery* (London: Thomas Newcomb, 1651), 2.

4. Wyman Herendeen, "Milton and Machiavelli: The Historical Revolution and Protestant Poetics," in *Milton in Italy: Contexts, Images, and Contradictions,* ed. Mario A. Di Cesare (Binghamton: Medieval and Renaissance Texts and Studies, 1991), 443.

5. Milton's position here, favoring rashness instead of discipline, would seem to contradict what he himself taught in earlier treatises such as *Of Education.*

6. Plutarch, *Lives of Illustrious Men,* trans. John Dryden (New York: Little, Brown, 1859), 645.

7. Valerius Maximus, *Memorable Deeds and Sayings* (London: For Benjamin Crayle and John Fish, 1684), 115.

8. William Camden, *Britannia,* trans. P. Holland (London: G. Bishop and J. Norton, 1610), 37. Like both Plutarch and Valerius, Camden makes Scaeva's hero-

ism generate from Caesar's larger military organization: "Scaeva, one of Casars Souldiers, with four other fellow Servitours," says Camden.

9. John Speed, *The History of Great Britaine* (London: G. Humble, 1627), one of Milton's seventeenth-century sources, observes that Scaeva had "formerly fled to Caesar" (184), which fact Milton omits, probably because it would make Scaeva appear less loyal.

10. Henry of Huntingdon, *Historia Anglorum*, VI *Rerum Anglicarum*, ed. Savile (Frankfurt, 1601), 364.

11. Ibid., 361.

12. William of Malmesbury, *Chronicle of the Kings of England*, ed. and trans. J. A. Giles (London: Henry G. Bohn, 1847), 256–57.

13. Robert Ward, *Animadversions of Warre; or, A Militarie Magazine of the Truest Rules, and Ablest Instructions, for the Managing of Warre* (London: John Dawson, 1639), 172.

14. Huntingdon, *Historia*, 368.

15. Bede, *Ecclesiastical History of the English People*, ed. and trans. Leo Sherley-Price (London: Penguin, 1968), 69–70.

16. Geoffrey of Monmouth, *History of the Kings of Britain*, trans. Sebastian Evans (London: Everyman's Library, 1966), 155.

17. David Loewenstein, *Milton and the Drama of History: Historical Vision, Iconoclasm, and Literary Imagination* (Cambridge: Cambridge University Press, 1990), 87.

18. Loewenstein cites the *History of Britain:* "The Saxons were now full as wicked as the Britans were at their arrival, brok'n with luxurie and sloth" (259).

19. John Milton, *The Second Defense of the English People*, in *Complete Poems and Major Prose*, 836.

20. Herendeen, "Milton and Machiavelli," 443.

21. Milton, *Second Defense*, 834.

22. This passage refers to Augustine the lesser, not the author of *The City of God*.

23. See Barry Coward, *Cromwell* (Essex, England: Longman, 1991), 15.

24. Ibid.

25. Archbishop William Laud, *Divine and politike observations newly translated out of the Dutch language* (Amsterdam, 1638), 47.

26. Ibid.

27. Ibid., 48–49.

28. Ibid., 45.

29. See Ronald Hutton, *The British Republic: 1649–1660* (New York: St. Martin's, 1990), 72.

30. Laud, *Divine and politike observations*, 41.

31. King James Version.

"An Equal Poise of Hope and Fear": A Fraternal Harmony of Extremes

Jay Russell Curlin

> Yet where an equal poise of hope and fear
> Does arbitrate the event, my nature is
> That I incline to hope, rather than fear,
> And gladly banish squint suspicion. (409–12)

Since Enid Welsford declared in 1927 that "*Comus* is a dramatized debate" that one can read or act "and hardly realize that there are dances,"[1] modern scholarship has done much to bring the music back to the masque. Especially since John Demaray's detailed study of the genre in 1968, *Milton and the Masque Tradition*, contemporary discussions of the masque have shifted from its subject to its genre and the purpose for which it was written. One thinks of Angus Fletcher's *The Transcendental Masque*, where the focus is on magic symbolism and musical iconography, of Barbara Traister's *Heavenly Necromancers*, which places Comus and the Attendant Spirit in the tradition of the magician in Renaissance drama, or even of Maryann Cale McGuire's *Milton's Puritan Masque*, where the emphasis is on the tension presumably inherent in the paradox of a courtly masque that is nonetheless "Puritan" in content and authorship.[2]

An unfortunate consequence of this otherwise healthy shift in focus is that questions of genre have come to overwhelm the actual *subject* of the masque, to the extent that the reader of today, to reverse Welsford's claim, could read or act *Comus* and hardly realize that there is a debate. While some have noted the importance of disputation in the masque, others have gone so far as to say that the central conflict is not between Comus and the Lady; rather than being "about" chastity or temptation, the masque is a drama of warring magicians, of the overthrow of Comus by the Attendant Spirit and Sabrina.[3] Scholars more interested in what the Lady and her brothers have to say have nonetheless failed to observe the form of their argument. In his seminal essay, "The Argument of Milton's *Comus*," A. S. P. Woodhouse discussed the Elder Brother's speeches as a single

77

developed train of thought and ignored altogether the Second Brother's refutation, which effects a radical shift in focus in the other's argument.[4] E. M. W. Tillyard thought *Comus* a confused mixture of "poetical experiments,"[5] and Don Cameron Allen considered the entire masque "Milton's ill success" and "an attempted reconciliation of opposites that failed."[6]

Allen considered all attempts to explain *Comus* since 1780 "answers to Dr. Johnson," who declared the masque "deficient" as a drama, its dialogue composed of "declamations deliberately composed and formally repeated, on a moral question."[7] It is from this point that I too would like to redirect attention; for no matter what its other qualities or deficiencies as a masque may be, *Comus* is at the core "declamations deliberately composed and formally repeated." As Johnson recognized, the matter of the work is chiefly indebted to formal orations and disputations, the sort Milton had learned at St. Paul's and Cambridge. In his 1791 edition of Milton, Thomas Warton declared *Comus* "a suite of Speeches."[8] For Johnson, this fact constituted a "deficiency," a dramatic failure; but I would argue that this fusion of academic declamation with drama is, rather, further evidence of Milton's success in experimenting with literary form. In commenting on Milton's modification of genre, Northrop Frye remarked that "In listening to the Kyrie of the Bach B Minor Mass we feel what amazing things the fugue can do; in listening to the finale of Beethoven's Opus 106, we feel what amazing things can be done with the fugue. This latter is the feeling we have about *Comus* as a masque, when we come to it from Jonson or Campion. . . . Milton, like Beethoven, is continually exploring the boundaries of his art, getting more experimental and radical as he goes on."[9]

The two debates in *Comus* show something of this experimentation. Only one is immediately recognizable as a disputation, and it displays both the problems and the virtues of the tradition. The other, a friendly "disagreement" between brothers, is a vision of what disputation could be.

In the polemical exchanges, involving Comus and the Lady in Milton's masque, we find the traditional structure of university disputations. In the "gay rhetoric" (789) and "dazzling fence" (790) of Comus's orations, Milton exposes the "false rules . . . in reason's garb" (758) that he has attacked throughout his *Prolusiones Oratoriae*, most specifically in Prolusion 3, "Against Scholastic Philosophy." Although Comus's oration is eloquent and structurally flawless, the technique only barely conceals dangerously fallacious reasoning, and Milton uses the Lady's refutations to show that disputation can also unclothe "reason's garb" and confute error.

The debate between the Elder and Second Brothers, "an introduction to the main dispute,"[10] is of a much different nature. In this very private dispute, Milton shows a much less formal version of what disputation can be when its purpose is other than that of the endless bickering he had found so unproductive at Cambridge. Since the "disputants" are not obliged to hold tenaciously to a proposition, not only do they listen to each other's argument, but each is obviously swayed by what the other has to say. They are both naive to some degree, and each is irrational in his own way. Together, however, they manage to reach the conclusion at which their older sister has already arrived: "Virtue may be assailed, but never hurt" (588). Unlike disputants trying to annihilate each other's argument, the two brothers work far more in harmony in a mutual quest for truth; each is influenced and aided by the other's opinion. Their debate therefore ends with their having reached the same conclusion and seems in retrospect to be more like discussion than disputation. The Second Brother concludes their debate by remarking "How charming is divine philosophy!" thus giving a name to this very different form of disputation (475).

The debate of the two brothers, the first that occurs within *Comus*, has been generally treated as a single train of thought, rather than as a dialogue occurring between two speakers of completely opposite natures and viewpoints. The tendency to regard the arguments as one is understandable, however, because there is very little contesting of individual points within the debate. The two are brothers, after all, and one would have to go far to find more "fraternal" disputants. Each is in some degree swayed by the other's remarks, so that what would seem to be rebuttal is more an acceptance and redirection of points made. The Elder Brother is the idealistic optimist who worries too little about his sister's safety, the Second Brother the practical pessimist who worries too much.[11] Together, their separate temperaments complement each other and temper their irrational extremes.

From the point at which the two brothers make their first entrance, their debate is clearly of a much different nature from the public disputations of which the *Prolusiones Oratoriae* speak. The most basic difference sets the tone of the dispute and has much to do with its structure: they are alone. The academic disputations of Milton's university days were very much public performances, and both *defens* and *opponens* were concerned exclusively with an audience outside the arena of their contest. In none of the prolusions does Milton ever address his opponent in the second person, and he frequently addresses the audience to whom his oration is directed. Certainly no literary form would better suit such accommodation of the audience than the masque, the intimate staging of which places the action in the very midst of the audience and often calls for audience participation in its spectacles and for masquers and audience to join in dancing at the conclusion. And of course there was much of this element of the masque involved in the initial occasion of *Comus*, when the principal characters were the children and the music teacher of the family for whom it was performed. When the Egerton children were presented to their parents in the midst of the Attendant Spirit's song at the conclusion of the action, the audience was clearly being drawn into the action; however, no such awareness of the audience appears in this first debate. The brothers are disputing with, and actively attempting to persuade, only each other.

Their solitude is underscored by the combined exordium to their debate, in which the Elder Brother's call for light and the Second Brother's call for sound show them to be enveloped in darkness and silence. The traditional exordium attempted to capture the attention and sympathy of the audience and occasionally to invoke an agent of inspiration. In the exordium to Prolusion 6, for example, Milton combines flattery with invocation in saying that his listeners are incarnations of the Muses and that they therefore provide all the inspiration he needs. The two brothers similarly appeal to Nature to provide both illumination and sound, the physical parallels of the inspiration and the eloquence that the orator requests in the standard exordium. Later in the debate, the Elder Brother makes the connection between illumination and spiritual enlightenment all the stronger in his claim that "He that has light within his own clear breast / May sit i' the centre, and enjoy bright day" (380–81).

This exordium is also our first indication of the harmony that exists between the two disputants. Technically, each addresses a different audience: the Elder Brother addresses the stars and moon, while the Second calls on the more abstract spirit of sound. Indeed, since the Second Brother does not actually name his audience, his request resembles prayer: "might we but hear" (342). Yet the two requests are so tightly connected that they could have easily passed for a single two-part exordium had Milton not assigned each portion to a different speaker:

> *Eld. Bro.* Unmuffle ye faint stars, and thou fair moon
> That wont'st to love the traveller's benison,
> Stoop thy pale visage through an amber cloud,
> And disinherit Chaos, that reigns here
> In double night of darkness, and of shades;
> Or if your influence be quite dammed up
> With black usurping mists, some gentle taper
> Though a rush-candle from the wicker hole
> Of some clay habitation visit us
> With thy long levelled rule of streaming light,
> And thou shalt be our star of Arcady,
> Or Tyrian Cynosure.
>
> *Sec. Bro.*   Or if our eyes
> Be barred that happiness, might we but hear
> The folded flocks penned in their wattled cotes,
> Or sound of pastoral reed with oaten stops,
> Or whistle from the lodge, or village cock

Count the night-watches to his feathery dames,
'Twould be some solace yet some little cheering
In this close dungeon of innumerous boughs.

(330–48)

This "double exordium" is very much one in spirit, for each requests relief from "this close dungeon of innumerous boughs," and the Second Brother's continuation of the thought simply supports the first request by asking for a subordinate favor if the first cannot be granted. He even echoes his brother's request with his opening clause, "Or if our eyes / Be barred that happiness."

The exordiums are also tightly connected in form, being fused in a single iambic line. When we contract "Tyrian" with the synaeresis typical of Milton,[12] we find that the Elder Brother concludes his exordium with the first three iambic feet of line 341: "Or Tyrian Cynosure." The Second Brother concludes the line with the iambic fourth and fifth feet: "Or if our eyes." The pause is no longer than any natural caesura. Indeed, in both the Trinity and the Bridgewater manuscript versions of the masque and the first edition of 1637, the line is unbroken, and "2 bro" is merely inserted in the space following "Cynosure": "or Tirian Cynosure: 2 bro: or if o'eyes."[13] From neither the meter nor the contextual turn could one expect a change in speaker were it not for the stage direction. As we shall see, such metrical and contextual fusion is characteristic of this debate; in only one instance is the change in speaker effected with separate lines.[14] The technique occurs only twice in the debate between Comus and the Lady, where it achieves a much different effect. With the brothers, the fusion always supports agreement and seems far more dialogic than polemical. When the Lady completes a line begun by Comus, it is either to interrupt or contradict.

As complementary as the two exordiums are, it is significant that Milton assigns the first to the Elder Brother. The central theme of the Elder Brother's remarks is the presence of a spiritual illumination, a "radiant light" that enables the virtuous to "enjoy bright day" even if the "sun and moon / Were in the flat sea sunk" (373–81). He claims by contrast that "he that hides a dark soul, and foul thoughts / Benighted walks under the midday sun" (382–83). It is therefore consistent that his first thought would be to dispel the "double night of darkness" that obstructs his physical vision, though the optimism and resoluteness of his subsequent remarks show that he does not share his younger brother's fear of the dark. In similar fashion, the Second Brother requests sound because he needs to *hear*—not the noise of "folded flocks" or "pastoral reed" but the instruction of his Elder Brother, which gives him far more of the "solace" he requests in line 347. Though he plays an active part in the debate, it is in the subordinate role of the attentive *listener* whose questions and objections lead the "teacher" to new insights.

The description of the enveloping darkness and silence initiates the debate; for the Second Brother knows that if such a "double night of darkness" is frightening to him and his brother, how much more so it must be for their sister, who is even more alone than they. After his plaintive call for "some solace" in "this close dungeon," the Second Brother nervously considers the possible fate of their sister, whom he assumes to be in danger. We know in fact that she *is*, for we have just seen her led away by the disguised Comus as the result of a strange academic naïveté: being worldly enough to know that "courtesy ... is sooner found in lowly sheds ... than in tap'stry halls / And courts of princes, where it first was named, / And yet is most pretended" (322–25), she nonetheless moves to the ingenuous assumption that a shepherd must therefore be trustworthy. It is the same type of one-sided reasoning with which the Elder Brother first dismisses his brother's fears for her safety.

To the Second Brother's concerns for his sister's fate, the Elder Brother gives three reasons to "be not over-exquisite / To cast the fashion of uncertain evils" (358–59). The advice is good enough in itself for a number of reasons, not the least of which is that over-anxious pessimism that assumes the worst paints no truer a picture than unrealistic optimism. But the three propositions of the Elder Brother's opening argument are neither the best of reasons nor at all applicable to the situation of the Lady's danger. They have the ring of a clichéd general admonition against pessimism, with no thought of whether the formulaic response truly fits the present case. William Kerrigan maintains that every contention of the Elder Brother is "validated by the subsequent action of the masque,"[15] but Milton shows him to be much more naive than such a reading suggests. With the help of this dialogue with his brother, he comes close to the central truths argued in the masque, but he begins the debate as hardly the "privileged interpreter" Kerrigan has claimed him to be.[16]

First Proposition

> Peace brother, be not over-exquisite
> To cast the fashion of uncertain evils;
> For grant they be so, while they rest unknown,
> What need a man forestall his date of grief,
> And run to meet what he would most avoid?

(358–62)

In addition to being hardly helpful to the Lady's case, the comfort the Elder Brother first offers his brother is something of a red herring as an argument. To begin with, the dangers listed by the younger brother are by no means the inevitable doom suggested by "date of grief." While the younger brother wants to speed his sister's rescue, the other seemingly wishes to delay it for fear of its being necessary.

Robert Frost stated something of the same argument in "The Bearer of Evil Tidings," but with greater logic:

> As for his evil tidings,
> Belshazzar's overthrow,
> Why hurry to tell Belshazzar
> What soon enough he would know?[17]

Since the fate of Belshazzar is already sealed, there is little point in spoiling what little time he has left. But the case is much different with the fears that the Second Brother has mentioned; he has stated no irreversible fate:

> Perhaps some cold bank is her bolster now
> Or 'gainst the rugged bark of some broad elm
> Leans her unpillowed head fraught with sad fears,
> What if in wild amazement, and affright,
> Or while we speak within the direful grasp
> Of savage hunger, or of savage heat?
>
> (352–57)

If the Lady is indeed cold, frightened, and alone, her rescuers should certainly make whatever haste they can; if in actual danger, the greater should be their speed. It is very poor advice indeed, then, to remind the younger brother that the wise man does not "run to meet what he would most avoid."

Second Proposition

> Or if they be but false alarms of fear,
> How bitter is such self-delusion!
>
> (363–64)

The strange implication in the Elder Brother's second proposition is that the younger brother would be much happier for his fears to be true than to find his sister safe and sound. Of course, the Elder Brother is hardly so coldhearted as this sounds; he is merely giving an academic response to irrational pessimism, though without giving much thought to how well reasoned that pessimism is. His argument is in considerable need of refinement, which he will achieve in answering his brother's objections.

The Elder Brother shows his initial equanimity to be, in fact, less logical than his brother's anxiety. Simply dismissing the possibility of his sister's being in danger "(Not being in danger, as I trust she is not)" (369), he reduces her situation to "the single want of light and noise" (368–69). However "over-exquisite" the Second Brother has been in his description of possible evils, he has certainly remained within the realm of possibility: it *is* cold in the forest, especially in this "double night of darkness," and there is the possibility of attack from both man and beast. Against these very real possibilities, the Elder Brother's claim that her only inconveniences are the dark and the silence is surprisingly reductive, especially since the reader knows that she has just been led off by Comus.

Having reduced the possibility of danger to a safe darkness, the Elder Brother moves to his third proposition, an ethical claim that largely circumvents rational debate:

Third Proposition

> Virtue could see to do what Virtue would
> By her own radiant light, though sun and moon
> Were in the flat sea sunk. And Wisdom's self
> Oft seeks to sweet retired solitude,
> Where with her best nurse Contemplation
> She plumes her feathers, and lets grow her wings
> That in the various bustle of resort
> Were all to-ruffled, and sometimes impaired.
> He that has light within his own clear breast
> May sit i' the centre, and enjoy bright day,
> But he that hides a dark soul, and foul thoughts
> Benighted walks under the midday sun;
> Himself is his own dungeon.
>
> (372–84)

Milton's readers have found such praise of "sweet retired solitude" before, most notably in "Il Penseroso." The important questions here are whether that solitude has been elected and whether it is an adequate parallel to the situation of a woman lost in the woods. The Elder Brother claims that "Wisdom's self / Oft seeks to sweet retired solitude," thus suggesting that the lost sister has purposefully removed herself to something like the "peaceful hermitage" (168) of "Il Penseroso." The result of such reasoning is that the Elder Brother has moved from dismissing any possible danger to suggesting that being lost in the woods is actually preferable to the "bustle of resort" which the Lady would find were she still in her brother's company.

As peculiar as such reasoning may appear upon examination, it appears persuasive enough to the Second Brother, who not only lets pass the reductive and irrelevant first two propositions but actually concedes the truth of the third:

> 'Tis most true
> That musing Meditation most affects
> The pensive secrecy of desert cell.
>
> (384–86)

As with his first response, the Second Brother completes the closing line of his brother's oration and continues his theme, voicing his agreement all the more emphatically with the spondaic "most true." The metrical fusion is also tighter than in the first example we noted; for, in addition to completing the line, the response actually shares the split pyrrhic fourth position, in which the caesura is hardly long enough to change speakers:

> Himself | is his | own dun | **geon.** ‖ **'Tis** | most true.

The Second Brother's response and his agreement are immediate. If he has not forgotten his earlier fears for his sister's woodsy discomforts, he has been strangely swayed by the argument that one should not run to meet what one does not want to see.

Were this his only response—immediate agreement with his "opponent's" argument—we could hardly regard the scene as a debate. But he goes on to qualify his agreement with the demur that, while the gray-haired hermit usually associated with Meditation has nothing to tempt the villain, the meditating female is too lovely to pass up:

> But Beauty like the fair Hesperian tree
> Laden with blooming gold, had need the guard
> Of dragon-watch with unenchanted eye,
> To save her blossoms, and defend her fruit
> From the rash hand of bold Incontinence.
>
> (392–96)

The Second Brother appears to have missed the point entirely. The idealistic Elder Brother has been addressing only the question of darkness, claiming that the sister's inner virtue provides all the illumination she needs, while the Second Brother's thoughts are still on the question of safety. Associating his brother's remarks on meditation very literally with aged hermits, he assumes that the security of Virtue and Wisdom lies only in the poverty of those who have it—after all, who could possibly wish to rob an old man with just a few books, some beads, and a maple dish?

> 'Tis most true
> That musing Meditation most affects
> The pensive secrecy of desert cell,
> Far from the cheerful haunt of men, and herds,

> And sits as safe as in a senate-house,
> For who would rob a hermit of his weeds,
> His few books, or his beads, or maple dish,
> Or do his grey hairs any violence?

(384–91)

To his brother's idealism, the Second Brother presents an almost humorous practicality: if the brigand gives a wide berth to the saintly hermit, it has nothing to do with any quality inherent in him. He simply has nothing a villain would want.

The Elder Brother then makes no attempt to correct this misunderstanding of his metaphor. Instead, he is obviously moved by his brother's argument that

> You may as well spread out the unsunned heaps
> Of miser's treasure by an outlaw's den,
> And tell me it is safe, as bid me hope
> Danger will wink on opportunity,
> And let a single helpless maiden pass
> Uninjured in this wild surrounding waste.

(397–402)

His agreement with this refutation is as swift as the Second Brother's agreement with his first argument, and it also completes the fourth foot of the regularly iambic line:

of our | unown | ed sis | ter. ‖ I | do not [brother].[18]

The Elder Brother reverses his earlier dismissal of the dangers and more or less throws in the towel on the question of danger:

> I do not, brother,
> Infer, as if I thought my sister's state
> Secure without all doubt, or controversy.

(406–8)

As if to apologize for being overly cavalier in his first response, the Elder Brother admits to being an optimist by nature:

> Yet where an equal poise of hope and fear
> Does arbitrate the event, my nature is
> That I incline to hope, rather than fear,
> And gladly banish squint suspicion.

(409–12)

As we have seen, this is hardly the substance of his first response; it directly contradicts his flat claim" (Not being in danger, as I trust she is not)." Yet it does help to explain the seeming offhandedness with which he has dismissed his brother's fears: he is not so much callous as irrationally optimistic. He has warned his brother against an irrational pessimism that is "overexquisite / To cast the fashion of uncertain evils" but has shown himself to be equally extreme in the natural optimism that he now confesses.

Having made this admission, the Elder Brother shifts his argument to address the element of danger that he has previously dismissed. He reminds his brother of the "hidden strength" of their sister, which will serve as the theme of the masque:

> My sister is not so defenceless left
> As you imagine, she has a hidden strength
> Which you remember not.
> *Sec. Bro.*   What hidden strength,
> Unless the strength of heaven, if you mean that?
> *Eld. Bro.* I mean that too, but yet a hidden strength
> Which if heaven gave it, may be termed her own:
> 'Tis chastity, my brother, chastity.
>
>   (413–19)

This reversal of his earlier position, though no less optimistic in nature, reveals the degree to which the opposing opinion has influenced the progression of the debate. The Second Brother has insisted on the danger that their sister is in, and the Elder Brother has conceded the point, while giving his consistent optimism a new channel.

With this shift in his argument, the Elder Brother not only faces his brother's fears head on but actually adds to the list of dangers. The worst the Second Brother has imagined of natural ills has been "chill dew" and "rude burs and thistles" (351), but the Elder now imagines their sister weathering "huge forests, and unharboured heaths, / Infamous hills, and sandy perilous wilds" (422–23). To the more ominous danger posed by man, the nervous younger brother has been unable to put a face and has had to resort to such vague abstractions as "savage hunger" (357) and "bold Incontinence" (396), but the Elder Brother fleshes out these abstractions as "savage fierce, bandit, or mountaineer" (425). Nor does he stop there. Coming much closer to the truth of the matter with the magical Comus, the Elder Brother catalogues the possible supernatural dangers:

> Some say no evil thing that walks by night
> In fog, or fire, by lake, or moorish fen,
> Blue meagre hag, or stubborn unlaid ghost,
> That breaks his magic chains at curfew time,

No goblin, or swart faëry of the mine,
Hath hurtful power o'er true virginity.

(431–36)

This final claim is, of course, the point of the Elder Brother's "worst-case scenario": no matter what the danger, whether natural or supernatural, their sister is sufficiently protected by the "complete steel" (420) of her chastity. Having given name to his brother's less articulate fears, the Elder Brother shows that their sister's means of protection is much more formidable than the dangers he has described. It had enabled the "huntress Dian" (440) to tame beasts and "set at nought / The frivolous bolt of Cupid" (443–44), and armed with her Gorgon-headed shield, Minerva had "freezed her foes to congealed stone" with her "rigid looks of chaste austerity" (448–49).[19]

Far more convincing than these non-Christian allusions to antiquity is the Elder Brother's subsequent claim for "saintly chastity" (452) that "A thousand liveried angels lackey her, / Driving far off each thing of sin and guilt" (454–55). While this may seem the most outrageous of Milton's claims to the supernatural protection of chastity, it is in fact the most theologically orthodox. Describing the person who makes the Lord his "habitation," the psalmist writes: "For he shall give his angels charge over thee, to keep thee in all thy ways. They shall bear thee up in their hands, lest thou dash thy foot against a stone" (91.11–12).[20] We know from the Attendant Spirit's introduction that the Lady is indeed among those who "by due steps aspire / To lay their just hands on that golden key / That opes the palace of eternity" (12–14) and is therefore due such divine protection as promised in Psalms. The Attendant Spirit has been dispatched for that very purpose: "by quick command from sovran Jove / I was dispatched for their defence, and guard" (41–42). And when we first find the Lady lost in the woods, she invokes her qualities of Conscience, Faith, Hope, and Chastity as separate entities that she can see "visibly" (214) and that are as a "hovering angel girt with golden wings" (213). An even more explicit reference to her angelic protection is the Lady's claim that God "Would send a glistering guardian if need were / To keep my life and honour unassailed" (218–19). Stressing the Renaissance Platonism of the masque, Sears Jayne argues that we should think of the Attendant Spirit "not as an angel from St. Peter's heaven, but as a Platonic airy spirit," but the frequent references to biblical angels and the Attendant Spirit's own description of his commission are quite explicit.[21]

Associating such angelic aid with his sister's chastity is a considerable remove from the Elder Brother's earlier claim of chastity's self-protection. When the only danger he acknowledged was darkness and solitude, the Elder Brother spoke of internal illumination and the joys of meditation. Granting his brother's claim of a far more tangible danger compels him to use a more convincing optimism: not only is their sister not truly alone, but she is surrounded by guardian angels who both protect and rarefy her:

> Till oft converse with heavenly habitants
> Begin to cast a beam on the outward shape,
> The unpolluted temple of the mind,
> And turns it by degrees to the soul's essence,
> Till all be made immortal.
>
> (458–62)

In one respect, the argument has come full circle, having returned to the Elder Brother's initial claim of the type of invulnerable perfection at which their sister had already arrived. When his description of her "radiant light" (373) has failed to convince, he describes the external forces that have nurtured that light. If the Second Brother concedes the truth of their sister's unusual perfection, he must also acknowledge its source: "oft converse with heavenly habitants." And if he grants this, he must also admit that their sister is hardly in any danger since she is neither unprotected nor alone. Despite such emphasis on heavenly aid, Maryann McGuire has stated that the Elder Brother "makes a significant advance when he admits the limitations of human powers" *only* after the Attendant Spirit has "enlightened" him and he prays, "And some good angel bear a shield before us" (657). If he is overly optimistic by nature, his optimism is grounded on the faith in a "thousand liveried angels," and the Attendant Spirit has done nothing to alter that.[22]

Far from presenting a rebuttal, the Second Brother totally submits to his brother's argument, coming just short of applauding the victor of the debate:

> How charming is divine philosophy!
> Not harsh, and crabbed as dull fools suppose,
> But musical as is Apollo's lute,
> And a perpetual feast of nectared sweets,
> Where no crude surfeit reigns.
>
> (475–79)

If we hear in this an echo of Milton's attack against scholastic philosophy and the "pretty disputations of sour old men" in his third prolusion,[23] we should note that Milton is making a very definite distinction between scholastic and "divine" philosophy here and suggesting that the two are often confused. Scholastic philosophy, according to the third prolusion, *is* "harsh, and crabbed" and the stuff of "dull fools." Divine philosophy is another thing altogether, and Milton has just given us an example of it with this first, very undisputatious debate. In its suppression of the "zeal of contradiction" and its subordination of human reason to religious faith, this form of "divine philosophy" largely answers Francis Bacon's call to Cambridge for a greater fusion of faith and reason: "Surely the grace of the divine light will attend and shine upon you, if humbling and submitting Philosophy to Religion you make a legitimate and dexterous use of the keys of the senses; and putting away all zeal of contradiction."[24]

Angus Fletcher has called this first debate "ineffectual,"[25] and Barbara Traister has pronounced it a "fruitless" debate that gets the brothers nowhere until the Attendant Spirit shows up for their "enlightenment,"[26] while both Cedric Brown[27] and John Creaser have suggested more mildly that this debate chiefly shows the operation of juvenile reason, an "enchanting" instance of "idealistic eagerness" but unrealistic expectations.[28] I would argue, however, that the debate is far more successful than these readings suggest. The resolution is reached before the Attendant Spirit arrives, and he adds nothing to the brothers' conclusions. Indeed, when his information shows the Lady to be in definite danger and the Second Brother lapses into his former despair, the Elder Brother declares emphatically that this "enlightenment" has not changed a thing. The development of their debate has led them to imagine the greatest evils possible and, for the Elder Brother at least, to enforce a bedrock faith in divine protection. To hear their worst fears realized, then, is to learn nothing the Elder Brother has not already imagined and for which he has not already provided an answer: "this I hold firm, / Virtue may be assailed, but never hurt" (587–88). If this sounds overly naive, it is certainly confirmed in the crisis to follow.

Notes

John Milton, *Comus*, in *Complete Shorter Poems*, ed. John Carey (London: Longman, 1971). All references to *Comus* and "Il Penseroso" are to this edition and are cited parenthetically in the text.

1. Enid Welsford, *The Court Masque* (Cambridge: Cambridge University Press, 1927), 317–18.

2. John Demaray, *Milton and the Masque Tradition: The Early Poems, "Arcades," and "Comus"* (Cambridge: Harvard University Press, 1968); Angus Fletcher, *The Transcendental Masque* (Ithaca: Cornell University Press, 1971); Barbara Traister, *Heavenly Necromancers: The Magician in English Renaissance Drama* (Columbia: University of Missouri Press, 1984); Maryann Cale McGuire, *Milton's Puritan Masque* (Athens: University of Georgia Press, 1983).

3. The latter view has been espoused by A. Fletcher, *Transcendental Masque*, and Traister, *Heavenly Necromancers*. I would agree, however, with Harris Fletcher that the "disputing between the two forces constitutes the main action of the poem" (*The Intellectual Development of John Milton*, 2 vols. [Urbana: University of Illinois Press, 1956], 2:269). Christopher Hill has also connected *Comus* chiefly with the academic disputations of Milton's youth: "*Comus* is a dramatic dialogue, recalling

debates in which Milton was accustomed to take part at Cambridge" (*Milton and the English Revolution* [New York: Viking, 1977], 46).

4. A. S. P. Woodhouse, "The Argument of Milton's *Comus*," *University of Toronto Quarterly* 11 (1941): 46–71.

5. E. M. W. Tillyard, *Milton*, rev. ed. (London: Chatto and Windus, 1966), 58–66.

6. Don Cameron Allen, "The Higher Compromise: 'On the Morning of Christ's Nativity' and a Mask," in *The Harmonious Vision: Studies in Milton's Poetry* (Baltimore: Johns Hopkins University Press, 1954), 24.

7. Samuel Johnson, "Milton," in *Lives of the English Poets*, cited in Allen, *Harmonious Vision*, 63.

8. Cited in A. Fletcher, *Transcendental Masque*, 150.

9. Northrop Frye, *The Return of Eden: Five Essays on Milton's Epics* (Toronto: University of Toronto Press, 1965), 90, 92.

10. H. Fletcher, *Intellectual Development*, 2:269.

11. In commenting on what he considers an "ineffectual but charming debate" between the two brothers, Angus Fletcher has claimed that "the Elder Brother, who philosophizes skeptically, is a champion of faith, the younger a champion of hope" (170), but surely the reverse is true. In soothing the Second Brother's pessimistic fears, in which there is not a single ray of hope, the Elder Brother is not skeptical in the least. His argument *is* based on faith, but this makes him endlessly hopeful: "my nature is / That I incline to hope, rather than fear" (410–11).

12. In standard handbooks on prosody, for the "y-glide" contraction of synaeresis, which keeps a Miltonic line decasyllabic by combining two vowels to create a single diphthong, an example cited almost invariably is *disobed-yence* from the first line of *Paradise Lost*: "Of man's first disobedience, and the fruit . . ." (John Milton, *Paradise Lost*, ed. Alastair Fowler [London: Longman, 1971]. All references to *Paradise Lost* are to this edition and are cited parenthetically in the text). See, for example, Paul Fussell, *Poetic Meter and Poetic Form*, rev. ed. (New York: Random House, 1979), 26.

13. Line 343 in the Bridgewater manuscript, printed in *A Maske: The Earlier Versions*, ed. S. E. Sprott (Toronto: University of Toronto Press, 1973), 91.

14. In 415–16, the Second Brother interrupts the Elder Brother's speech to ask him what "hidden strength" he is speaking of:

Sec. Bro.   What hidden strength,
Unless the strength of heaven, if you mean that?
Eld. Bro. I mean that too, but yet a hidden strength
Which if heaven gave it, may be termed her own.

(415–18)

This is the only time within the debate in which a speaker closes a line before the other begins. Yet even here the dialogue is nicely connected by the interrogatory nature of the Second Brother's interruption. The question breaks into the Elder Brother's oration in the middle of a line, and the answer completes the fusion.

15. William Kerrigan, *The Sacred Complex: On the Psychogenesis of "Paradise Lost"* (Cambridge: Harvard University Press, 1983), 42.

16. Ibid.

17. Robert Frost, "The Bearer of Evil Tidings," in *The Poetry of Robert Frost*, ed. Edward Connery Lathem (New York: Holt, Rinehart, and Winston, 1964), 313, lines 41–44.

18. I have bracketed the vocative as hypermetrical to what is otherwise a pure iambic pentameter. This is the only instance known to me in Milton's poetic dialogues in which the vocative is not incorporated into the decasyllabic line. However, James Anderson Winn suggested to me on March 25, 1993, that a staging of *Comus* could easily render the lines as "contrapuntal": if the Elder Brother's entrance is perceived as an interruption of the Second Brother's speech, the first foot of the interruption could be read simultaneously with the closing syllable of the Second Brother's speech and thus preserve the pentameter line:

of our | unown | ed sis | ter. |
                                        | I do | not
brother.

19. Milton's interpretation of the symbolic value of the Gorgon shield is a creative modification of contemporary interpretations of Homer: "She wore the gorgon's head on her breast, because no one can turn his eyes against the light of the sun or against wisdom and remain unharmed" (Conti, cited in Carey, ed., *Complete Shorter Poems*, 198 n. 447). Though this passage has no direct connection to chastity, Milton has described the virtue earlier in the *Comus* debate in much the same terms: "Virtue could see to do what Virtue would / By her own radiant light" (372–73).

20. All biblical references are to the King James Version.

21. Sears Jayne, "The Subject of Milton's Ludlow *Mask*," in *Milton: Modern Essays in Criticism,* ed. Arthur E. Barker (New York: Oxford University Press, 1965), 88–111. For other biblical sources of "a thousand liveried angels," compare Psalms 68.17: "The chariots of God are twenty thousand, even thousands of angels," and Zechariah 1.10: "These are they whom the Lord hath sent to walk to and fro through the earth." Consider also Adam's promise to Eve in book 4 of *Paradise Lost,* a promise confirmed by what we see of Gabriel and his legions searching Eden for Satan: "Millions of spiritual creatures walk the earth / Unseen, both when we wake, and when we sleep" (677–78).

22. McGuire, *Milton's Puritan Masque,* 152.

23. John Milton, *Complete Prose Works of John Milton,* 8 vols., ed. Don M. Wolfe et al. (New Haven: Yale University Press, 1953–82), 1:241.

24. Cited in John Milton, *Milton: Private Correspondence and Academic Exercises,* ed. E. M. W. Tillyard, trans. Phyllis B. Tillyard (Cambridge: Cambridge University Press, 1932), xx.

25. A. Fletcher, *Transcendental Masque,* 170.

26. Traister, *Heavenly Necromancers,* 172.

27. Cedric Brown, *John Milton's Aristocratic Entertainment* (Cambridge: Cambridge University Press, 1985), 95.

28. John Creaser, "'The Present Aid of This Occasion': The Setting of *Comus,*" in *The Court Masque,* ed. David Lindley (Manchester: Manchester University Press, 1984), 132.

From Woman Warrior to Warrior Reasoner:
Lady Alice and Intellectual Freedom in
A Mask

HOPE A. PARISI

THE evaluation of Milton's women as reasoners stirs much of the debate for or against an implied feminism in the major poetry.[1] The sure-spoken Lady of *A Mask Presented at Ludlow Castle* provides an example. Combatting Comus, she quickly moves past the awkwardness of a woman breaking silence in this period. Reason justifies her:

> I had not thought to have unlockt my lips
> In this unhallow'd air, but that this Juggler
> Would think to charm my judgment, as mine eyes,
> Obtruding false rules prankt in reason's garb.
> I hate when vice can bolt her arguments,
> And virtue has no tongue to check her pride.
>
> (756–61)[2]

At her words, Comus, not Alice, becomes the "cold" and "shudd'ring" one, "feel[ing] . . . fear" (802, 800).[3] For her, reason points to virtue and virtue to a psychological *integritas*. As an able female reasoner, she is *self*-affirmed: "Thou canst not touch the freedom of my mind" (663).

Certainly if there is any mark of Miltonic fortitude, it is that of standing strong in reason. So even when Milton's women err, their ability to reason points to their "freedom and sufficiency,"[4] and so exemplifies what later becomes a major proof of women's equality with men. Unfortunately, however, to consider Alice virtuous in light of reason occasions a comparison with Milton's other females tempted, Eve and Dalila, who do not benefit. As a model of reason, Alice shows up her counterparts by setting an example they fall short of. She resists temptation; they cannot. Reason as a sign of virtue that marks Adam's and Samson's best moments is the measure against which Milton's women are decried in their worst. Dalila's point about women in argument with men is proven by the basis that exists in Milton for dividing his women into two camps: when they are judged according to criteria for behavior or worth that also serve to circumscribe them, women "ever / [Go] by the worse" (*Samson Agonistes*, 903–4).

Alice's relationship to reason anticipates later feminists' efforts to abstract reason from among the differences between the genders in order to support women's claim for education. It would be difficult to read Mary Astell's references to women, *schooled* in their religion, as "eminently and unmovably good . . . too firm and stable to be mov'd by the pitiful Allurements of sin" without thinking of Alice, especially Comus's captive Alice, in whom "Reason and Truth . . . firm and immutable"[5] form her to be literally frozen. So it is tempting to ascribe feminist feeling to Milton for allowing Alice, a female, to in some sense pioneer his call for Christian liberty.

The problem comes with eliding the difference between Lady Alice as a mouthpiece for Milton's libertarian concerns and as an embodiment of feminist consciousness.[6] The reasoning women for whom Alice is a prototype, and to whom well-intentioned readers join her, formulate their identities in response to discourses that set women apart from reason, forcing them to dissociate from the *especially* female (e.g., emotional, trivial, and pleasure loving) of their sex and so from aspects of themselves. Thus, as a proof of moral fortitude, the ability of these women to keep integrity largely as a function of reason includes self-rejection. Insofar as their "mind[s] and . . . bod[ies] are invaded by a social definition of . . . femininity that threatens to disconnect [them] from their own experience,"[7] or makes it impossible to articulate that experience coherently, they are self-alienated. Now Alice, Eve, and Dalila meet in the *same* camp—with real women of the period whose lives and writings suggest the difficulties of a woman's coming to speak at all.

To rephrase at least part of my thesis, readings that would appropriate Alice for feminism argue from basically the same standpoint as Renaissance (and then later) philosophers who assert the sexlessness of virtue or, relatedly, the nongendered nature of the intellect. In the "new sciences" of the seventeenth century, "law" came to inhabit the universe at the same time that the principle of self-rule, reason, now defined the individual. As a way to ensure that the "truth" of divinely ordered hierarchies might be seen, a connection obtained between who was reasonable and who was virtuous. "The law itself was fulfilled by the expectation that if human beings were good, they would be reasonable; and conversely, that if they were not reasonable, they would be neither good nor fully human."[8] Theoretically, the principle pertained equally to men and women. Reason was a potential democratizer, centralizing an essentially genderless aspect of selfhood.

It is easy to understand how women of the seventeenth century would want to appropriate a genderless intellect, if possible, in order to share a greater part in letters, literacy, and the public life. Margaret Cavendish wrote that without the popular acknowledgment of women's intellect, "we are become like Worms that only Live in the Dull Earth of Ignorance, Winding our Selves sometimes out by the Help of some Refreshing Rain of good Education, which seldome is given us, for we are Kept like Birds in Cages to Hop up and down in our Houses."[9] Following Descartes, who "wanted even women to understand something"[10] of his philosophy, women like Cavendish, most often already joined to humanist households, took up the notion of a genderless intellect for the new freedom it offered.[11] Disdaining the "dull insipid Trifles" and "debasing Impertinences"[12] of the rituals and pastimes foisted upon them as leisured women, they sought a part in the period's burgeoning scientific and philosophic activity. They advised each other to "learn Descartes's philosophy . . . not only because it disabuses us of a million commonly held errors but also because it teaches us how to think properly." The writer adds, "Without it we would die of boredom in this province."[13]

For others, women's exhortations to reason registered urgency and even anger. As Bathsua Makin wrote "To all Ingenious and Vertuous Ladies":

The Barbarous custom to breed Women low, is grown general amongst us, and hath prevailed so far, that it is verily believed (especially amongst a sort of debauched Sots) that Women are not endued with such Reason, as Men; nor capable of improvement by Education, as they are. . . . To offer to the World the liberal Education of Women is to deface the Image of God in Man, it will make Women so high, and men so low, like Fire in the House-top, it will set the whole world in a Flame.[14]

By 1703, the martial "Zeal" of Sarah Fyge Egerton would carry the feminist insistence against "Tyrant Custom" even further. She wrote,

> We yeild like vanquish'd Kings whom Fetters bind,
> When chance of War is to Usurpers kind;
>
> . . . .
>
> We will our Rights in Learning's World maintain,
> Wits Empire, now shall know a Female Reign.[15]

And to some extent, it did. Cavendish, Chudleigh, Lady Anne Finch Conway, and Elizabeth Thomas, among others, initiated relationships with some of the most noted philosophers and scientists of the day, often spurring their mentors to develop or amend allegedly original claims and theories.[16]

Alice's withstanding of Comus spins on a self-possessiveness that is rooted in her capacity to reason, in the manner of Sarah Fyge Egerton and others. Alice's circumstances and rhetoric, as well as the lives and writings of these women, model similar dilemmas of social inscription. All have dubious relationships to the authority they claim. As I mean to show,

Alice's remarkable confidence in debating Comus must be read in the context of the culture's safeguards against women's actually attaining the full freedom of mind and conscience it held out to them. While the humanists had already established the universality of the mind in their advocacy for women's education, and while the idea of comparable intellects between the sexes was—and has been—revolutionary in its implications, changes in family structure were solidifying patriarchal authority.[17] Women's agency was undermined also despite Paul's notion of spiritual equality. At the same time that they were acknowledging women's autonomy insofar as they were to be held accountable for their own actions, Renaissance philosophers disputed women's freedom of conscience when it conflicted with their "natural" obligations as childbearer and nurse.[18]

As Catherine Belsey notes, it is this frequent jolting of identity across a range of discourses that "exert[s] a pressure on concrete individuals to seek new, non-contradictory subject-positions." Women, defined and redefined by others' terms, are especially open to such determinative action. Toward this end, the "liberal humanist discourse of freedom, self-determination and rationality"[19] attracted many women of the mid to late seventeenth century. But these women claimed rationality from different starting points than men did. As intellects, men abstracted themselves from a network of social obligations. Reason supported men's reach for greater self-sufficiency in the social realm and also ameliorated the threat that individuals would suddenly feel isolated.[20] Similarly in their own way reaching for social self-sufficiency, so-called "Cartesian" women sought retreat from the family. Erica Harth notes: "seventeenth-century literature by and about women was generally consistent with [the idea of the separability of mind and body] and included variations on the theme, 'the mind has no sex.' With the diffusion of Cartesianism, this phrase became something of a feminist rallying cry."[21] Not only did it validate women's capacity for intellectual pursuits by virtue of their owning, like men, their own "seamlessly unified" and "gloriously autonomous" selves,[22] but it also made possible a degree of escape from "the obligations and prejudices attached to their female bodies."[23]

Still, women were tapping into a discourse that was principally for shaping new positions of authority for *men*. Women pitched their voices in a sense, projecting themselves beyond spheres of constricted female activity. But "it was precisely Descartes's dualism . . . seem[ing] to support [women] as thinking subjects" that "seemed to drain the thinking subject of all feeling and emotion connected to the body and to reduce the body to a mere machine."[24] Women's discourses of reason surface at the same time that bourgeois values of family are being strengthened. The wave of female prophecy during the Interregnum, when women's bodies could physically and symbolically disrupt social conventions, saw women, by 1700, rejected as spiritual authorities. As Phyllis Mack shows, there is a relationship between certain women's loss of power positions within radical politics and a rhetoric of introspection. It appears that with the evacuation of women's bodies from public mediation comes the cultivation of individual *voice*.[25]

Readings that would appropriate Alice (especially the captive Alice) for feminism take up an Enlightenment ideal of selfhood that in its essence privileges voice. Humanism draws on the power of voice—i.e., the power of self-naming. But as my argument already suggests: "The subject is not only a grammatical subject, 'a centre of initiatives, author of and responsible for its actions,' but also a *subjected being* who submits to the authority of the social formation."[26] Alice's "real" subjectivity, as it pertains to that authority as it variously claims subjectivity *for* her, must be negotiated by a social framework (represented by the Attendant Spirit and his band) by the end of the mask that helps reincorporate her into various relationships that will define her identity from that point on. Thus, given the relationship with the social framework, how far can we go in claiming Alice for individualism or its liberal brand of feminism?

To see reason as a mode of expression for women that reflected changes in family structure and perceptions of women moves us closer to reading the *inert* Alice, with voice resounding, of the palace scene. Alice's reasoned self-defense certainly shares the temper and assumptions of her Cartesian contemporaries. First, the implicit right to speak claimed by Alice denotes Descartes's support for a nongendered intellect. As a fellow human being, she has all the mental wherewithal to discern and name truth—"a mind entirely free of all prejudice,"[27] in Descartes's words—and in hers, an "[un]-charm[ed] judgment" (758) so as to see "false rules prankt in reason's garb" (759). She also has stable measures by which to check her assumptions. She knows that Comus's "cordial Julep" (672) is "treasonous" (702), for instance, for

> none
> But such as are good men can give good things,
> And that which is not good, is not delicious
> To a well-govern'd and wise appetite.
>
> (702–5)

(Is she telling us that she wouldn't like the cordial *anyway?*) The equivalent of scientific principles drawn from experience minimizes the threat of variable results that a test of her virtue could yield. These and other lines of Alice's speech can point toward readings that figure or refute questions of unacknowledged desire—as in Leah Marcus's reference to Margery Evans, a fourteen-year-old servant girl whose reputed volition in her own rape in 1631 may stand behind the mask; or William Kerrigan's suggestion that

Alice is fighting with Comus against her own sexual impulses.[28] In a philosophical world in which the movements of both heart and mind act according to a capricious will, Alice's body, now made inert, signals women's
general transition to a new and more gendered moral plane. Coming to
speak, Alice enters discourse at a place predeterminative of desire and/or
its fracturing. She exhibits a new kind of verbal effluence that, as it is
spoken, subjects itself to the analysis of the speaker. As reasoner, Alice is
in full ownership of her words while making audible—for herself and her
audience—an internal process of self-scrutiny.

Second, Alice's tone and rhetoric in the palace scene have something in
common with an emerging tradition of women's reactive polemic. As the
earliest form of women's debate, it gained wide currency in the mid and
late seventeenth century with "Cartesian women" like Chudleigh and Fyge
Egerton, along with pseudonymous writers- like Jane Anger, Ester
Sowernam, and Joan Sharpe. Its first occasions were the "injustice" of an
unsolicited misogynist attack, to which women felt compelled to respond,
despite the injunctions against their speaking or writing. Once they broke
silence, they went at their detractors with abandon, "respond[ing] fierce[ly]
in tone and intensity . . . return[ing] blow for blow."[29] It was the new
mode of scientific inquiry that enabled women, along with men, to claim
both reason and experience as a way to tear at arguments upheld by custom,
authority, and shared assumptions among men.[30]

Perhaps Alice does not read into Comus's invitation to make "Beauty
. . . current" (740) as "nature's coin" (739) an explicitly misogynous attack,
but his suggestion does provoke her to fill the "unhallow'd air" (757) of the
palace with words defending the honor of a force that Comus and she
personify as female. The Lady corrects Comus's view of nature as indulgent
mother: "she, good cateress" (764), "most innocent nature" (762),

> Means her provision only to the good
> That live according to her sober laws
> And holy dictate of spare Temperance.
>
> (765–67)

Like the female reactives emerging in society, Alice attacks not only her
detractor, nor even principally her detractor, but "a specified opinion or
doctrine."[31] She rejects Comus's argument that spending all the currency
of nature shows gratitude for nature's gifts and pays her homage:

> If every just man that now pines with want
> Had but a modest and beseeming share
> Of that which lewdly-pamper'd Luxury
> Now heaps upon some few with vast excess,
> Nature's full blessings would be well dispens't

> In unsuperfluous even proportion,
> And she no whit encumber'd with her store,
> And then the giver would be better thank't,
> His praise due paid.

(768–76)

Moreover, she castigates "not only the offending male but the behavior of men in general,"[32] that is, all who uphold Comus's assumptions.

Most striking, however, is the tone of her arguments. Had she not disdained the attempt to have Comus "convinc't" (792),

> the uncontrolled worth
> Of this pure cause would kindle my rapt spirits
> To such a flame of sacred vehemence,
> That dumb things would be mov'd to sympathize,
> And the brute Earth would lend her nerves, and shake,
> Till all thy magic structures rear'd so high,
> Were shatter'd into heaps o'er thy false head.

(793–99)

As with some late seventeenth-century women writers, her words warn of an apocalyptic overturning of the established order. For Alice, the source of resistance is reason's sheer forcefulness. Containing her, it is a power that is itself contained. Let loose it could enflame the world and tumble it. In fact, she has followed reason so far here that she is on the cusp of losing reason, losing her grasp on self. Like early Quaker prophetesses whose forceful identification with the voice of divine authority prompted their experience of self-transcendence, Alice nears a transformation into pure superego. However, it is a temporary modulation, and one that Alice cannot sustain, just as the Quakers' move away from radical politics would soon mollify such passion in prophecy, a development occuring at the same time that post-Revolution politics would redefine women's role in the family.[33] Ironically coinciding with a toning down of women's voices and roles within an important realm of reactive politics for women, these are the last words in the mask that Alice speaks.

Subtending the historical specificity of Alice's problem as speaker is the shift in women's agency from the time of myth and hagiography. Among Alice's literary prototypes are the desert wanderers of the saints' lives that share their motifs with classical mythology and medieval romance. Whether as the Amazon of the woods, the woman warrior in disguise, or the androgyne, the virtuous woman of literature traditionally keeps close ties to the male world of militancy and independence. As tradition progresses, woman's independence moves closer to militancy against the self. Diana and her band used their virgin powers to ward off external enemies. The

story of Acteon's cruel fate after intruding upon Diana demonstrated the
dangers of violating the sacred space of female power.[34] By the time of
Milton's mask, the realm of inviolability is becoming the female body. Now
the nymph acts as huntress of her own impure impulses.

In Marcus's reading of A Mask with Margery Evan's story of rape in the
background, a woman's sincerity decides her complicity or innocence when
others sexually affront her. (Alice's sincerity, her inviolateness of mind,
marks virginity from chastity, the latter being a determinative aspect of
character.[35]) The Elder Brother praises Alice as a daughter of Diana, but
he also leaves room for condemning her, or women like her, should they
"clot" their souls "by contagion" (467) of

> lust
> By unchaste looks, loose gestures, and foul talk,
> But most by lewd and lavish act of sin.
>
> (463–65)

Diana's strength derived from a mystery of power that females *shared*. In
the world of· A Mask, the shared space of power closes around each female·
until ideally she becomes "clad in complete steel" (421), inviolate not only
to intruders or to the "savage fierce, Bandit or mountaineer" (426) but also
to her own potential for self–defilement.

Renaissance philosophers wrote that women's self-vigilance was war-
ranted. Pierre Le Moyne, for instance, inverted models of the *femme forte*
tradition to turn the woman against herself. He wrote that "women have
not everyday Holoferneses's to vanquish [as Judith did], but everyday [their
own] excess vanity, delights, and all pleasing and troublesome passions."[36]

To further their interests in education, women would soon parrot similar
sentiments: "A rational mind will be employ'd, it will never be satisfy'd in
doing nothing, and if you neglect to furnish it with good materials, 'tis like
to take up with such as come to hand."[37] For Mary Astell, plays and ro-
mances presented this danger. For other women, female "Exorbitancies . . .
those Toyes and Trifles, they now spend their time about" were familiar
enough to need little specifying. Affirming women's intellect also meant
offering a picture of women's penchant for pleasure. "Bad women," wrote
Bathsua Makin, are uneducated women, "weak to make Resistance," and
thus "strong to tempt to evil: Therefore without all Doubt great Care ought
to be taken, timely to season them with Piety and Virtue."[38] Culture's
drive to observe, classify, and otherwise dominate an unwieldy nature is
epitomized in women's own efforts to claim education as a potential means
for achieving *power over* self.

It is the course of this modulation, from woman warrior to warrior
reasoner, that A Mask charts. Despite the tradition of strong women that

surrounds Alice,[39] she progresses away from rather than toward it. She is that tradition's vagrant. From her first efforts to stave off "a thousand fantasies" (205) from crowding her psyche, reason has been the Lady's "Land-Pilot" (309). Along with "Conscience" (212), she enlists as guardians "pure-ey'd Faith" (212) and "white-handed Hope" (213)—reason's retinue for Christian liberty—in order to control perception's sometimes unorganizable nature and the threat it poses to a humanist conception of self.

In good part, it is the Lady's rationality that locks her into Comus's power in the first place. Throughout the mask, Alice places great stock in words and the ear's ability to "[attend]" (272) them. She overtrusts in the period's new emphasis on the worthy man's integrity in matters of speech, demanding no further assurance of Comus's promise to lead her from the woods. "Shepherd," she says, "I take thee at thy word" (321). She also tries to reason impending harm away:

> In a place
> Less warranted than this or less secure
> I cannot be, that I should fear to change it.
>
> (326–28)

She weighs two potential dangers—one of staying, the other of going. Choosing to go, she enters into a kind of liberal contract, a sign of freedom, and reaffirms her powers of rational autonomy.

Following her inclination to chart her course by reason, the Lady practices a rational piety, one driven by the period's interest in "the word"—doctrines, sermons, credos, catechisms and their recitations—which often sought out women as their first pupils. Many times during A Mask, it is possible to hear Alice's spontaneous protestations as a rehearsal of the rote learning that was a part of women's religious education. Her statement "These thoughts may startle well, but not astound / The virtuous mind" (210–11) bears this quality, especially in that the idea surfaces in response to sensations that potentially could lead her away from reason's path. The observation especially seems to hold in her debate with Comus. She meets the offer of Comus's drink, another potential destabilizer, with a precept to which I referred earlier ("none / But such as are good men can give good things" [702–3]). And her most potent rebuttal, on keeping to the "sober laws / And holy dictate of spare Temperance" (766–67), mounts one principle on top of another: "If every just man that now pines with want. . . ."; "swinish gluttony / Ne'er looks to Heav'n" (768, 776–77). The question is not whether she is capable of debating Comus; at issue is to what extent she has been *prepared* to debate and in the interest of which ideology as it concerns women?

Part of her rational piety is a penchant for anticipating the future rather than grasping the present. As with many religious women, hope and faith come to substitute intellectually for pleasure, which is removed to the next world or to an ideal one. In her conjuring a "glist'ring Guardian" (219) at the onset of danger, we see where Alice first depends upon imagination, although she evokes such a guardian through the exertions of reason and also of virtue as reason's nearly tangible corollary. For her dreams and fears

> may startle well, but not astound
> The virtuous mind, that ever walks attended
> By a strong siding champion Conscience.
>
> (210–12)

In the threat of danger, she peoples her consciousness with agents who will keep her mind, and thus her body, on track. "Faith . . . Hope" (213) and "Chastity" (215) she "see[s] . . . visibly" (216) and "now believe[s] / That he, the Supreme good" (216–17) would take ultimate measures—as the "glist'ring Guardian"—to keep Alice's "life and honor" (220).[40]

In the palace scene, the force of her argument trips up its own progress headlong into the future. "Shall I go on?" she asks, "Or have I said enough?" (779–80). Her incentive to quit arguing is that her words might precipitate a cataclysm within Comus's castle. Perhaps this would be the first step toward ushering in a more just society. But she is future abstracted, *there* instead of *here*. At the very end of her defense she edges toward a moment of ecstatic prophecy that would leave reason behind. As Beverly Harrison and Carter Heyward write of Christian religious dualism in general: "This disembodied sensibility, in which *pleasure is fundamentally a state of mind*, is steeped in the eschatological promise that the realm of the divine . . . is, for Christians, here but not quite here; now but not quite yet."[41] Alice's hopefulness, manifest in her "rapt spirits" (794), betrays the extent to which she has removed herself from the present. For the mind is the only realm that she can safely occupy being virtuous.

Alice's mode of faith stands in contrast to Comus's paganism, whose roots are a sense of place and present time (which the mask's benevolent genii also share). The fervor with which Comus dances toward ecstasy compares to the near-convulsiveness that the Lady reaches through her own speech. For Comus, "Nature [did] pour her bounties forth / With such a full and unwithdrawing hand" that *now* "no corner" is "vacant of her plenty" (710–11, 717, 718). As his rounds and revels demonstrate, religion relinks the individual to the group. It celebrates the communicant's sense of immediacy. Alice's piety, by contrast, more closely typifies religion's general shift with Protestantism to conceptual realms of social ethics and belief. Given the conflation of rhetorics in Alice's speech (her passionate prophetic utterance that has reason as its underpinning), Alice emerges as a cultural contradiction of sorts. Reason restrains her liberty to take ecstatic flight through prophecy at the same time that her movement toward prophecy destabilizes rational speech.

On various levels, then, Alice relates to women of the seventeenth century who define themselves chiefly in terms of reason, while she also speaks to the circumstances under which they engaged such intellectual discourse. To return specifically to the palace scene, Alice's words offer a glimpse of a subjectivity so fiercely coherent, so staunch in its sense of self, that Comus, the master of metamorphosis, shakes in his boots. But the scene, the culmination of the Lady's course of travel, through culture, also represents Alice's enunciative movement from woman warrior to warrior reasoner. What we see provides Alice's words with their own situational context. Immobilized in her chair, Alice embodies physical stasis, virtue forever frozen in time. What has her enchantment by Comus effected? It has brought about the arrest of her body from movement, desire, and change. Like the saints of icons and statues, she is preserved from the flux of time. Simultaneously, patriarchal society, having fixed her as image, rests safe from the danger of her sexuality.

It is something close to this kind of cessation, on the level of the family and state, that Renaissance treatises sought by advocating that women eradicate "all pleasing and troublesome passions." Here is the danger of Comus's cup: to drink from it would reengender the problem of desire if we reconceptualize that desire as "the jugular of social relatedness and psychological integration."[42] When readers see Alice's "no" to Comus in terms of liberty exercised by reason, they speed past the ways in which culture forces women perpetually to respond to the same types of question. (Will she? Did she? How much does she want to or *not* want to?) The magician's offer to "restore all soon" (689) threatens an even deeper choice Alice regrettably already has had to make. For her as a would-be "Cartesian," the choice has been either of retaining agency on the intellectual level or resubmitting to popular conceptions of woman in terms of "lyghte and triflynge" diversions, "fantasies," and "wanton and pyvyshe" pleasures.[43] Remember, we do not see the moment when Comus binds Alice; Comus has had assistance from many factors, including the enforced complicity of his subject herself.

Notes

1. Eve's reasoning in the separation scene is central to arguments that criticize her, and it is "excusable" in those that support her. Similarly, Dalila receives only slight commendation for daring to debate Samson, the "wavering" quality of her argument receiving the attention. See, for example, Dennis Burden, *The Logical Epic* (Cambridge: Harvard University Press, 1967), 83–91; H. V. S. Ogden, "The Crisis of *Paradise Lost* Reconsidered," *Philological Quarterly* 36 (1957): 1–19; Joan

Bennett, *Reviving Liberty: Radical Christian Humanism in Milton's Great Poems* (Cambridge: Harvard University Press, 1989), chapter four; and Thomas Kranidas, "Dalila's Role in *Samson Agonistes*," *SEL* 6 (1966): 125–37. For more positive views, see Diane McColley, *Milton's Eve* (Urbana: University of Illinois Press, 1983); John C. Ulreich, "'Incident to All Our Sex': The Tragedy of Dalila," in *Milton and the Idea of Woman*, ed. Julia M. Walker (Urbana: University of Illinois Press, 1988), 185–209; and Stella Revard, "Dalila as Euripidean Heroine," *Papers on Language and Literature* 23 (1987): 291–302.

2. John Milton, *A Mask Presented at Ludlow Castle*, in *John Milton: Complete Poems and Major Prose*, ed. Merritt Y. Hughes (New York: Odyssey, 1957). All references to Milton's poetry are to this edition and are cited parenthetically in the text.

3. Since Lady Alice Egerton played the role of the Lady in *A Mask*, I use her name interchangeably with that of the character.

4. McColley, *Milton's Eve*, 158.

5. Mary Astell, "A Serious Proposal to the Ladies" (London, 1701), in *First Feminists: British Women Writers 1578–1799*, ed. Moira Ferguson (New York: Feminist Press, 1985), 184.

6. Joseph Wittreich, *Feminist Milton* (Ithaca: Cornell Univeristy Press, 1987), shows the degree to which Milton's treatment of women and liberty supported the creation of a feminist consciousness in the eighteenth century. While Wittreich alludes to the presentation of Alice in *A Mask* as yet another example of a Milton who was sympathetic to women's causes, he also acknowledges that in *Paradise Lost* there are "discrepancies between . . . two consciousnesses" (68)—between that of a feminist and Milton's own, of which an eighteenth-century female readership was keeping aware. Elaine Pagels's point that "contradictory attitudes toward women reflect a time of social transition" (quoted by Wittreich, 68) is well-taken, with Milton perhaps himself divided.

I enter the debate on Milton's feminism not trying to negotiate hermeneutically among protofeminist and masculinist references in Milton. Rather, I want to deal with what a protofeminist reading of Milton might start with—a woman's speaking virtuously as itself a compromised and compromising act in the light of a specific cultural climate.

7. Muriel Dimen, "Power, Sexuality, and Intimacy," in *Gender / Body / Knowledge: Feminist Reconstructions of Being and Knowing*, ed. Alison M. Jaggar and Susan R. Bordo (New Brunswick: Rutgers University Press, 1990), 37.

8. Constance Jordan, *Renaissance Feminism: Literary Texts and Political Models* (Ithaca: Cornell University Press, 1990), 65.

9. Margaret Cavendish, "To the Two Most Famous Universities of England," preface to *Philosophical and Physical Opinions* (London, 1655), quoted in *First Feminists*, ed. Moira Ferguson, 85.

10. René Descartes, Letter to Father Vatier, in *Oeuvres*, ed. Adam and Tannery (Paris: Leopold Cerf, 1897), 1:560, quoted in Erica Harth, "Cartesian Women," *Yale French Studies* 80 (1991): 147.

11. Harth, "Cartesian Women," 148–50.

12. Mary Chudleigh, "To the Reader," in *Essays Upon Several Subjects in Prose and Verse* (London: T. H. for R. Bonwicke, W. Freeman, T. Goodwin, 1710), quoted in Hilda Smith, *Reason's Disciples: Seventeenth-Century English Feminists* (Urbana: University of Illinois Press, 1982), 64–65.

13. Jean Corbinelli, Letter of 23 August 1673 to Mme. de Sévigné, in *Corre-*

spondance, vol. 1, ed. Duchene (Paris: Gallimard, 1972–78), quoted in Harth, "Cartesian Women," 151.

14. Bathsua Makin, "An Essay to Revive the Antient Education of Gentlewomen" (London, 1673), quoted in *First Feminists*, ed. Moira Ferguson, 129.

15. "The Emulation," 11.1, 15–16, 32–33, quoted in *First Feminists*, ed. Moira Ferguson, 169–70. Carol Barash writes that Egerton's aggressive tone suggests a "feminist imperialism" that arises in the writing of women during Queen Anne's reign. See "'The Native Liberty . . . of the Subject': Configurations of Gender and Authority in the Works of Mary Chudleigh, Sarah Fyge Egerton, and Mary Astell," in *Women, Writing, History 1640–1740*, ed. Isobel Grundy and Susan Wiseman (Athens: University of Georgia Press, 1992), 55–69.

16. Ruth Perry, "Radical Doubt and the Liberation of Women," *Eighteenth-Century Studies* 18 (1985): 477–89.

17. Smith, *Reason's Disciples*, 60, 53–54.

18. Jordan, *Renaissance Feminism*, 21–23.

19. Catherine Belsey, "Constructing the Subject: Deconstructing the Text," in *Feminisms: An Anthology of Literary Theory and Criticism*, ed. Robyn R. Warhol and Diane Price Herndl (New Brunswick: Rutgers University Press, 1991), 597–98.

20. My ideas about abstract individualism were suggested in part by Jackie DiSalvo, who developed the concept in "Gender and Liberal Political Theory in *Paradise Lost*," read at the Third International Milton Symposium, Florence, Italy, June 1988, and forthcoming in *The Idolatry of Woman, the Ideology of Progress and the Masculinization of Culture in the Works of John Milton*. I am indebted to Professor DiSalvo for sharing her thoughts with me as I developed this reading of Alice.

21. Harth, "Cartesian Women," 149.

22. Toril Moi, *Sexual / Textual Politics: Feminist Literary Theory* (New York: Methuen, 1985), 8.

23. Harth, "Cartesian Women," 150.

24. Ibid.

25. Phyllis Mack, *Visionary Women: Ecstatis Prophecy in Seventeenth-Century England* (Berkeley: University of California Press, 1992), especially chapter four. Mack sees the physically transgressive behavior of female Quaker visionaries—the "loosening of all bodily inhibition in tears, groans, and shaking" (150)—as weakening distinctions between individuals existing in different social categories. She argues that introspection and self-analysis are more prominent in Quaker texts by women as allowances for women's physical expressiveness diminish. This shift toward greater restraint of the body in women's religious expression coincides with a growing emphasis on proper female decorum in general. See, for example, Ruth Yeazell, *Fictions of Modesty: Women and Courtship in the English Novel* (Chicago: University of Chicago Press, 1991), especially part 1.

I am not suggesting that Alice can be identified with Quaker prophetesses of the mid 1600s. But they are another group of women, like the Cartesian women and early female reactives, with whom I do align Alice, who typifies a problem of women's enunciative positions.

26. Belsey, "Constructing the Subject," 596.

27. René Descartes, *Discourse on Method*, trans. L. Lafleur, quoted in Perry, "Radical Doubt," 478.

28. Leah Marcus, "The Earl of Bridgewater's Legal Life: Notes toward a Political Reading of *Comus*," *Milton Quarterly* 21 (1987): 13–23. William Kerrigan, *The Sacred Complex: On the Psychogenesis of "Paradise Lost"* (Cambridge: Harvard University Press, 1983, chapter 2).

29. Moira Ferguson, introduction to *First Feminists*, 28.

30. See the collection of pamphlets by women (using real and pseudonymous names), *The Women's Sharpe Revenge: Five Women's Pamphlets from the Renaissance*, ed. Simon Shepherd (New York: St. Martin's, 1985). On Mary Astell, see Catherine Sharrock, "De-ciphering Women and De-scribing Authority: The Writings of Mary Astell," in *Women, Writing, History*, ed. Grundy and Wiseman, 109–24.

31. Moira Ferguson, *First Feminists*, 27, 28.

32. Ibid., 28.

33. Mack, *Visionary Women*, 406–12.

34. See Thomas Bulfinch, *Bulfinch's Mythology: The Age of Fable* (Philadelphia: Running Press, 1987), 40–42.

35. Marcus, "The Earl of Bridgewater's Legal Life," 13–23.

36. Pierre Le Moyne, *The Gallery of Heroik Women*, trans. Marquesse of Winchester (London: Henry Seile, 1652), 35, quoted in Mary Garrard, *Artemesia Gentileschi: The Image of the Female Hero in Italian Baroque Art* (Princeton: Princeton University Press, 1989), 166.

37. Astell, "A Serious Proposal," 189.

38. Makin, "An Essay to Revive," 130–31.

39. The affinities that Alice shares with Diana are well noted in Milton criticism. See as examples Kathleen Wall, "*A Mask Presented at Ludlow Castle*: The Armor of Logos," in *Milton*, ed. Walker, 52–65; Richard Halpern, "Puritanism and Maenadism in *A Mask*," in *Rewriting the Renaissance: The Discourses of Sexual Difference in Early Modern Europe*, ed. Margaret Ferguson et al. (Chicago: University of Chicago Press, 1986), 88–105.

40. The world of imagination, especially as it concerns the power of poetry, will play a major role in the Lady's rescue. See Cedric C. Brown, "Presidential Travels and Instructive Augury in Milton's Ludlow Masque," *Milton Quarterly* 21 (1987): 9–10.

41. Beverly Harrison and Carter Heyward, "Pain and Pleasure: Avoiding the Confusions of Christian Tradition in Feminist Theory," in *Christianity, Patriarchy, and Abuse: A Feminist Critique*, ed. Carole Bohn and Joanne Carlson Brown (New York: Pilgrim, 1989), 154.

42. Dimen, "Power, Sexuality," 38.

43. Juan Luis Vives, *Instruction of a Christen Woman*, trans. Richard Hyrde (London: Thomas Berthelet, 1521, 1529), 9, quoted in Betty Travitsky, ed., *The Paradise of Women: Writings by Englishwomen of the Renaissance* (New York: Columbia University Press, 1989), 17.

"Freely We Serve":
Paradise Lost and the Paradoxes of Political Liberty

Steven Jablonski

John Selden, a contemporary and possibly an acquaintance of John Milton, made the following observations regarding the puzzling relationship between the political and theological divisions of his day: "The Puritan . . . will allow no free-will, but God does all, yet will allow the subject his liberty to do or not to do, notwithstanding the king, the god upon earth. The Arminians . . . hold we have free-will, yet say, when we come to the king there must be all obedience, and no liberty must be stood for."[1] This is indeed a paradox: the same Puritan Calvinists who denied metaphysical free will asserted political liberty, while the same Arminians who asserted metaphysical free will denied political liberty. Yet however paradoxical, Selden's assessment seems quite accurate. Any list of the people who wrote works in defense of free will in the first half of the seventeenth century would have to include such individuals as Richard Montague, Robert Shelford, Thomas Jackson, Samuel Hoard, Herbert Thorndike, John Bramhall, Henry Hammond, and Thomas Pierce, all of whom were also notable supporters of the Stuart monarchy.

The paradox raised by Selden should interest literary scholars because it suggests another paradox that has long puzzled readers of *Paradise Lost.* This second paradox can be stated as follows: how could Milton, an Arminian, be both a professed enemy of earthly kings and a proponent of liberty and yet represent God in his greatest work as a king and Satan as a proponent of liberty? In this essay I will attempt to answer this second paradox by first resolving the paradox posed by Selden. To do this, I will begin by examining the differing ways the Calvinists and Arminians of Milton's day conceived of the relation between free will and political liberty. Then, I will turn to Milton's depiction of Heaven in *Paradise Lost* as a monarchy where "there must be all obedience, and no liberty must be stood for." Finally, I will conclude by more briefly attempting to reconcile Milton's republican beliefs about political liberty as expressed in his prose with his seeming support for monarchy in his epic poem.

To be sure, one might deny that Milton and the above-named Royalists possessed a common Arminianism. Thus, both Christopher Hill and Joan S. Bennett distinguish between what they consider the admirable radical Arminianism of Milton and John Goodwin and the disreputable High Church Arminianism of the Laudians and other Royalists.[2] Yet while Hill, Bennett, and others are surely justified in recognizing the very real differences between the beliefs of Milton and the Royalist Arminians on such subjects as church government and the role of ritual and ceremony in worship, these differences must not be allowed to obscure equally real similarities on other subjects. Specifically, no one who has actually read the ample writings of the Royalist Arminians on free will can deny that they hold essentially the same position on this subject as does Milton. Therefore, unless one confuses the question by bringing in issues unrelated to free will, the paradoxes suggested by Selden remain.

The differing ways in which the Calvinists and Arminians understood free will are best examined as part of their broader conceptions of the relation between God and humanity.[3] For simplicity's sake, the two groups can be seen as occupying opposite ends of two philosophic spectra, the first spectrum ranging from voluntarism to rationalism and the second from determinism to nondeterminism. The Calvinists were *voluntarists* in that they believed that God's will was the supreme rule of what was right or wrong, just or unjust, and *determinists* in that they believed that everything that occurs in the created world was willed by God and thus could not happen otherwise. The Arminians, by contrast, were *rationalists* who claimed that God's will was itself ruled by an intrinsic and inviolable standard of rational law and *nondeterminists* who believed that God allows humanity a significant portion of free will so that not all events are inevitable. To sum up, then, one might loosely say that whereas the Calvinists believed that God was free while humanity was bound, the Arminians believed that humanity was free while God was bound.

The Royalist Arminians argued that the political disobedience of the Calvinists followed from their pernicious combination of voluntarism with determinism. In the eyes of these Arminians, the Calvinists posed a threat to a settled state because they could justify any illegal action against it by claiming to be following the will of a God who was not bound by any law, let alone any mere civil law. Thus, Samuel Hoard argued that the Calvinistic conception of divine determinism leads to political rebellion because "By it all our doings are Gods ordinances, all imaginations branches of his predestination, and all events in Kingdomes and Common-weales the necessary issues of the Divine decree."[4] Henry Hammond, chaplain to Charles I, concurred that "to deny all liberty of man's choice toward good or evil, and to affix all events to Gods predetermination" was "utterly irreconcileable with the *nature* of *civil government*." As he explained,

When the *People*, which think their *liberty*, of which they are very *tender* and *jealous*, to be retrenched or impaired by the restraint of *Laws*, can answer their *Rule[r]s* . . . that they *cannot* observe their *Laws*, being led by *irresistible decrees* to the *transgressing* of them, the consequence is easie to foresee, the *despising* and *contemning* of *Laws*, and hating and detesting of those who are obliged to *punish* them, when they have *offended*.[5]

This, then, is the Arminian explanation for the paradox noted by Selden between the Puritans' denial of free will and their justification of political disobedience.

The Arminians' own position on free will and its relation to political obedience is complex and deserves further explanation. One might begin by examining the different ways in which the concept of liberty has been understood historically. According to Isaiah Berlin in an influential essay, people in the Western world have generally conceived of liberty in either a negative or a positive sense.[6] On the one hand, negative liberty can be loosely described as *freedom from* outside interference. It is measured solely by the absence of coercive or restraining forces. Positive liberty, on the other hand, implies the *freedom to* develop one's capacities or fulfill one's own nature. It emphasizes active self-direction and self-realization rather than the mere absence of constraint. Looking at this same distinction from another angle, Charles Taylor describes positive liberty as an "exercise concept" that requires a person actually to follow a certain course in order to be free, while negative liberty is an "opportunity concept," in which a person is free so long as he has different options available to him, whether he chooses to exercise these options or not.[7]

The Arminians, we have seen, were both rationalists and nondeterminists. While their nondeterminism meant that they believed in a certain form of negative liberty, their rationalism demanded that they also adopt a positive conception of liberty as well. In a negative or "opportunity" sense, the Arminians believed that humanity was free because people were not predetermined toward a single choice of action. In a positive or "exercise" sense, they believed that people were truly free only when they actually chose rightly. This positive conception of liberty informs the Arminian position on the roles of free will and grace in a person's salvation. The Arminians insisted that "free" will implies both that the will is free from the necessity of sinning and also that it is free to cooperate with grace. To be sure, the Arminians agreed with the Calvinists that people could neither achieve salvation nor avoid sin without God's gift of grace. They differed from them in that the Arminians believed that a person was free to accept or reject this grace, whereas the Calvinists believed that a person could be only the completely passive recipient of grace. As the Arminian Herbert

Thorndike put it, "though the grace of Christ's cross be the medicine, yet, till it be freely taken, it worketh not the cure."[8]

The positive conception of liberty held by the Arminians was not unique to them, nor was it a historical innovation. Rather, it was developed by the medieval and Renaissance Thomists from sources in Cicero, the ancient Stoics, and, ultimately, Aristotle. According to the Thomists, God appointed a determinate end to everything that he created. Since human beings are rational creatures, they fulfill their own end when they act in accordance with reason. Human beings are not impelled by any internal necessity to obey the promptings of reason, yet they must choose to do so in order to experience the true freedom that comes only from adhering to God's predetermined purpose. As summarized by Hiram Haydn, the Thomists believed that

> true Christian liberty is not freedom *from* anything, but freedom *to become* something—specifically, freedom to grow to the full stature of a Christian man in the likeness of God. . . . The difference betwen [sic] man's position and that of the sub-rational creatures lies in the fact that although man is naturally impelled toward his goal, as are the rest, he is not *obliged* to follow it. Yet if he does not, he cannot retain his true and characteristic freedom as a man, a person, and he cannot grow to the full stature of a man—for if he deserts the end prescribed by reason, he loses his rational standing.[9]

God built rational law into the very structure of the universe, and true freedom cannot be understood apart from it.

Following the paths blazed by the Thomists before them, the Arminians of the seventeenth century believed that true freedom was identical with obedience to rational law. In the words of Hammond, "the nature of *Angels* or men, which have the bounds of *Vertue* and *Conscience*, and have *Laws* prescribed them, within which they are to move . . . cannot thereby be said to have lost the *liberty* of their *species*." Hammond supported this claim by appealing to the law-abiding nature of God himself:

> And this *regulation of indefinite power* by such prudent limits as these, (*i.e.* by the *Universal* law of *Reason* and *Justice*, or by particular conclusions, which the wisdom of the *Law-givers* hath thought fit to deduce from thence) cannot justly be quarrell'd, as a *retrenchment of power*, any more, than the infinite goodness of God which permits him not to be able to do anything which is contrary to that attribute, is a *manacling*, or restraining his *Omnipotence*; but is only a cultivating and dressing of it, a *paring off the excess*, and exorbitances of it, and leaving it a *form'd channel*, instead of a vast or *unbridled Ocean*.[10]

In the eyes of Hammond and his fellow Arminians, law was not a chain restricting the will but a channel directing it—not a retrenchment of freedom but the perfection of it.

The passages from Hammond quoted above are taken from a political pamphlet defending the rights of monarchs rather than from a theological tract, and it is easy to see how the Arminians reconciled political liberty with obedience to a monarch once one recognizes how they identified free will with obedience to rational law. The Royalist Arminians denied that their support for obedience to the Stuart monarchy compromised their own freedom because they believed that this obedience was completely in harmony with right reason. They saw the position of Charles I, if not all his actions, as guaranteed by fixed principles of rational law, including the ancient laws of England that undergird the rights of kings as well as of subjects, the law of nature that upholds peace and the settled state of order, and the positive law of God that commands subjects to "obey the powers that be." The Royalist Arminians claimed that their horror at rebellion stemmed from their reverence for law rather than any fondness for absolutism. As they saw it, neither the subject's nor the monarch's freedom exempted them from obedience to law. In the words of Hammond, God subjects a monarch "to *reason*, and *rules of Justice*, and . . . to *the positive municipal Laws* . . . and hath been as particular in prescribing *Laws* to the *Prince*, to avoid *Oppression* or *acts of Height*, as to *Subjects* to abstain from *Resistance*."[11] The difference between a monarch and a subject was that a monarch could punish a subject for disobeying a law, while only God could punish a monarch for the same offense.

Hammond's belief that Charles I both ruled by divine right and yet was under the ultimate sovereignty of rational law was not unusual in his day. Indeed, as Conrad Russell and others have pointed out, the belief that even a divine right monarch was limited by law was held by many Royalists as well as Parliamentarians in the Civil War.[12] Milton himself replied to Salmasius's claim that a king was above law by stating that "Many of those among us most favorable toward the king have ever been guiltless of a belief so base."[13] Yet the willingness of Royalists to see their monarchs as under the sovereignty of law is not surprising given their willingness to see God himself as a law-abiding monarch. This position was stated best, albeit after the Restoration, by Ralph Cudworth:

The right and authority of God himself is founded in justice; and of this is the civil sovereignty also a certain participation. It is not the mere creature of the people, and of men's wills, and therefore annihilable again by their wills at pleasure; but hath a stamp of Divinity upon it. . . . Neither ought [the ultimate authority of justice] be thought any impeachment of civil authority, it extending to all, even to that of the Deity itself. The right and authority of God himself, who is the supreme sovereign of the universe, is also in like manner bounded and circumscribed by justice.[14]

To put this another way, the Royalist Arminians believed that kings were like God because both God and kings were constitutional monarchs and their constitution was right reason.

Turning from the views of the Royalist Arminians to those of Milton himself, we can now see how he created a heaven where God was "Sovran King" (8.239)[15] and where "there must be all obedience, and no liberty must be stood for." Like his fellow Arminians and the Thomists before them, Milton acknowledged the value of negative liberty in his epic, but he did not believe that this kind of freedom should be "stood for" in opposition to positive liberty, an erroneous opposition that Milton attributed to Satan. On the contrary, Milton defended obedience to his heavenly monarch with the same appeal to positive liberty and rational law that the Royalist Arminians used to defend obedience to earthly monarchs.

Milton made it clear in *Paradise Lost* that the angels, humanity, and even God himself all possess some sort of negative liberty, and this statement is equally valid whether one chooses to understand negative liberty in the traditional sense as the absence of coercion or to follow Taylor and define this liberty by the presence of opportunities for choice. In the "absence of coercion" sense, the angels and humanity are free because their wills are not "over-rul'd by Fate" (5.527), and God is free because he can say that "Necessity and Chance / Approach not mee" (7.172–73). Likewise, in the "opportunities for choice" sense, the angels are free "To love or not" (5.540), humanity is free "to stand or fall" (8.640), and God is free "To act or not" (7.172). Milton took care to underscore the negative liberty of the angels and humanity in large part because this was essential to his theodicy. As God himself somewhat testily explains, Adam and Eve's freedom from necessity makes them "Authors to themselves in all" (3.122) and therefore absolves him from any responsibility for their fall (3.95–128).

But while Milton assuredly insisted upon humanity's negative liberty and believed that this liberty was a great good, he also distinguished another form of liberty, a positive or "exercise" concept in which freedom consists of obedience to rational law. "[T]rue Liberty," says Michael, "always with right Reason dwells" (12.83, 84). The unfallen Adam is equally blunt: "what obeys / Reason, is free, and Reason [God] made right" (9.351–52). Since God's rule is completely in harmony with rational law—"God and Nature bid the same" (6.176)—the angels believe that they maintain their freedom when they obey God. As Adam says in other circumstances, one can "yet still free / Approve the best, and follow what [one] approve[s]" (8.610–11). For his own part, God links the rebel angels' opposition to the kingship of his Son with their opposition to rational law. As he puts it, the rebels

> reason for thir Law refuse,
> Right reason for thir Law, and for thir King
> Messiah, who by right of merit reigns.
>
> (6.41–43)

And even Satan himself has no difficulty attributing his own preeminence simultaneously to both "the fixt Laws of Heav'n" and "free choice" (2.18, 21).

Despite this singular instance, however, Satan usually imagines "Servility with freedom to contend" (6.169) because his conception of liberty is almost exclusively negative. By his own admission, he incites the War in Heaven to protect the freedom of his fellow angels, "to cast off" a newly imposed "Yoke" (5.786), rather than to assume any more power for himself. He can claim that he and his fellow rebels will "dwell free" (6.292) in their corner of Heaven and console himself in Hell that "Here at least / We shall be free" (1.258–59) because he believes that freedom begins where obedience ends. For Satan and his followers, one is free to the extent that one is not immediately subject to God. This is why Satan boasts that he "in one Night freed / From servitude inglorious well nigh half / Th' Angelic Name" (9.140–42), why he promises "to set free" Sin and Death "From out this dark and dismal house of pain" (2.822–23), why Nisroch praises him as a "Deliverer from new Lords, leader to free / Enjoyment of our right as Gods" (6.451–52), and why Sin claims "Thou hast achiev'd our liberty, confin'd / Within Hell Gates till now" (10.368–69). The two fallen angels and Sin are explicitly appealing to a "freedom from" conception of liberty, and all of their statements are valid according to this conception.

Satan opposes the liberty of the angels not only to the monarchy of Heaven but also to God's imposition of laws. Indeed, Satan is a "Rebel to all Law" (10.83), one who first broaches his rebellion against God's rule by invoking what he sees as God's attempt to impose "new Laws" (5.679) and "new commands" (5.691) on the angels. He later claims that the angels are "Equally free" (5.792) and uses this as an argument not only against God's monarchy and the exaltation of the Son but also against God's introduction of "Law and Edict on us, who without law / Err not" (5.798–99). In a similar move, Mammon associates what he calls the angels' "Subjection" with "Strict Laws impos'd" (2.239, 241). Both these fallen angels imagine that freedom is incompatible with command or prohibition, and here they seem to be taking the view of Thomas Hobbes, another theorist of negative liberty, who likewise believed that a subject's liberties "depend on the silence of the Law" and that "where the Sovereign has prescribed no rule, there the Subject hath the liberty to do, or forebeare, according to his own discretion."[16]

Abdiel affirms a positive conception of liberty in his response to Satan. He refuses to accept Satan's contention that it is "Flatly unjust, to bind with Laws the free" (5.819). Abdiel, it should be stressed, neither denies that the angels are free nor that they are bound by laws. What he does deny is that this arrangement is "unjust." He continues,

> Shalt thou give Law to God, shalt thou dispute
> With him the points of liberty, who made
> Thee what thou art, and form'd the Pow'rs of Heav'n
> Such as he pleas'd, and circumscrib'd thir being?
>
> (5.822–25)

This passage deserves close attention. On the one hand, Abdiel's words allude to Romans 9.20: "Nay but, O man, who art thou that repliest against God? Shall the thing formed say to him that formed *it*, Why hast thou made me thus?" (King James Version). This verse, however, was a favorite of those Calvinists who wished to claim that God was *exlex*, a position that Milton assuredly did not hold. Abdiel's point appears to be quite different: rather than arguing that God is lawless, Abdiel maintains that law, and with it liberty, proceeds *from* God into the universe he created. God has built law into the very identity of the angels; he has "circumscrib'd thir being," and "the points of [their] liberty" cannot be understood apart from this.

Satan falls short in his self-professed role as "Patron of Liberty" (4.958) neither because he asserts a false liberty nor because he falsely asserts liberty. In fact, Satan's view of liberty as precious birthright that must be zealously protected from monarchial encroachment is precisely the traditionally English negative conception of liberty enshrined in the Magna Carta.[17] Milton himself often drew upon this view of liberty in his political writings, most notably in *The Tenure of Kings and Magistrates*. Thus, just as Satan defends his rejection of the Son's kingship by appealing to the angels' rights as "Natives and Sons of Heav'n" (5.790) who are "free / Equally free" (791–92) and who possess "Imperial Titles which assert / Our being ordain'd to govern, not to serve" (801–2), so, too, did Milton invoke humanity's native freedom and God-given mandate to govern in *The Tenure of Kings and Magistrates*: "No man who knows ought, can be so stupid to deny that all men naturally were borne free, being the image and resemblance of God himself, and were by privilege above all the creatures, born to command and not to obey" (3:198–99). There is little difference between Satan's insistence that the angels are "ordain'd to govern, not to serve" and Milton's that humanity is "born to command and not to obey."

But while Satan's arguments are Milton's arguments, they are not Milton's arguments in their entirety, for Milton also held a positive conception of liberty. The same appeal to negative liberty that Milton made in *The Tenure of Kings and Magistrates* and that Satan makes to his followers in Heaven appears once more in *Paradise Lost*, this time in Adam's condemnation of Nimrod's usurpation:

> O execrable Son so to aspire
> Above his Brethren, to himself assuming
> Authority usurpt, from God not giv'n:

> He gave us only over Beast, Fish, Fowl
> Dominion absolute; that right we hold
> By his donation; but Man over men
> He made not Lord; such title to himself
> Reserving, human left from human free.
>
> (12.64–71)

Michael, of course, replies to Adams's "freedom from" conception of liberty by outlining an ideal of positive, or "Rational Liberty" as Michael terms it:

> Justly thou abhorr'st
> That Son, who on the quiet state of men
> Such trouble brought, affecting to subdue
> Rational Liberty; yet know withal,
> Since thy original lapse, true Liberty
> Is lost, which always with right Reason dwells
> Twinn'd, and from her hath no dividual being:
> Reason in man obscur'd, or not obey'd,
> Immediately inordinate desires
> And upstart Passions catch the Government
> From Reason, and to servitude reduce
> Man till then free.
>
> (12.79–90)

We can see, then, that Satan errs not by asserting negative liberty, which is valuable in its own place, but by refusing to acknowledge positive liberty and, in fact, by pitting negative liberty against the claims of positive liberty and rational law.

If Satan's insistence on an entirely negative conception of liberty disqualifies him as a spokesperson for Milton's views, it also disqualifies him from being a republican. As J. H. Hexter has noted, the Machiavellian or classical republican tradition is based on a positive notion of liberty.[18] It stresses public duty and civic virtue over the freedom to be left alone. For this reason, Blair Worden is not strictly accurate when he states that Satan adopts a republican language in *Paradise Lost*.[19] It is true that Satan's language is highly antimonarchial, but one did not have to be a republican to be antimonarchial nor antimonarchial to be a republican. More important, however, Satan's language is not republican in any positive sense because he does not advocate a republican ideal of political liberty. Indeed, Worden himself acknowledges in another essay that "Republican freedom was not a mere absence of constraint,"[20] and "a mere absence of constraint" is the only freedom that Satan values.

Milton was undoubtedly a republican of some sort when he wrote *Paradise Lost*, and like other republicans, he advocated a positive conception of liberty. There is, however, more than one type of positive liberty. Isaiah Berlin argues that the goal of self-direction that lies at the heart of any positive conception of liberty has taken on two major historical forms: "the first, that of self-abnegation in order to attain independence; the second, that of self-realization, or total self-identification with a specific principle or ideal in order to attain the selfsame end."[21] The first kind of liberty is based on individual autonomy and self-sufficiency; people master the world by mastering their own minds, by constricting their desires to fit their circumstances and deliberately choosing to accept their lot.[22] Such a form of liberty is perhaps best suited to a dejected and restricted people, and indeed its sole advocate in *Paradise Lost* is the fallen Mammon. He argues that the defeated and imprisoned angels should

> rather seek
> Our own good from ourselves, and from our own
> Live to ourselves, though in this vast recess,
> Free, and to none accountable, preferring
> Hard liberty before the easy yoke
> Of servile Pomp.
>
> (2.252–57)

Mammon's "Hard liberty," the freedom which comes when one lives "to none accountable," is essentially the Stoic conception of freedom. Milton scorned its premises both in *Paradise Lost* and in *Paradise Regained*. In this latter work, Christ explicitly repudiates the Stoics and their notion of the wise man "perfect in himself, and all possessing" (4.302),

> contemning all
> Wealth, pleasure, pain or torment, death and life,
> Which when he lists, he leaves, or boasts he can.
>
> (304–6)

In Milton's opinion, this was not admirable independence but foolish pride.

Berlin's second form of positive liberty, that of self-realization, can itself be divided into at least two major historical forms, although Berlin himself does not make this particular subdivision. These two forms, both of which we have already encountered, are, first, the Aristotelian or Thomistic tradition of positive liberty and, second, that of the Machiavellians or classical republicans. While both traditions identify freedom with self-realization, the Thomistic tradition with its emphasis on rational law and divinely ordained ends defines this realization more narrowly than does the Machiavellian. As Quentin Skinner explains, writers in the Machiavellian tradition differ from those in the Thomistic because the Machiavellians "never argue, that is, that we are moral beings with certain determinate purposes, and thus that we are only in the fullest sense in possession of our liberty when these purposes are realised."[23] On the contrary, Machiavelli and many of his followers acknowledged that different classes of people have different interests and that the resulting conflict of these interests might be conducive to political health.[24]

Although Milton was influenced by Machiavelli, the tradition of positive liberty that he favored was Thomistic rather than Machiavellian. Milton certainly believed "that we are moral beings with certain determinate purposes." In Adam's words,

> to observe
> Immutably [God's] sovran will . . . [is] the end
> Of what we are.
>
> (7.78–80)

Moreover, we have already noted how the Machiavellian or classical republican tradition insists on political participation as the cornerstone of liberty. Milton, however, was determined in his *The Readie and Easie Way to Establish a Free Commonwealth* to propose a model republic where participation would be severely limited once his perpetual senate was established. He begrudged even a partial rotation of this senate and sneered at "the ambition of such as think themselves injur'd that they also partake not of the government" (7:434). In doing so, he came remarkably close to echoing no less a Royalist than Charles I himself, who said on the scaffold that although he desired the liberty of the people, he nonetheless believed "that their liberty consists in having of Government those laws by which their life and goods may be most their own. It is not having a *share* in Government, Sirs; that is nothing pertaining to them."[25] Likewise, Milton insisted that his free commonwealth could be legitimately established without the consent of even a bare majority of an already severely limited English electorate, and he rejected out of hand the proposal that a popular assembly balance his perpetual senate. Yet all of this is not surprising because for Milton the key component of positive liberty was not participation in government but obedience to rational law.

With the mention of rational law, we return once more to the Royalist Arminians. The reason for Milton's rejection of the Royalism held by so many of his fellow Arminians was not that he did not share their political ideals. Rather, he questioned their application of these ideals to the monarchy of England. Both Milton and the Royalist Arminians believed that the ideal commonwealth would be one where "reason only swaies" (*The Readie and Easie Way*, 7:427), but unlike them he came increasingly to doubt that such a commonwealth was possible in England without a complete restructuring of its inherited institutions. Thus, he insisted that an erring monarch be held accountable by his subjects for any violation of law. One could not simply hope that a king would always conform to God's law-abiding example. Moreover, because the problem for Milton was not simply that earthly monarchs seldom behaved like God but that earthly subjects seldom behaved like angels, he eventually decided that only a well-designed and carefully limited republic would secure through its institutions the sovereignty of reason that he could not otherwise take for granted. However, Milton had no need to compensate for human imperfections in imagining his heaven. And the heaven he imagined was one that a Royalist could applaud.

Notes

1. John Selden, *The Table Talk of John Selden,* ed. Frederick Pollock (London: Quaritch, 1927), 49. I have modernized Selden's spelling and punctuation.

2. Christopher Hill, *Milton and the English Revolution* (New York: Penguin, 1977), 268–78; Joan S. Bennett, *Reviving Liberty: Radical Christian Humanism in Milton's Great Poems* (Cambridge: Harvard University Press, 1989), 6–32.

3. For more on the differing ways the Calvinists and Arminians conceived of God and his relationship with humanity, see Steven Jablonski, "Evil Days: Providence and Politics in the Thought of John Milton and his Age" (Ph.D. diss., Princeton University, 1994).

4. Samuel Hoard, *Gods Love To Man-kinde. Manifested by Dis-proving his Absolute Decree for their Damnation* (London, 1658), 79.

5. Henry Hammond, *The Works of the Reverend and Learned Henry Hammond, D.D.,* 2d ed., 4 vols. (London, 1684), 1:489.

6. Isaiah Berlin, "Two Concepts of Liberty," in *Four Essays on Liberty* (New York: Oxford University Press, 1970), 118–72.

7. Charles Taylor, "What's Wrong With Negative Liberty," in *The Idea of Freedom: Essays in Honour of Isaiah Berlin,* ed. Alan Ryan (Oxford: Oxford University Press, 1979), 175–93.

8. Herbert Thorndike, *The Theological Works of Herbert Thorndike,* 4 vols. (Oxford: J. H. Parker, 1845–53), 3:483.

9. Hiram Haydn, *The Counter-Renaissance* (1950; reprint, Gloucester, Mass.: Peter Smith, 1966), 300.

10. Hammond, *Works,* 1:346.

11. Ibid., 1:345.

12. Conrad Russell, "Divine Rights in the Early Seventeenth Century," in *Public Duty and Private Conscience in Seventeenth-Century England: Essays Presented to G. E. Aylmer,* ed. John Morrill, Paul Slack, and Daniel Woolf (Oxford: Oxford University Press, 1993), 101–20; Glenn Burgess, "The Divine Right of Kings Reconsidered," *The English Historical Review* 107 (1992): 837–61.

13. John Milton, *Complete Prose Works of John Milton,* 8 vols., ed. Don M. Wolfe et al. (New Haven: Yale University Press, 1953–82), 4:341. All references to Milton's prose are to this edition and are cited parenthetically in the text.

14. Ralph Cudworth, *The True Intellectual System of the Universe,* 2 vols. (Andover: Gould and Newman, 1838), 2:356, 358.

15. John Milton, *Paradise Lost,* in *John Milton: Complete Poems and Major Prose,*

ed. Merritt Y. Hughes (New York: Odyssey, 1957). All references to Milton's poetry are to this edition and are cited parenthetically in the text.

16. Thomas Hobbes, *Leviathan*, ed. C. B. Macpherson (New York: Penguin, 1968), 271.

17. J. H. Hexter, review of *The Machiavellian Moment*, by J. G. A. Pocock, *History and Theory* 16 (1977): 331–37.

18. Ibid., 331.

19. Blair Worden, "Milton's Republicanism and the Tyranny of Heaven," in *Machiavelli and Republicanism*, ed. Gisela Bock, Quentin Skinner, and Maurizo Viroli (Cambridge: Cambridge University Press, 1990), 235–38.

20. Blair Worden, "English Republicanism," in *The Cambridge History of Political Thought 1450–1700*, ed. J. H. Burns with the assistance of Mark Goldie (Cambridge: Cambridge University Press, 1991), 468.

21. Berlin, "Two Concepts of Liberty," 134.

22. Ibid., 135–41.

23. Quentin Skinner, "The Republican Ideal of Political Liberty," in Bock, Skinner, and Viroli, *Machiavelli and Republicanism*, 306–7. Oddly enough, Skinner himself considers republican liberty to be a kind of negative liberty, presumably because he acknowledges only one type of positive liberty, that of Aristotle and the Thomists.

24. Worden, "English Republicanism," 465–66.

25. Quoted in David Masson, *The Life of John Milton*, 7 vols. (London: Macmillan, 1859–94), 3:725.

The Politics of Love in *Paradise Lost*

ROBERT THOMAS FALLON

Modern commentary on a poet's political imagery invariably attempts to position the artist somewhere within the ideological spectrum. Critical inquiry seems intent upon labeling a work, and its author, with one or the other of the currently fashionable ideological tags, and in the case of a great work of literature, one with which the critic of the moment is altogether comfortable. Such commentary can be skillful and enlightening, of course, but by its nature it restricts the critical imagination to a narrow range of inquiry.

When applied to Milton's works, this method ends only in confusion. When Satan sounds like Oliver Cromwell, the champion of the English Revolution, and God Almighty for all the world like the king of England, one is hard-pressed to know where to place the poet within the spectrum of allegiances of his day. One can deconstruct, of course, analyze silences, and read between lines so as to locate the poet on the proper ideological wavelength; but one is forced to exercise such ingenuity only because those lines keep telling us something we don't want to hear. Milton's God is an absolute monarch, but since Milton clearly had little sympathy for absolute monarchs, it is difficult to reconcile the Almighty of *Paradise Lost* with the poet's known political preferences. What to do?[1] Well, once it can be shown that Milton drew on *both* Cromwell and King Charles to depict his splendid devil, *and* to represent God Almighty as well, all that ingenuity seems pointless.[2]

Readings of the poetry that place Milton within a political spectrum go astray from the outset by assuming that *Paradise Lost* is a political testament, in the same way that *Eikonoklastes* is a political testament, that is, the poet's statement of his position on the ideological issues that divided his age. Both works are crowded with political figures, but it is abundantly clear that Milton composed the poem and the tract for very different purposes, the one to justify the ways of God, the other the ways of the English Republic; hence, those figures play very different roles in their respective lines. Similarly, in *The Readie and Easie Way to Establish a Free Commonwealth*, Milton urges his readers to adopt a particular form of government; but among the governments of *Paradise Lost*, the structure that most closely resembles the design in the tract is the one in Hell, where there is a degree of representation, open debate of issues, and decision by ballot, rather than the celestial one, where an absolute monarch rules by inalterable decree. This is not to imply that Milton was of the Devil's party, but to argue that the political structures of *Paradise Lost* do not reflect the poet's political allegiances.

But if the political imagery does not make a political statement, what sort of statement does it make? Whatever their position on the murky controversy over authorial intent, even the most modern of postmodern scholars can agree that Milton expected his readers to contrast his Heaven and Hell and, presumably, to prefer the former. Those readers were to judge, however, on the basis of the distance between the spiritual qualities of the two realms, not on the surface impression left by their separate political structures. Each of the governments of *Paradise Lost* is predicated on a different quality of the spirit, which we may call the "governing principle" of its political structure. There are four such realms in the poem, those in Heaven, Hell, Chaos, and Eden—five when one distinguishes between the governing principles that order the lives of prelapsarian and postlapsarian humankind. Let us consider each in turn, starting with the lowest.

The structure of Hell allows for the expression of some of the common concerns of fallen human beings—a desire to better their condition, find relief from pain, and live in freedom—as well as some of their less admirable qualities—obsessive ambition, the drive of self-interest thoughtless of the cost to others, a compulsion for revenge, and unprincipled hatred. Satan and his followers demonstrate all these qualities at one time or another, but the one that chiefly defines them is hatred.

Initially, Hell is a place much in need of structuring. Disobedience is a political act, a denial of authority; it is a step that, once taken, immediately thrusts the rebel into a political world, where choices must be made from among alternative governing principles to replace the one rebelled against. Satan's leadership brings order out of disorder; paralyzed initially by fear that God's forces will pursue the war and "with linked Thunderbolts / Transfix us to the bottom of this Gulf" (1.328–29),[3] the rebel angels are ultimately restored to their former military discipline and unity. Once the limits of the divine will have been tested and found to permit the reestablishment of order, their fear gives way to hatred, which acts as a unifying force for the damned, who, brought together by the shared desire to seek revenge on the power condemning them to their terrible punishment, embrace a common cause. It is not Milton's purpose, however, to depict the forces of evil as mere puppets of a single diabolical will. Each of the fallen angels is dangerous in his own right, and they all retain the gift of reason, which they exercise in agreeing on a scheme to seek vengeance. The "great Seraphic Lords and Cherubim" (1.794) approve Satan's plan of action, not out of loyalty or devotion to him, to be sure, but because they are persuaded that it is the best means of relieving their pain and avenging their outcast state without risking annihilation.

As for Chaos, to speak of structure there is, of course, to talk nonsense. The governing principle of that realm is discord; it is a kingdom wracked with "the noise / Of endless wars" (2.896), where "four Champions fierce / Strive . . . for Maistry, and to Battle bring / Thir embryon Atoms" (898–900) and where "Chance governs all" (910). Milton chose to depict that "dark / Illimitable Ocean" (891–92) in political allegory, however, and conceived a court of corulers, "Chaos and ancient Night" (970), with a retinue of eight attendants, Orcus, Ades, Demogorgon, Rumor, Chance, Tumult, Confusion, and Discord (964–67), a structure reflecting the cosmic scheme of governance to be found as well in both Heaven and Hell.[4] It is an uneasy allegory, to be sure, where substance is imposed upon elements resolutely insubstantial; but Milton may have taken the risk to demonstrate further Satan's diplomatic skills. By promising to restore the newly created World, once conquered, to the realm of "ancient Night," an agreement that he has no intention of honoring, he succeeds in securing the aid of a distraught Chaos, who willingly points the way to the newly created universe.

Heaven is a place where the will of God is immediately manifest as the will of the body politic, a phenomenon explainable only in terms of the love between the Deity and his creation. God decrees and the heavenly host concur, not because they are puppets of the Almighty—they too can reason—but because of the mutual love between the king and his subjects; he acts, through the Son, and they burst into hymns of praise, perceiving that his actions manifest his love. In this respect, Heaven really has no need of government; and Milton's decision to give it one was motivated perhaps by his desire to magnify the glory of God to such a degree as to chastise all earthly rulers who seek to emulate him. Those who pretended to that glory, and their subjects who joined in such worship, he branded as idolaters (3:343–44, 601).[5]

The rule of Earth, as much as we see of it, is a manifestation of the same divine love. Eden is a place where two beings gifted with reason can debate issues, such as working conditions, and arrive at agreement; but as a governing principle, that love is expressed in terms not evident in the other realms, that is, as a personal relationship. What we see of the interaction between individual fallen angels gives some evidence of envy, competing ambition, and disagreement; but hate as a governing principle does not extend to individual relationships. The devils' hatred of God does not produce a hatred for one another. In like manner, we do not see evidence of God's angels loving one another. Though in answer to Adam's rather forward question ("Love not the heav'nly spirits, and how thir Love / Express they . . . ? [8.615–16]), Raphael reveals that "Spirits embrace" (8.626), it is clear that he would rather not discuss the matter further. For Milton, then, human love is a means of expressing a dimension of the divine not elsewhere demonstrated—the love of God inspires the love of one's fellow being—and a way of describing the effects of the governing principle of Heaven in terms accessible to human understanding.

The Fall precipitates dramatic changes, many of which are figured in terms of a shift in political power. On the cosmic scene, the angelic guards are recalled, the stairs to Heaven "drawn up" (3.516), and Adam and Eve expelled from Eden, which then is placed under divine protection, a celestial foothold in a corrupted world.[6] God's love is not withdrawn, but his presence is; henceforth, the race will be deprived of "His blessed count'nance" (11.317), which "to behold" was, for Adam, the "highth / Of happiness" (10.724–25). Michael comforts Adam with the assurance that "God is as here [in Paradise] . . . still compassing thee round / With goodness and paternal Love" (11.350, 352–53); however, he will no longer "visit oft the dwellings of just Men" (7.570), but be known to them only as an insubstantial "Omnipresence" (11.336).

If the governing principle of Eden was love, that of the fallen world will be something else entirely. The initial reaction of the fallen pair to one another and Michael's long account of the sorry history of humankind paint a picture of incessant conflict. The race, it seems, will rule itself through the clash of conflicting interests, resolved all too often by resort to arms. Conflict is not to be confused with the discord of Chaos, however; divine love still holds Creation together, but henceforth human affairs will be characterized by forces competing for power and wealth rather than the joyful accord that united God and prelapsarian human beings, a relationship now shattered by disobedience. Milton was ambivalent about conflict. In *Areopagitica*, the young controversialist exults in the "disputing, reasoning, reading, inventing, discoursing, ev'n to a rarity, and admiration" (2:557) of the citizens of London. The poet of *Paradise Lost*, however, perhaps because he had seen too much of conflict, deplores the incessant wrangling of the race, citing the fallen angels' unanimity at the close of the "great consult" (1.798):

> O shame to men! Devil with Devil damn'd
> Firm concord holds, men only disagree
> Of creatures rational.
>
> (2.496–98)

But he had only to survey his own times to be convinced that conflict shaped human government, in England's case the clash of royalist and republican factions that led to civil war and in the 1650s the economic competition that erupted into hostilities with the United Netherlands, Denmark, and Spain.[7]

In describing the government of Heaven as an absolute monarchy and the one in Hell as a representative assembly, Milton is not urging his readers to choose one political structure over the other; he is asking them to choose love over hatred. His artistic problem arises from the fact that hatred is much more readily represented in political terms than is its opposite; hence, the government of Hell is more vivid and immediate than the rule of Heaven. Hate begets a compulsion to act, set traps, hatch plots, and strike by night. It *demands* action, and with its restless energy will precipitate conflict, whether in debate over issues, the struggle for power, or the clash of arms, all readily represented in imagery of the political arena. Further, the demonic regime is closer to the poet's own experience, from which he drew most readily for the materials of his art.

Love, conversely, connotes rest, contentment, and a joyful acceptance of the bond that satisfies all yearning. It has no counterpart in the practice of governance except in the image of the absolute monarch in perfect accord with his subjects, a bond that earthly monarchs fervently claimed for their kingdoms and that Milton with equal fervor condemned wherever claimed. The kings of Milton's time were fond of citing the reciprocal love they shared with their subjects and among their "cousins," the crowned heads of nations, who were all related in one way or another. (Louis XIV and Charles II, for example, were first cousins.) Milton considered such monarchal posturing idolatrous, which helps explain why he avoids mention of love in his praise of Cromwell and the other leaders of the Republic in *The Second Defence of the People of England*. In the Lord Protector's letters to heads of state, there can be found frequent references to friendship, amity, union, and goodwill; but the personal relationship is never said to go beyond "affection." Divine love, then, though essential to the justification of God's ways, is not represented in political terms. The angels sing of it and the Deity demonstrates it by surrendering his Son to death; but it lies outside human experience and defies description in the language of governance.

Thus, Milton was confronted with the challenge of somehow expressing that inexpressible love of the Deity for his creation, and for humankind especially—the latter in the face of evidence that would seem to call it into question. In the *Christian Doctrine*, he lays little stress on divine love, perhaps because his systematic theology is designed to make Scripture accessible to human reason rather than emotion. In his list of God's attributes, Milton describes him as "SUPREMELY KIND" (6:150); and in his citation of the familiar lines from John 3.16, "For God so loved the world," he is discussing other matters entirely. But love is the single attribute of God upon which any justification of his ways must rest. Divine love is the central principle of all creation, the reciprocal bond that makes it work, uniting its fallen and unfallen creatures in a celebration of existence; and although it may not lend itself to representation in a systematic theology devoted to forming "correct ideas about God guided by nature or reason" (6:132), it is a quality appropriate to expression in poetry, whose music reaches out to an understanding beyond the merely rational. In the *Christian Doctrine*, Milton can only interpret God's ways; in *Paradise Lost* he seeks to justify them, and he does so in terms of God's love for humankind.

Any effort to represent divine love in political terms invariably ends up as an argument suspiciously circular—I love God because I am free; I am free because I love God. But that same love resolves the many paradoxes of the political imagery that distinguish the human experience from the divine—such puzzling contradictions as: in absolute obedience lies absolute freedom; within the elaborate "Orders and Degrees" (5.792) of Heaven all its creatures are equal; and the Son's "Humiliation shall exalt" (3.313) him, to which may be added the oxymoron, "government of Heaven." Though the politics of Paradise, lost and regained, is a pervasive metaphor, it makes sense only in terms of the love that binds God's creatures to one another and him to his creation. Thus, the harsh punishment for Adam's sin can only be justified once it is understood that obedience to God is the political equivalent of that love returned and that disobedience is the political equivalent of that love betrayed.

When one speaks of "justifying," the language is legal, raising the question as to whether the acts or laws are "just" or not. God's judgment of what is right or wrong need not conform to that of human beings, of course; but if God as the ruler of the universe wants to engage the allegiance of a being he has endowed with reason, he will have to present himself as a "just" ruler insofar as the individual is given to know the meaning of justice. It is immaterial that humankind cannot fully comprehend the mind of God, however true that may be; but his mind must be made accessible to a human understanding of justice, else God will lose his creatures' devotion. Having endowed men and women with reason, God must reason with them. And this is no easy task, for Milton's God must condemn them to death in such a way as to retain their love. It is difficult to feel affection for a distant, unbending judge who proclaims his word as law; but if it can be shown that he does so out of love, the bond between human and divine can be sustained. The alternative is unthinkable; once God's universe is deprived of the ordering principle of mutual love between the creator and his creation, it reverts to the condition of Chaos, a place of endless discord, ruled by an "Anarch" who "imbroils the fray / By which he Reigns" (2.908–9).

Thus, in *Paradise Lost* Milton celebrates the belief that God created all things solely to express that quality of his nature through the person of the Son:

in him all his Father shone
Substantially express'd, and in his face
Divine compassion visibly appear'd,
Love without end, and without measure Grace.

(3.139–42)

And he gave his creatures the gift of reason so they could respond in kind: "Not free, what proof could they have giv'n sincere / Of true allegiance, constant Faith or Love?" (3.103–4). When the Son offers himself for man, "mee for him, life for life" (236), God foresees the Incarnation as a victory by which "Heav'nly love shall outdo Hellish hate" (3.298), and the celestial choir celebrates the sacrifice, "O unexampl'd love, / Love nowhere to be found less than Divine" (3.410–11).

But Milton had to do more than simply sing about God's love; he had to show it; and the means of doing so arise from his familiar definition in *Areopagitica*: "It was from out the rinde of one apple tasted, that the knowledge of good and evill as two twins cleaving together leapt forth into the World. And perhaps this is that doom which *Adam* fell into of knowing good and evill, that is to say of knowing good by evill" (2:514). In a striking series of parallels between Hell and Heaven, and between Satan and the Son of God, Milton defines love in terms of its opposite. His readers, who can only know good *by* evil, are presented with an image of celestial governance beyond their comprehension, but whose quality can be brought within the scope of human understanding when it is placed alongside the regime in Hell, whose structure mirrors the governments of Earth, and is, hence, all too familiar to them. The essential difference between the two realms can be grasped only through a vision of what they, like "two twins cleaving together," have in common.

The parallels between the celestial and demonic trinities are frequently cited to illustrate Milton's intent to depict Hell as a parody of Heaven, that is, to underline the rather self-evident commonplace that one is inferior to the other.[8] The similarities between the two trinities, however, the family relationships and the commitment of their members to a common goal, are designed to emphasize their disparate ends, the one motivated by hatred, the other by love. The purpose of these parallels is not to mock evil, but to define good.

Further, the political hierarchy of Hell mirrors that of Heaven; their conclaves are comparably splendid, and, after the "great consult," their subjects equally united in purpose. The similarities serve to accentuate the different purposes, the one to divide human beings from God, the other to draw them closer. Beelzebub and God ask for volunteers for their separate missions, and both are greeted with silence, as the two bodies ponder the consequences; in the one, none "could be found / So hardy as to proffer or accept / Alone the dreadful voyage" (2.424–26), and in the other, none "durst upon his own head draw / The deadly forfeiture, and ransom set" (3.220–21). However, there is a discernible difference in the responses to the two offers. The response to Satan's acceptance speech is relatively subdued: the fallen angels "bend / With awful reverence prone; and as a God / Extol him equal to the highest in Heav'n" (2.477–79); in contrast, the Son's offer, once God has explained its significance, is greeted by "a shout / Loud as from numbers without number, sweet / As from blest voices, uttering joy" (3.345–47), and the angels burst into a long hymn of praise (372–415). The similarities here set up responses appropriate to the different motives of the two. Satan's personal ambition, his need to perform some exemplary act to prove himself worthy "to reign in Hell" (1.263), is greeted with begrudged admiration, touched with awe. The Son, with nothing to prove, having already demonstrated his right to the throne by his victory over the rebel angels, acts out of perfect love for humankind, bringing joy to the heavenly host, who respond with "sacred Song" (3.369).

Both Satan and the Son embark on voyages to the world, the one to subvert Adam and Eve, and thereby the human race, the other to save them; and their missions have similar political consequences. Satan secures his right to reign in Hell, with his enhanced status defined by Sin. "Thine now is all this World" (10.372), she declares, "here thou shalt Monarch reign" (375), and God must "henceforth Monarchy with thee divide / Of all things" (379–80). Satan, very full of himself, confirms that he has "made one Realm / Hell and this World, one Realm, one Continent" (391–92) with him as sole ruler. The Son is similarly confirmed as king of Heaven, for as the Father proclaims, as a result of his sacrifice,

> Here shalt thou sit incarnate, here shalt Reign
> Both God and Man, Son both of God and Man,
> Anointed universal King.
>
> (3.315–17)

Both suffer humiliation on Earth, Satan's "foul descent" (9.163) into the serpent, the Son's crucifixion; both triumph, Satan over Adam and Eve, the Son over Death; both assume humble guises, Satan on his return to Hell as a "Plebian Angel militant / Of lowest order" (10.442–43), the Son on Earth as man; and both are greeted with animation on the return to their respective realms, Satan to the loud acclaim and joy of all "the great consulting Peers" (10.456), and the Son "exalted high / Above all names in Heav'n" (12.457–58), as Michael foretells. Satan silences his followers with a gesture, proclaims his victory, and directs them to "enter now into full bliss" (10.503). Rather than the hymns of praise that will greet the "Son . . . of God and Man" (3.316), however, he hears only "A dismal universal hiss, the sound / Of public scorn" (10.508–9). The Son's "Humiliation shall exalt" him; but Satan's exaltation, in ironic contrast, ends only in further humiliation. God's love is confirmed, and defined, by its opposite. We come to know good by evil.

There is more to be said, of course, on all these matters; but I raise them here chiefly to illustrate the freedom with which the critical imagination may range in examining the political imagery of Milton's lines, once it is relieved of the tiresome burden of reconciling his poetic figures with what is known of his political ideology. Milton is an unusual instance of a poet who served at the center of the political life of his country, not on its fringes; and his imagination clearly drew heavily on that experience. But his political figures play a very different role in his epic poetry than they do in his polemic prose or than they did in his political life; and the tedious scanning of his art in search of hints to confirm or deny his ideology can add little to our regard for his poetic achievement. Our concern should not be what he thought of his political experience, but what he made of it.

Notes

1. Two recent studies accept God as a king, but strive to assure readers that he is the right kind of king: Joan S. Bennett, *Reviving Liberty: Radical Christian Humanism in Milton's Great Poems* (Cambridge: Harvard University Press, 1989), 33–58; and Stevie Davies, *Images of Kingship in "Paradise Lost": Milton's Politics and Christian Liberty* (Columbia: University of Missouri Press, 1989).

2. For Charles I as a source, see Bennett, *Reviving Liberty*, 33–58. For Cromwell, see Robert Thomas Fallon, *Captain or Colonel: The Soldier in Milton's Life and Art* (Columbia: University of Missouri Press, 1984), 161–62, 171–72, 191–92, 199.

3. John Milton, *Paradise Lost*, in *John Milton: Complete Poems and Major Prose*, ed. Merritt Y. Hughes (New York: Odyssey, 1957). All references to Milton's poetry are to this edition and are cited parenthetically in the text.

4. Robert H. West, *Milton and the Angels* (Athens: University of Georgia Press, 1955). West describes Milton's use of the traditional eight orders of angels, a hierarchy duplicated in Hell.

5. John Milton, *Eikonoklastes*, in *Complete Prose Works of John Milton*, 8 vols., ed. Don M. Wolfe et al. (New Haven: Yale University Press, 1953–82). All references to Milton's prose are to this edition and are cited parenthetically in the text.

6. See Fallon, *Captain or Colonel*, 145–49, for the postlapsarian status of Eden as a political image.

7. For the Republic's wars with these nations, see Robert Thomas Fallon, *Milton in Government* (University Park: Pennsylvania University Press, 1993), 73–99. Seeking economic advantage, England engaged in three wars with the United Netherlands during Milton's lifetime.

8. See, for example, Balachandra Rajan, *"Paradise Lost" and the Seventeenth Century Reader* (New York: Oxford University Press, 1948), 50.

"Among Unequals What Society": The Dynamics of Punishment in *Paradise Lost*

ALICE M. MATHEWS

IN her study of the punishment theme in *Paradise Lost*, Wilma G. Armstrong claims that Milton's poem anticipates the principles of Michel Foucault's work *Surveiller et Punir*. Referring to Barry Cooper's *Michel Foucault: An Introduction to the Study of His Thought*, Armstrong summarizes Foucault's outline of how penal systems have developed throughout history. Foucault notes four distinctive systems of punishment: classical Greek and Roman, involving exile, banishment, or loss of property; the old Germanic tradition, which included "atonement, compensation, and fines"; the medieval period, in which bodily pain including torture was required; and modern punishment with its emphasis on rehabilitation through "surveillance."[1] Armstrong maintains that Adam and Eve experience all four systems of punishment, whereas Satan undergoes only the classical and the medieval.[2] Armstrong then focuses on the modern concept of punishment, with imprisonment providing the means for overseeing the offender and perhaps reforming him or her. Like Foucault, Milton shows discipline to be the "ultimate goal of surveillance."[3]

Although Armstrong succeeds in applying to Milton's poem Foucault's historical outline of judicial methods, she fails to establish any causal relationship between that outline and the poem. In fact, I would argue that Milton's depiction of punishment is less a result of his understanding of judicial history than of his recognition of natural principles. One of these important principles involves physical and psychological movement, the subject of Elizabeth Ely Fuller's study of motion in *Paradise Lost*, which provides another critical framework for reexamining the patterns of punishment in the poem. Expanding on Isabel MacCaffrey's observation of the rising and falling action in the poem,[4] Fuller argues that "the primary mode of both his [Milton's] vision and his poetry is kinesthetic."[5] Milton constructs an imaginative realm with its own laws that ultimately "subsume" the physical laws of "the Newtonian frame."[6] The main law of Milton's imaginative world is that learning occurs through "forcing the mind through various kinds of motions"[7]—through shifting perspectives, dimensions, and faculties. Fuller's emphasis on movement, and the energy and knowledge that it produces, helps to reveal another approach for understanding Milton's conception of punishment, which likewise depends on a system of motions.

Whereas Foucault argues that punishment and discipline are the expression of power and the means by which that power is maintained,[8] I believe that Milton depicts justice as an interplay of movements that work toward the preservation or restoration of purity. Obviously the power of God is an essential component in Milton's masterpiece. However, there is some evidence in the poem to suggest the existence of movements that operate in concert with God's power and in the interest of purity.

Before examining the various manifestations of punishment in the poem, we should consider the prologue to the punishment. The first step that Milton shows in the punishment process is the judging of the offender. Armstrong claims that Milton follows the medieval tradition of trying the accused in secret and "in the absence of the accused." She maintains that the trial of Adam and Eve occurs in book 3, "where, in feudal fashion, they are judged and condemned *in absentia* for a crime they have not as yet committed."[9] However, the poem does not suggest any sort of duplicity against the accused. And though the accused are absent for the deliberations concerning their fates, they are told clearly and unequivocally the results of those deliberations. One could also argue that they are not really judged until book 10, when the Son pronounces the sentence, and that the heavenly council in book 3 is more a depiction of God's foreknowledge and of the Son's sacrifice for man than of "the exercise of sovereign power" that precedes "torture and execution."[10] Indeed, Dick Taylor's exhaustive study of the various accounts of the judgment excludes Milton's depiction of the heavenly council, focusing only on the Son's pronouncing judgment in the garden.[11]

The important point is that judgment provides a means of formally stating the crime and the sentence. In *Paradise Lost* Abdiel is the first agent of judgment. When Satan tells Abdiel to inform God of his revolt, Abdiel's reply carries judicial authority:

> O alienate from God, O Spirit accurst,
>
> . . . .
>
>   henceforth
> No more be troubl'd how to quit the yoke
> Of God's Messiah: those indulgent Laws
> Will not be now voutsaf'd, other Decrees
> Against thee are gone forth without recall;
> That Golden Sceptre which thou didst reject
> Is now an Iron Rod to bruise and break
> Thy disobedience.
>
>   (5.877, 881–88)[12]

Later, after Satan has compounded his crime by entering the serpent to seduce Eve, the Son judges the serpent and, by extension, Satan, sentencing the serpent to grovel on its belly, to eat dust, and to be bruised by the woman's seed. When the Son convicts the serpent, he repeats a key word that Abdiel used in judging Satan—"bruise"—an implication that Satan will share the serpent's doom. Moreover, Satan and his rebel troop feel the immediate effects of the sentence when they are changed into the shape of serpents. At the same time that the Son pronounces judgment on the serpent, he sentences Eve to sorrow in childbirth and Adam to labor for survival. First Satan, then Eve, and finally Adam—the order in which they are sentenced follows the order in which they transgress. The process of judging the accused is systematic.

Judgment does not determine guilt but rather announces it. Although the offenders argue the reasons for their crimes, they do not deny the actual deeds they have committed. Judgment is thus a formality. However, the ceremony of judgment is translated into a pragmatic act—ejection of the offender from the society of the offended. The fall or the crime produces a corruption that cannot be tolerated among the uncorrupted. Indeed, as Belial points out during the infernal debate, ejection of the impure is a natural law, which, according to Fuller's paradigm, would transcend Newtonian laws. Refuting Moloch's recommendation that the rebels invade Heaven, Belial explains:

> th' Ethereal mould
> Incapable of stain would soon expel
> Her mischief, and purge off the baser fire.
>
> (2.139–41)

The benefits of this process are especially clear in the account of the heavenly war when the conflict is ravaging the celestial environs. If God had not given the Son power to pursue "these sons of Darkness, [to] drive them out / From all Heav'n's bounds into the utter Deep" (6.715–16), Heaven would have been destroyed. The upturned mountains, the storm of flaming arrows, the cannon's explosive charges all violate the physical integrity of Heaven. The Son goes against the rebels armed with thunderbolts and driving a fiery chariot, and his show of power in ousting the fallen angels is graphically portrayed in the description of the chariot, which emits a "whirl-wind sound" (6. 749) and flashes flames of fire. Moreover, the chariot is drawn "By four Cherubic shapes, four Faces each" (6.753), an anticipation of the four-faced cherubim that accompany Michael on his similar mission to Eden.[13] The obvious source of the angels with four faces is the first chapter of Ezekiel, which describes the prophet's vision of God; and the charges given to the Son and later to Michael, to eject the transgressors from their pure environments, correspond to the task God assigns to Ezekiel immediately after his vision: "I send thee to the children of Israel, to a rebellious nation" (2.1). And the primary message Ezekiel is to deliver concerns the Israelites' exile in Babylon.

The inability of the pure, the unfallen, to endure the presence of corruption is a principle that governs both Earth and Heaven: hence, the need to expel the offender, in the classical manner described by Foucault. In Heaven, the Son's ejection of the rebels is necessary not only to restore order but also to prevent corruption of the pure by the impure, an infection that Abdiel intuits even in the first moments of Satan's rebellion:

> I see thy fall
> Determin'd, and thy hapless crew involv'd
> In this perfidious fraud, contagion spread
> Both of thy crime and punishment.
>
> (5.878–81)

After receiving the Father's commission to drive out the angels, the Son explains the desired end:

> Then shall thy Saints unmixt, and from th' impure
> Far separate, circling thy holy Mount
> Unfeigned Halleluiahs to thee sing.
>
> (6.742–44)

On Earth Adam and Eve are to experience the effects of that same principle, for the Father announces to the Son their imminent exile from Eden:

> But longer in that Paradise to dwell,
> The Law I gave to Nature him forbids;
> Those pure immortal Elements that know
> No gross, no unharmonious mixture foul,
> Eject him tainted now, and purge him off
> As a distemper.
>
> (11.48–53)

The threat of contamination is further demonstrated by a reversal of the ejection theme, as described in book 12, when God commands Abraham to leave the idolatry and wickedness of his native land, Ur of Chaldea. In this case, purity is promoted not by ejecting the impure but by withdrawing from it.

Not only does Milton portray the practical concern about permitting evil to remain in the camp of good, he also emphasizes the instinctive, involuntary repulsion to evil. Even the fallen can be moved to disgust by the presence of evil because, as the narrator explains, the damned spirits do not "Lose all thir virtue" (2.483). The virtue that remains is thus capable of recognizing evil. Even after experiencing the pains of Hell, Satan is not immune to perceiving this horror, for when he meets the embodiments of evil—Sin and Death—he calls them the most "detestable" sights he has ever seen (2.745). Likewise, Adam's reaction to his partner in disobedience is one of loathing:

> Out of my sight, thou Serpent, that name best
> Befits thee with him leagu'd, thyself as false
> And hateful.
>
> (10.867–69)

And if the sinful feel antipathy toward evil, how much more repulsive is evil to the sinless? As Taylor observes, Milton emphasizes the gulf between fallen man and God by his unique depiction of the Son's pronouncing judgment on the sinful pair, thus simultaneously showing God's mercy for and withdrawal from them.[14] Much later, as the descendants of Ham become increasingly depraved, God withdraws from them and determines to confine his presence to one nation, the descendants of Abraham (12.105–13). As Adam witnesses the future sinfulness even of the chosen people, he asks Michael how God's presence can tolerate such impurity:

> This yet I apprehend not, why to those
> Among whom God will deign to dwell on Earth
> So many and so various Laws are giv'n;
> So many Laws argue so many sins
> Among them; how can God with such reside?
>
> (12.280–84)

In this query Adam assumes the validity of this same principle—that purity resists mixing with impurity. Michael does not deny the principle but explains that God plans to purify the sinful through the Son, thereby effecting a true society shared by God and humankind.

Earlier Adam shows an inherent understanding of a true society. When he explains to God his need for a mate, he argues the unfitness of brutes to be his companions: "Among unequals what society / Can sort, what harmony or true delight?" (8. 383–84). In other words, the joining of likes produces order, and the joining of unlikes produces disorder. In *The Doctrine and Discipline of Divorce*, Milton cites the authorities that had addressed this issue: Homer, who had credited God with bringing together "like to . . . like" (2:271);[15] the author of Deuteronomy, the twenty-second chapter of which contains this admonition: "Thou shalt not sowe thy vineyard with divers seeds, lest thou defile both. Thou shalt not plow with an

Oxe and an Asse together" (270); and the writer of 2 Corinthians, which "forbid[s] mis-yoking marriage" (270). Milton concludes that God always seeks "to bring the due likenesses and harmonies of his workes together" (272) and that he "forbids all unmatchable and unmingling natures to consort" (272). The desire to unite contrarities, says Milton, emanates not from God but from "error, or some evil Angel" (272).

Raphael confirms the views Milton presented in the divorce tract as he explains to Adam the orderly creation of the world, when the spirit of God "conglob'd / Like things to like" (7. 239–40). Raphael also says that his task during the Creation was to guard the "Gates of Hell" (8.230), to prevent "Destruction" from mixing with "Creation" (236). Adam witnesses the effects of an improper mixture when Michael shows him scenes of carnage, murder, and "factious opposition" (11.664). All the violence and degradation of Enoch's time, Michael says, are the result of righteous men uniting with fair, lustful women—"ill-mated Marriages" in which "good with bad were matcht" (11.684–85). Even Chaos is portrayed as a combination of unlikes, where the four elements "in thir pregnant causes mixt / Confus'dly" (2. 913–14).[16] Finally, the forbidden fruit itself, plucked from the tree of knowledge of good and evil, is the archetypal mixture of unlikes. When opposing principles confront each other, destructive effects are inevitable.

The impulse to remove (or withdraw from) evil in order to stop its spread prompts Adam's wish to die without issue, thereby ejecting evil from the world. But, as Adam begins to learn, evil is a permanent resident in the lapsarian world, clinging so closely to good that the two are "almost inseparabl[e]."[17] The natural antipathy between them remains, as Milton's image of Truth "grappl[ing]" with Falsehood demonstrates,[18] but evil has a role to play in effecting God's will—to reveal good: "this is that doom which Adam fell into of knowing good and evil, that is to say, of knowing good by evil."[19] Eve's response to Adam's bitter realization of the "Fair Patrimony" (10.818) that he will leave his offspring provokes Adam to a deeper understanding of this interplay of good and evil. When Eve suggests either suicide or sexual abstinence as a means of stopping evil from further corrupting the world, Adam recalls the promise of the Seed to "bruise / The Serpent's head" (10.1031–32), the fulfillment of the Son's offer to be the agent of God's love and mercy.

Unfortunately, Adam's impulse to halt the spread of sin does not govern his action when he learns of Eve's fall. His first response reveals the instinctive antipathy of good to evil:

> horror chill
> Ran through his veins, and all his joints relax'd;
> From his slack hand the Garland wreath'd for Eve
> Down dropp'd, and all the faded Roses shed:
> Speechless he stood and pale.
>
> (9.890–94)

While Adam recognizes that Eve is devoted to death, he fails to follow the example of the Son. As Dennis Danielson suggests, Adam should have offered to die in Eve's place.[20] But lacking the heavenly charity shown by the Son, Adam chooses instead to join her in sin. He neither intercedes for her nor renounces her. By seeking no remedy for her and failing to cut humankind free of her, Adam acts irrationally—in effect, retaining a gangrenous limb. He does not eject the offender in order to prevent the corruption of an entire race.

Although expelling the offender halts the spread of corruption among the uncorrupted, it also increases the degree of corruption in the offender. At the conclusion of Raphael's account of the rebels' expulsion from Heaven, the narrator explains this principle as a means of automatic punishment for evil:

> the evil soon
> Driv'n back redounded as a flood on those
> From whom it sprung, impossible to mix
> With Blessedness.
>
> (7.56–59)

When evil is expelled from the pure, that evil turns back on itself, feeding its own corruption. Based on Armstrong's use of Foucault's framework, this action would fit into the medieval tradition of punishment, in which the offender's body experiences the effects of his transgression.

Milton depicts this torture in both physical and psychological terms. The physical terms include various deformities and defacements such as the serpent form for Satan and his followers, the pain of childbirth for Eve, Adam's sweat in working, and all the maladies that Michael shows besetting the human race. The psychological suffering, however, seems worse. As the Father and the Son watch Satan's voyage from Hell to Earth, on his mission to contaminate the new world, God predicts Satan's torture:

> so bent he seems
> On desperate revenge, that shall redound
> Upon his own rebellious head.
>
> (3.84–86)

The narrator describes Satan's suffering as a boiling "in his tumultuous breast" that "like a devilish Engine back recoils / Upon himself" (4.16, 17–18). Later as Satan prepares to enter the serpent, he bewails his tortured condition whereby he experiences the pain of containing opposing principles within himself:

> the more I see
> Pleasures about me, so much more I feel

Torment within me, as from the hateful siege
Of contraries; all good to me becomes
Bane, and in Heav'n much worse would be my state.

. . . .

Nor [do I] hope to be myself less miserable
By what I seek, but others to make such
As I, though thereby worse to me redound.

(9.119–23, 126–28)

Although it may seem that God is administering the punishment, it is ultimately "self-generated in the way that Sin was generated from Satan."[21]

The prelapsarian Eve realizes this truth and even uses it in her debate with Adam. Believing that she will repel Satan's advances on her innocence, she argues,

his foul esteem
Sticks no dishonor on our Front, but turns
Foul on himself.

(9.329–31)

Her argument, of course, assumes that evil will confront her undisguised, whereas Uriel's inability to pierce Satan's masquerade as a cherub shows that deceit can foil the reaction of good to evil:

For neither Man nor Angel can discern
Hypocrisy, the only evil that walks
Invisible, except to God alone.

(3.682–84)

But the relevant issue here is that evil's attack on good spontaneously provokes its own punishment, a principle that the Elder Brother asserts in *Comus:*

But evil on itself shall back recoil,
And mix no more with goodness, when at last
Gather'd like scum, and settl'd to itself,
It shall be in eternal restless change
Self-fed and self-consum'd.

(593–97)

Sin and Death, the allegorical characters in *Paradise Lost*, demonstrate in a graphic way the operation of this principle. Before Sin and Death are allowed to roam the earth, "to lick up the draff and filth / Which man's polluting Sin with taint hath shed / On what was pure" (10.630–32), they must, in a sense, feed on themselves in an endless cycle of gorging without satisfaction. The incestuous union of Sin and Death thus produces the Hell Hounds, "hourly conceiv'd / And hourly born," which continually return to the womb of Sin, to gnaw the bowels of her that bore them (2.796–800). Death, who provokes his offspring to torment their mother, has such a strong appetite for prey that he would devour his mother if he did not know she would "prove a bitter Morsel, and his bane" (2.808). Evil, contained but ever perpetuating itself, is also mirrored in the description of Hell—"a fiery Deluge, fed / With ever-burning Sulphur unconsum'd" (1.68–69). In an image of constriction bursting for release, the newly ejected Satan prepares to address the angels who have followed him to Hell: "Thrice he assay'd, and thrice in spite of scorn, / Tears such as Angels weep, burst forth" (1.619–20).

The fallen Adam also grieves as he contemplates the implications of his state. Realizing that all generations will be contaminated by his sin, he bewails the multiplication of curses on his head:

> for what can I increase
> Or multiply, but curses on my head?
> Who of all Ages to succeed, but feeling
> The evil on him brought by me, will curse
> My Head; Ill fare our Ancestor impure,
> For this we may thank Adam; but his thanks
> Shall be the execration; so besides
> Mine own that bide upon me, all from mee
> Shall with a fierce reflux on mee redound.
>
> (10.731–39)

Adam understands that sin cannot long be contained; its spread will begin with the next generation.

Although the containment of evil within the guilty cannot persist, the original ejection of the corrupt is permanent. The fallen angels and the fallen Adam and Eve can never return to the society that they offended. When the Son drives out the rebel angels, they know they are forever barred from Heaven by God's "Eternal wrath" (6.865). In the devils' council not one of the speakers suggests returning to Heaven as a serious possibility. Mammon theorizes that even if God forgave them, the conditions for being restored would be too humiliating to endure (2.237–49). Satan also realizes the impossibility of restoration, for the breech in original unity is permanent: "never can true reconcilement grow / Where wounds of deadly hate have pierc'd so deep" (4.98–99). And God declares his unwillingness to grant the rebels grace because they were "Self-tempted" (3.130).

Despite God's plan to provide a means of rehabilitating Adam and Eve, in the old Germanic tradition of atonement, their exile from Eden is also

irrevocable. God's command to Michael underscores the permanent nature
of ejection:

> Haste thee, and from the Paradise of God
> Without remorse drive out the sinful Pair,
> From hallow'd ground th' unholy, and denounce
> To them and to thir Progeny from thence
> Perpetual banishment.
>
> (11.104–8)

Though comforting Adam by reminding him of future redemption, Michael
also explains that God's grace will not restore Eden to him—"But longer
in this Paradise to dwell / Permits not" (11. 259–60).

The depiction of punishment in *Paradise Lost* does seem to validate the
historical precedents outlined by Armstrong via Foucault. However, the
text of the poem indicates that Milton does more than imitate cultural traditions: he constructs a system of punishment that can be enforced both with
and without an agent, a system based on harmony as an essential good in
God's creation and on motion as a means of dealing with sin. Thus Milton's
law expands the law of motion that Fuller describes as a perpetual movement
from one point or state to its opposite. Fuller stresses the dynamic effect
of movement without much considering the moral principle that invokes
the movement, or, as MacCaffrey describes it, "the dynamic orientation of
moral action."[22] In depicting punishment as an ejection of impurity followed by a recoiling of impurity upon itself, Milton transforms a dynamic
principle into a divine plan for handling the problem of sin.

Notes

1. Wilma G. Armstrong, "Punishment, Surveillance, and Discipline in *Paradise Lost*," *SEL* 32 (1992): 93.

2. Ibid., 93–94.

3. Ibid., 104.

4. Isabel Gamble MacCaffrey, *"Paradise Lost" as "Myth"* (Cambridge: Harvard University Press, 1959), 44–73.

5. Elizabeth Ely Fuller, *Milton's Kinesthetic Vision in "Paradise Lost"* (Lewisburg, Pa.: Bucknell University Press, 1983), 20.

6. Ibid., 40.

7. Ibid., 21.

8. Barry Cooper, *Michel Foucault: An Introduction to the Study of His Thought*, Studies in Religion and Society, vol. 2 (New York: Edwin Mellen, 1981), 79–132.

9. Armstrong, "Punishment," 99.

10. Ibid.

11. Dick Taylor, "Milton's Treatment of the Judgment and the Expulsion in *Paradise Lost*," *Tulane English Studies* 10 (1960): 51–82.

12. John Milton, *Paradise Lost*, in *John Milton: Complete Poems and Major Prose*,

ed. Merritt Y. Hughes (New York: Odyssey, 1957). All references to Milton's poetry are to this edition and are cited parenthetically in the text.

13. This entire discussion of the chariot is adapted from my note in *Explicator* 40 (1982): 20. In contrast, Armstrong considers the cherubim with their many eyes as "surveillants" with a "deterrent" role (102).

14. Taylor, "Milton's Treatment," 71.

15. John Milton, *The Doctrine and Discipline of Divorce*, in *Complete Prose Works of John Milton*, 8 vols., ed. Don M. Wolfe et al. (New Haven: Yale University Press, 1953–82).

16. See MacCaffrey's analysis of the images of disruption in *"Paradise Lost" as "Myth,"* 136–44.

17. John Milton, *Areopagitica*, in *John Milton: Complete Poems and Major Prose*, ed. Hughes, 728.

18. Ibid., 746.

19. Ibid., 728.

20. Dennis Danielson, "Through the Telescope of Typology: What Adam Should Have Done," *Milton Quarterly* 23 (1989): 124.

21. Armstrong, "Punishment," 96.

22. MacCaffrey, *"Paradise Lost" as "Myth,"* 68.

"The Rising World of Waters Dark and Deep": Chaos Theory and *Paradise Lost*

MARY F. NORTON

W HEN Milton denies creation *ex nihilo* in the *Christian Doctrine*, he renders Chaos, as a place, integral to the creation of the universe. In *Paradise Lost*, the principle of chaos is therefore the beginning of a continuum of creation and must be evaluated as an intrinsic, inexorable force in the poem's physical and moral universe. Though contemporary scientific "Chaos Theory" has not previously been applied to *Paradise Lost*, it explains the chaotic features of the poem's physical and epistemological cosmos, while also illuminating the poem's significant fusion of order and chaos. Milton's treatment of Chaos anticipates the primary claim of chaos theory, that chaos is "order's precursor and partner rather than its opposite."[1] For example, chaos theory enables a new interpretation of Milton's Eden and Earth as both a contrast to and a replication of Chaos: direct correlations between the places reveal their general symmetry. Chaos theory additionally reveals that chaos, as a principle, itself contains an inherent tendency toward change that serves in Milton's poem to generate increasingly complex moral systems. Thus, in *Paradise Lost*, Chaos as both a place and principle has constructive, generative features that make new orders possible and that impel moral and intellectual evolution. The changes Chaos instigates are not merely, as some critics contend, degenerative or evil, nor is the principle of chaos the mere antithesis of order. The poem shows how order evolves out of Chaos, and simultaneously how order generates its own chaos. Chaos is the deep structure of creation, and Milton's Chaos is not only the universe's material origin, but also creation's ontological prototype.

Most critical theories up to now impose order upon texts in part by disregarding textual incongruities and contradictions. As a result, critics have oversimplified and also widely disagreed about the role and moral status of Chaos in *Paradise Lost*. Chaos has variously been determined to be exclusively good, exclusively neutral, and exclusively evil—but none of these in conjunction. A. S. P. Woodhouse based his assessment of Chaos's goodness on Milton's statement in the *Christian Doctrine*: "For this original matter was not an evil thing, nor to be thought of as worthless: it was good, and it contained the seeds of all subsequent good" (6:308).[2] Michael Lieb and Robert Adams instead interpret Chaos as neutral because it is, by nature, only amoral potentiality.[3] In contrast, A. B. Chambers, Harinder Marjara, and, perhaps most convincingly, Regina Schwartz evaluate Chaos as unequivocally evil.[4] However, this most recent evaluation of an evil Chaos that Schwartz presents in *Remembering and Repeating* overemphasizes Chaos's role as a destructive catalyst in *Paradise Lost*, reducing it merely to an evil that makes good possible. Refuting such a view, Stephen Fallon contends that "Chaos is not metaphysical evil. Nor is he even morally evil."[5] Refuting Schwartz's oversimplification of Chaos as evil, Fallon perceptively observes Chaos's tenuous nature, claiming that Chaos is instead "a mirage of evil; the illusory sense of a fund of evil existing prior to Satan's sin."[6] John Rogers concurs that "Milton's account of chaos goes further than painting a poeticized, Manichean battle between good and evil."[7] Chaos theory, on the other hand, contradicts historical, theological, and Hegelian evaluations because they do not allow for the generative features of chaos and they misrepresent the poem's important relationship between order and change.

Chaos theory enables a new way of reading *Paradise Lost* that displaces the poem's primary focus from a good-evil dichotomy to a nonmoral continuum; such a reading also reveals that, for Milton, "knowing by contraries" is not the only way to understand or to explain forces within the universe. In *Areopagitica*, Milton describes "Truth" as fragmented, her wholeness "hewd . . . into a thousand peeces, and scatter'd . . . to the four winds" (2:549). *Paradise Lost* acknowledges such fragmentation, and Milton's treatment of Chaos presents an additional epistemology, one not solely bound to moral codification. Milton maintains the moral categories of good and evil while simultaneously offering nonmoral categories of chaos and order because both represent effective, plausible ways of perceiving and describing this world. Milton's treatment of Chaos recognizes that unpredictability and complexity are not synonymous with randomness nor antithetical to a monist conception of the world. Nonetheless, for Milton, like his contemporary, physicist Robert Boyle, "Religion rather than science was the foundation of his being."[8] Chaos theory, like religion, however, celebrates how "Pattern [is] born amid formlessness,"[9] and it offers a conceptual framework that complements rather than threatens the poem's biblical, moral, and theological statements because it illuminates the poem's "combination of simplicity and complexity, determinism and unpredictability."[10] Modern scientific chaos theory gives new, rich insight into Milton's Chaos and into what critics previously cited as its moral as well as theological disparities or its sometimes inexplicable "absurdities,"[11] which existed without philosophical or artistic precedent.

It is necessary to acknowledge that Milton's Chaos is the combination of all dimensions of morality—goodness, neutrality, evil—yet it is none of these dimensions exclusively and perhaps even all partially. Change in itself is neither good nor evil, though both the impetus and results of change may be. In *Chaos Bound: Orderly Disorder in Contemporary Literature and Science,* N. Katherine Hayles outlines the main traits of chaotic systems as "complexity through increased dimensionality," "nonlinearity," "recursive symmetries," and "sensitivity to initial conditions."[12] Each of these chaotic properties functions throughout *Paradise Lost,* demonstrating that Milton's Chaos itself contains and impels an inherent tendency toward change that in turn generates incrementally complex moral systems throughout the poem. Because chaos theory analyzes the functionings and the forces of chaos, it can be used to examine the many systems, paradigms, and patterns of morality and being to be found in *Paradise Lost,* and it can explain why these do not remain stable or static, but rather are created, revised, renewed, and dynamic.

Renaissance systems—any uniform set of principles, doctrines, and beliefs forming a complex unity—traditionally have been interpreted as explaining the world's apparent natural, physical, and spiritual order. An emphasis on order was manifest in such systems as "a chain, a series of corresponding planes, and a dance,"[13] as well as in systemic constructs for cosmic and natural phenomena: angels, stars, elements, humors. These outlines of order revealed, claims Harinder Marjara, an "integrated vision of the truth of nature."[14] Such systems were generally based on a hierarchy, usually of "forces or powers or categories extending from God to Nature and through all manifestations of Nature,"[15] and *Paradise Lost* accommodates such a connection between spiritual and natural systems, most obviously perhaps in Raphael's presentation of the *scala naturae* in book 5 (469–99).[16] Importantly, however, epistemological systems in the Renaissance were often more than mere exhibits of order. For instance, in *Leviathan* Hobbes describes the connected complexity of political systems: "By Systems; I understand any numbers of men joined in one interest, or one business. Of which, some are *regular,* and some *irregular. Regular* are those, where one man, or assembly of men, is constituted representative of the whole number. All other are *irregular.*"[17] In *Paradise Lost,* it is interactions and complexities within the systems, the irregularities that chaos theory explicates, rather than hierarchies or differentiations. Instead of the moral or natural schemes of organization presenting universalized order, chaos theory explains the characteristics that do not fit neatly or in an orderly way into the overriding scheme. The particular dynamical law controlling the moral systems in *Paradise Lost* is neither order nor disorder. While the poem presents moral and natural systems that do possess patterns and structures of order, order is not the exclusive characteristic of any system in the poem. Paradoxically, its systems are both deterministic and unpredictable.

In *Paradise Lost*, at least four different moral systems function with explicit rules and codes. First, in the Heaven system, God and the Son peacefully reign over angels who possess free will. Because of Satan's choice to rebel, however, a new system, that of Hell, is activated. In it the physical space of Hell (and for Satan its corresponding psychological state) is governed by a new set of laws that now includes physical and psychological punishment. This moral system, which still allows free will for the now fallen angels, governs potent and active evil. Next, Adam and Eve in Eden operate within a new moral system and power structure where they have

> Dominion giv'n
> Over all other Creatures that possess
> Earth, Air, and Sea.
>
> (4.430–32)

In the prelapsarian or Eden system, the moral scheme includes free will, "One easy prohibition" (4.433), and the promise of death for transgression. The postlapsarian system subsequently contains mortality, free will, and the new possibility for "renovation" (11.65). In each case, a new system emerges from the initial one but incorporates features of its predecessor. There is replication without exact duplication, a key concept in chaos theory, particularly fractal replication. Thus, in *Paradise Lost* the postlapsarian system is in fact more complex than the Eden system, which was more complex than the Hell system, which was more complex than the Heaven system prior to Satan's rebellion, which was more complex than a solitary God prior to any of his creations. A Heraclitean dynamic of change brings about all moral and epistemological progress in the poem.

A newly instigated moral system—for example, the postlapsarian system—that is perceived as "increased dimensionality" and "complexity," instead of as the debased outcome of Adam and Eve's moral failure, accentuates the effect of action instead of the cause, the Fall. And though "Sacred history" may indeed "speak, not of entropy, but of disobedience,"[18] as Hayles suggests, chaos theorists Ilya Prigogine and Isabella Stengers view entropy as "an engine driving the world toward increasing complexity, rather than toward death."[19] Of course, in scientific as well as moral systems, "fragmentation and unpredictability are not . . . always cause for celebration."[20] Where Christianity has traditionally conceived of the Fall as the *felix culpa*, chaos theory enables a new interpretation of Eve's act of disobedience and its consequences as "dissipative reorganization."[21] Chaos theory demonstrates that in *Paradise Lost* destruction and discord are not a chaotic system's sole features nor its sole epilogues. Instead, new, interrelated, thus more complex moral and intellectual patterns and systems evolve.

Milton's complex, multidimensional, enigmatic Chaos reveals the connection between the results of chaos and the force and constitution of chaos. In his extensive analysis of Milton's Chaos, Walter Clyde Curry twice comments on Milton's presentation, once calling it "unusually original" and later noting its "remarkable originality."[22] He also cites Milton's diversity of philosophical and artistic sources but generally concentrates on the innovative and paradoxical Chaos depicted in *Paradise Lost*. For example, Curry observes that Chaos is at once "formless infinite" (*Paradise Lost*, 3.12) and yet has a palpable, perceptible subsistence. It is a void nonetheless, containing like elements that coalesce according, in part, to Epicurean and Democritean principles of atomism:[23]

> then conglob'd
> Like things to like, the rest to several places
> Disparted.
>
> (7.239–41)

These aggregate atoms form moments of light, darkness, water, and other elements:

> For hot, cold, moist, and dry, four Champions fierce
> Strive here for Maistry, and to Battle bring
> Thir embryon Atoms.
>
> (2.898–900)

Such descriptions show that Chaos paradoxically possesses and does not possess distinct material formations; it is and is not capable of generating and maintaining tangible structures, for it is concurrently generative and destructive. Chaos is, after all, "The Womb of nature and perhaps her Grave" (2.911).

Chaos possesses other paradoxical traits, and Curry also observes that Milton's conception of space is relative as well as infinite, which allows the poet to "give direction to movements of individuals in and over chaos."[24] That is, Chaos talks with and directs Satan out of Chaos toward Earth in book 2, and consequently Death and Sin are able to follow a coherent course in building their bridge through Chaos from Hell. Such paradoxical qualities of space and subsistence attest to Stephen Fallon's recent description of Chaos as existing on the "border of being and non-being."[25]

Ironically, then, the narrator describes Chaos in book 2 as

> a dark
> Illimitable Ocean without bound,

> Without dimension, where length, breadth, and highth,
> And time and place are lost.
>
> (891–94)

Yet, the poem also presents a contradictory view by *showing* that all such features are indeed present, though only temporarily. In his journey, for example, Satan does plummet a measurable depth:

> he drops
> Ten thousand fadom deep, and to this hour
> Down had been falling, had not by ill chance
> The strong rebuff of some tumultuous cloud
> Instinct with Fire and Nitre hurried him
> As many miles aloft.
>
> (2.933–38)

Dimensions may be "lost" but are certainly not absent, for disorientation and confusion are not the equivalent of absence. Chaos is therefore not absolute disorder but contains unpredictable, transient moments as well as structures of order that are also perceptible to others. As Fallon contends, "Chaos represents an order of reality different from creation."[26] Most importantly, Chaos is a form of order; it is a form of reality, for "different from creation" does not denote opposition to creation.

Milton debates the substance of the *prima materia* in the *Christian Doctrine*, arguing that God could not have created this world out of nothing, and in deciding that the world was not created *ex nihilo*, Milton determines that at some point Chaos must have originated from God (6:307). In also claiming that the "original matter was not an evil thing, nor to be thought of as worthless: it was good, and it contained the seeds of all subsequent good," Milton refutes those who would be "dissatisfied" because they misunderstand not just the original substance but also God's nature and essence (6:308–9). Milton acknowledges the intrinsic nature of God's virtue, which is "heterogeneous, multiform, and inexhaustible" (6:308). Thus, in the beginning, God

> created all
> Such to perfection, one first matter all,
> Indu'd with various forms, various degrees
> Of substance, and in things that live, of life.
>
> (5.471–74)

On a nonmoral continuum, both God and Chaos possess the same characteristics, which will become infused in the shaping and the *materia* of the world. God's diversity is inherent in Chaos, which is inherent in the created world.

God's circumscribing the world from and within Chaos does not negate
Chaos's existence because the encircling act is both exclusive and inclusive:
Chaos both contains and is contained in the elements of ordered creation.[27]
Milton's sources for the Creation, including Genesis, Proverbs, Hesiod's
Theogony, and Ovid's *Metamorphoses,* emphasize the process of differenti-
ating forms. Milton's "great Architect" of *Paradise Lost* (8.72), like Plato's
"Great Constructor" (*Timaeus*), chooses for the universe the shape of the
circle, the sphere, which traditionally in Christian iconography as well as
classical mythology implies wholeness, totality, inclusion.[28] Uriel's account
of the creation in book 3, therefore, presents images and a rhetoric of
containment, not eradication:

> I saw when at his Word the formless Mass,
> This world's material mould, *came to a heap:*
> Confusion heard his voice, and wild uproar
> Stood *rul'd,* stood vast infinitude *confin'd.*
>
> (708–11; emphasis mine)

While Plato presents the world's form as cohesive and coherent, more important for Milton is the idea that structural totality and stability do not
preclude epistemological fragmentation or instability. Coherence and order
are not the equivalent of stasis or inertia: as the process of creation is
dynamic, so the created structure is inherently dynamic.

What is "Adverse to life" (7.239) about Chaos as a place, therefore, is
not the totality of Chaos itself, but merely specific elements indigenous to
it. Chaos contains *all* elements from which the "great Architect" will select
and arrange. The "dregs," "The black tartareous Infernal dregs" (7.238)—
the excess, not the essence—are "downward purg'd" (237), and Chaos consequently "continues to exist, in part, even after creation."[29] Since God
does not destroy Chaos as a place or principle, but transforms it with order,
Chaos remains the submerged infrastructure of order. The *essentia* of Chaos
is not destroyed in a new *substantia* of creation, just as with the *kenosis* the
Son's divinity is not destroyed in his human form. Similarly, to perceive
chaos as chaos theorists do, as a "presence rather than absence" that "combines pattern with unpredictability," is to acknowledge that Chaos in *Paradise Lost* offers a limitless potential for evolution and is "capable of
development and innovation."[30]

Milton's Chaos does not simply follow Augustine's "passive principle of
matter," which A. B. Chambers asserts "becomes chaos when implanted
with certain active powers or causes."[31] Neither does Milton's Chaos per-
sonified derive only from Spenser's Demagorgon or Boccaccio's "Anarch
old" (*Paradise Lost,* 2.988).[32] In fact, Milton empowers his artistically original Chaos with an active form and function in his allegorical personification.

Chaos himself is also a point of focus for Satan in the otherwise "unessential" (2.439), unordered place. Chaos paradoxically comprehends order and generates his own order within the context of disorder, in part because the character Chaos is "inseparable from the realm he personifies."[33] Chaos embodies and is consistent with the abstract principles of chaos and thus serves the generative agency of an allegorical character. More significantly, Milton's Chaos is given an aggressive role, which the poet describes in the prose *Argument* of book 2: "with what difficulty he [Satan] passes through, directed by Chaos, the Power of that place, to the sight of this new World which he sought." Chaos deliberately divulges to Satan the structural design of the universe as well as the sequence in which it was implemented—the very workings of both space and time:

> first Hell
> Your dungeon stretching far and wide beneath;
> Now lately Heaven and Earth, another World
> Hung o'er my Realm, link'd in a golden Chain
> To that side Heav'n from whence your Legions fell.
>
> (2.1002–6)

Expanding his aggressive role, Chaos next intentionally points Satan in the right direction—providing a version of order—in his wanderings toward Earth: "If that way be your walk, you have not far" (2.1007). Chaos's actions demonstrate that he apprehends and can generate and enact order; he is obviously not simply the passive *prima materia* whose domain is "Encroacht on" (2.1001) for God's use in creation. Chaos constructively brings more of his own unordered essence to Earth, the reward of which is expansion of an already boundless realm: "Havoc and spoil and ruin are my gain" (2.1009). Milton fuses Chaos's character, principle, and spatial dimensions in this scene with Satan; Chaos, without the intervention of God, nevertheless enacts his own generative capabilities.

Chaos's multidimensionality in *Paradise Lost*—a coalescence of person, place, force, and principle—parallels scientific chaotic systems that are "interactive instead of inert."[34] In empowering an agent who will replicate him outside of his physical matter, beyond his own initial physical boundaries, Chaos propagates his own force and constitution. In scientific terms, such duplication of an original shape parallels fractal generation. Fractal geometry, which helps reveal some patterns of chaotic systems, expresses structural variations in a figure as complexity and as fractionalized pieces that will reveal an "increased dimensionality" of the original figure.[35] The Latin verb *fractus*, "to break," denotes creation of irregular fragments,[36] and the Latin *complexus*, "to embrace," "to encircle," implies that as new coordinates are added to a shape, a more intricate composite will evolve. In *Areo-*

pagitica, Milton explains fractal replication metaphorically in his description of the building of Solomon's temple:

> there should be a sort of irrationall men who could not consider there must be many schisms and many dissections made in the quarry and in the timber, ere the house of God can be built. And when every stone is laid artfully together, it cannot be united into a continuity, it can but be contiguous in this world; neither can every peece of the building be of one form; nay rather the perfection consists in this, that out of many moderat varieties and brotherly dissimilitudes that are not vastly disproportionall arises the goodly and the gracefull symmetry that commends the whole pile and structure. (2:555)

Milton graphically presents a hermeneutical model of change and evolutionary action that is analogous to fractal generation. The concept of fractals perhaps most usefully and accurately expresses complexity's constructive evolution in the forms of increasingly complex moral systems in *Paradise Lost*.

By perceiving chaos and order as opposite ends of a continuum, it is possible to interpret Milton's origin of all systems—an "uncircumscrib'd" (7.170) God, "who fill[s] / Infinitude" (168–69)—as an extreme on the continuum. God is therefore absolute ordered complexity, a self-contained system of "All," the ultimate fractal configuration. As James Gleick states in *Chaos: Making a New Science*, "in the mind's eye, a fractal is a way of seeing infinity."[37] God's multiplication of himself and of the universe is analogous to the multiplication of fractals. Further, the creation of the universe with compasses in book 7 metaphorically describes fractal generation:

> He took the golden Compasses, prepar'd
> In God's Eternal store, to circumscribe
> This Universe, and all created things:
> One foot he centred, and the other turn'd
> Round through the vast profundity obscure,
> And said, Thus far extend, thus far thy bounds,
> This be thy just Circumference, O World.
>
> (225–31)

A sphere is created by multiplying infinitely the proportion of the circle that has been circumscribed by the compass. The infinite form of Chaos becomes a finite form with infinite capacity for complexity. Multidimensionality is, therefore, inherent in the very shape of the whole,[38] and it renders the structure and systems within the structure chaotic.

However, the sphere of the world is not uniformly smooth since Eden

> delicious Paradise,
> . . . Crowns with her enclosure green,

As with a rural mound the champaign head
Of a steep wilderness.

(4.132–35)

Further,

God had thrown
That Mountain as his Garden mould high rais'd
Upon the rapid current.

(4.225–27)

The topography of Eden reveals it to be irregular, dynamic, and projecting upward from the smooth sphere of the world. It is not, therefore, on the sphere's uniformity that Milton focuses, but on this Eden, this fractal.

Not surprisingly, the poem imparts an important symmetrical relationship between, on the one hand, Chaos and Eden, and, on the other, Chaos and propagation. Fractals, being self-similar, possess symmetries; anything fundamentally symmetrical possesses a measure of constancy in relation to something else. Symmetry "emphasize[s] the similarities between different fields."[39] Regina Schwartz's lucid illustrations of the similarities between Chaos, the War in Heaven, and Hell substantially illustrate Chaos's indisputable destructiveness.[40] Yet such correlations also, and very importantly, emphasize order within Chaos, and Chaos within order. Point-by-point correlations reveal a total symmetry between Chaos and Eden and also reveal that Chaos and Eden both are dynamic and multidimensional. Chaos and Eden are not opposites but different regions on a chaos-order continuum: Chaos is less created, and thus less ordered, than Eden. Creation is not Chaos's antithesis, but Chaos's ordering.

Topographical descriptions of Chaos consequently parallel topographical descriptions of Eden. Typically, critics, recognizing that "the dynamic character of Milton's Eden is apparent in the landscape as a whole,"[41] see this variety as coalescing into order, and, as Arnold Stein puts it, as "a great variety fulfilling itself in greater harmony."[42] However, critics consistently have overlooked the intrinsic disorder of Eden. Yet the disorder of Chaos is present there. However, because Eden exists closer on the continuum toward order, its systemic disorder is embedded in its order. Thus, where Chaos is described as the "wild Abyss" (2.910, 917), a "universal hubbub wild" (2.951), the "wild expanse" (2.1014), and "Chaos wild" (5.577), Eden is similarly "Wild above Rule or Art" (5.297), an "enclosure wild" (9.543), and, as Eve says, "Tending to wild" (9.212). Eden is "steep wilderness, whose hairy sides / With thicket overgrown, grotesque and wild" (4.135–36). Like the darkness of Chaos, Eden also contains dark and indistinct places to which, in his postlapsarian anguish, Adam would later yearn to escape:

> O might I here
> In solitude live savage, in some glade
> Obscur'd, where highest Woods impenetrable
> To Star or Sun-light, spread thir umbrage broad,
> And brown as Evening.
>
> (9.1084–88)

Not only does Eden's physical space contain chaotic characteristics, but certain physical actions occurring in Eden correlate with those that occur in Chaos. For example, Satan's journey through Eden to find Adam and Eve parallels his journey through Chaos to find Earth. Through Chaos,

> nigh founder'd on he fares,
> Treading the crude consistence, half on foot,
> Half flying.
> . . . . . .
> So eagerly the fiend
> O'er bog or steep, through strait, rough, dense, or rare,
> With head, hands, wings, or feet pursues his way,
> And swims or sinks, or wades, or creeps, or flies.
>
> (2.940–42, 947–50)

To travel through Eden,

> Satan had journey'd on, pensive and slow;
> But further way found none, so thick entwin'd,
> As one continu'd brake, the undergrowth
> Of shrubs and tangling bushes had perplext
> All path of Man or Beast that pass'd that way.
>
> (4.173–77)

As he had traveled through Chaos "With head, hands, wings, or feet," so Satan similarly travels through Eden by flying, leaping, walking, stalking, and slithering, pursuing his way, first as a "stripling Cherub" (3.636); next as a "prowling Wolf" (4.183); then "like a Cormorant" (196) sitting on the "Tree of Life" (194); then as various "fourfooted" (397) animals; next as "Lion" (402), then "Tiger" (403) as he "began / Through wood, through waste, o'er hill, o'er dale his roam" (537–38), until, finally, he is discovered by Ithuriel and Zephon, "Squat like a Toad, close at the ear of Eve" (800). Satan's physical metamorphosing to adapt to the environment of Eden in order to accomplish his goal of corrupting Adam and Eve parallels the physical activities he has found necessary to adapt to and travel through the environment of Chaos. Eden is not ordered rigidly enough to navigate through simply.

In addition to the physical and spatial correlations of Eden and Chaos,

Milton suggests their epistemological similarities as well. He describes Chaos's limitless potentiality with adjectives of absence, not moral privation: "*un*bottomed" (2.405), "obscure" (406), "void" (438), "hollow" (953), "*Il*limitable" (892; emphasis mine). In itself, however, the absence of limits does not merely suggest the absence of goodness, as Schwartz contends in her analysis of Chaos's perimeters and the Bible's iteration of boundaries.[43] Importantly, Chaos's scope and essence are emphasized and must be considered: as an allegorical character it consists of its abstract principle, so its form also imitates its matter. Therefore, as Chaos is unpredictable, multidimensional, and unlimited, so also in Eden, Adam and Eve

> enjoy
> Free leave so large to all things else, and choice
> Unlimited of manifold delights.
>
> (4.433–35)

And the trees in Eden "bear delicious fruit / So various" (4.422–23), and "all sorts are here that all th' Earth yields, / Variety without end" (7.541–42). Eden's variety reveals that its complexity correlates with Chaos's multiplicity. Both are wild without being entirely random, and both provide the potentiality for the creation of higher forms of order. Adam and Eve are always laboring to "prune, or prop, or bind" (9.210) the growth in Eden, and Eve looks forward to a time when there will be "more hands" (9.207) to help bring more order to Eden. The relationship between order and disorder in Eden and Chaos provides "a new way to think about order, conceptualizing it not as a totalized condition but as the replication of symmetries that also allows for asymmetries and unpredictabilities."[44]

Further, Chaos's paradoxical potential for both creation and destruction correlates with Eden's juxtaposition of the Tree of Life with the Tree of Knowledge, which possesses the capacity to bring Death: the "Tree / Of Knowledge, planted by the Tree of Life, / So near grows Death to Life" (4.423–25). In *Areopagitica*, Milton also insists that "Good and evill we know in the field of this World grow up together almost inseparably" (2:514). The trees, therefore, represent not only the temptation that Adam and Eve face, but also Eden's potential, in its vitality, to possess the tangible means of destruction. Further, the "morning Sun" (4.244) in Eden is once described as it paradoxically

> first warmly *smote*
> The open field, and where the un*pierc't* shade
> Imbrown'd the noontide Bow'rs.
>
> (4.244–46; emphasis mine)

The surprising military descriptions of the sun's generative force simultaneously suggest its destructiveness. Additionally, the summary of classical
paradises in book 4 (268–84), meant to contrast with biblical Eden, nonetheless juxtaposes Eden's beauty and fertility with images of death; in one
example,

> Proserpin gath'ring flow'rs
> Herself a fairer Flow'r by gloomy Dis
> Was gather'd, which cost Ceres all that pain.
>
> (4.269–71)

Here Milton indicates the potential for turbulence and constant change that
reverberates in the descriptions of both Eden and Chaos, thus revealing
their systemic symmetry. Closer to order's extreme on a continuum, Eden
is not a Chaos "writ small," but it possesses elements symmetrical with
Chaos, because both exist within the same cosmological field, both contain
the same fundamental elements, and both are fundamentally dynamic.

In the mathematical terms of chaos theory, Eden's instabilities and disorder could be described in a nonlinear equation. Such an equation expresses
episodes of instability that punctuate stable periods, but it is also unsolv-
able. As Gleick says, nonlinear "terms tend to be the features that people
want to leave out when they try to get a good, simple understanding."[45]
Linear equations, in contrast, project a system's surface stability and order,
leaving out its inherent instabilities and disorder. Nonlinearity importantly
reveals a system's intrinsic complexity and mutability,[46] which in scientific
terms parallels God's unknowability and the mysteries of his ways. Intrinsically dynamic and mutable, nonlinear systems also reveal the "often star-
tling incongruity between cause and effect, so that a small cause can give
rise to a large effect."[47]

Paradise Lost suggests this incongruous but inexorable relationship between small and large in, for example, the declaration in book 1 that "mortal
taste / Brought Death into the World" (2–3). "Taste," of course symbolic
of the transgression of God's "sole command," does not suggest gluttony
or any extreme action that would inculcate an extreme result or macroscopic
change. Yet the "taste" is the catalytic action that implicitly furnishes the
potential to alter the entire moral and physical world's future; any action
in a dynamic, nonlinear system has the power to destabilize or alter—for
better or for worse—the entire system. Thus Adam and Eve's model for
living in the postlapsarian world is also based on incongruity, which Adam
recognizes after Michael's explicit descriptions of the world's future:

> and by small
> Accomplishing great things, by things deem'd weak
> Subverting worldly strong, and worldly wise
> By simply meek.
>
> (12.566–69)

The model thus affirms that no order within *Paradise Lost* is static, and that, most importantly, free will is the variable that renders the Eden system nonlinear.

Free will has the capacity either to stabilize or destabilize order within any of God's created, nonlinear, dynamic systems. The poem obviously focuses and insists on the variable of free will: how, when, and why choice functions, and how it affects moral systems. The individual can choose service and obedience in order to uphold the system's order, as Abdiel did—choosing to rebuff Satan and the other rebelling angels; thus he became "Among the faithless, faithful only hee" (5.897). Or individuals can decree "Thir own revolt" (3.117), as Satan did, to instigate a new order, to "reign in Hell, [rather] than serve in Heav'n" (1.263). Satan's new order may be evil in its intention, but not all choices lead to evil new orders, though all choices have some consequence, as Abdiel, Satan, and Adam and Eve exemplify. Moral order, however, is not static or immutable as long as there is free will, as long as the intellectual and moral beings that God creates are "Sufficient to have stood, though free to fall" (3.99), and as long as "(Reason also is choice)" (3.108). The conditional covenants God establishes, based on free will, assure an unstable and dynamic system of human morality, one that is inherently complex, inconsistent, mutable—even chaotic.

Because of free will, the promised reward for faith and obedience depends upon fulfilling the conditions set forth in a compact. For example, the protevangelium includes the condition of Eve's continued faith after the Fall, and any individual's "renovation" is only a possibility, accomplished "after Life / Tri'd in sharp tribulation, and refin'd / By Faith and faithful works" (11.62–64), and "Giv'n thee of Grace" (11.255). "Joy entire" (3.265) is contingent on repentance and active faith, as Michael reminds Adam:

> wherein thou mayst repent,
> And one bad act with many deeds well done
> May'st cover: well may then thy Lord appeas'd
> Redeem thee quite from Death's rapacious claim.
>
> (11.255–58)

Free will, reason, and faith render the moral system nonlinear; therefore, as God states in book 3:

> Authors to themselves in all
> Both what they judge and what they choose; for so
> I form'd them free, and free they must remain.
>
> (122–24)

Raphael also reminds Adam of the catalyst of free will:

> God made thee perfet, not immutable;
> And good he made thee, but to persevere
> He left it in thy power, ordain'd thy will
> By nature free.

>   (5.524–27)

Free will guarantees nonlinear instability in the moral and physical systems in the poem. Thus, although *Paradise Lost* follows the biblical tradition of sanctifying symbols of order—categories, divisions, boundaries, hierarchies[48]—just as significantly, the entire poem presents fewer demonstrations of stasis or serenity than of change, turbulence, and disorder—primarily because of its insistence on the powerful variable of free will, which renders all moral systems in the poem dynamic and mutable.

However, inherent instability within the poem's moral systems does not necessarily denote anarchy; rather it means that a dynamic system permits competing options for the direction of its motion. For example, Satan's free will enables him to make a choice to destabilize Heaven's period of peace both with the War in Heaven and afterward via his attempt to "interrupt" God's joy (2.371) by corrupting "some new Race call'd Man" (2.348). The result of this choice is the activation of the moral system of Hell, "the place of punishment prepar'd for them in the Deep" (6. *The Argument*). Adam and Eve's free will allows them to make a choice that destabilizes the Eden system, which requires active faith to avoid transgressing the "one easy prohibition." Their choice initiates the new postlapsarian system with its new "mortal Sin / Original" (9.1003–4).

Because nonlinear systems do not repeat themselves exactly but, weblike, replicate the same theme with variations, the postlapsarian system also includes some dimensions of Heaven and some of Eden's peace (as Eden includes some of Chaos's turbulence). After Adam and Eve's transgression in the garden, God directs Michael to "send them forth, though sorrowing, yet in peace" (11.117). Adam recognizes the peace of Eden as "peace return'd / Home to my Breast" (11.153–54). Similarly, the postlapsarian system will not exactly replicate, but will reinterpret and append to Eden's physical and moral dimensions new, additionally complex, psychological, and moral properties of being, such as guilt, remorse, mortality, forgiveness, and hope. Though forced from Eden as part of their punishment, Adam and Eve will be able to internalize Eden, though it will be transformed into a higher spiritual state and the promise for a future after death, rather than a state and place of totalized existence: They shall "possess / A paradise within . . . happier far" (12.586–87). As in all previous systems, in the postlapsarian moral system the potential for change and a new moral system (in this case a "happier" paradise) is still contingent on free will and "Faith and faithful works" (11.64).

The additional dimension that can multiply the complexity of the new postlapsarian moral system is, ironically, death, for the new system now includes mortality. Death can activate the "happier" paradise because death's power can be destroyed with the combination of the individual's faith and good works and with God's mercy through the Son's *kenosis*. The result is a New Testament, a new system, a new fractal:

> so Death becomes
> His final remedy, and after Life
> Tri'd in sharp tribulation, and refin'd
> By Faith and faithful works, to second Life,
> Wak't in the renovation of the just,
> Resigns him up with Heav'n and Earth renew'd.
>
> (11.61–66)

Further, the postlapsarian system not only activates death and mercy, but it also forces Adam and Eve to internalize a new dimension of time.[49] Adam's postlapsarian knowledge of time is necessarily more complex than his prelapsarian conception and experience where there was no end to time. In the postlapsarian world it gains an explicit beginning, middle, and end. Time will not only describe but also include the past (Raphael's lessons about Satan's fall, accounts of the Creation, and Adam's own life experiences) and "what shall come in future days" (11.114) through Michael's revelation of human history in books 11 and 12. Because death now ends life, the Fall gives time a concreteness and elasticity; it gives experience a more complex dimension of consequentiality that it did not possess in prelapsarian Eden.

The consequence of Adam and Eve's transgression, despite Raphael's illustrative instruction and God's direct warnings, is nonetheless not known to a degree of what physicist Mitchell Feigenbaum calls "infinite precision": in nonlinear systems, unpredictability in part arises because "unless the initial conditions are known to *infinite precision*, all known knowledge is eroded rapidly into future ignorance."[50] This means that the Eden system has always possessed some intrinsic potential for unpredictability. Though Adam and Eve did know their world's moral order and the promised result of their violating "one easy prohibition," Raphael's allegorical definition of disobedience in book 5 (570–72) and Adam and Eve's understanding of death reveal the imprecision of their understanding. In his explanation to Eve, Adam can only define it as

> whate'er Death is,
> Some dreadful thing no doubt; for well thou know'st
> God hath pronounc't it death to taste that Tree,
> The only sign of our obedience left

> Among so many signs of power and rule
> Conferr'd upon us.
>
> (4.425–30)

Because they understand the prohibition but not the consequence of their disobedience, Satan can easily manipulate Eve's ignorance about death in book 9, challenging her faith, experience, and knowledge:

> do not believe
> Those rigid threats of Death; ye shall not Die:
> How should ye? by the Fruit? it gives you Life
> To Knowledge: By the Threat'ner? look on mee,
> Mee who have touch'd and tasted, yet . . . live.
>
> (9.684–88)

Satan confuses Eve's knowledge of life by offering himself as an example of one who still lives and has bodily animation after the same disobedient action that Adam and Eve have been warned against. He presents an experience that contradicts her comprehension, and in this way he challenges her faith not only in Adam's report of God's interdiction but also in the face value of reality. Eve's confusion about death further reveals itself even after the Fall, as she contemplates telling Adam about eating of the Tree:

> but what if God have seen,
> And Death ensue? then I shall be no more,
> And Adam wedded to another Eve,
> Shall live with her enjoying, I extinct;
> A death to think.
>
> (9.826–30)

She understands that death is the absence of life—she will be "extinct"—yet she also equates it simply with loss and emotional pain: "all deaths / I could endure, without him live no life" (9.832–33). She minimizes the real force of the physical and moral death that would ensue, and her multiple definitions do not reveal a complexly precise apprehension of death but one confused and ambiguous.

Adam and Eve's initial apprehension of death may be "sufficient" because they can predict the future of an unfallen Eden (if they supplement their knowledge with faith). Yet their knowledge is not "exact" enough to guarantee that the Eden system will remain static in its way of knowing goodness. That is, knowing by "contraries"—knowledge of good by knowing evil—is merely a potential, but becomes a new dimension for knowing in prelapsarian Eden. Milton might agree with Aristotle that what is "probable" should happen, but what is improbable also can happen because chaos is endemic, and death is not known to infinite precision:[51] Adam's and Eve's knowledge did not after all sustain the surface linearity of the prelapsarian system in the face of the new version or revision of moral order that Satan extends in book 9.

Satan typically misleads by juxtaposing lies with truth and by distorting truth with lies that seem truthful. For instance, he not only redefines death but distorts the knowledge by defining it as cognizance of sin when he describes to Eve his apparent newfound "inward Powers" (9.600) that lead him to

> Speculations high or deep
> . . . [and thus] with capacious mind [he]
> Consider'd all things visible in Heav'n,
> Or Earth, or Middle, all things fair and good.
>
> (9.602–5)

Later, with renewed zeal, he claims power

> not only to discern
> Things in thir Causes, but to trace the ways
> Of highest Agents.
>
> (9.681–83)

In claiming this power for himself, he is obviously trying to diminish God's power while at the same time (and quite ironically) offering Eve the human equivalent of the same godly power he belittles:

> ye shall be as Gods,
> Knowing both Good and Evil as they know.
> That ye should be as Gods, since I as Man,
> Internal Man, is but proportion meet,
> I of brute human, yee of human Gods.
>
> (9.708–12)

Satan's interpretations, however, are like a linear equation that ignores details and complexities.

Yet, it is his appealing, though simplistic, explanation and reinterpretation of death, knowledge, God, and power that render Eve's initial understanding more chaotic. Eve's resulting choice, to disregard her prior understanding of the universe's order and replace it with a new, albeit distorted, one, has the capacity to activate Satan's system of morality. Change and complexity are features of any nonlinear, chaotic system, and though chaos and evil occur, in this case simultaneously within Eve's decision, chaos and evil are not, therefore, epistemologically equivalent.

The interaction between Eve and Satan demonstrates not so much the force of evil as the force of chaos, which impels change. And chaos theory helps to explain how and why a single act can generate immense change within an entire system, and how one system can be transformed into another system. Chaos theory recognizes that systems are ordered patterns, and that patterns replicate themselves, but never exactly: order generates its own chaos. This inevitability of change and of the forces impelling change fuses chaos and order in *Paradise Lost*—a fusion manifest in the very constitution of Chaos's multidimensional character, the symmetries of Eden and Chaos, the insistent variable of free will, and the evolution of the postlapsarian moral system.

Physicists like Stephen Hawking might take the question of order and chaos to its limit, considering a model of the universe that allows for "chaotic boundary conditions," which "implicitly assume either that the universe is spatially infinite or that there are infinitely many universes."[52] Milton was no post-Heisenburg physicist, but the Chaos he created in the seventeenth century is not merely an amalgamation of antecedent sources, for its originality both incorporates and anticipates features just now explicable using contemporary scientific chaos theory. Indeed, the poem's presentation of order and chaos operates on a continuum where Chaos "challenges and complements"[53] God's constructs of order. Because the world of *Paradise Lost* is nonlinear, no system in the poem is static, irreducible, or impervious to subsequent regeneration by Chaos. Thus, in attempting to justify God's ways, Milton anticipates the twentieth century's scientific quest to know "why it is we and the universe exist. If we can find the answer to that, it would be the ultimate triumph of human reason—for then we would know the mind of God."[54]

Notes

"'The Rising World of Waters Dark and Deep': Chaos Theory and Paradise Lost," originally appeared in *Milton Studies* XXXII, Albert C. Labriola, ed., ©1995 by University of Pittsburgh Press. This version is reprinted by permission of the publisher.

1. N. Katherine Hayles, *Chaos Bound: Orderly Disorder in Contemporary Literature and Science* (Ithaca: Cornell University Press, 1990), 9.

2. A. S. P. Woodhouse, "Notes on Milton's View on the Creation: The Initial Phases," *Philological Quarterly* 28 (1949): 211–36. John Milton, *Complete Prose Works of John Milton*, 8 vols., ed. Don M. Wolfe et al. (New Haven: Yale University Press, 1953–82). All references to Milton's prose are to this edition and are cited parenthetically in the text.

3. Michael Lieb, *The Dialectics of Creation: Patterns of Birth and Regeneration in "Paradise Lost"* (Amherst: University of Massachusetts Press, 1970), 17; Robert M. Adams, "A Little Look into Chaos," in *Illustrious Evidence: Approaches to*

English Literature of the Early Seventeenth Century, ed. Earl Miner (Berkeley: University of California Press, 1975), 76.

4. A. B. Chambers, "Chaos in *Paradise Lost," Journal of the History of Ideas* 24 (1963): 55–84; Harinder Singh Marjara, *Contemplation of Created Things: Science in "Paradise Lost"* (Toronto: University of Toronto Press, 1992), 91–102; Regina Schwartz, *Remembering and Repeating: Biblical Creation in "Paradise Lost"* (Cambridge: Cambridge University Press, 1988), 8–39.

5. Stephen M. Fallon, *Milton Among the Philosophers: Poetry and Materialism in Seventeenth-Century England* (Ithaca: Cornell University Press, 1991), 190.

6. Ibid., 191.

7. John Rogers, "Chaos and Consensus: The Liberal Science of *Paradise Lost"* (paper presented at the New York Milton Seminar, Franklin and Marshall University, spring 1993), 9.

8. Quoted in Richard Westfall, *Science and Religion in Seventeenth-Century England* (New Haven: Yale University Press, 1958), 40.

9. James Gleick, *Chaos: Making a New Science* (New York: Viking, 1987), 299.

10. Hayles, *Chaos Bound,* 149.

11. Walter Clyde Curry, *Milton's Ontology, Cosmogony, and Physics* (Lexington: University Press of Kentucky, 1957), 81.

12. Hayles, *Chaos Bound,* 9.

13. E. M. W. Tillyard, *The Elizabethan World Picture* (New York: Vintage, 1943), 25.

14. Marjara, *Contemplation,* 14.

15. Curry, *Milton's Ontology,* 160.

16. John Milton, *Paradise Lost,* in *John Milton: Complete Poems and Major Prose,* ed. Merritt Y. Hughes (New York: Odyssey, 1957). All references to *Paradise Lost* are to this edition and are cited parenthetically in the text.

17. Thomas Hobbes defines in detail different types for systems in *Leviathan* (*The English Works of Thomas Hobbes,* 11 vols., ed. William Molesworth [1839; reprint Germany: Scientia Verlag Aalen, 1966], 3:210–11). For an incisive critical discussion of Hobbes's ideas about mathematics, motion, and nature, see Fallon, *Milton Among the Philosophers,* 32–34.

18. Schwartz, *Remembering and Repeating,* 26.

19. N. Katherine Hayles, ed., *Chaos and Order: Complex Dynamics in Literature and Science* (Chicago: University of Chicago Press, 1991), 13.

20. Hayles, *Chaos Bound,* 27.

21. Ilya Prigogine and Isabella Stengers, *Order Out of Chaos: Man's New Dialogue With Nature* (New York: Bantam, 1984), 289.

22. Curry, *Milton's Ontology,* 87, 90.

23. Ibid., 76–77.

24. Ibid., 89.

25. Fallon, *Milton Among the Philosophers,* 191–92.

26. Ibid., 192.

27. Milton states in the *Christian Doctrine* that "nothing can be utterly annihilated" (6:310–11). Importantly, he also claims that "The addition of forms . . . did not make it [the universe] more perfect but only more beautiful" (6:308).

28. Plato writes in *Timaeus* (Loeb Classical Library, 1966), 61–63: "Now for that Living Creature which is designed to embrace within itself all living creatures the fitting shape will be that which comprises within itself all the shapes there are; wherefore He wrought it into a round, in the shape of a sphere." Additionally, see Proverbs 8.27. See also George Ferguson, *Signs and Symbols in Christian Art* (New

York: Oxford University Press, 1959); Edwin Panofsky, *Studies in Iconology* (New York: Harper, 1939); Joseph Campbell, *The Power of Myth* (New York: Doubleday, 1988). See A[nthony] Zee, *Fearful Symmetry: The Search for Beauty in Modern Physics* (New York: Macmillan, 1986), 9–12, for a discussion of the scientific and aesthetic symmetry of the circle.

29. Chambers, "Chaos," 83.
30. Hayles, *Chaos and Order*, 6–9, 263.
31. Chambers, "Chaos," 78.
32. See Merritt Y. Hughes, ed., *John Milton: Complete Poetry and Major Prose*, 255 n. 959–67, for Milton's adaptation of Spenser and Boccaccio.
33. Fallon, *Milton Among the Philosophers*, 190.
34. Hayles, *Chaos and Order*, 5.
35. Ibid., 12–13.
36. Benoit Mandelbrot, *The Fractal Geometry of Nature* (New York: W. H. Freeman, 1983), 4. For additional information on the mathematics of fractals, see Jenny Harrison, "An Introduction to Fractals," in *Chaos and Fractals: The Mathematics Behind the Computer Graphics*, ed. Robert L. Devaney and Linda Keen, Proceedings of Symposia in Applied Mathematics, vol. 39 (Providence, R.I.: American Mathematical Society, 1989), 107–26.
37. Gleick, *Chaos*, 98.
38. This idea was suggested in a discussion with Keith Hull.
39. Gleick, *Chaos*, 103. For explicit scientific information on symmetry, see J. P. Elliot and P. G. Dawber, *Symmetry in Physics: Volume I: Principles and Simple Applications* (New York: Oxford University Press, 1979). For a discussion of the aesthetics of symmetry, see A. Zee, *Fearful Symmetry*.
40. Schwartz, *Remembering and Repeating*, 8–39.
41. John R. Knott, *Milton's Pastoral Vision: An Approach to "Paradise Lost"* (Chicago: University of Chicago Press, 1971), 39.
42. Arnold Stein, *Answerable Style: Essays on "Paradise Lost"* (Minneapolis: University of Minnesota Press, 1953), 64–66.
43. Schwartz, *Remembering and Repeating*, 11–18.
44. Hayles, *Chaos and Order*, 10–11. Applying this concept to history, John T. Shawcross (letter to the author, 13 April 1993) suggests a connection between symmetry, patterning, and Giambattista Vico's notion of cyclical history, *ricorso*. See Giambattista Vico, *The New Science of Giambattista Vico*, trans. Thomas Goddard Bergin and Max Harold Fisch (Ithaca: Cornell University Press, 1968), books 4 and 5.
45. Gleick, *Chaos*, 24.
46. Ibid. Gleick explains nonlinearity in this way: a linear equation would signify the amount of energy needed to accelerate, for example, a hockey puck, yet the equation becomes nonlinear when it tries to account for friction.
47. Hayles, *Chaos Bound*, 11.
48. Schwartz, *Remembering and Repeating*, 11–18.
49. See John T. Shawcross, "Stasis, and John Milton and the Myths of Time," *Cithara* 18 (1978): 3–17.
50. Mitchell Feigenbaum, "Universal Behavior in Nonlinear Systems," *Los Alamos Science* 1 (summer 1980): 21.
51. See Aristotle's notion interpreted in modern scientific terms in Fritjof Capra, *The Tao of Physics: An Exploration of the Parallels Between Modern Physics and Eastern Mysticism* (Toronto: Bantam, 1977), 56.
52. Stephen Hawking, *A Brief History of Time: From the Big Bang to Black Holes* (Toronto: Bantam, 1988), 123.
53. Hayles, *Chaos Bound*, 3.
54. Hawking, *A Brief History*, 175.

"Pregnant Causes Mixt": The Wages of Sin and the Laws of Entropy in Milton's Chaos

Catherine Gimelli Martin

Wнɪle from the very beginning of their reception history most of the allegorical episodes in *Paradise Lost* have evoked problematic responses, no single character has provoked quite so much debate as Milton's Chaos. Despite the "shockingly" material nature of Sin and Death's agencies, and despite even the debate over their relative or complete unreality, their poetic presence and function are ultimately far clearer than that of Milton's allegorical *and* real Chaos.[1] Simultaneously representing a person, place, and thing, Chaos not only has an ambiguous ontological status but also an apparent hostility to his putatively divine origin, both of which pose extremely perplexing problems. While in one sense his kingdom merely represents the latent state of the manifestly material energies flowing within Raphael's "one first matter" (5.472), in another, both this chaotic realm and its "Anarch" (2.988) seem "naturally" drawn to the satanic camp. As he first encounters the arch rebel after his triumphant escape from Hell, Chaos thus actually seems to damn himself by extending a welcome not unlike that expressed by Satan's offspring, Sin and Death, in Hell. Even more damning, he accepts Satan's promise to redeem his kingdom from the tyranny of divine rule. Despite his quite different genetic origin, then, Chaos might be accused of sharing the psychology and the interests of the satanic family; all could equally proclaim with him that "Havock and spoil and ruin are my gain" (2.1009).[2]

Nevertheless, in an equally obvious sense, Chaos's complicity in the satanic goal of advancing "the Standard . . . of ancient Night" (2.986) on Earth is far more apparent than real.[3] While the reign of Satan, Sin, and Death actively excludes the benefits that the "Umpire Conscience" will offer to fallen humanity with its progressive "light after light" (3.195, 196), as the opposing "Umpire" (2.907), Chaos does not restrict but only "more imbroils the fray / By which he Reigns" (2.908–9). Hence in his volatile kingdom—"The Womb of nature and perhaps her Grave" (2.911)—no progressive "dark after dark" obscures or cancels Heaven's light, but this random darkness at once conceives and connects the strands of lighter worlds.

161

As a primordial "Womb" and source of matter, Chaos thus provides the source of the seamless path winding from the divine skirts, "dark with excessive bright" (3.380), to their earthly expression: the "bright consummate flowr" (5.581) whose "root" (479) lies in the "dark materials" of matter waiting "to create more Worlds" (2.916).

In this sense, far from a dualistic "hostility" to divine rule, Chaos actually demonstrates the monistic continuity of epic processes wholly in harmony with Milton's philosophical materialism.[4] As the organic base of God's cosmic plant, his Chaos seems not only logically consistent with but also poetically compounded from the *ex deo* form of creation described in the *Christian Doctrine*.

Nevertheless, regarding this indeterminate realm housing the "pregnant causes" (2.913) of matter as either neutral or as potentially benign does not wholly dismiss the textual cruxes outlined above.[5] As Regina Schwartz questions, if Chaos is actually neutral, why does its "Anarch" lend assistance to *both* God and Satan, and why does he openly declare his hostility to divine order?[6]

The novelty of the Miltonic version of Chaos only compounds this problem, which is then further compounded by the multitude of conflicting source studies attempting to isolate the "true" philosophical link between Milton's *potentia materiae* and his ontology of evil.[7] While the concept and representation of chaos appear early and continue late in literary history—originating in Hesiod, Plato, and Ovid, and continuing through Silvestris, Spenser, and Shakespeare—chaos has a quite different function and character in the *Theogony*, the *Cosmographia*, or even *The Faerie Queene* than in *Paradise Lost*. Thomas McAlindon proposes that its traditional character remains intact in Shakespeare's last tragedies where, in conformity with the Platonic tradition derived from the *Timaeus* and summed up in the *Cosmographia*, chaos is conceived of as a timeless "hellish . . . featureless, violent duration" rooted in "de-natured" nature. Yet this conception suddenly disappears in *Paradise Lost*, where spiritual rather than material degeneration is clearly held "responsible for the bleaker aspects of human history." Rather than being associated with what McAlindon calls *hyle*, *sylva*, or uncreated matter, hellish violence must thus be traced directly to the will and the psychology of Satan.[8] Even assuming that Chaos and Satan somehow remain in collusion, there can be little doubt that the epic function of the former is dramatically altered by conceiving the latter as the principle source of the Fall; that is, once *spirit* is accused of perverting matter, conventional spirit/matter dichotomies are effectively inverted.[9]

Even more radically, however, in this epic cosmos, Chaos's very volatility now seems to provide the basis of the essential goodness of elemental matter by insuring its regenerative capacity. Because the original sin of neither Satan nor Eve can be linked to the condition of Chaos, which is alternately conceived as the pre-material source of divine creation, harmony, and redemption (1.5–10, 17–26) or, for the demons, as the source of oblivion (2.149–51), the realm of Chaos and Night becomes the virtual repository of the potential for ascent and/or descent that God grants to "one first matter all" (5.472)—and most particularly to all spiritual bodies. Since after their creation both the perception and will of these bodies remain mutable, and since their capacity *either* to rise or fall remains both conditional and temporal, mutability itself becomes a beneficent ingredient in a divine plan that can never wholly be disrupted. Given the potential order *within* Chaos, not only this realm but also all material creation now reflects the simultaneous goodness and freedom of the godhead. After Satan's fall allows Earth to fill his "vacant room" (7.190) and even after the human fall alters the benign predispositions of both Earth and its inhabitants, material creation is no longer a punishment but a means of self-reflection essential to redemption. However "gross" (11.53) the chaotic inhabitants of Earth grow, acknowledging the encumbrances produced by sin can lead first to the "light" of temperance, then to a recovery not merely in but also *through* matter. At last death itself is no longer the mortal enemy of Donne's famous sonnet, but mankind's "final remedie" (11.62) which, assisted by internal resolve,

> after Life
> Tri'd in sharp tribulation, and refin'd
> By Faith and faithful works, to second Life,
> Wak't in the renovation of the just,
> Resignes him up with Heav'n and Earth renewd.
>
> (11.62–66)

In the larger cosmic framework, this altered perspective on the womb/tomb capacity of Chaos (as opposed to the purely destructive "wombs" of Sin and Death) suggests that *in itself* Chaos is no longer an evil "absence" that needs either the shaping power of spiritual good (or the divine order) to restore it, as it is in Silvestris, *or* the perpetual stability of eternity (or the divine presence) to redeem it, as it is in Spenser's *Mutabilitie Cantos*. In fact, the tables have now turned so far that uncreated matter, or flux, rather than stability is linked to spiritual good, which is conditional upon indeterminacy, change, mobility, self-determination and refinement, and of course freedom—the moral forces and values everywhere endorsed in this most Protestant epic. While its cosmos still ideally reflects a transcendent order, it remains both physically and metaphysically consonant with this order only through the immanent compliance of its agents, who must choose freedom over the tyranny of the satanic will—the only true antithesis of Chaos's innocent indeterminacy.

Because it remains innocent of what is externally imposed but wholly absent from its originally immanent state, in its final appearance Chaos is clearly vindicated of the satanic proclivities that had earlier seemed to "seduce" it. Thus, in book 10, the reader sees the newly "freed" Sin and Death repeat the sins of their father upon chaotic matter by swooping down into its fertile "damp and dark" and "Hovering upon the Waters" (10.283, 285) like an insane parody of the Holy Spirit's "brooding" (1.21) upon their "Abyss" (7.234). Parching and fixing its seas into an "aggregated Soyl" (10.293) that the poet pointedly compares to the bridge with which "Xerxes" tried "the Libertie of Greece to yoke" (10.307)—an imperial "scourge" (with tongue not much in cheek) he calls a work of "wondrous Art / Pontifical" (10.311–13)—Sin and Death reenact Satan's earlier attempt to link its energies to his cause. Then, should the reader miss the significance of this specious liberation of Chaos (10.368), the being metaphorically compared to the later Greek home of liberty and its oppression by double-speaking and acting tyrannic "reducers" (10.438),[10] Satan's legions are linked to subsequent oppressors and perverters of natural freedom in the course of history.

Likened next to a marauding oriental potentate who, like the "Tartar" (10.431), "leaves all waste beyond / . . . in his retreat" (434–35), the satanic forces abrogate the inherent potential of Chaos by "wasting" its indeterminacy. This poetic pun on their "waste," or ruin, of its once fertile "waste" (282), or undeveloped expanse, reemphasizes the continuity between their "wasteful" incursions into this expanse and those of Sin and Death, who "waste and havoc yonder World" (617)—the divinely authored world stretching from Earth all the way into Chaos. Hence, when Satan and his demons are at last appropriately "reduced" to "sharp and spare" (511), like the "barrs" (417) that Sin and Death enforce upon the indignant "Anarch," their punishment is made to fit their crime: they end up chewing the "bitter Ashes" (566) of a fire that its damp "Anarchie" (283) would have put out. Further, because these self-destructive incursions are caused by "the folly of Man" that "Let in these wastful Furies" (619–20), they are proportionally limited to the scope of that folly. Since unlike Satan's host, the majority of creation is neither "Self-tempted" nor "self-deprav'd" (3.130), like Chaos, it remains capable of renewal (175–77). Thus, ultimately, neither Satan nor his progeny can fully forestall the quenching capacities of a pregnant deep whose dynamic *priority* to sin-ful rigidity insures that its cleansing waters can at last swallow and digest their wasteful *rigor mortis,* which will at last not only stop the "mouth of Hell," but "For ever . . . seal up his ravenous Jaws" (10.636–37). In this final state as in every phase of the epic universe, the physical cosmos is conceived of as resulting from a "voluntary covenant between human will and divine commandment."[11] No static microcosm reflecting an eternal macrocosm, it is produced by and through spiritual forces as intrinsically *and* positively alterable as Chaos itself—especially since its "fixed" perversions prove the least stable of all its interchangeable parts.

Despite their awareness of these epic innovations, most critics remain uncomfortable with the depiction of an *ex deo* form of matter derived from God but still capable of evil. To explain this apparent theological inconsistency, they tend to assume that Milton fell back upon more primitive conceptions of Chaos either for poetic or philosophical purposes, either of which might have drawn him toward the rich and familiar legacy of the hostile Chaos. As Harinder Marjara has recently observed, however, this source-study approach has by now proved as inconclusive as it was universal, not least of all because it has usually ignored the influence of seventeenth-century science upon obviously physical fictions like that of Milton's Chaos.[12] Ignoring both the philosophically positive implications of Chaos and the fact that only Satan introduces truly entropic fire into it, such studies generally concur in making this "titanic" realm the virtual equivalent of the hell that in this cosmos it neither anticipates nor includes.[13] In itself, however, Chaos wholly lacks the power to generate *either* the ice of hate or the fire of desire that could "suffice" to trigger the universal conflagration that Robert Frost's "Fire and Ice" anticipates with its own quasi-Lucretian irony. Much as Frost begs the question of the sufficient cause of cosmic destruction with the illusory "either/or" of hate and desire, so Milton portrays Satan's self-destruction as proceeding not from the separation but from the *synthesis* of emotions essentially alien to the natural forces of disorder. As the antithesis of these destructive energies, chaotic entropy is as far beneath his God as it is above the ice and fire of Satan's transpersonal hell: an enduring void "where length, breadth, and highth, / And time and place are lost" (2.893–94) *only* to retain the plastic potential essential to both freedom and recuperation: the élan vital of life itself.[14]

However, even from an exclusively historical perspective, Marjara finds these studies objectionable because, contrary to the assumptions of traditional intellectual and literary scholars of both the period and the poem, no antagonism between science, religion, and literature, nor any cataclysmic shift from mystical or metaphysical to empirical accounts of the universe as yet existed. In *Paradise Lost,* as throughout the seventeenth century, scientific *and* theological interest in the primal state of matter is as evident as the numerous ways in which these interests overlap. By excluding contemporary atomist speculation from their explanations of the Miltonic cosmos, scholars have overlooked a far more influential source of references than the primitive mythology examined in their accounts. Thus, once these biases, along with the belief in the unimpeded march of scientific progress, are called into question, the cosmology of *Paradise Lost* no longer exhibits anything like what Marjara calls the "unduly conservative" structure ascribed to it by critics like Arthur O. Lovejoy, Kester Svendsen, Lawrence Babb, and most recently, Regina Schwartz. What instead emerges is a poem that not only mixes older teleological with more "objective" views of nature in ways resembling those of Milton's most advanced scientific contemporaries,[15] but that also in many ways anticipates some of the latest applications of atomism in the field of modern chaos theory.

However, because neither Marjara nor other recent critics who have explored Milton's epic in the context of contemporary materialism have been specifically concerned with his Chaos, not only its normative but also its prophetic physical aspects have yet to be examined.[16] As a result, the consensus view is still represented by more traditional scholars like Schwartz, who rely upon mythic/historical rather than scientific/contemporary means of "explaining" a principle that is either sinfully "at war . . . with heaven and with the world," or at least has "some affinity with, evil."[17] Yet in assuming that *Paradise Lost* rehearses the traditional theological dichotomy between a masculine father principle and the feminine principle of Tiamat/ Tehom, the pregnant "deep" that must be silenced and circumscribed by the Holy Spirit of Genesis working upon its waters (7.216–27), this school of thought obscures the much more benign ontology postulated by the alternate atomist tradition currently being revived in modern chaos theory. From this seventeenth-century *and* modern perspective, despite its obvious unruliness (216–17), unformed matter is "naturally" opposed neither to divine nor to any other form of universal order. Thus like his contemporary John Ray, Milton clearly entertains a distinctly Christian form of ancient atomism that views matter not merely as a neutral but also as a constructive and recuperative agency. From this perspective, Chaos's *materia prima* can be seen as "variously confused and confusedly commixed, as though they had been carelessly shaken and shuffled together; yet not so but that there was order observed by the most 'Wise Creator' in the disposition of them."[18] Hence, also like the modern geneticist Ilya Prigogine and the chemist Isabella Stengers, who similarly recall the tradition of Lucretian atomism by *refusing* to oppose randomness to order or chance to necessity, Milton seems to conceive "necessary" order as the dialectical result of his benignly unruly and eternally unruled Chaos.[19]

Nevertheless, if Milton's dark epic matter becomes "good" precisely by remaining random, how can it be connected to the eternal *im*mutability of the God from which, through light (3.1–6), it seems to originate? How can a fully omniscient and beneficent deity create a fully indeterminate form of matter? Given the traditional, seemingly insurmountable theological dichotomy between the freedom of the spirit and the fixity of matter, and confronted with the odd relationship between an unruly "Anarch" and a divine monarch, who if he should not, *does* seem to oppose him, the critical reader might continue to suspect that rather than presenting a *literarily* pre- or postmodern paradoxical (if not actually confused) conception of prime matter, Milton's Chaos inadvertently represents a *literally* and malignly late reversion to the dichotomies present in the more primitive cosmogonies. Despite being praised as nature's "eldest birth" (5.180), the material "cause" (7.90) upon which God builds whenever he is "late[ly] . . . Mov'd" (92, 91) to lay aside "his holy Rest" (91),[20] Chaos would thus remain a dualistic opponent of divine order, an epic recapitulation of the deep that must be silenced lest its "troubl'd waves" (216) overturn creation with their "loud misrule" (271). To remove the suspicion that this realm is not only a sign but actually also a *means* of the Sin whose deadly path it "Tamely endur[es]" (2.1028), further exploration of both the sources and functions of the complex dynamism of Milton's Chaos is in order.

As outlined above, the dynamic ambiguity of this perplexing realm generally can be traced to the rudimentary yet radically synthetic dialecticism that characterized Milton's period, when it was "a mode of thinking bred in the bone" and a hallmark of the contemporary attempt to fuse metaphysical with physical law.[21] More importantly, however, it should be associated with Milton's own idiosyncratic "solution" to the scientific debate over natural entropy, the approach announced in his academic exercise, *Naturam Non Pati Senium*. While in this as in every other aspect of the ongoing "battle of the books" Milton places himself on the side of the "steady-state," or progressive, faction in the debate against the ancients (the faction that saw the possibility of empirical progress safeguarded by the fundamental rationality and stability of nature's laws),[22] he evidently needed to modify the thesis of his early prolusion, that "Nature Is Not Subject to Old Age," in order to account for the Fall. Not surprisingly, then, his solution to this epic "problem" is characteristically dialectical; rather than a steady-state universe in which energy is always conserved, *Paradise Lost* features a threefold and *reversible* state of original matter evolving in time.[23] In thus conserving the monistic underpinnings of his epic cosmos by imagining divine order as continuous with physical disorder, Milton comes startlingly close to anticipating the three phases of matter of modern thermodynamics. That is, both the threefold reversible processes at work in his Chaos *and* the irreversible time thereby initiated are remarkably similar to equilibrium (the condition implied by the first law of thermodynamics); inertia or decline (the "linear" condition implied by the second law); and reintegrative flux (the uncertainty principle postulated by modern molecular biology and chaos theory).[24] This extraordinary feat may seem less remarkable if we accept Jacob Bronowski's quasi-Miltonic claim that scientific and literary genius obey essentially the same principles: in either case "the mind decides to enrich the system as it stands by an addition which is made by an unmechanical act of free choice."[25]

In any case, the theology of this choice is clearly dictated by material monism, a solution to the ontological problem of evil that can maintain the essential benignity of creation only through the "randomness" of free will—a state of indeterminacy that can be *physically* imagined only by providing an ongoing state of chaos. Without this innovation, Milton's material monism would contradict his more traditional metaphysics, so that the top (God or good) and bottom (Satan or evil) of his cosmic scale of being would be logically at odds not only with one another but also with the unity of the scale itself. Milton seems to have grasped the potential (in every sense) of the grand "Anarch" as a neutral and plausible mediator of the scale's extremes, and of Chaos as an incipient condition of good. To provide further differentiation and ambiguation *within* "one first matter all," he then allows the entropic *pre*-matter of his universe to exist in three quite different states: a first or original phase in which it can accurately be addressed as nature's respected "eldest birth," a neutral, balanced, and inherently benign agency; a second inertial or regressive phase once its energies are "freely" misappropriated for malign ends; and a final phase, in which its original potential is restored by the necessary recoil of these malign energies themselves, which transform their own "waste" into forces facilitating recuperation.

Thus, Milton's syncretic but not therefore unscientific solution suggests that only when a determined alienation from God replaces an indeterminate one, that is, only when evil enters Chaos, does the second definitional sense of the word *entropy* replace the first: instead of existing simply as a "measure of the amount of energy unavailable for useful work in a system undergoing change," evil makes entropy "a measure of the degree of disorder in a substance or a system [where] entropy always increases and available energy diminishes" (*Webster's New World Dictionary*). If like energy itself Chaos must remain *available* to the influx of sin, it also remains true to its divine origin in providing an arena for disorder that both initiates and at last conserves the immanently benign plan of the Protestant universe.

Although resembling the "randomness" of free will in its openness to the influx of both positive and negative forms of entropy, Chaos most resembles the unfallen or redeemed will in its original and final states, which are inherently hostile to evil and *not* to order. As an unborn rather than a firstborn creation, even after being diverted from God this realm retains sparks of its original source, the power of his pure light (3.1–6), the energy fueling its regenerative capacity. Both the ingenuity and complexity of this solution to the problem of allowing for a matter at once free *and* divine is suggested by Marjara's quandary over how to describe the place of Chaos. Ignoring its ambiguous and evolutionary potential and considering it only in its pre-creation or "God-filled" state, he unwittingly overemphasizes a positivity that is *implicit* in but not *necessary* to this state. Yet precisely this lack of necessity explains its relation to Milton's God, the deity free either

"To act or not" (7.172), who pronounces that "Necessitie and Chance / Approach not mee" (172–73).[26] In equal but opposite senses, both are maximally free of necessity, God providing the positive ground of freedom, and Chaos its negative or passive counterpart; both contain a potential for spontaneous creation that is distinctly if differently divine. Insofar as their freedom also remains antithetical—divine liberty being infinitely integrative and its chaotic counterpart infinitely disintegrative, except in the presence of a positive will to good *or* evil—it is finally only *through* this antithesis that an *ex deo* creation can be reconciled with divine or free will, both of which (as an absence of external determination) are virtually the same. That is, only in an essentially benign but also fundamentally alterable and free sphere of physical action can God's goodness be reconciled with authentic liberty, which as Sonnet 12 suggests, is at once supremely good and supremely subject to decay, or license.[27] By inserting a capacity for decay in a material substance that remains good only to the extent that it remains free, Milton depicts evil as a compression or limitation of this substantive freedom.

In the process, the traditional dualism between good (spirit) and evil (matter) is effectively overcome: now matter can be regarded as the ground of freedom, even though it can never be freedom itself (which is God). Hence, while Marjara is undoubtedly right in supposing that this imagination of Chaos is made possible in part by the reinvigoration of the idea of vacuous space that "came into prominence with the revival of Platonism, Stoicism, and especially atomism," he errs in failing to see how its alternative conception of absence and flux as naturally positive rather than "abhorred" kinds of neutrality turns the divine presence in Chaos into a noncontradiction.[28] Containing both vacuums and unformed matter, which are now reconcilable with nature, Chaos thus becomes a benign reflection of the unimaginably pure potentiality of a God who says he fills

> Infinitude, nor vacuous the space.
> Though I uncircumscrib'd my self retire,
> And put not forth my goodness, which is free
> To act or not.
>
> (7.169–72)

As John T. Shawcross notes, this invisible withdrawal of divine influence into its own freedom can be conceived of as a place as well as a state, wherein it can refer only to Chaos, the divine efflux it resembles in being at once empty and full.[29]

Two general corollaries can be derived from these material premises. Since Chaos is not in itself constructive, but is in its original state neither destructive *nor* subject to old age, its entropic matter paradoxically can be regarded as *essentially* benign—an ongoing source or "Womb" of nature. Yet since due to this very benignity it is also receptive (like Heaven itself) to evil—in this case it becomes the "Grave" that perverted matter unconsciously craves, the "final remedie" for the "filth" (10.630) of Sin and Death. However, as argued above, in either case its very passivity has positive implications. If superficially incompatible, these related womb/tomb principles are no more logically contradictory than the laws concerning the conservation of matter/energy from which the laws of entropy currently derive. Moreover, though these thermodynamic principles were not formally stated until much later, their basic assumptions are generally implicit both in seventeenth-century science and in Milton's epic processes. As Marjara explains,

> The process of change from one element to another and from one substance to another is not, in Milton, a mechanical process of rarefaction or condensation, though the images of "dense" and "rare" occur frequently in *Paradise Lost*. A qualitative change is taken for granted, but at the same time, Milton assumes that the essential matter which they are made of remains the same. There is no real duality between corporeal and incorporeal substances, and the vertical rise is merely a change from a lower to a higher degree, and not a transformation into a different kind.[30]

There remains only the task of tracing how these interchanges work in their most subtle instances, which occur generally in Chaos and particularly in the passages depicting its intermediary or transformative phase, the state of entropy that seems to identify it with evil. Because this stage deals with the disruption of benign or "natural" entropy, clarifying the empirical processes at work in this evolution and counter-evolution should not only defuse most of the by now routine charges against this notorious epic "aberration," but also illuminate the fully integrated nature of the poet's apologetic purposes. These purposes include the simultaneous vindication of God, matter, and the universal freedom that ultimately connects them, themes that unite the epic to the underlying philosophy—or, in another sense, the Protestant ideology—of the much earlier academic exercise.[31] The result is a theodicy in praise of a material continuum that is humanly knowable and malleable to the extent that it is *not* subject to decay, which is also the extent to which it remains free of the "license" of moral evil. Because this moral evil can no longer be conceived of simply as contaminating a static cosmos *or* its Chaos, both freedom and progress thereby become entropy's only actual "determinants," forces that *through* self-determination fuel the self-extermination of its malign elements. Here, as throughout Milton's work, destruction is inherent in creation, but in a positive and strikingly contemporary sense; in giving every action an equal and opposite reaction, he makes both satanic destruction and human recuperation necessary concomitants of the eternal recreation implicit within the plan of God's material creation.

Yet, as observed at the outset, *initially* to distinguish the perverse entropic energies of Satan, Sin, and Death from those of the "embryon Atoms" (2.900) randomly clashing in Chaos demands not only careful reading, but also scrupulous rereading. Characteristically, clues to the relatively small but actually substantial differences between Chaos's "vast vacuitie" (932) and the forces that propel Satan's fatal journey to Earth must be excavated from the details of similes that, unlike those of less empirical epics, are never merely ornamental or "digressive."[32] A case in point is the little noted simile in which, as he slogs through the chaotic liminality of "neither Sea, / Nor good dry Land" (939–40), Satan is described

> As when a Gryfon through the Wilderness
> With winged course ore Hill or moarie Dale,
> Pursues the Arimaspian, who by stelth
> Had from his wakeful custody purloind
> The guarded Gold: So eagerly the fiend
> Ore bog or steep, through strait, rough, dense, or rare,
> With head, hands, wings or feet pursues his way,
> And swims or sinks, or wades, or creeps, or flyes.
>
> (2.943–50)

At one level, this description foreshadows Satan's later entropic descent into the "creeping" and "flying" animals that the spread of Sin and Death will turn into beasts of prey (the half-lion, half-eagle "gryfon" in this case taking on serpentine qualities); at another, it emphasizes the griffin's traditional moral alienation from the "warmth of the Holy Spirit."[33] But at a still deeper and more significant level, the analogy underscores the monistic underpinnings of its universe by exhibiting the same pattern of three-phase energy or light symbols that operate in the poem's unfallen as in its fallen terrain. By calling attention to the griffin's attempt to recover his hoarded gold, the simile emphasizes not only the common yet disparate uses of gold in Heaven and on Earth, but also suggests its use in Hell, where, in its "freer" or more "liquid" state, gold is hardened and frozen into the deadly capstone of Pandaemonium, the native seat of the griffin.[34] As when evil enters Chaos, originally random or benign matter is entropically enclosed, limited, and objectified—that is, "purloind" from the native indeterminacy of "strait, rough, dense, or rare." In place of a chaotically potent mixture of "hot, cold, moist, and dry" (2.898), satanic or negative entropy purges and pollutes elements that would otherwise remain "in thir pregnant causes mixt / Confus'dly" (913–14)—but also fertilely.

In accordance with another characteristic epic pattern, this simile then recontextualizes an earlier and more central one. When challenged by [a deathly son] whose kingdom serves only "to enrage thee more" (2.698), Satan confronts his entropic alter ego, a shape "tenfold / More dreadful and deform" (705–6), which

> Unterrifi'd, and like a Comet burn'd,
> That fires the length of Ophiucus huge
> In th' Artick Sky, and from his horrid hair
> Shakes Pestilence and Warr.
>
> (708–11)

As Shawcross notes, this confrontation with his son Death depicts Satan as a "combiner of fire and ice," which, like his astronomical counterpart, the "'serpent-bearer'" comet, favors the "'cold' instruments of death, pestilence and war."[35] In the lower realms, the collision of satanic or positive negation with the utter negation of Death then appears as

> when two black Clouds
> With Heav'ns Artillery fraught, come rattling on
> Over the Caspian, then stand front to front
> Hov'ring a space, till Winds the signal blow
> To joyn thir dark Encounter in mid air:
> So frownd the mighty Combatants, that Hell
> Grew darker at thir frown, so matcht they stood;
> For never but once more was either like
> To meet so great a foe.
>
> (2.714–22)

Here, the appropriate opponent of the father is found in his still "icier" son, whose midair encounter (cf. *Paradise Regain'd*, 4.568) threatens Satan with a premature head wound. The grim appropriateness of Death's misappropriation of the heavenly Son's role is suggested both by substitution of the latter's righteous sword with the former's mortal dart, and also by the halting or "freezing" effect of this encounter, one that causes Hell's fires thereby to grow darker, not brighter, as they might in a more naive epic cosmos. These innovations emphasize that Sin's "merciful" preservation of Satan from Death's "mortal dint" (2.813) or thunderclap (as the *OED* defines "dint" [1b]) promotes a still more deadly cold collusion of energies diverted from their proper source, the benign balance and mediation springing from divine warmth and energy.

At the dramatic level of the poem, a parallel perversion appears in Satan's initial attempt to distance himself from these children, to whom he declares, "I know thee not, nor ever saw till now / Sight more detestable then him and thee" (2.744–45). This ironic echo of the final judgment upon those who fail to reconcile themselves to God—"I never knew you: depart from me" (Matthew 7.23)[36]—increases the degree of Satan's icy alienation from the Almighty's divine *and* his own creation, whom he "helps" only by "hoarding" the truth beneath ever deeper layers of lies. Precisely *because* he has known Sin carnally, he now knows her not (his incestuous desires and their fruits having deformed her beyond recognition); like a gothic self-portrait, his "perfect image" (2.764) more resembles him the more he tries to disown her, who is by now also the "perfect image" of his internal alienation. Through the same "attractive graces" (762) that produced her self-consuming conceptions, Death and his pack of "yelling Monsters" (795), Sin reflects the deadly kind of "love" her father and son have for her and the narcissistic hardening and inversion of the divine, life-giving love that all three reflect in each other.

Nevertheless, once he has recovered sufficiently from his initial shock to learn "his lore" (2.815) from his daughter, Satan gladly "claims" this dreadful duo—for a price. Bartering his recognition of them for their own acceptance of the wages of sin—their further brutalization in exchange for the spurious liberation that any acceptance of their "double" betrayer and begetter must buy—he further increases their mutual hardening and psychic decay.[37] These effects are already implicit in Satan's answer "smooth" (816):

> Dear Daughter, since thou claim'st me for thy Sire,
> And my fair Son here showst me, the dear pledge
> Of dalliance had with thee in Heav'n, and joys
> Then sweet, now sad to mention, through dire change
> Befall'n us unforeseen, unthought of, know
> I come no enemie, but to set free
> From out this dark and dismal house of pain,
> Both him and thee, and all the heav'nly Host
> . . . .
> And bring ye to the place where Thou and Death
> Shall dwell at ease.
> . . . .
>   there ye shall be fed and fill'd
> Immeasurably, all things shall be your prey.
>   (2.817–24, 840–41, 843–44)

Trusting in his false promises to free them from a perpetual state of famine that can be filled neither in Hell nor on Earth, Sin and Death ironically await a new world of light and bliss, even as their father effectively consigns them to the forces of "original darkness" (984). Although for both himself and them the prospect of an ascent to light is clearly a hallucinatory inversion of their actual state of entropy, the material ingredients of this delusion are not unreal in themselves. In another sense, however, they are also less real than the "pregnant causes" further "imbroil[ed]" (2.908) by Chaos and

Night. Unlike the elements contained in a realm *bordered* by light (1035–39), satanic darkness contains a *positive* form of negation whose degrees of fire and ice increase in geometrical proportions inconceivable in a "Nethermost abyss" (956) that is capable of neither geometry nor proportion. In the real yet also *mixed* "darkness" of a quite different state of "Eternal Anarchie" (896)—in which dimension, time, and place are lost—"confusion stand[s]" (897), but does not fall.

In this sense Sin and Night represent the consorts of two utterly different kings. While the darkness of Sin constructs a progressively deepening abyss where, as her sire later discovers, "in the lowest deep a lower deep / Still threatning . . . opens wide" (4.76–77), the darkness of Night is visited by ceaselessly alternating forces, "Light-arm'd or heavy, sharp, smooth, swift or slow" (2.902). These rapid reversions alternately sink Satan himself into the depths, then blast him back "As many miles aloft" (938). Because none of Night's "four Champions" (898) ever achieves "Maistrie" (899), combinations like "Fire and Nitre" (937) can by "ill chance" (935) advance Satan's progress, but they can sustain it no more than they can sediment into his fire and ice. In fact, from a scientific viewpoint, the very presence of "Fire and Nitre" in Chaos would associate it with the nondestructive, random entropy of primary matter, not with the negations of Hell. Because of the privilege that seventeenth-century scientific theory granted to analogy, "exhalations" common to "water and other materials" were thought to govern both "the report of the explosion of gunpowder and the peal of thunder," leading to the conclusion that thunder and lightning were similarly produced by "particles of sulphur and niter in the air."[38] The universal distribution of these chemical reactions allowed their random "reports" to be contrasted with their purely inimical uses, perverse distillations of unformed substance such as Satan and his demons use to convert heavenly rays to cannon fire. Thus, in contrast with Moloch's hellish oath that God shall yet "hear / Infernal Thunder, and for Lightning see / Black fire and horror shot with equal rage" (2.65–67), Chaos and Night's "ruinous[ly]" (921) noisy state merely *counterfeits* a war it can never wage: they can threaten no throne, nor overturn any realm capable of lasting creation *or* destruction. Theirs is a realm of all sound and no fury, much thunder and no lightning.

Only with richly appropriate irony, then, does Chaos sympathize with Satan, confusing his own *un*arrayed confusion with the determined disarray of the forces he sees falling "With ruin upon ruin, rout on rout / Confusion worse confounded" (2.995–96). Whatever Chaos's "natural" sympathies with this melee, no concerted effort on his part can actually affiliate him with Satan: his entropic drives are limited by the very "Illimitab[ility]" (892) of the material energies (both positive and negative) that define his realm. Consequently, he can neither accurately recognize *nor* aid a fiend whose banishment from light consists in the pseudo-liberation that is limitation itself: fire, ice, and negative entropy. Rather than real assistance, his pathetic offer of "all I can . . . [to] serve, / That little which is left so to defend" (999–1000) merely marks his inevitable confusion and incompetence in the face of a ruin whose direction and "speed" (1008) is far better organized than he can possibly imagine. In this case still greater irony is generated by the fact that the good angel Uriel, the "fire of God," will unwittingly render far more aid and comfort to the enemy (3.722–35) than Chaos ever affords his so-called "friends."[39] Although, like Satan, Chaos thinks himself "impaird" (5.665) by the recent encroachments on his realm, *un*like him, Chaos actually opposes more, not less, order.

While Satan champions the static "Orders and Degrees" (5.792) that the new heavenly order has leveled, Chaos prefers the "hubbub wild" (2.951) of an endless dissonance that he correctly associates with demonic ruin but that he incorrectly assumes is identical with his own. Here again, his very illimitability makes it impossible for him to conceptualize the process whereby satanic misrecognition inevitably descends into psychic dissonance, a regular and predictable process whose causes are intimately and nonrandomly bound to their effects. His misunderstanding is further compounded by the fact that these discordant effects are the result of a dialectical pattern of decay originally alien to Chaos, a pattern whereby objectification and projection, diseases of too much consonance, eventually produce their own inversion, diseases of too much dissonance.[40] For these reasons, Chaos is as inept as he is confused: a true "Anarch" and no monarch, he completely miscalculates the fact that the Infernal Triad will encroach far more upon his territory than the heavenly forces now at rest. However, the discerning reader easily perceives the quite different "dissonances" of Chaos and his guest, which are marked in their contrasting aspects—the "Anarch['s]" "faultring speech and visage incompos'd" (2.989) shares none of the tyrant's "obscur'd" (1.594) yet "Original brightness" (592) and glory.

Although Chaos's erratic entropy does and must contrast with the heavenly irregularity (5.622–24) and its counterpart, an earthly fertility "Wild above Rule or Art" (5.297), its differences from the hyperorganized depredations of satanic fire and ice go far deeper. Of course, as appropriate to an unformed, neutral state of matter, some residual parallels with negative entropy remain: if the noisy combustions of Chaos are less pernicious than those of Hell, neither can induce the peaceful generation that results from an ordered alternation of dark with light. Yet, despite its lack of the benign dichotomies that organize Heaven and Earth, Chaos's greater distance from Hell is clear from the stark contrast between the comic vehemence of the former and the harshly repetitive reverberations of the latter. When Sin gives birth to her "inbred enemie" (2.785), her outcry of "Death" (787) echoes throughout Hell's "Caves" (789) and deflects back upon her (789) with deadly effect. First taking the hollow no-shape of a form possessed only of a "lust . . . [and] rage" (791) to repeat himself—and consequently his father—by raping his mother, Death's repetition of Sin punishes her incestuous repetition of their father through the "ceasless cry" (795) of his devouring sons, the hounds of Hell. This abortive dissonance not only reflects their "hollow" affections, but also contrasts with Chaos's "hollow dark assaults [upon the] . . . ear" (953), which at least suggest its noisy *potential* for the "*kindly* rupture" (7.419; emphasis mine) inherent in its "pregnant causes." As opposed to these chaotic birth pangs, the cruel ruptures of a Sin-ful body can only bring forth sterile Death and increasingly alienate their malformed progeny from the light. But because original chaotic entropy cannot be destroyed, it remains fertilely receptive to reorganization in the presence of *either* light or darkness, as it is when it is molded first by the Son's golden compasses opening Earth's dark warmth (7.225–36), and then by Death's "Mace petrific, cold and dry" (10.294), pounding out his bridge to Hell.

In contrast, by *controlling* the winds of "Fire and Nitre" that had once played havoc with him in Chaos, Satan bequeathes his integral fire and ice to his heirs, which in turn regularly increases the depths of the internal "Hell" (4.75) they share regardless of where they crawl, creep, or fly. By placing the nutritive properties of "hot, cold, moist, and dry" in the crucible of his lust and rage, Satan can create no indeterminate or alterable domain, but only the truly hostile chaos of the northerly comet that presides over pestilence and war. Extracted from but essentially unlike the merely uncreative entropy of Chaos and Night, this anticreative entropy can produce *only* icy thunder or burning wastes, not the generative storms whose lightning brings the rain.[41]

Thus, if satanic or negative entropy has a temporal materiality as real as that of Chaos that, like it, operates through attractions of like kind—"Faction" or "Clanns" (2.901)—it differs insofar as its reified attractions are permanently and irreversibly degenerative. Lacking the generative capacity of the chaotic matter that hears the Son's voice as he comes to create the Earth (7.221), satanic or negative entropy thrives only upon those elements "purg'd" (237) from it: "the black tartareous cold infernal dregs / Adverse to life" (238–39). If originally part of nature's balance, once these "dregs" are isolated and "reduced," they are made hostile to divine order and friendly only to its "reducers." However, when still diffused throughout the "fluid Mass" (237), even these elements can scarcely be hostile to the light that also vitalizes the tragi-comic entropy of Chaos, which contains, without being limited to, their influence.

Ancient but not subject to old age, chaotic entropy can thus decline from its benignly random condition and be turned to destructive substances only in the presence of evil. No more intrinsically inimical to God than the heavenly subsoil where his freedom permits a similarly real yet temporary perversion, this entropic state is not merely consistent with Milton's mature belief that "original matter was not an evil thing, nor . . . worthless: it was good, and it contained the seeds of all subsequent good . . . a confused and disordered state at first . . . [that] afterwards God made . . . ordered and beautiful."[42] More than that, it is also logically *opposed* to the "hot" of Sin and the "cold" of Death, the negative or "pure" entropy inherent in Satan's fire and ice. Understood as ironically as the later Lucretian poet also portrayed them, Milton's entropic elements of perverse desire are even more inevitably redemptive than the fully human hate and desire of Frost's apocalyptic "Fire and Ice." Yet if Frost's satiric poem suggests his more stoical response to the downward drift of fallen creation, as outlined above, it may also be considered a belated gloss on a problematic ontology of metaphysical evil that Milton's Chaos physically resolves. In *Paradise Lost,* due to the purgative potential implicit in the imbalances of negative entropy, the universe is empirically imagined as being renewed through the wisest of Providence's provisions: the primeval *im*balance of uncreated matter, the divine check on the balances of the rest of God's creation. Because the most "eccentric" (5.623) of angelic dances cannot in themselves nullify the over-organization of satanic energies, it is only through Chaos's power to extinguish the self-consuming fires that initiate the "sling[ing]" (10.633) of Earth's "Hell-hounds" (630) back through nature's "Womb" and "Grave" that primal entropy can be restored. In this most voluntaristic of all theodicies, higher spiritual agencies cannot destroy lower and more degenerate ones but must allow the latter's "heavier" and "colder" entropic energies gradually to succumb to the downward drift of their own self-created material substances. Then, freed at last from Satan's "Universe of death . . . / Where all life dies, death lives, and nature breeds, / Perverse" (2.622, 624–25), the fundamental alterability of primal entropy becomes the agency whereby "Heav'n and Earth renewd shall be made pure" (10.638) from its source—in Chaos.

Therefore, the truly "de-natured" nature of *Paradise Lost* can no longer be identified with Chaos, but only with "its [very] own place" (1.254), the satanic mind. As Satan himself claims, his is an originally free psychic state, but as the reader soon understands, it is a state whose icy entropic drives lead to inalterable, fused metaphysical and physical forms of combustion. Of course, in the same sense that Satan's hellish mind is "its own place," Chaos's realm has also become more state than place: at once the atomic substrate of the physical universe, the medium of its metaphysical agents, and the potential for their own on-going creation. Because its unintegrated and potentially dis- *or* re-integrating matter can be found in the subsoil of Heaven as well as in the "high Winds" (9.1122) of "Discord" (1124) that immediately reign in the animal spirits of the newly fallen couple, Chaos is ultimately like Hell, an everywhere. However, unlike Hell, *in potentia* its universal physical properties remain essentially on the side of the life rather than the death principle, as Adam and Eve later discover.

By affiliating its vacuities with those of divine freedom, Milton makes his reformed Chaos far more positive than negative, a medium of regeneration as well as choice. Hence, this deceptively "minor" epic deviation provides an important key to the major metaphysical *and* physical innovations at work in Milton's poetic conception as a whole. In valorizing vicissitude, his poem also valorizes relativity in ways that expand the scope of moral human choice far beyond the dimensions imagined in the poem's Shakespearean or Spenserian "originals." In *Paradise Lost*, although "up" and "down" preserve some of their ancient moral implications, due to Milton's temporalization of space these meanings have become merely local and/or mutable; Satan falls by "rising" to the challenge of invading Earth, the Son rises by "falling" to serve a sinful race, while Raphael both falls and rises in completing his own faithful service to humankind. These and a wealth of other details illustrate the atomic and relatively random basis of a natural philosophy strikingly in accord with its libertarian metaphysical outlook, which emphasizes Arminian self-determination, empirical self-discovery, and (as in *Areopagitica*) the essentially benign nature of mutability and flux.[43] As a result, both Milton's Chaos and the cosmos on which it is founded must be situated in "a physics that transcends the physical laws of a finite universe," as Marjara remarks, but also (actually to reverse the argument) in one whose "moral symbolism" becomes apparent only in the "literal truth" of its natural laws of birth, decay, and regeneration.[44]

In this sense, at least, the normal processes of myth have been reversed: moral meaning is not projected on to the symbolic screen of the physical universe, but the laws of natural action and reaction are made the paradigm for the "physics" of the moral law. At least partly because modern science does originate in metaphysics,[45] in the imagination of one of its early admirers as in contemporary theory, matter must be allowed two contrary but not antithetical attributes. Given the proper influences, its originally steady state in the subatomic forces of Chaos (or dark matter) has the potential either to explode in the super-atomic evolution of the galaxies (or angels), or to implode under the adverse gravitational pull of negative entropy (or demons). However, because matter is always conserved, it is also always subject to reconfiguration after the death of stars like Satan/Lucifer. From this final perspective, then, it should seem no coincidence that in his early poetic expression of a later "Big-Bang" theory, Milton would consistently associate the ordered movement of his most integrated or refined spirits "with that of astronomical bodies,"[46] and their elliptical "dance[s]" (5.620) with the "starrie Sphear / Of Planets" (620–21): planets that their movement not only "Resembles nearest" (623), but outside of which his angels can now scarcely be imagined at all.

Notes

1. As Samuel Johnson remarked, "To give [the allegorical figures] any real employment, or ascribe to them any material agency, is to make them allegorical no longer, but *to shock the mind by ascribing effects to non-entity*" (emphasis mine). See Samuel Johnson, "Life of Milton," in *Johnson's Lives of the English Poets: A Selection*, ed. J. P. Hardy (Oxford: Clarendon, 1971), 108.

2. John Milton, *Paradise Lost*, in *The Complete Poetry of John Milton*, ed. John T. Shawcross, rev. ed. (New York: Doubleday, 1971). All references to Milton's poetry are to this edition and are cited parenthetically in the text.

3. Currently, the primary advocate of this position is Regina Schwartz; see *Remembering and Repeating: Biblical Creation in "Paradise Lost"* (Cambridge: Cambridge University Press, 1988), especially 10–11.

4. Two important recent studies examine the implications of this system in detail; see Dennis Danielson, *Milton's Good God: A Study in Literary Theodicy* (Cambridge: Cambridge University Press, 1982); and Stephen M. Fallon, *Milton Among the Philosophers: Poetry and Materialism in Seventeenth-Century England* (Ithaca: Cornell University Press, 1991).

5. Shawcross notes, "The causes are Ramus' forces by which things exist: nothing has been born yet from their confusion but potential birth is imminent." See *Complete Poetry*, 294 n. 49.

6. Schwartz examines the evidence for a consistently hostile Chaos that does not even *appear* friendly to the divine faction (*Remembering and Repeating*, 26–31). This position will be refuted in what follows.

7. While much of Milton's portrait of Chaos may be derived from Ovid, chaotic matter was, traditionally, sharply distinguished from, but also reconciled to, God through the doctrine of *ex nihilo* creation, as John Carey and Alistair Fowler point out (John Milton, *The Complete Poems of Milton*, ed. John Carey and Alistair Fowler [London: Longman, 1968], 549 n. ii895–903). As most subsequent critics agree, both Milton's monism and his insistence on an *ex deo* doctrine of creation considerably confuse the situation, so that in his poem the potential of matter must now logically be reconciled—or fail to be reconciled, as Schwartz argues—to God and not merely to "nothing." See *Remembering and Repeating*, 9–10.

8. Thomas McAlindon, *Shakespeare's Tragic Cosmos* (Cambridge: Cambridge University Press, 1991), 16, 23; see also 267 n. 15. Significantly, Schwartz mistakenly *identifies* Milton's attitude toward vacuous space with Shakespeare's; see Schwartz, *Remembering and Repeating*, 19–20.

9. While McAlindon describes a view of the traditional chaos and its contribution to a "tragic vision" of the cosmos that is more dualistic than that of *Paradise Lost*, it does exhibit some of the tragic *consciousness* that Lucien Goldmann associates with Pascal, and Frank Kermode with Milton. See McAlindon, *Shakespeare's Tragic Cosmos*, 16, 23, 263; Lucien Goldmann, *The Hidden God* (London: Routledge and Kegan Paul, 1964), especially 142–50; and Frank Kermode, "Adam Unparadised," in *The Living Milton*, ed. Frank Kermode (London: Routledge and Kegan Paul, 1960), 85–123.

10. See also Sin's important speech in which, turning to Satan, she looks forward eagerly to the "Monarchie" being forced "with thee [to] divide / Of all things"

(10.379–80), when in fact the bridge between Hell and Earth will only reapportion the universe by negatively dividing and reducing the richness of its potential. Shaw-cross comments that Sin has here "fallaciously contrasted" concepts of "squareness and circularity . . . male, female; imperfect, perfect; justice, mercy." See *Complete Poetry,* 460 n. 37.

11. Anna K. Nardo, *Milton's Sonnets and the Ideal Community* (Lincoln: University of Nebraska Press, 1979), 13. See 4–26 for a convenient summary of the Weber-Tawney-Hill hypothesis regarding the rise of Puritanism, the hypothesis to which I allude here.

12. For a fuller and more detailed defense of this point, see Harinder Singh Marjara, *Contemplation of Created Things: Science in "Paradise Lost"* (Toronto: University of Toronto Press, 1992), 12–14.

13. For Satan's associations with fire and ice, see Shawcross, *Complete Poetry,* 289 n. 36.

14. In this sense Blake's misunderstanding of Milton's Satan in "The Marriage of Heaven and Hell" is actually an understanding of Milton's God: the divine lawgiver who is also the divine poet working *within* a creation that, at least in Chaos, literally unites the potential of Heaven and Hell. These points are further developed below.

15. As Marjara concludes, since "A blend of older ideas and newer scientific speculations is to be found in several Renaissance scientists, among whom we may count many standard-bearers of the new science such as Kepler, Helmont, Harvey and Boyle [,] . . . Milton's attitude . . . must be considered contemporary in his response to science" (*Contemplation,* 14).

See also 7–8, where in critiquing Lovejoy, Svendson, Babb, and others, he also explodes the myth of the inimical relationship between religion and science, a point differently developed in my article, "'Boundless the Deep': Milton, Pascal, and the Theology of Relative Space," *ELH,* 63 (1996): 45–78.

16. An important exception is Danielson, who in *Milton's Good God* underscores the importance of Chaos in Milton's literary theodicy, although not in conjunction with his science. Another is S. Fallon *(Milton Among the Philosophers),* who in a useful footnote argues that Schwartz creates the "mirage" of an evil Chaos by bracketing out not only Milton's prose but also too much of his poem (190–91 n. 44). Marjara seems unaware of or uninterested in the issue of a hostile Chaos.

17. A. B. Chambers, "Chaos in *Paradise Lost,*" *Journal of the History of Ideas* 24 (1963): 55–84; A. S. P. Woodhouse, "Notes on Milton's Views on the Creation: The Initial Phases," *Philological Quarterly* 28 (1949): 229 n. 30. As both quotations indicate, Schwartz's mythic perspective fails to produce very different findings from Chambers's reliance on Plato's *Timaeus* or Woodhouse's reliance on the Neoplatonic tradition, even if it *seems* more relevant than John Rumrich's speculations upon the ancient Hebrew concept of *kabod.* Drawing heavily upon Bernhard Anderson's study of the persistence of the Canaanite chaos/creation opposition in the Hebrew Bible, Schwartz largely confines herself to anthropological approaches to primitive myth: Mary Douglas's analysis of the prohibitions of Leviticus in *Purity and Danger: An Analysis of Concepts of Pollution and Taboo* (London: Routledge and Kegan Paul, 1966); Arnold van Gennap, *The Rites of Passage,* trans. Monica B. Vizdom and Gabrielle L. Cafee (Chicago: University of Chicago Press, 1960). See *Remembering and Repeating,* 12–18, and also John Peter Rumrich, *Matter of Glory: A New Preface to "Paradise Lost"* (Pittsburgh: University of Pittsburgh Press, 1987), 14–25.

18. John Ray, *Three Physico-Theological Discourses* (London, 1693), 6; the comparable passage from Milton's *Christian Doctrine* is cited below.

19. Ilya Prigogine and Isabella Stengers, *Order Out of Chaos: Man's New Dialogue with Nature* (New York: Bantam, 1984), 14.

20. Although I have taken a few liberties with word order, my use of this quotation reflects Adam's own perplexity in the matter. As his question to Raphael suggests, he too has difficulty imagining

> what cause
> Mov'd the Creator in his holy Rest
> Through all Eternitie so late to build
> In Chaos, and the work begun, how soon
> Absolv'd, if unforbid thou maist unfould.
>
> (7.90–94)

In this way, both Chaos and God are recognized as part of a holy but not wholly inexplicable mystery, one that inevitably links the "Boundless . . . Deep" (7.168) of God to the "vast immeasurable Abyss / Outrageous as a sea" (211–12), the chaotic "Deep" (216) extracted from, but not formed by, his own nature. For a more extended exploration of this theme, see Martin, "'Boundless the Deep.'"

21. McAlindon, *Shakespeare's Tragic Cosmos*, 11.

22. See Richard Jones, *Ancients and Moderns: A Study of the Rise of the Scientific Movement in Seventeenth-Century England* (Berkeley: University of California Press, 1965).

23. For a comparable if ultimately quite different analysis of the "triadic" dialectical structure of *Paradise Lost*, see Sanford Budick, *The Dividing Muse: Images of Sacred Disjunction in Milton's Poetry* (New Haven: Yale University Press, 1985).

24. See Prigogine and Stengers, *Order Out of Chaos*, 131–76.

25. Jacob Bronowski, *The Identity of Man* (New York: Doubleday, 1971), 136. While Bronowski argues that this is the way that great science and literary minds work at *all* times, his account is obviously at odds with the objectivist models of scientific progress still dominant when he wrote—which perhaps makes him a similarly prophetic poet and philosopher of science.

26. See Stephen Fallon, "'To Act or Not': Milton's Conception of Divine Freedom," *Journal of the History of Ideas* 49 (1988): 425–49.

27. Although Shawcross (*Complete Poetry*) numbers this Sonnet 11, I here defer to the more common numbering.

28. Marjara, *Contemplation*, 97; see 96–100. While seeming to endorse something *like* my position, Marjara remains vague and inexplicit about what he calls the "(absence of) nature of the most vague ontological entity in *Paradise Lost*" (96), a state concerning which he finds Milton similarly vague. Ironically, the same resistance to vacuums and adherence to Aristotelian orthodoxy—particularly the idea that "Nature abhors a vacuum" (which, as Steven Fallon points out, contradicts Milton's cherished concept of plenitude)—underlies Lovejoy's exasperation with Milton. See Fallon, *Milton Among the Philosophers*, 11–13, and Martin, "'Boundless the Deep,'" for further challenges to this orthodoxy.

29. See Shawcross, *Complete Poetry*, 392 n. 21.

30. Marjara, *Contemplation*, 234.

31. A contrary position is presented by Annabel Patterson, who suspects the early Milton of "aristocratic" or "elitist" leanings ("'Forc'd fingers': Milton's Early Poems and Ideological Constraint," in *"The Muses Common-Weale": Poetry and Politics in the Seventeenth Century*, ed. Claude J. Summers and Ted-Larry Pebworth [Columbia: University of Missouri Press, 1988], 9–22, especially 12, 15). A similar (and to my mind equally erroneous) view is presented by David Loewenstein, "'Fair

Offspring Nurs'd in Princely Lore': On the Question of Milton's Early Radicalism,"
Milton Studies 28 (1992): 37–48.

32. On this point, see the classic studies of James Whaler, "The Miltonic Simile,"
PMLA 46 (1931): 1034–74; and Harry Berger, Jr., *The Allegorical Temper: Vision
and Reality in Book II of Spenser's "Faerie Queene"* (Hamden: Archon, 1967).

33. Carey and Fowler take these symbols from "an allegory of Raban Maur's
(Migne cxi 342)," but also note that "The legend of the 'gold-guarding griffins' in
Scythia, from whom the one-eyed Arimaspi steal, was often retold out of Herodotus
(iii 116) and Pliny (*Nat. hist* vii 10)." See *Complete Poems*, 552 n. ii943–7.

34. As an embodiment of the original Golden Age, Eden abounds with organic
forms of gold, perhaps among the more memorable of which is its "vegetable Gold"
(4.220), while Heaven's golden floor is usually understood as representing the free
righteousness of the Son, the "ground" of his being "misconceived" and misappropriated by demons like Mammon and Satan.

35. Shawcross, *Complete Poetry*, 289 n. 236.

36. King James Version.

37. For this aspect of Satan, see John T. Shawcross, "The Mosaic Voice in *Paradise
Lost*," *Milton Studies* 2 (1970): 25–26; and Samuel S. Stollman, "Satan, Sin, and
Death: A Mosaic Trio in *Paradise Lost*," *Milton Studies* 22 (1986): 101–20. According
to Stollman, "Sin and Death and their encounters with Satan act out one of Milton's
major doctrines, namely, his . . . antinomian view of the Mosaic Law and of the
Law's impediment of the attainment of Christian liberty" (101).

38. Harinder Singh Marjara, "Analogy in the Scientific Imagery of *Paradise
Lost*," *Milton Studies* 26 (1990): 86.

39. For Uriel as the "fire of God," see Shawcross, *Complete Poetry*, 314 n. 38.

40. For a suggestive consideration of satanic or sinful narcissism that causes *copia*
to degenerate into a "mere copy," see R. A. Shoaf, *Milton, Poet of Duality: A
Study of Semiosis in the Poetry and the Prose* (New Haven: Yale University Press,
1985), 27–29.

41. Marjara notes that "In Milton's universe, the images of feeding interrelate
the earth with the heavens." See "Analogy," 89. In contrast, one might postulate
that Hell cannibalizes Chaos in anticipation of its putrefying influence on Earth.

42. John Milton, *Christian Doctrine*, in *Complete Prose Works of John Milton*, 8
vols., ed. Don M. Wolfe et al. (New Haven: Yale University Press, 1953–82), 6:308.

43. See Danielson, *Milton's Good God*, and Jones, who, in *Ancients and Moderns*,
shows that the methods, aims, and ideology of supposedly "other-worldly" Puritans
and of empiricists were fundamentally the same.

44. Marjara, *Contemplation*, 150–51.

45. This point is brought out by Marjara, *Contemplation*, 5. See also Edwin A.
Burtt, *The Metaphysical Foundations of Modern Physical Science* (London, 1924),
and Prigogine and Stengers, *Order Out of Chaos*.

46. Carey and Fowler, *Complete Poems*, 715 n. v620–4.

Angelic Visitations:
Raphael's Roles in the Book of Tobit and
Paradise Lost

Janna Thacher Farris

For centuries, readers of *Paradise Lost* have recognized that Milton's treatment of the subject of marriage is unorthodox. He purposefully develops a mutuality between Adam and Eve as he presents the perfect marriage in prelapsarian Eden. Also in a radical vein for his time, Milton chooses to present angels as corporeal beings, having Raphael stress,

> one first matter all,
> Indu'd with various forms, various degrees
> Of substance, and in things that live, of life.
>
> (5.472–74)[1]

A study of the angel Raphael reveals that he has an apocryphal history of walking among human beings and an even more specific tradition of intervening in human marriages. Considering this history, Raphael's appearance in the Book of Tobit must be closely examined as Milton's source for Raphael's intervention into Adam and Eve's prelapsarian world. As Virginia Mollenkott notes, "The reference to Raphael and the Book of Tobit is . . . the most obvious of all Milton's Apocryphal borrowings."[2] Through a comparison of Raphael's visits to Tobias and Sarah in Tobit and to Adam and Eve in *Paradise Lost*, one finds that Milton intentionally reduces the hierarchical distance between Raphael and the prelapsarian humans in order to stress the perfection of paradisal existence.

Beverly Sherry points out that "Milton knew Raphael from the apocryphal Book of Tobit, and it seems . . . that he wanted to evoke that story as a primary association around Raphael."[3] Sherry also focuses on the Raphael of Tobias's story as the logical basis for Milton's Raphael since Milton knew the text of the "legend of Tobias and the angel" and recognized the popularity of the Book of Tobit in his England.[4] Mark Wollaeger stresses that Milton regarded the Apocrypha as "'closest to the scriptures of authority,' though not the word of God," as is made clear in Milton's own *Chris-*

tian Doctrine.[5] Direct evidence of Milton's consideration of the Book of Tobit exists in the narrator's references to the story of Tobias in 4.166–71 and 5.219–23. Mollenkott also includes the mention of Asmadai that appears in 6.365—a reference more important to the relationship between Raphael and Satan than to the one between the angel and the human couple—as another reference to the Book of Tobit.[6]

The connection between the Book of Tobit and *Paradise Lost* becomes evident when reading the apocryphal account of Tobias and Sarah's wedding night. In their nuptial bower, Tobias offers a prayer to the Lord saying, "Thou madest Adam and gavest him Eve his wife as a helper and support. From them the race of mankind has sprung. Thou didst say, 'It is not good that the man should be alone; let us make a helper for him like himself'" (8.6).[7] Furthermore, "Like Tobias and Sara, Adam and Eve come together with prayer (PL IV.720 ff.); and the prayers are similar except for Tobias' awareness of danger,"[8] a purposeful omission for Adam on Milton's part. Directly following the wedding prayer in Tobit, Tobias asserts that he takes Sarah not in lust, "but with sincerity" (8.7). Milton echoes this apocryphal act in *Paradise Lost* when "into thir inmost bower / Handed they [Adam and Eve] went" (4.738–39), following their evening prayer, which was "said unanimous" (736). The newly married couple in Paradise enjoys "the Rites / Mysterious of connubial Love" (742–43), participating in sexual intercourse as a part of "wedded Love, mysterious Law, true source / Of human off-spring" (750–51). It is this perfect wedded love that drives "adulterous lust" (753) from humankind. As in Tobias and Sarah's story, Adam and Eve first share a prayer, theirs specifically heralding "mutual love" (728), then experience the physical consummation of their wedded love.

Mollenkott believes that Milton uses "the Tobias-Sara relationship as a prototype for his Adam and Eve" because "[r]egarding Tobias and Sara as the ideal couple may have been rather traditional, for in the earliest Book of Common Prayer (1549) the marriage service refers to Tobias and Sara as providing the ideal pattern for a good marriage."[9] It cannot be ignored, however, that chronologically the Tobias story follows the story of Adam and Eve in Paradise, and, logically, Milton had to consider this point as he created his Raphael who would visit a prelapsarian couple participating in the perfect marriage. This important fact causes Milton to shape his Raphael differently from the Raphael of Tobias's story.

With the basis for Milton's Raphael placed in the Book of Tobit, a close comparison of Raphael's communion with human beings both in Tobit and in *Paradise Lost* highlights the more human qualities of Milton's Raphael. The actual reasons for each angel's descent vary with the narratives and underline the human aspect of Milton's angel. God calls Raphael in *Paradise Lost* in response to Satan's visitation to Eve while she sleeps, specifically charging Raphael: "Go therefore, half this day as friend with friend / Converse with Adam" (5.229–30). God gives Raphael specific instructions to advise and warn Adam on particular topics (233–45), and it is later revealed to the reader in book 7 that Raphael has received an additional commission "to answer thy [Adam's] desire / Of knowledge within bounds" (119–20). It is apparent, then, that Raphael in *Paradise Lost* has a charge from God not only to act as a counselor, but also to share information with the couple as a humanlike companion.

Raphael's visit to Tobias specifically answers the prayers of both Tobit and Sarah. Raphael, whose name means "God heals," "was sent to heal the two of them: to scale away the white films from Tobit's eyes; to give Sarah . . . in marriage to Tobias . . . and to bind Asmodeus the evil demon, because Tobias was entitled to possess her [Sarah]" (3.17). It is evident that God's intention in Tobit's postlapsarian scene is for the angel to enter the human realm as an active superior. There is no implication in the Book of Tobit of the equality of "friend to friend" that God's charge to Raphael in *Paradise Lost* contains. Additionally, in Tobit, Raphael is sent on a mission which appears at odds with producing a marriage of mutuality such as Milton presents in the prelapsarian garden. While the purposes of the visits are different, the basis of Tobit as Milton's source is still apparent, for each Raphael is "certainly the go-between of gods and men,"[10] and each acts as an intervening force against a satanic presence.

The next difference between the two Raphaels is apparent in their entrances into the scenes and the human beings' recognition of the angels. In *Paradise Lost*, after an elaborate description of Raphael's descent, Adam readily recognizes the approach of the angel and encourages Eve to prepare extra food in order "to honor and receive / Our Heav'nly stranger" (5.315–16). As Raphael arrives at the nuptial bower, "Adam though not aw'd, / Yet with submiss approach and reverence meek, / As to a superior Nature, bowing low" (358–60) speaks first to his guest. It is clear that Adam shows proper respect to his guest, as to a superior, but the superiority of his guest seems forgotten as Adam initiates conversation. Raphael further diminishes the hierarchical distance between his race and the prelapsarian humans by emphasizing that he

> came, nor art thou [Adam] such
> Created, or such place hast here to dwell,
> As may not oft invite, though Spirits of Heav'n
> To visit thee.
>
> (372–75)

Obviously the prelapsarian Paradise affords Adam and Eve privileges and a certain degree of familiarity with heavenly beings that are absent in their postlapsarian state and in the Book of Tobit.

In the Book of Tobit, Raphael's arrival and his recognition by the human race are much different. Tobias searches for a man to accompany him to Media, without any knowledge of the possibility of his marriage, and "he found Raphael, who was an angel, but Tobias did not know it" (5.4–5). Much like Adam in *Paradise Lost*, "Tobias invited him [Raphael, who has assumed the identity of Azarias] in; he entered and they greeted each other" (5.9). This postlapsarian scene is reminiscent of Hebrews 13.2, in which it is stated that "some have entertained angels unawares." It is not until Tobias and Sarah have successfully married and several days later returned to the home of Tobit where he is cured of his blindness that Raphael admits to Tobit and Tobias, whom he has brought together privately, that "God sent me to heal you and your daughter-in-law Sarah. I am Raphael, one of the seven holy angels who present the prayers of the saints and enter into the presence of the glory of the Holy One" (12.14–15). Tobit and Tobias's reaction to Raphael's revelation is one of fear as "they fell upon their faces" (12.16).

Their reactions recall Adam's postlapsarian response to Michael's approach: "carnal fear that day dimm'd Adam's eye" (11.212). When Michael visits Eden after the Fall, Adam states that this heavenly visitor will not be "sociably mild, / As Raphael, that I should much confide" (234–35). The postlapsarian Adam bows before his heavenly guest after the Fall, but "hee [Michael] Kingly from his State / Inclin'd not"; and, he speaks first to the fallen man (249–50). Adam's relationship with the visiting angel after the Fall is more in accordance with the hierarchy demonstrated in the Book of Tobit. Milton shows an amiable, sociable relationship between human beings and angels prior to the Fall, but afterward, although Adam, unlike Tobit and his family, still readily recognizes the angel, the hierarchical distance between beings human and heavenly is greater.

Yet another example of the diminished hierarchical distance between prelapsarian Adam and Eve and Raphael as opposed to the distance between Raphael and Tobit's family is illustrated in the time that Milton's Raphael spends with the human couple. Interestingly, however, in both the Book of Tobit and *Paradise Lost*, the angel enters the human realm with foreknowledge of the couples' futures. In both instances, God has provided Raphael with an understanding of what is to come, which corresponds with contemporary opinion in Milton's day, expressed by scholars such as John Salkeld, that "As for the future, it is dark to the angel unless God discovers it to him."[11] In the case of Tobias and Sarah, the future looks positive, and Raphael's mission is directly involved in providing the instructions, which he does with dispatch, that ensure the future of the couple. In Milton's story, Thomas Copeland claims that "as Raphael approaches the bower and beholds Eve, his burden of foreknowledge becom[es] heavy."[12] Copeland continues by asserting, "In his kindly acceptance of Adam's invitation,

Raphael . . . disguises the urgency of his errand, conceals for the moment the fact of God's having sent him."[13] Copeland cites Raphael's words, "these mid-hours, till Ev'ning rise / I have at will" (5.376–77) as a misrepresentation to the couple, "for he is on a mission, not on leave."[14] However, Copeland's labeling of Raphael's statement as a "misrepresentation" seems harsh in that God has charged the angel to talk with Adam as "friend with friend." The willingness of Raphael to do more than quickly warn, instruct, and leave emphasizes the difference in Milton's presentation of prelapsarian human relations with angels. Raphael and Adam can enjoy each other's company, even though Raphael does have important information to relate. The Raphael of the Book of Tobit has so little in common with his human listeners that he quickly accomplishes his task and leaves their realm.

Significantly, Raphael will eat or appear to eat human food in both stories. In *Milton and the Angels,* Robert H. West cites a number of scholars, including Augustine, Tertullian, and Henry More, who debate the question "of whether angels eat and of how they eat, or seem to."[15] West importantly acknowledges elsewhere in his study that "like Salkeld, most Scholastics preferred to say with Aquinas that as angels did not assimilate [as Calvin maintained], they did not truly eat."[16] Notably, after Adam offers Raphael food in *Paradise Lost,* fearing that it may be "unsavory food perhaps / To spiritual Natures" (5.401–2), Raphael replies:

> food alike those pure
> Intelligential substances require
> As doth your Rational; and both contain
> Within them every lower faculty
> Of sense, whereby they hear, see, smell, touch, taste,
> Tasting concoct, digest, assimilate
> And corporeal to incorporeal turn.
> For know, whatever was created, needs
> To be sustain'd and fed.
>
> (407–15)

In the Book of Tobit, however, Raphael is careful to explain to his human hearers that "All these days I merely appeared to you and did not eat and drink, but you were seeing a vision" (12.19). Mollenkott contends that "Milton differs from Tobit *because* Tobit seems to contradict Genesis xviii and xix, in addition to contradicting the information in both canon and Apocrypha that manna is 'angel's food'" (emphasis mine).[17] However, Mollenkott is not considering Milton's creation of a prelapsarian Adam. Tobit and Tobias note after Raphael's departure that "the angel of the Lord had appeared to them" (12.22). The choice of the word *appeared* downplays any implications that the angel might be a corporeal visitor to them, unlike the Raphael of *Paradise Lost.* In Genesis 18.1, too, the word *appeared* is used to initially introduce the Lord's visit to Abraham and Lot in the form of angels. Milton's intention in differing from Tobit is to highlight a division between angel and human being that is much more distinct in postlapsarian existence than that between angel and Milton's prelapsarian human couple. As West states, "The only angelologist who could assert with Milton that angels profited by earthly food would be one who wanted also to assert a basic resemblance of man to angel in the whole of their beings."[18] Perhaps few, if any, angelologists would embrace this assertion, but Milton indeed did in describing prelapsarian existence in *Paradise Lost*.

Although Raphael's visit to the family of Tobit originates with God's giving a clear mission to the angel, the visiting angel in the Apocrypha stays only as long as needed to instruct, see the instructions completed, and finally reveal himself and further advise his charge. Raphael of *Paradise Lost* stays and shares information with Adam on many subjects, accenting the likenesses of angels and humans on many points. For instance, he stresses to Adam the common free will of both angels and human beings and their service and obedience to God. He says, "Our voluntary service he requires, / Not our necessitated" (5.529–30), emphasizing the inclusive pronoun for angels and humanity, and he continues,

> Myself and all th' Angelic Host that stand
> In sight of God enthron'd, our happy state
> Hold, as you yours, while our obedience holds;
> On other surety none.
>
> (535–38)

He also reveals to Adam the limited nature of angelic might through his description of the War in Heaven (6.229). Milton additionally makes it clear through Raphael that the angels have no foreknowledge beyond that provided to them through experience and by God. When Adam offers to "relate / My Story, which perhaps thou [Raphael] hast not heard" (8.204–5), Raphael welcomes the information, telling Adam to "say therefore on; / For I that Day was absent" (8.228–29), referring to the sixth day of the Creation when Raphael guarded "the Gates of Hell" (8.231). Milton is showing an exchange of information between beings who are often considered incapable of a reciprocal sharing of knowledge. In prelapsarian Eden, Adam is able to supply information to Raphael that the angel has not received previously, again reaffirming the limited hierarchical distance between angels and humans in prelapsarian existence.

A final area that perhaps most greatly highlights Raphael's reduced hierarchical distance from human creatures in *Paradise Lost* is his potential fallibility. In his visit to the created universe, Raphael makes statements that provide questionable assistance to his human companions, and he interprets situations wrongly. Wollaeger, for instance, points to the ability of Milton's Raphael to make choices during his visit, citing Raphael's first words to Adam, "these mid-hours, till Ev'ning rise / I have at will" (5.376–77), as the moment when "Raphael introduces the possibility that he may stray from his commission."[19] Although God has outlined exact thoughts to express to Adam and Eve, when Raphael converses with the couple on varying subjects, he must rely at his discretion on his own limited knowledge. For example, when Raphael focuses on the similarities between humans and angels when it comes to the intake of food, he states:

> time may come when men
> With Angels may participate, and find
> No inconvenient Diet, nor too light Fare:
> And from these corporal nutriments perhaps
> Your bodies may at last turn all to spirit,
> Improv'd by tract of time, and wing'd ascend
> Ethereal.
>
> (493–99)

Although Raphael follows his statement with the qualification, "If ye be found obedient, and retain / Unalterably firm his love entire / Whose progeny you are" (501–3), it is possible that Eve has Raphael's promising words in mind at her temptation. It might be possible, too, that Satan has heard Raphael's words in the garden since for seven days, including the day of Raphael's visit to the couple, he was "compassing the Earth" by night, "cautious of day" (9.59). According to the serpent Eve meets, the fruit he offers can provide her qualities such as Raphael mentions—"ye shall be as gods . . . participating God-like food" (9.708, 717). Adam does appear to understand Raphael's message when he tells the angel,

> Well hast thou taught the way that might direct
> Our knowledge, and the scale of Nature set
> From centre to circumference, whereon
> In contemplation of created things
> By steps we may ascend to God.
>
> (5.508–12)

However, how many steps there will be in this ascension is not clearly defined. Although Eve is no doubt "Sufficient to [stand]" (3.99), Raphael's decision regarding what information to reveal to his human companions may have been a mistake.

A more recognized instance of Raphael's fallibility exists in his discussion with Adam of Adam's fascination with Eve (8.540–617). Claudia Champagne maintains that when Adam questions Eve's separate gardening, "he

strikes the pose of masculine intellectual superiority that Raphael tells him
he must embody and that Eve tries to excel by eating the fruit."[20] Although
Champagne's analysis perhaps places too great a blame on the angel, Copeland also notes Raphael's error in his discussion of Eve and human sexuality
with Adam. Copeland asserts, "Adam is certainly swayed by sensuality,
but he is by no means a slave in the mill of servile copulation, as Raphael
has portrayed him."[21] Copeland also offers an excuse for the angel's reduc-
tion of human sexuality to lust, stating, "His overemphasis arises from . . .
alarmed concern for Adam."[22] Anne Ferry, however, provides a rationale
for Raphael's odd stance on women and human marriage. She notes that
"Raphael preaches St. Paul's view of woman's relation to man."[23] She identifies Adam's reply to Raphael's interpretation of human sexuality as "not
an apology or an excuse, but a correction of the Angel's view of human
marriage. . . . Adam's reply is a lesson in human marriage."[24] Ferry's interpretation clearly supports the position that Milton has designed an angelic
being, an assumed superior being, who has much to learn from his human
companion. With neither Tobias nor Tobit will Raphael reciprocally share
information. The sharing of information in the Book of Tobit is through a
one-sided instructor/pupil relationship, whereas in *Paradise Lost* Milton
purposefully illustrates a relationship in which knowledge between prelapsarian human beings and angels is shared. Such conveniences and pleasures
are allowed to humans prior to the Fall, but like other free gifts of Eden,
this sharing relationship with the angels and easy access to beings from the
heavenly realm is altered in postlapsarian existence. Mollenkott, citing 2
Esdras 7.113, says that "this concept of free access to God in the prelapsarian world and difficulty of access in the postlapsarian world is implied
in the Canon, but is stated outright in the Apocrypha."[25] She notes, too,
Milton's adherence to the idea that access to God was "relatively easy"
before the Fall, using 3.528–29, "A passage down to th' Earth, a passage
wide, / Wider by far than that of after-times," as support.[26]

The only instance in which Tobit's Raphael seems to exhibit a more
human feature than Milton's Raphael is in his recognition of female beauty.
In the Book of Tobit, Raphael acknowledges Sarah's looks, saying, "The
girl is also beautiful and sensible" (6.12). In *Paradise Lost*, when Raphael
first meets Eve in the bower, Milton's narrator stresses her unfathomable
beauty, but Raphael greets Eve using the "holy salutation" (5.386), taking
no note of her appearance. Once again the narrator emphasizes Eve's physical beauty as she serves the meal, but again there is no response from
Raphael (5.443–50). Later, Raphael is disturbed by Adam's rapture over
Eve's beauty, responding, "For what admir'st thou, what transports thee
so, / An outside?" (8.567–68). The only instance in which the angel comments on Eve's beauty is when, in the midst of scolding Adam, he says in
regard to Eve, "fair no doubt" (8.568). Despite the apparent concession

here, mild though it is, Milton's emphasis on Raphael's inability to fully understand everything human once again diminishes the hierarchical distance between angels and human beings. Although in noticing Sarah's beauty Tobit's Raphael seems more attuned to human sense, Milton's choice to have Raphael largely ignore Eve's beauty does not diminish Milton's effectiveness because it allows Adam an opportunity to share some human understanding with his angelic companion.

Raphael undoubtedly plays a significant role in the lives of each couple in their respective narratives. However, the nature of Raphael's relationship with prelapsarian Adam and Eve is significantly different from his relationship with Tobias and Sarah in the Book of Tobit. Similarly, Adam and Eve's postlapsarian relationship with Michael will be noticeably distinguished from their sociable experience with Raphael. The fulcrum of the change in the nature of human and angelic relationships is the Fall. Sherry recognizes that "As we watch Adam conversing with 'the sociable Spirit, that deigned / To travel with Tobias,' we know very well that Adam is not Tobias, that—rather—Tobias is a remnant of Adam."[27]

This point is exactly what Milton intends to indicate to his audience. Adam will take privileges with and will freely socialize with an angel only before the Fall. Paradise allows Adam and Eve a familiarity with their hierarchical superior, so much so that Adam can quite casually say to Raphael, "thou to mankind / Be good and friendly still, and oft return" (8.650–51). Wollaeger argues, "Had they been able to, Adam and Eve would have been better off exchanging Milton's 'affable angel' for Tobit's guardian angel."[28] Hearing only instructions from Raphael and following them exactly provide Tobias a happy outcome for himself, his wife, and their families. However, the apocryphal Raphael does not have a place in *Paradise Lost*. Milton's Adam and Eve consistently exhibit characteristics which imply greater freedom and responsibility for prelapsarian humans, and even more importantly, Milton's narrative has a prescribed ending that is less happy.

> No more of talk where God or Angel Guest
> With Man, as with his Friend, familiar us'd
> To sit indulgent, and with him partake
> Rural repast, permitting him the while
> Venial discourse unblam'd.
>
> (9.1–5)

In *Paradise Lost*, Milton presents an interesting variation in Raphael's character by making him an available companion for the prelapsarian Adam and Eve, unlike the superior role Raphael assumes in the story of Tobias. In doing so, Milton successfully illustrates yet another significant loss to humankind as a result of the Fall of Adam and Eve.

Notes

1. John Milton, *Paradise Lost*, in *John Milton: Complete Poems and Major Prose*, ed. Merritt Y. Hughes (New York: Odyssey, 1957). All references to *Paradise Lost* are to this edition and are cited parenthetically in the text.
2. Virginia R. Mollenkott, "Milton and the Apocrypha" (Ph.D. diss., New York University, 1964), iv.
3. Beverly Sherry, "Milton's Raphael and the Legend of Tobias," *Journal of English and Germanic Philology* 78 (1979): 230.
4. Ibid., 234.
5. Mark A. Wollaeger, "Apocryphal Narration: Milton, Raphael, and the Book of Tobit," *Milton Studies* 21 (1985): 137.
6. Mollenkott, "Milton and the Apocrypha," 198.
7. *The New Oxford Annotated Bible with the Apocrypha*, eds. Herbert G. May and Bruce M. Metzger (New York: Oxford University Press, 1962). All scriptural references are to this edition and are cited parenthetically in the text.
8. Mollenkott, "Milton and the Apocrypha," 195.
9. Ibid., 194–95.
10. Sherry, "Milton's Raphael," 229–30, 232.
11. Quoted in Robert H. West, *Milton and the Angels* (Athens: University of Georgia Press, 1955), 47.
12. Thomas A. Copeland, "Raphael, the Angelic Virtue," *Milton Quarterly* 24 (1990): 119.
13. Ibid.
14. Ibid.
15. West, *Milton*, 164.
16. Ibid., 56.
17. Mollenkott, "Milton and the Apocrypha," 197.
18. West, *Milton*, 167–68.
19. Wollaeger, "Apocryphal Narration," 146.
20. Claudia M. Champagne, "Adam and His 'Other Self' in *Paradise Lost:* A Lacanian Study in Psychic Development," *Milton Quarterly* 25 (1991): 55.
21. Copeland, "Raphael," 125.
22. Ibid.
23. Anne Ferry, "Milton's Creation of Eve," *SEL* 28 (1988): 123.
24. Ibid., 124.
25. Virginia R. Mollenkott, "The Pervasive Influence of the Apocrypha in Milton's Thought and Art," in *Milton and the Art of Sacred Song*, ed. J. Max Patrick and Roger H. Sundell (Madison: University of Wisconsin Press, 1979), 38.
26. Virginia R. Mollenkott, "Apocrypha and Pseudepigrapha," in *A Milton Encyclopedia*, 9 vols., ed. William B. Hunter, Jr., et al. (Lewisburg, Pa.: Bucknell University Press, 1978), 1:62.
27. Sherry, "Milton's Raphael," 239.
28. Wollaeger, "Apocryphal Narration," 149.

The Education of Milton's Good Angels

Anna K. Nardo

> One gets the impression that in some mysterious way there is a drama going on in heaven which corresponds to the drama going on on earth, and that the angels are being educated in the same kind of epic quest that the human race is being educated in.
>
> Northrop Frye

According to Raphael, he and his fellow angels must make the choice to stand or fall every minute of eternity:

> Myself and all th' Angelic Host that stand
> In sight of God enthron'd, our happy state
> Hold . . . while our obedience holds;
> On other surety none; freely we serve,
> Because we freely love, as in our will
> To love or not; in this we stand or fall.
>
> (5.535–40)[1]

This heretical and eccentric doctrine of angelic freedom gives Milton's good angels the potential for conflict, failure, and growth. This potential, I want to argue, creates a subplot in *Paradise Lost*—the story of the education of the good angels. Through attempting to fulfill charges that sometimes appear futile, they receive an education in God's salvific plan and in what roles they will perform in its unfolding. The more the angels learn about man and woman—their vulnerability, mutual love, and sorrows—the better they are able to teach God's ways with compassion, love, and respect.[2]

Of course, the central story of *Paradise Lost* is the struggle for the souls of Adam and Eve, but epic is typically complex and includes multiple dramas related to the central event. On one side, Satan's story records his repeated failures to learn from Abdiel's logic (5.803–95), from Michael's sword (6.418–36), from the Son's terrifying power (6.785–99), from his own misery (4.79–110), or from Adam's and Eve's beauty and innocence (4.373–92, 9.455–72). Like those mortals who, God predicts, will scorn his "long sufferance and . . . day of grace," Satan will "hard be hard'n'd, blind be blinded more," to "stumble on, and deeper fall" (3.198, 200–1). On the other side, the story of the Son and his angels records their continued growth in understanding God's ways with humankind as well as their own angelic role in the history of salvation. Like those mortals who, God predicts, "will hear" his guiding conscience, the Son and his angels shall attain "Light after light well us'd . . . And to the end persisting, safe arrive" (3.195–97). How the angels listen, what light they attain, and where they arrive is my interest here.

We first encounter the good angels of *Paradise Lost* at the heavenly synod in book 3, as all about God's throne

> the Sanctities of Heaven
> Stood thick as Stars, and from his sight receiv'd
> Beatitude past utterance.
>
> (60–62)

After hearing the dialogue in which Father and Son work out man's salvation, the angelic host shout hosannas, bow "lowly reverent," and cast down their crowns of amaranthus and gold "With solemn adoration" (349–52). This spontaneous, yet almost liturgical, gesture of worship leads naturally to song. Reaching for the harps they keep "ever tun'd . . . glittering by thir side / Like Quivers" (366–67), they sing in perfect harmony, apparently without conductor, without discussion of the tune, without even setting the pitch. This comparison of harps to quivers suggests that spontaneous joy that erupts in song is heroic service equal to fighting God's wars. In this introduction to good angels, Milton imagines wholly other kinds of beings whose passionate love and zeal sustain them in a state of blissful anticipation, always ready to rejoice or fight or fly at command.

At key points in both *Paradise Lost* and *Paradise Regained*, God summons his ready angels to heavenly synods for the express purpose of instruction. The angels witness earthly deeds as if on a vast stage, and these dramas of God's ways with humankind confirm their faith and instruct them in God's redemptive plans. At other times, however, God charges the angels to enter the drama. Raphael tells Adam and Eve that God sends angels

> upon his high behests
> For state, as Sovran King, and to enure
> [Their] prompt obedience.
>
> (8.238–40)

Although God needs nothing to insure that what he wills occurs, the angels ornament his kingship and accustom themselves to obedience by doing his bidding. "But is that all?" many readers have asked. "Does God command the good angels to perform such futile tasks as driving Satan out of Heaven or guarding Eden against Satan's entry simply in order to create a magnificent show and exercise their faith?" If that were true, then the good angels would deserve the slights they have received from critics: to Dryden they were mere "machinery"; to others they have seemed "ornately pointless" or "little more than automata."[3]

Abdiel, that wise and brave angel, has learned from experience that God has other goals in setting tasks for his angels. To confute Satan's logic that God's command to bow before the Son diminishes the angels, Abdiel protests,

> by experience taught we know how good,
> And of our good, and of our dignity
> How provident he is, how far from thought
> To make us less, bent rather to exalt
> Our happy state under one Head more near
> United.
>
> (5.826–31)

The faithful angel knows that God commands angels to perform tasks in order to provide for their "good" and their "dignity." In citing the evidence for his knowledge, Abdiel demonstrates the central good God provides in his commands—education. "By experience," Abdiel has learned that God's goal is provident care for his angels.

Even though created perfect, unfallen Adam and Eve can learn more about their happy state. Likewise, angels can grow in knowledge of their bliss. Angelic knowledge, however, both resembles and exceeds human knowledge. Raphael explains to Adam and Eve that angelic reason has two forms:

> Discursive, or Intuitive: discourse
> Is oftest yours, the latter most is ours,
> Differing but in degree, of kind the same.
>
> (5.488–90)

Here Milton agrees with most previous commentators on angelic nature that, whereas humans learn through dialogue, angels can reason intuitively. He departs from tradition, however, in allowing for the possibility of angels learning through discourse as well.[4] In calling the synods to instruct the good angels in his ways, God expects them to learn discursively about events on earth or in the future that they could not intuit. In sending them on missions to discipline their obedience, he also expects them to learn through experience.

The War in Heaven is the turning point for this kind of experiential learning. It gives the good angels the opportunity to enact what they have

learned from experience and intuition about God's purpose for them and
to learn more in particular from their experience of warfare. By fighting
the good fight and failing, they learn in ways that no proclamation, even
from God, can teach that the Son, who rescues them on the third day
of battle, is "worthiest to be Heir / Of all things, to be Heir and to be
King" (6.707–8).

The command to drive out the rebels gives the faithful angels the opportunity to put themselves on the line for what they love most. They thrill
with zeal:

> each on himself reli'd
> As only in his arm the moment lay
> Of victory.
>
> (6.238–40)

On meeting Satan in the first day's battle, Michael is

> glad as hoping here to end
> Intestine War in Heav'n, the Arch-foe subdu'd
> Or Captive dragg'd in Chains.
>
> (258–60)

Michael does not want to claim the glory of Satan's defeat for himself;
he warns Satan that "Heav'n casts thee out," not Michael himself (272).
Nevertheless, the mighty angel does hope that his own "avenging Sword"
will be the agent of "vengeance wing'd from God" (278–79). When he
swings his sword "with huge two-handed sway" and "the horrid edge"
shears Satan's right side, he learns, however, the limits of even the famous
"sword / Of Michael," albeit forged in "the Armory of God" (251–52,
320–21). The war is not ended, Satan not subdued or chained. Despite his
pain, the nectarous humor of angelic blood closes the wound, and Satan
will return to battle with worse weapons the next day. The narrator focuses
our attention on Satan, who is

> Gnashing for anguish and despite and shame
> To find himself not matchless, and his pride
> Humbl'd by such rebuke.
>
> (340–42)

Surely, however, Michael is humbled as well. He has experienced his first
lesson in the limitation of military might. This lesson is confirmed the next
day when the good angels are so encumbered by their armor that Satan's
cannonballs, useless against spiritual forms, knock the good angels flat—

literally, although not morally, undermining their firm stance for God (590–97).

Abdiel, the angel who triumphed in reason first (29–43) before Michael was dispatched to battle, sees more clearly the purpose of angelic warfare. When Abdiel again meets Satan, this time on the battlefield, he taunts the taunter:

> th' Omnipotent . . .
> with solitary hand
> Reaching beyond all limit, at one blow
> Unaided could have finisht thee, and whelm'd
> Thy Legions under darkness; but thou seest
> All are not of thy Train; there be who Faith
> Prefer, and Pietie to God.
>
> (136–44)

Here, at its beginning, Abdiel intuits what the experience of the war will demonstrate to the faithful angels: their dependence on God to defeat the enemy.[5] He further intuits the purpose of their fighting on, even though they cannot defeat Satan alone. By fighting for God, they realize their love, faith, and piety in actions that will later win them the Son's commendation, and they manifest this true heroism before Satan, who refuses to know God through intuition, discourse, or experience. Through their futile and failed actions, the good angels learn by experience the limitations of might and bring into being the truth of their own intuitions about God's providential plans for them.[6]

Like their fellows in Heaven, Gabriel and Uriel apparently fail to accomplish their missions—but only apparently. Although, according to Uriel, Gabriel and his band are charged to keep evil out of Eden (4.561–63), they fail, and Gabriel himself seems to know that their task is impossible. When Uriel warns him of Satan's flight to Earth, Gabriel replies, "hard thou know'st it to exclude / Spiritual substance with corporeal bar" (584–85). When confronting Satan, Gabriel claims only to "have power and right / To question thy bold entrance on this place," not to be able to prevent Satan's entry (881–82). If they cannot keep Satan out of Eden, and if God knows that Satan will in fact enter Eden and that his entry will result in mankind's temptation, fall, and redemption, why does he send angels to guard the gates of Paradise? After the Fall, God even consoles the good angels with the reminder that they knew that their "sincerest care could not prevent" (10.37) Satan's success. Their divinely assigned task seems pointless.

Their commission of guardianship, however, serves the angels themselves, not their charges; it is the gift of an opportunity to serve and learn. In the flyting between Satan and Gabriel, the guardian angel—like Abdiel,

Michael, and the other warrior angels in Heaven—exercises his zeal in
God's service and his reasoning in finding the flaws in Satan's argument
about why he escaped from his bonds in Hell (4.946–50). Through his
defense, Gabriel also learns the limitation of his own abilities. In the heat
of zeal, he threatens to "drag [Satan] chain'd, / And Seal" him in "th'
infernal pit" (965–66). But God's golden scales remind him that his and
Satan's strength are

> Neither our own but giv'n; what folly then
> To boast what Arms can do, since thine no more
> Than Heav'n permits, nor mine.
>
> (1007–9)

Unlike the typical flyting hero of epics of warfare, Gabriel corrects his
mistaken assumption of prowess, withdrawing his boast and giving all the
credit to the source of his strength.

At first, Uriel seems as inept as Eden's angelic guardians. He gives the
vulture directions to his prey, because, despite being "The sharpest-sighted
Spirit of all in Heav'n" (3.691), he cannot recognize Satan's true nature
beneath his angelic disguise. Goodness is simple, the narrator remarks, and
"thinks no ill / Where no ill seems" (688–89). But the narrator also informs
us that Uriel's prime charge is readiness; he is

> one of the sev'n
> Who in God's presence, nearest to his Throne
> Stand ready at command, and are his Eyes
> That run through all the Heav'ns, or down to th' Earth
> Bear his swift errands over moist and dry,
> O'er Sea and Land.
>
> (648–53)

He seems to be both a contemplative angel, who stands in the divine presence, and a messenger angel, who runs throughout the cosmos bearing
errands. When Satan first spies him, Uriel seems rapt; then, after giving
directions to Earth, Uriel turns abruptly away saying, "Thy way thou canst
not miss, me mine requires" (735), as if merely standing on the sun were
some "way" that "requires" attention—some compelling task, like contem-
plating the divine radiance, "ready at command."

Indeed, Uriel's rapt attention to God's overflowing goodness renders
him blind to evil. When asked the way to Earth, he does not merely give
directions, but discourses at length on the wonder and delight of God's
work of creation. He makes the mistake of assuming that the motive of the
curious "stripling Cherub" (636) is his own:

> to know
> The works of God, thereby to glorify
> The great Work-Master.
>
> (694–96)

Of course, Uriel's joy and wonder at the creation are proper angelic work. But what he learns from witnessing Satan's disfiguring rage on the Assyrian mount is how very vulnerable that creation is. It requires more than contemplation; it requires action. Uriel, Gabriel, and all the guardian band have to act to protect Adam and Eve from the imminent satanic threat. Although Adam and Eve alone guard their own reason and will, the angels can and do protect their charges from physical assault. Still, their actions serve more as angelic education than as protection of Adam and Eve. Evil is quite young in this world, and the good angels have only experienced it so far in warfare, not in the form of guile. Through their failures to prevent Satan's entry into Eden, Uriel, Gabriel, and his band receive experiential instruction in the skills of guardianship—skills that, as we shall see later, they will need in future human history.

Just as Gabriel's band know that they could not prevent the Fall, so does Raphael, whom God charges to warn Adam and Eve of the danger posed by Satan.[7] After the Fall, the Father reminds "multitudes" of "Assembl'd Angels," not just the unsuccessful guardians, that he had

> Foretold . . . what would come to pass,
> When first this Tempter cross'd the Gulf from Hell.
> I told ye then he should prevail and speed
> On his bad Errand, Man should be seduc't.
>
> (10.38–41)

Here God reminds the good angels of the great synod in book 3 at which he foretold humankind's fall and the Son prepared their redemption. Surely, Raphael was also present when "all the Sanctities of Heaven / Stood thick as Stars" (60–61) around God's throne and heard that Satan

> now
> Through all restraint broke loose . . . wings his way
> . . . .
> Directly towards the new created World,
> And Man there plac't, with purpose to assay
> If him by force he can destroy, or worse,
> By some false guile pervert; and shall pervert.
>
> (86–92)

Later, Raphael's long conversation with Adam suggests that the angel remembers this prophecy of the Fall, as he imagines the results of human ingenuity: devilish engines like the ones Satan used in the War in Heaven and ridiculous systems to explain the movements of the planets and stars.

So, both Raphael and God know the angel's errand is futile, and this knowledge has puzzled critics. Apparently God's only purpose is to fulfill "All Justice," "Lest wilfully transgressing [Adam] pretend / Surprisal, unadmonisht, unforewarn'd" (5.247, 244–45). Doesn't such a motive, asks Thomas Greene, make God petty, legalistic, and self-righteous?[8] But the narrator describes God as moved "With pity" (220) upon hearing Adam and Eve's morning prayers after Eve's satanic nightmare and upon observing their innocent gardening. How can we find pity in God's dispatch of a warning he knows will fail? According to Philip Gallagher, God sends Raphael as "the harbinger of prevenient grace" before the Fall in order to facilitate Adam and Eve's regeneration after the Fall. These repeated prelapsarian warnings will soften their postlapsarian hearts so that they will convict themselves of sin, and thereby admit God's grace.[9] According to Hideyuki Shitaka, moreover, God shows both justice (by forewarning Adam and Eve) and pity (by sending "Raphael, the sociable Spirit") (5.221). God foreknows that Raphael will give the couple "a comprehensive, if shadowy, preview of the fallen world," thereby preparing them for their future.[10]

But what can any creature yet know about the fallen world? According to Aquinas, although angels can intuit the truth of what pertains to God or their own natures, they cannot know the future without divine revelation.[11] According to Milton himself, Abdiel can intuit the truth of God's ways with angels in the War in Heaven, but Raphael cannot intuit the details of Adam's and Eve's creation: he must learn them discursively through Adam's story. So, as Raphael narrates what he does know—the stories of the War in Heaven and the Creation—he can only make inferences about what he does not know, human life in the fallen world. Whereas Greene, Gallagher, and Shitaka focus on God's feelings and motives in his charge to Raphael, I want to analyze Raphael's response to that charge—a response that may reveal something about God's motives.

As Raphael wings toward Eden, his knowledge is partial. Although he learned at the synod in book 3 that humankind will fall and the Son will die to redeem them, the angel can have no knowledge as yet of the time between Adam's sin, Christ's death and resurrection, and the Last Judgment. In book 3, when the Son predicts these future events, he collapses human time so that the Resurrection seems to be immediately followed by Christ's final destruction of death and his entry into Heaven with the multitude of redeemed humanity, inaugurating the reign of bliss (3.238–65). So Raphael knows both that Adam and Eve will fall and that they may join the angelic host in this final "Joy entire" (3.265). What he cannot comprehend is the human experience of the time in between.[12]

With this burden of knowledge, what must Raphael feel when he meets the first humans? In response to Adam's humble offer of hospitality, the angel assures his anxious host that Eden and its lord are a delight comparable to the bliss of Heaven (5.371–75). At the first sight of Eve, so "lovely fair" (380), he salutes her with respect, even reverence, as the mother of a world of sons to come (388–91). Apparently, the angel is much taken with the human couple. But the language of Adam's invitation,

> voutsafe with us
>
> . . . .
>
> in yonder shady Bow'r
> To rest, and what the Garden choicest bears
> To sit and taste, till this meridian heat
> Be over, and the Sun more cool decline,
>
> (365–70)

prompts the angel to think temporally, and he replies,

> lead on then where thy Bow'r
> O'ershades; for these mid-hours, till Ev'ning rise
> I have at will.
>
> (375–77)

There is a poignancy in these lines—an awareness of the short time he has to enjoy their company and the short time of innocent bliss they have. Earlier in a soliloquy after spying on Adam and Eve, Satan had drawn our attention to the brevity of Edenic life in an ironic rendering of the carpe diem trope:

> Live while ye may,
> Yet happy pair; enjoy, till I return,
> Short pleasures, for long woes are to succeed.
>
> (4.533–35)

Of course, the fallen Satan would understand the poignancy of time that will bring loss, but how could an unfallen angel, who hymns his joy throughout eternity, know anything about time or about how it feels to love innocence and beauty that you know will fade? Raphael gains this experience while awaiting the cool of the evening in the company of mortals. By performing God's apparently futile charge to warn Adam and Eve, Raphael draws close to fellow servants (8.225), who—with all their "whole posterity," all Eve's sons—he knows must die (3.209).

Although Raphael cannot know precisely what time will bring to Adam, Eve, and their children, he can share with them his own experiences of time, the three days of the War in Heaven and the seven days of God's creation. If he cannot prevent their fall with his warnings, he can tell them his own story in the faith that God's ways with the faithful are constant. "What if," he wonders,

> Earth
> Be but the shadow of Heav'n, and things therein
> Each to other like, more than on Earth is thought?
>
> (5.574–76)

Critics have noted how Raphael's stories of Heaven—the war, the Son's rescue of the good angels, and God's responding to satanic destruction with creation—are applicable to Earth, but to the fallen more than the unfallen world.[13] After the Fall, Adam and Eve's progeny must, like the soldier angels, fight on against evil in what appears to be a stalemate, and they are to be sustained only by their faith that God will one day fulfill his promise to bruise the serpent's head.[14] Typologically, Raphael's stories prefigure Christ's defeat of death in his resurrection on the third day, his creation of a new world in believers' hearts, and finally his Second Coming to save the good, damn the evil, and create a new Heaven and Earth—all of which Raphael learned at the synod when the Son volunteered to save mankind. Raphael, of course, knows nothing about typology, but he trusts God's justice and mercy, and gives Adam and Eve a story of God's ways with angels that can sustain their hope and faith in his ways with humankind, no matter what follows their foreknown fall.

So during Raphael's visit to Adam and Eve, he takes Adam as his friend, experiences the poignancy of beauty he knows will fade, and begins the long history of angelic intervention in human history. While he fulfills God's justice by directly and repeatedly warning Adam and Eve of Satan's wiles, he also bestows a gift of friendship on his host—a story from his own past that teaches hope for humankind's future. The angel gains a boon too. To carry out their future tasks of guarding and guiding humankind, angels must feel love and pity for their charges. Toward the end of his visit, Raphael confesses his admiration for his new friend:

> Speaking or mute all comeliness and grace
> Attends thee, and each word, each motion forms.
> Nor less think wee in Heav'n of thee on Earth
> Than of our fellow servant, and inquire
> Gladly into the ways of God with Man.
>
> (8.222–26)

In sending Raphael to Eden, God forges the bond that will wing angels joyfully to Earth, even after the Fall.

So far, however, the bond is forged only with Adam. Although Adam converses with Raphael for an entire afternoon, Eve is silent, even when she is present. Raphael does not know much about women to start with, and without talking to Eve, he has little chance to learn more. As we have seen, angels know about their own natures and relation to God through intuition, but they learn about humans through discourse and experience. Although one exegetical tradition found biblical evidence of sexual intimacy between "the sons of God," interpreted to be angels, and women,[15] the narrator of *Paradise Lost* goes to some lengths to deny this tradition: although naked and beautiful, Eve has no need to fear improper advances from the virtuous angel (5.443–50).[16] Such narrative asides establish a decorous distance between Raphael and Eve. Likewise, when the discussion turns to astronomy, Eve leaves because "Her Husband the Relater she preferr'd / Before the Angel" (8.52–53). Innocence and a sense of decorum keep woman and angel apart.

Although Raphael hails Eve, when he first meets her, as "Mother of Mankind" (5.388), his understanding of her role in creation is partial. When narrating his version of the Creation story, he addresses Adam only, although Eve is present: "Male [God] created thee, but thy consort / Female for Race" (7.529–30). This account adds the extrabiblical phrase "for Race" (compare Genesis 1.27–28) and omits any mention of God's opinion that "It is not good that the man should be alone; I will make him an help meet for him" (Genesis 2.18). Whereas according to the angel, Adam's consort was made "Female for Race," the author of *The Doctrine and Discipline of Divorce* believed that the prime end of marriage is the "apt and cheerful conversation of man with woman," not procreation.[17]

Later, when Adam tells Raphael his own story of creation, we see that— even though they eat together, converse as friends all afternoon, and value each other's company highly—the man and the angel are very different kinds of creatures. Adam, in a paradise teeming with life, feels incomplete. Could a hymning angel among the heavenly host ever feel alone, "In unity defective" (8.425)—that is, defective because he is a unit? In Adam's creation story, Raphael encounters for the first time a loneliness so intense that it impels a creature to argue with his Creator to get a mate. When Adam asks his new friend to help him understand his powerful feelings for that mate, the angel is at a distinct disadvantage. He has just heard for the first time what it feels like to want a wife, for there is, according to Matthew 22.30, no marriage in Heaven. His rather stiff response confirms and bolsters Adam's own assumption of superiority. But both he and Adam seem to have temporarily forgotten what Adam asked for (8.383) and what God gave—an equal, "Thy likeness, thy fit help, thy other self" (8.450).[18]

Adam does correct the angel's misconception about his love. Eve is not a mere object of carnal enjoyment or a "Female for Race," as Raphael had assumed. She is the helpmate, solace, and complement that no angel needs. Still, the first young lover distrusts the validity of the "vehement desire . . . passion . . . Commotion strange" (8.526, 530, 531) that he feels in Eve's presence. The reader, at a safe distance from such powerful emotions, may see that, just as God's stern justice sometimes bows to mercy, so Adam's confident male superiority yields at times to unfallen Eve's radiant beauty, grace, and goodness. But Adam and Raphael—the one bewildered by love's intensity, the other put on the spot by a question beyond his knowledge— respond defensively. Adam assures Raphael (and himself?) that he knows "in the prime end / Of Nature [Eve is] th' inferior" (8.540–41), and Raphael sagely advises Adam that masculine "self-esteem" will prompt Eve to "ac- knowledge thee her Head" (8.572, 574). In this intimate conversation be- tween man and angel, both run the risk of mistaking God's open dialectic between male and female, justice and mercy, spirit and flesh, for an inflex- ible hierarchy. As a result, both have trouble understanding woman.[19]

Raphael cannot give the advice Adam needs most. At the moment of Eve's fall, Adam should not, as the angel had advised,

> weigh with her thyself;
> Then value: Oft-times nothing profits more
> Than self-esteem, grounded on just and right.
>
> (8.570–72)

He should not value Eve less and himself more, but Eve more and himself less. He should offer to die for her sin. Adam, however, lacks the boundless love of the Son. Likewise at the synod in book 3, when God asks who among the "Heav'nly Powers" will die to redeem mankind, "all the Heav'nly Choir stood mute, / And silence was in Heav'n" (3.213, 217–18). Whereas the good angels fail to volunteer to die for humankind, and Adam fails to volunteer to die for his wife, Eve offers to take all Adam's sin on her head (10.930–36). Her love will reenact the Son's offer, "Account mee man" (3.238).

Eve's and the Son's willing humiliation contrasts markedly to Adam's proper "self-esteem" and the good angels' "dignity" (5.827). Although the angels eagerly serve humanity at God's behest, the debasement required to enter human flesh, suffer, and die would be uncharacteristic behavior for angels. They are radiant in their contemplation of God and his universe, splendid in their hallelujahs and hymns of praise, magnificent as messengers posting throughout the cosmos, and grand as soldiers; they are for "state" (8.239) and "dignity" and zealous obedience, not humility and self-sacrifice. Apparently, they are, like Adam, for "contemplation . . . and valor form'd,"[20] not, like both Eve and the Son, for "softness . . . and . . . Grace"

(4.297–98). And they have lessons yet to learn about love, if they are to serve humankind throughout salvation history.[21]

These are lessons that even Michael, the "Princely Hierarch" (11.220), must learn. Whereas Raphael learns about time, loss, and love from meeting Adam and Eve, Michael learns about the horrors and heroism of fallen life as he previews human history. Whereas Raphael gives Adam and Eve the gift of a story from his past that may sustain them and their progeny in their fallen future, Michael sees and tells of this fallen future, thereby learning what role he and his fellow angels will play in salvation history.[22]

As soon as the warrior angel arrives on earth, the narrator reminds the reader of the roles of angels in human history. Michael's band is a "glorious Apparition" (11.211), which the narrator compares to two Old Testament hosts:

> Not that more glorious, when the Angels met
> Jacob in Mahanaim, where he saw
> The field Pavilion'd with his Guardians bright;
> Nor that which on the flaming Mount appear'd
> In Dothan, cover'd with a Camp of Fire,
> Against the Syrian King, who to surprise
> One man, Assassin-like had levied War.
>
> (213–19)

The angels who appear to Jacob before he meets Esau and who rescue Elisha from the treacherous Syrians exemplify for the reader the primary tasks of angels in human history: guarding the good and chastising the wicked. In the *Christian Doctrine*, Milton argues that the angels' "ministry relates especially to believers," but they "are sometimes sent from heaven as messengers of the divine vengeance, to punish the sins of men" (991). As soon as Michael arrives, before he announces his mission, the narrator reminds us of specific biblical incidents of angelic intervention about which Michael as yet knows nothing. This description thus alerts the reader to the potential for dramatic irony in Michael's account. The angel's knowledge is partial until he completes his charge; thus, at times, readers of the Bible know more than the angel about his future.

The first exchange between Michael and Adam activates this potential irony. As soon as Adam learns of his coming expulsion from the garden, he laments the loss of God's presence and asks, "In yonder nether World where shall I seek / His bright appearances, or footstep trace?" (11.328–29). Michael assures him,

> God is as here, and will be found alike
> Present, and of his presence many a sign
> Still following thee, still compassing thee round

With goodness and paternal Love, his Face
Express, and of his steps the track Divine.

(350–54)

What Michael learns only in telling his story is that the angels will at times "bear the appearance of the divine glory and person, and even speak in the very words of the Deity" (*Christian Doctrine*, 945). In the *Christian Doctrine*, Milton says that, when the biblical patriarchs see or hear God, "it was not God himself . . . but perhaps one of the angels clothed in some modification of the divine glory" (945). When Michael later tells Adam how Moses parted the Red Sea and how God led the Israelites in their flight from Pharaoh, the angel marvels,

Such wondrous power God to his Saint will lend,
Though present in his Angel, who shall go
Before them in a Cloud, and Pillar of Fire,
By day a Cloud, by night a Pillar of Fire,
To guide them in thir journey, and remove
Behind them, while th' obdúrate King pursues.

(12.200–205)

First as the Israelites' guard and guide, then as the destroyer, who "will trouble all [Pharaoh's] Host / And craze thir Chariot wheels" (12.209–10), the angel in the cloud and pillar bears God's presence. Michael learns what divine charges to expect in his own future as he relates Adam's future.

The prophetic visions Michael interprets and the stories he relates are the product of God's enlightenment of his angelic intuitive intellect. Michael both receives God's revelation of humankind's future and conveys that revelation to Adam. Without divine revelation, not even this prince among angels could know of murder, sickness, old age, war, or the flood—the panorama of future human misery that passes before both him and Adam. And this sight moves him profoundly. When he sees the first vision of Cain's murder of Abel, not Adam alone is horror-struck; "hee [Michael is] also mov'd" (11.453). With eyes purged of the film bred of sin, Adam sees this gory spectacle and does not need a graphic description to feel its horror. Nevertheless, Michael uses vivid language to describe what he and Adam both see: "here thou see [Abel] die, / Rolling in dust and gore" (459–60). The superfluous but powerful image he chooses reveals Michael's own shock at this first glimpse of human death.

Of course, Michael has seen violence before. He himself had sheared Satan's side in the War in Heaven, but that wound healed instantly, and angels cannot, except by annihilation, die (6.344–47). In Abel's death, Michael as well as Adam learns what death is:

                                      sight
Of terror, foul and ugly to behold,
Horrid to think, how horrible to feel!

                                    (11.463–65)

While Adam must learn from Michael's story how to live in a world of death, Michael must learn how to guard and guide humankind through that future.

In the final scene of expulsion, this mutual education culminates as angel, man, and woman begin to enact what they have learned. Although the angels at the gate, "With dreadful Faces throng'd and fiery Arms" (12.644), threaten punishment for re-entry, Adam and Eve enter the fallen world with an angelic guide. Surely one aspect of "Providence thir guide" (647) is the lessons of God's faithfulness that they have learned from Raphael and Michael. Likewise, in expelling Adam and Eve from the garden, Michael and his band perform the angelic roles Michael has just learned through vision and narration; they become guardians, guides, and agents of punishment. While his cohort raises the "flaming Brand" (643) to guard the gate of Paradise, Michael takes Adam and Eve in hand, leads them down from Eden, and turns them out of one paradise toward their quest for another (625–49).

Now, however, Michael takes Eve's as well as Adam's hand. Despite his military aspect, his exalted position in the angelic ranks (*Christian Doctrine*, 991), and his charge to expel the sinners, Michael comes closer to Eve than did Raphael, who became Adam's friend. The "Princely Hierarch," not "the sociable Spirit," actually converses with the woman. Albeit "unseen" (11.265) in the "place of her retire" (267), Eve grieves openly that she must leave the garden. Michael listens to her lament at the loss of those flowers she had "bred up with tender hand / From the first op'ning bud" (276–77) and the "nuptial Bower" she had "adorn'd / With what to sight or smell was sweet" (280–81), and he responds directly to her lament with "mild" instruction (286). Then later, while interpreting the vision of the "Bevy of fair Women" (11.582), he dismisses these "fair Atheists" (625) as mere toys for men's pleasure, while valorizing women's domesticity as worthy of praise. In his condemnation, Michael echoes what he heard in Eve's earlier lament; women's work nurtures life and creates beauty, and Michael, therefore, accords it due "honor."[23] An angel has learned something from a woman.

As Michael narrates salvation history, he learns more about women; he sees beyond Raphael's assumption that Eve and her daughters serve primarily as men's mates "for Race" (7.530), as their "weaker" (6.909), and as beauties "Made so adorn for [their] delight the more" (8.576). Eve, he discovers, will become the vessel of humankind's deliverance. Although he tells Adam to instruct her about the "great deliverance by her Seed to come" (12.600), he has given her more direct instruction, a portentous dream (595–96).[24] Eve—having understood the angel's communication through her dream, without Adam's mediating instruction—knows immediately upon waking that she will bear "the Promis'd Seed" that "shall all restore" (623). In contrast to her earlier silence before Raphael, her preference for Adam's instruction, and Raphael's confusion about women, Eve and Michael communicate directly and learn from each other. The angel teaches the woman to face her expulsion from the garden with courage and hope, and the woman teaches the angel compassion and respect for women's work and their role in salvation history.

Only at the moment of expulsion—with Adam chastened but faithful, with Eve submissive but consoled, with Michael enlightened but "mov'd"— do man, woman, and angel finally comprehend what lies behind Raphael's hopeful surmise that humankind, "Improv'd by tract of time" (5.498), might one day participate in heavenly feasts with angels, "If ye be found obedient" (501). In fulfilling God's charge to "reveal / To Adam what shall come in future days" (11.113–14), Michael has learned what Raphael did not know— the sorrows and terrors the "tract of time" will bring—as well as what Raphael did know—the final reward to the obedient.

What I have tried to show in this discussion of Abdiel's, Gabriel's, Uriel's, Raphael's, and Michael's roles in *Paradise Lost* is that the good angels are not dismissible as mere "machinery," as "ornately pointless," or as "little more than automata." They are characters with the potential to fail and learn in a subplot of angelic education. Through their apparent futility in guarding Eden and Heaven, the good angels learn their own limitations, experience and manifest the truth of their intuitions about God's love, and discover the vulnerability of the human charges they must learn to love. Through their relations with humankind, they confront what they could never have known intuitively—the poignancy of human time, the love of man and woman, the misery of fallen humanity, and their future roles in salvation history.

This angelic subplot expands the vision of *Paradise Lost* in a baroque sweep beyond its focus on Satan, Adam, and Eve. In sinless, but narcissistic naïveté, Eve asks why the stars shine when she and Adam are asleep, and Adam's answer calls her attention to the angels: "Millions of spiritual Creatures . . . with ceaseless praise [God's] works behold / Both day and night" (4.677–80). Likewise, the experiences and feelings of the good angels remind readers, prone as we all are to narcissism, that human beings are not God's only beloved creations and that the drama of their fall and redemption is not God's only care. His providence extends to his radiant, ready angels, whom he instructs and assigns tasks so that "Light after light well us'd they shall attain" (3.196).

Notes

Northrop Frye, *Five Essays on Milton's Epics* (London: Routledge and Kegan Paul, 1966), 34.

1. John Milton, *Paradise Lost*, in *John Milton: Complete Poems and Major Prose*, ed. Merritt Y. Hughes (New York: Odyssey, 1957). All references to Milton's poetry and prose are to this edition and are cited parenthetically in the text. See also "Of the Special Government of Angels," in the *Christian Doctrine*, 990. Robert H. West, *Milton and the Angels* (Athens: University of Georgia Press, 1955), argues that Milton's heretical doctrine of angelic free will "is of no importance in *Paradise Lost*," 164; see also 125, 162–63.

2. Critics have studied the way angels look (Roland Mushat Frye, *Milton's Imagery and the Visual Arts: Iconographic Tradition in the Epic Poems* [Princeton: Princeton University Press, 1978], 169–88); their relation to previous epic messengers from the gods (Thomas Greene, *The Descent from Heaven: A Study in Epic Continuity* [New Haven: Yale University Press, 1963], 363–411); their place in the history of angel lore (West, *Milton and the Angels*); and their role as educators for Adam and Eve (Kathleen M. Swaim, *Before and After the Fall: Contrasting Modes in "Paradise Lost"* [Amherst: University of Massachusetts Press, 1986], and Michael Allen, "Divine Instruction: *Of Education* and the Pedagogy of Raphael, Michael, and the Father," *Milton Quarterly* 26 [December 1992]: 113–21). Seldom, however, have the good angels been taken seriously as characters who can feel and develop.

3. Critics who address the role of the good angels in the epic plot often dismiss them as merely useful "machines" (John Dryden, "A Discourse Concerning the Original and Progress of Satire," in *Essays of John Dryden*, 2 vols., ed. W. P. Ker [New York: Russell and Russell, 1961], 2:34); as ineffectual ("Voltaire on Milton: 1727," in *Milton: The Critical Heritage*, ed. John T. Shawcross [London: Routledge and Kegan Paul, 1970], 256); as "ornately pointless" (West, *Milton and the Angels*, 107–20); as "absurd" and unimaginative (J. B. Broadbent, *Some Graver Subject: An Essay on "Paradise Lost"* [New York: Barnes and Noble, 1960], 199–200, 212); even as "automata—and sterile, promiscuous, monosexual automata at that" (John Peter Rumrich, *Matter of Glory: A New Preface to "Paradise Lost"* [Pittsburgh: University of Pittsburgh Press, 1987], 175).

Two analyses of the War in Heaven, however, have emphasized the heroism of the good angels' faithful stand for God (Boyd M. Berry, *Process of Speech: Puritan Religious Writing and "Paradise Lost"* [Baltimore: Johns Hopkins University Press, 1976], 170–90) and their education in the limits of warfare (Stella P. Revard, *The War in Heaven: "Paradise Lost" and the Tradition of Satan's Rebellion* [Ithaca: Cornell University Press, 1980], 126–27, 190). I am indebted to these studies.

4. According to Aquinas, angels know themselves and God "by an act that rises from a power of which their essence is a condition. They know other creatures by intellectual forms or species." According to Duns Scotus, general intellectual forms are infused by God, but particular ones are received from the things themselves. Aquinas, however, contends "that all these species are infused at the beginning of the world as perfect forms to be actuated at need by the angel's perfect understanding."

Although angels understand consequences in nature, claims Aquinas, they cannot know the future without divine revelation (West, *Milton and the Angels*, 47, 140).

West assumes that Milton followed the Catholic tradition, derived from Aquinas, in which angels "know the world by intuition rather than discourse" (126). Raphael, however, does not make this claim: he says (1) that discourse is "oftest" Adam's mode of reasoning, (2) that intuition is "most" often the angels' mode of reasoning, and (3) that the two modes are of the same kind, differing only in degree (5.487–90). So, according to Raphael, discourse is also a mode of reasoning available to angels, and Abdiel states directly that he has learned from experience (5.826–28).

5. Revard, *War in Heaven*, 127.

6. Ibid., 247.

7. The following studies call attention to Raphael's foreknowledge: Thomas A. Copeland, "Raphael, the Angelic Virtue," *Milton Quarterly* 24 (December 1990): 119; Hideyuki Shitaka, "'Them thus employed beheld / With pity heaven's high king': God's Dispatch of Raphael in *Paradise Lost*, Book 5.219–47," *Milton Quarterly* 24 (1990), 130–31; Philip J. Gallagher, *Milton, the Bible, and Misogyny*, ed. Eugene R. Cunnar and Gail L. Mortimer (Columbia: University of Missouri Press, 1990), 140.

8. Greene, *Descent from Heaven*, 409.

9. Gallagher, *Milton, the Bible, and Misogyny*, 137–50.

10. Shitaka, "'Them thus employed beheld,'" 130.

11. West, *Milton and the Angels*, 47.

12. Throughout *Before and After the Fall*, Swaim describes the knowledge that Raphael teaches in Platonic terms: "Raphael is preparing for a human future that can grow toward perfection without the trauma of the fall" (231). At dinner, the angel does express his hope that Adam and Eve, "Improv'd by tract of time," may one day become spirits, dwelling in heaven, "If ye be found obedient" (5.496–503). Nothing in this passage contradicts the Son's vision of humankind's future, confirmed by the Father, that Raphael heard at the synod in book 3 (260–65, 334–41). All the angels heard that, although Adam and Eve will fall, humankind will eventually be reunited with God through the Son's act of atonement. But, because human time is collapsed in the Son's prediction, Raphael cannot yet know what ages of suffering the "tract of time" between the Crucifixion and the Last Judgment will bring.

13. William G. Madsen, *From Shadowy Types to Truth: Studies in Milton's Symbolism* (New Haven: Yale University Press, 1968), 110–11; Revard, *War in Heaven*, 278–300; Shitaka, "'Them thus employed beheld,'" 130.

14. Berry, *Process of Speech*, 179–83.

15. West, *Milton and the Angels*, 129–31; James Grantham Turner, *One Flesh: Paradisal Marriage and Sexual Relations in the Age of Milton* (Oxford: Clarendon, 1987), 268–71.

16. For Eve's innocence in the sight of angels, see *Paradise Lost*, 4.319–20. Also compare 5.383–85 to 1 Corinthians 11.1–15, and compare 5.445–50 and 11.573–627 to Genesis 6.2–4.

17. *The Doctrine and Discipline of Divorce*, 703.

18. This intimate scene between two males, both confused, trying to decide what to do with the first woman, does not, as several critics have noted, give Milton's final word on gender hierarchy: David Aers and Bob Hodge, "'Rational Burning': Milton on Sex and Marriage," *Milton Studies* 23 (1979): 23–27; Diane Kelsey McColley, *Milton's Eve* (Urbana: University of Illinois Press, 1983), 88; F. Peczenik, "Fit Help: The Egalitarian Marriage in *Paradise Lost*," *Mosaic* 17 (1984): 31; Barbara

.Kiefer Lewalski, *"Paradise Lost" and the Rhetoric of Literary Forms* (Princeton: Princeton University Press, 1985), 216–18; Stevie Davies, *The Idea of Woman in Renaissance Literature: The Feminine Reclaimed* (Brighton: Harvester, 1986), 228–29; Turner, *One Flesh*, 273–81; Rumrich, *Matter of Glory*, 101; Copeland, "Raphael, the Angelic Virtue," 124–25; Allen, "Divine Instruction," 116. Rather, Adam's conversation with Raphael dramatizes the limitations of angelic advice about marriage.

19. The Son seems to confirm Raphael's insistence on Adam's superiority when he judges the couple after the Fall (10.145–56), but he is responding to Adam's lie. To excuse his trespass, Adam whines that God made Eve so perfect that he could not have suspected any evil from her. At the moment of the Fall, however, Adam knows full well that accepting the fruit is evil (9.998). His motive is self-love, not love for Eve: "How can *I* live without thee" (9.908; emphasis mine), he laments. Later in the judgment scene, the Son emphasizes Adam's "dignity" and greater fitness "to bear rule" (10.151, 155) in order to place the blame for his own fall squarely on Adam. After exercising God's justice, however, the Son reassumes his role as servant and vessel of love and mercy, clothing the couple's naked bodies with skins of beasts and their "inward nakedness" with "his Robe of righteousness" (10.215–23). Here, as elsewhere throughout the epic, the dialectic between justice and love complicates easy assumptions about hierarchy.

20. Although in the catalogue of demons the narrator claims that angels can assume either sex (1.422–31), all the angels we meet in *Paradise Lost* are male.

21. In particular, Raphael and Adam's conversation about Eve gives the angel the opportunity to learn about human love and marriage before his future charge to help Tobias win his bride away from her demon lover Asmodeus (see 4.166–71; 5.221–23).

22. See Swaim's differing view of the contrasts between Raphael and Michael (*Before and After the Fall*, 1–25). She sees Raphael's perspective as Platonic, Michael's as typological.

23. For Milton's valorization of woman's work, see McColley, *Milton's Eve*, 110–39, and "Eve and the Arts of Eden," in *Milton and the Idea of Woman*, ed. Julia M. Walker (Urbana: University of Illinois Press, 1988), 100–119.

24. See West (*Milton and the Angels*, 126) for a discussion of the angelic ability to control bodily humors in order to produce dreams and visions.

"Conscious Terrours": Seventeenth-Century Obstetrics and Milton's Allegory of Common Sin in *Paradise Lost*, Book 2

Louis Schwartz

IN the course of research into the lives and untimely deaths of Mary Powell and Katherine Woodcock for an essay on Milton's Sonnet 23, I discovered a wealth of very disturbing information about the nature of sixteenth- and seventeenth-century obstetric practices, and this has made me rethink the significance of birth imagery in a number of sixteenth- and seventeenth-century poems.[1] Perhaps one of the most surprising facts I have discovered is that of all poets in the period, Milton stands out as one of the most concerned with poetry's ability to respond to the emotional and spiritual problems presented by what can only be described as catastrophic circumstances. In sixteenth- and seventeenth-century London, women of the middle and upper classes were dying in childbed at a rate of approximately one death per forty births.[2] With fertility rates of as high as one birth every eighteen to twenty-two months (an average of eight to fifteen births in a lifetime), a married woman stood approximately a one-in-four chance of dying in childbirth in the course of her fertile years.[3] Both Mary Powell and Katherine Woodcock in fact died of childbed complications.

Milton not only wrote one of the few and one of the most poignant poems concerning a husband's grief over death in childbed (Sonnet 23), but he also wrote one of the most elaborate of the few conventional funeral epitaphs that deal explicitly with childbed death ("An Epitaph on the Marchioness of Winchester") and, as this essay argues, he made disastrous childbirth an important motif in the structure of *Paradise Lost*. In my essay on Sonnet 23, I argued not only that Milton's sonnet was best understood in relation to certain obstetric rituals and practices, but that, by echoing the sonnet's first and last lines in Adam's description to Raphael of the creation of Eve in book 8, he draws the childbed deaths of his first two wives into *Paradise Lost*. The moment of the creation of the first woman and hence of the conditions of sexuality and marriage comes to us in the form of an evocative reversal of one of the most troubling aspects of postlapsarian married life. In fact, Adam's description contains several details that suggest obstetric surgery (a kind of painless caesarian section with God serving as male surgeon). Milton's treatment of this "birth" stretches the limits of traditional literary and theological birth imagery, tying it to concrete contemporary conditions and practices.

The allegory of Sin and Death at the end of book 2 is another important instance in which Milton alludes to birth in ways that go beyond traditional literary and theological usage. The passage in fact contains obstetric imagery of an uncommon specificity, and this has very important implications for the way we read figures of birth in the epic. The allegory of Sin and Death is the crux of a complex rhetorical strategy by which Milton represents the transmission and reversal of sin. Birth has always been a central figure in the narratives of the Fall and the nativity.[4] It was, however, also one of the central and most appalling ways in which fallenness was experienced by human beings in the seventeenth century. In associating Sin with contemporary obstetric conditions, Milton is therefore emphasizing something that is both inherent in Eve's curse (Genesis 3.16) and very vivid for seventeenth-century Christians: that the childbed was a place in which men and women regularly confronted some of the most difficult aspects of the human condition (the vulnerability of the body to pain and disease, the suffering of the innocent, and the death of loved ones).

The naturalistic referents of Milton's allegory, which most critics have warned against taking too literally, provide more than merely the narrative connections necessary for the expression of the theology of sin or the ontology of evil in Milton's system. Their obstetric content complicates the referentiality of the episode, drawing the reader into an elaborate network of identifications with its allegorical figures. The obstetric content of Milton's imagery also suggests that the ways we have traditionally read the episode's references to moral and theological abstractions have been too narrow. The allegorical reference of Sin should not be limited, as most readings would have it, to the experience of temptation to what Milton calls in the *Christian Doctrine* "individual sin" (6:382–92).[5] Readings that make this assumption necessarily construct a temptation narrative whose subject is male. Satan or the reader is enticed by Sin's original beauty only to see her transformed into something terrible (or after her fall by the alluring upper half of her body, only to discover her scaly lower half and stinging tail). I would instead suggest that the allegory, while still making use of the more traditional narrative, complicates it with reference to "common sin," the sin that, again according to Milton in the *Christian Doctrine*, is common to all human beings after the Fall and that to a large extent limits and challenges the individual's exercise of free will. "Common sin," as Milton defines it (6:382–92), is best understood as the context in which the temptation to "individual sin" is acted out. The obstetric focus that Milton's unconventional manipulation of his literary and theological sources gives the passage leads to a reading that, therefore, places birth at the center of a complex allegorical tableau, making it a central figure for the fallen condition itself and providing subject positions that are gendered both male and female.

1

To a reader familiar with the suffering of women in childbed during the seventeenth century, Sin's pitiable and extravagant account of her own experiences has a referential concreteness not wholly accounted for by an allegorical reading. The account, in fact, closely follows several specific ideas about birth held by most educated Londoners of the age and suggests some of the consequences of seventeenth-century surgical solutions to various forms of abnormal childbirth. For example, the account concerning Death's tearing through his mother's entrails, effecting his own birth and leaving her terribly disfigured, strikingly parallels descriptions of birth typically found in seventeenth-century medical literature. Here is Sin's description of the birth of Death:

> Pensive here I sat
> Alone, but long I sat not, till my womb
> Pregnant by thee, and now excessive grown
> Prodigious motion felt and rueful throes.
> At last this odious offspring whom thou seest
> Thine own begotten, breaking violent way
> Tore through my entrails, that with fear and pain
> Distorted, all my nether shape thus grew
> Transform'd.
>
> (2.777–85)[6]

The following is a passage describing the onset of labor and birth from Ambroise Paré's *Works,* one of the most often cited medical texts of the time:

When the naturall prefixed and prescribed time of child-birth is come, the childe being then growne greater, requires a greater quantity of food: which when he cannot receive in sufficient measure by his navell, with great labour and striving hee endeavoreth to get forth: therefore then hee is moved with a stronger violence, and doth breake the membranes wherein he is contained. . . . [T]he wombe, because it is not able to endure such violent motions . . . by reason that the conceptacles of the membranes are broken asunder, is relaxed. And then the childe pursuing the aire which hee feeleth to enter in at the mouth of the wombe, which then is very wide and gaping, is carried with its head downewards, and so commeth into the world, with great pain both unto it selfe, and also unto his mother.[7]

The belief that the infant was physically active in its birth was very strong in the period, and almost all the obstetric literature contains descriptions of birth that are remarkable for the violence they ascribe to the infant.[8] William Harvey, for example, in his *Anatomical Exercitations*, argues that "the assistance of the *foetus* is chiefly required in the *birth*," relating several anecdotes of postmortem deliveries and ruptured wombs explained by the still-living infant's action.[9] He also tells a story about a woman whose genital tissues were closed off by the scars she had acquired in a particularly difficult delivery only to have the passage opened again by the action of her next child:

> I also knew a *Woman*, who had all the interior part of the neck of her *Womb* excoriated and torne, by a *difficult* and *painful delivery:* so that her time of *Lying in* being over, though she proved with Child againe afterward, yet not onely the sides of the *Orifice* of the *Neck* of the *Womb* neer the *Nymphae* did close together, but all the whole *Cavity* thereof, even to the *inner Orifice* of the *Matrix*, whereby there was no entrance even for a small *probe*, nor yet any egress to her *usual fluxes*. Hereupon the time of her delivery being now arrived, the poor soul was lamentably tortured, and laying aside all expectation of being delivered, she resigned up her keys to her Husband, and setting her affairs in order, she took leave of all her friends. When behold, beyond expectation, by the strong contest of a very lusty Infant, the whole tract was forced open, and she was miraculously *delivered;* the lusty Child proving the *author of his own*, and *his Parents life*, leaving the passage open for the rest of his Brethren who should be borne in time to come.[10]

The birth of Death in *Paradise Lost* is unnaturally violent and a grotesque exaggeration, but it follows the same basic and familiar etiology. In a terrible parody of a normal healthy infant, Death, "breaking violent way," tears unnecessarily through his mother's pregnant, though presumably still "heav'nly fair" (2.757), body. His birth is announced by the "prodigious motion" of the monstrous infant and the "rueful throes" of the womb that cannot contain him. His birth goes through the sequence thought normal in the seventeenth century. And in both cases (and in that of the hounds he later forcibly engenders on his mother), the child emerges hungry.

Like the women in Harvey's anecdotes and Paré's medical account, Sin in addition is portrayed as entirely subject to the actions of her infant. The child, not the mother (or even her body), is understood as the agent of birth. We will return to the significance of this below, but a good deal of the episode's pathos derives from Sin's helplessness. This child not only causes "great pain both unto it selfe, and also unto his mother," but it also causes her to undergo the process, while, like Scylla, she in fear and pain watches helplessly as her formerly beautiful body is distorted and trans-formed into something terrible.

Sin's transformation from heavenly beauty to detestable monstrosity is essentially allegorical in its meaning. It is like the transformation of Satan and the other rebel angels, whose tarnished and ruined appearance in Hell is the external, figurative measure of their fall from grace. The permanent transfiguration of the lower half of Sin's body, which Milton adapts from Ovid's account of Scylla (with some telling alterations), also, however, has its correlative in the contemporary experience of childbirth. Practices that led to permanent external disfigurement of women were very common in the period. Although a certain amount of tearing of the perineal tissues is common in normal childbirth, beliefs among seventeenth-century obstetric practitioners, mostly deriving from the recommendations of the single most influential midwifery handbook of the period, *The Birth of Mankind*,[11] caused a good deal of extra harm. This was further exacerbated by a sort of "cult of difficulty" among middle class women who believed that difficult birth was a sign of greater cultural and spiritual refinement.[12] Many otherwise normal births were, as a result, far more torturous and disfiguring than they had to be.

Percival Willughby, a male midwife and obstetric surgeon active in Derby, Stafford, and London from 1621 to 1670, railed against the hastiness of untrained midwives who went for a knife, a makeshift hook, or manual dilation of the cervix and vagina when more sensible, gentler techniques could do the job with greater safety and less pain.[13] Willughby gives some terrifying accounts of cases in which he and his sister (his partner in the practice and later a midwife on her own) were called in to aid women who were harmed by disturbingly common practices. Accounts like the following give us a glimpse of what many women had to suffer, describing another set of beliefs and circumstances that resonate in Sin's narrative.

> Let all cruelties, as cutting of children in pieces in the mother's womb, with all violent wayes in every difficult labour, bee forborn. For it retardeth the births, and, oft lacerating the body of the woman, maketh her paines intolerable, which renders her so weake, and heartles, that shee hath no strength left to endure her throws, and the child's enforcements. Whosoever useth such harshnes, may well be branded with cruelty, and ignorance in midwifery.
>
> A London midwife, very officious, endeavouring to have a speedy delivery, through haling, and stretching those tender parts, made a labour of long continuance, and, with her halings, a breach about an inch long into the fundament. With this affliction the woman was much disquieted. For ever afterward her excrements came forth by the birth place; yet this woman did much commend her laborious midwife, and said that she took great paines to deliver her, to save her life.
>
> This fact was done in Fleet-street. The woman came to me for help, and shewed me her torn body.[14]

Cases of this kind were not only common, but also occasioned more than temporary trauma. As the anecdote from Harvey that I quoted earlier shows, the injuries suffered in a difficult birth could follow a woman for years as a permanent disfiguration, one that could make her subsequent births even more frightening and painful. Willughby goes on to recommend, for this reason, that if a woman can endure the kind of problem he describes, it is better to leave it than to cure it: "Where this grief can, without trouble bee suffered, it will bee much better not to meddle with it, then to endeavour to cure it. For it will cause the next labour to bee more dolorous, and difficult, by making new laceration, or incision." He argues that the woman's physical state should be left in the condition most conducive to further childbearing: "not being cured, the ensuing births will bee more easy, by reason of the spaciousnes of the breach, the vulva and intestinum rectum being laid together, and making but one passage."[15] Audrey Eccles, in her study of Tudor and Stuart gynecology, notes that this practice was common: "It seems likely," she states, "that unless the tear was too extensive to live with it was more usual to leave the cure to nature, or to use medicines only."[16] *The Birth of Mankind* recommended a two-part bandage that could be sewn together to facilitate healing, but it was uncommon for a practitioner to attempt actually stitching a woman's perineal tissue. The rigidity of the scar, it was believed, would make another breech unavoidable, and this was thought undesirable despite the fact that Paré and other French writers recommended stitching for reasons related as much to sexual pleasure as to procreation: "the Excrements coming that way disgust the Husband," noted one French physician, "and the Woman is by no means fit for his Caresses."[17]

For a reader who lived in Milton's London, such incidents and practices were a part of the texture of everyday life. For such a reader, Sin's account of the birth of Death and its permanently disfiguring transformation of her lower half could very well have brought to mind the painful and lingering suffering of women like those described in these passages. Sin's transformation makes her unrecognizable and repugnant to the father of her child. Tearing her open Death is like the child in Harvey's account preparing the way for his siblings. Thus begins a cycle of painful repetitions of an event that many women would experience over and over again every eighteen to twenty-two months until they either died or entered menopause.

Sin's narrative also suggests a host of other conditions and beliefs. The passages in book 2 present the relationships between Satan, Sin, and Death as a set of incestuous sexual acts (one a rape) and, as a result, they associate the operations of Sin and Death with other extremely painful aspects of human experience: with female vulnerability to male sexual violence and also to widowhood and abandonment.[18] Sin speaks of herself in her narrative as a sort of war widow and "single mother," abandoned and deformed, until she meets Satan again at the gates of Hell. The episode is a ghastly reunion, and Satan himself, after hearing Sin's story and recognizing who she is, behaves like an aristocratic libertine confronted with the illegitimate results of some courtly backstair work.

In their repeated regress into the womb and their gnawing at Sin's bowels, the behavior of the hounds who are born of her rape may evoke images of the fevers and hemorrhaging that killed many women in the days or weeks particularly following their giving birth, particulary since these conditions followed many women for years after a particularly difficult birth and since each new birth brought fears of further pain.[19] Furthermore, the goading on of these monsters by Death, the "conscious terrours" (2.801) with which they vex his mother at his instigation, suggests an allegorization of the role that fear of death, disease, and deformity played in the imaginations of women who were about to give birth and who, given their high fertility rate, lived approximately half of their lives pregnant.

There is evidence that obstetric anxieties were, in fact, a significant cause of mental illness among women. For example, Michael McDonald's study of the medical-practice notes of Richard Napier, an astrological physician and Anglican divine who was active in Oxford and Buckinghamshire from 1580 to 1634, cites the tribulations of childbirth as an important factor in mental disorders: "Women who survived were sometimes irreparably mangled. The suffering childbirth caused cannot be estimated accurately, but the fear, stress, and illnesses induced by difficult births contributed to the mental disorders of 81 of Napier's patients, including one man who was so frightened by his wife's awful pain that he went mad."[20]

Because of Death's shapelessness and voracity, his birth should also be understood as a monstrous birth, something that the Renaissance found deeply fascinating (Death is called a "Monster" at line 675, his movements in Sin's womb at the onset of delivery are "prodigious"; the hounds are also called "Monsters" at line 795). Medical and zoological texts as well as broadside ballads and wonderbooks provided an almost endless stream of tales of monstrosity in the period, a rich and strange literature that itself deserves further study.[21]

The birth of death, because it is "Death" being born, finally suggests a grotesquely deforming stillbirth. Stillbirth was one of the most common causes of obstetric complications in the period, in part because it was believed that a dead infant could not effect its own birth and strenuous measures had to be used to remove it.[22] These often included the dismemberment of the dead infant with special cutting tools and hooks. Stillbirth also brought with it increased risk of infection from the often putrefying corpse of the dead infant, and this risk was increased further by unskillful midwives and surgeons who often severely lacerated the inside of a woman's womb in the process of surgical, or manual, removal of the infant.[23] The birth of a dead infant, in other words, often meant death for the mother. This last suggestion stands paradoxically juxtaposed with the suggestions of a violently active infant, but the juxtaposition actually supports the moral allegory, giving Death a resonant double nature. Just as he seems to the narrator at line 669 to be both shadow and substance, he is both active and static, the sign of an event that brings the cessation of all events.

"[R]est or intermission none I find" and "Before mine eyes in opposition sits / Grim Death" (2.802–4). These are words from *Paradise Lost* that a typical seventeenth-century married woman was likely to find echoed her own sentiments, given that in the course of her fertile years, if she lived through them at all, she was likely to be pregnant between ten and fifteen times, and often sick, and perhaps disfigured. The passage provides in the voice of Sin a position from which a female reader can recognize very "conscious terrours" indeed.

2

In constructing the allegory of book 2, Milton drew on traditional materials, but he reworked these materials in order to emphasize figures of birth in his narrative. Pregnancies and their effects, therefore, become central to the function of his allegory in ways not encompassed by the original literary sources (for example, Fletcher, Ovid, and Spenser) or by the oft-cited genealogies of Sin found in the espistle of James and in St. Basil.[24]

Milton draws, for example, on Redcross Knight's confrontation with Error in *The Faerie Queene*, altering and refocusing certain Spenserian details. Both Sin and Error are described as grotesque mothers. Milton's images retain some of the force of perverted nurturing and cannibalism, but he exchanges Spenser's scatology for a focus on obstetrics. Not only does the womb replace the mouth as the place of regress, but the fathering and birthing of the children are described with attention to the physical consequences for the mother.[25]

It is important that the transformation of Sin's lower half and also the fear and pain caused by the "conscious terrours" that vex her after she is raped by her son and gives birth to the hounds are results of her painfully giving birth twice, and that these births alter her original beauty. This is, in fact, perhaps the most striking change Milton rings on his literary antecedents. Both Spenser's Error and Fletcher's Hamartia are born in their deformed state. Ovid's Scylla is transformed, but the metamorphosis has no obstetric connection (though this is where Milton probably got the idea of the dogs). Milton's change not only gives birth pride of place in the narrative, but his descriptions emphasize the physicality of birth and the fact that it is something that happens to a woman as a result of sex with or without the cooperation of her will.

This is, as I have said, in large part responsible for the peculiar pathos of the narrative. Sin's pregnancies, especially the second one, are unwanted, and her experience of them is of processes beyond her control, enforced from without, occurring within, and then exploding out again and repeating the cycle with further pain and mutilation. The description of these processes gives the passage an affective complexity that belies simple allegorical reference. The difference between Sin's own speech and that of the narrator, the first to describe her to us, is, for example, telling. He focuses on the loathsome appearance of the allegorical pair, but she delivers an account of her life that seems designed to provoke a very different response. She begins by lamenting her ugliness, tells of her "birth" from Satan's head, speaks with pride of her original beauty and with nostalgia of her dalliance with her father and their subsequent separation by the War in Heaven. She then goes on to detail a gruesome family romance. The pregnancies and births that resulted from her congress with her father and her subsequent rape by her newborn son, Death, are described carefully and with a pathos that is surprisingly affecting, given the name of the speaker and our understanding of her present rhetorical need to move Satan (*Paradise Lost*, 2.777–87, 790–809).

Because her physical suffering is so fully imagined by Milton, and because suffering of this kind was so familiar to seventeenth-century Londoners, it is hard not to sympathize with Sin's helplessness and pain—and this despite the satiric grotesquery of other parts of the episode. Hers is a story of a transformation that has been forced upon her and is beyond her control. She is in this sense very close to her model in Scylla, and just like that Ovidian character, she becomes first deformed and then demonic. At this moment, however (as it is in the first part of Ovid's narrative), the primary effect is of pathos. And the effect is meant to be disarming, though not just for Satan and not only to lure us into identification with Sin in a Fishian way.

Her lines pull us in two directions. On one hand we are presented with an unfolding moral allegory that reveals to us certain things about the nature of individual sin as a temptation that confronts the will. On the other hand, we are confronted with a highly affecting dramatic voice, one that expresses pain in language that is poetically rich and allusive and that forefronts birth as it is experienced by a woman.[26]

Milton's language also suggests to us how we are to read. Though the syntax of the second sentence in the passage I quoted earlier (2.777–85, the description of the birth of Death) is knotty, the words seem best paraphrased as follows: "At last this odious offspring . . . tore through my entrails, so that, distorted with fear and pain, my nether shape thus grew transformed." This paraphrase makes the force of the phrase that modifies the second clause more explicit. It is significant that Milton did not write: "so that with fear and pain all my nether shape thus grew transformed" (which is much simpler, telling us only that an experience of fear and pain accompanied the transformation). Instead, Milton complicates matters by adding the seemingly superfluous participle "distorted" to the prepositional phrase. The additional word does more than just emphasize the physical change (certainly the main thing on Sin's mind) by giving us two words for it. The effect is to momentarily reify the physical and emotional experience of fear and pain, which are properly experienced by Sin herself and not by her lower half. Even if we allow that pain might be said to be "experienced" by one part of the body, the same cannot be said of fear. If "distort" etymologically denotes the twisting of something from its original or natural shape (a meaning very dear to Sin at this point), here it also suggests a common figurative usage as a term to describe perception.[27] Milton's syntax and diction suggest that Sin's being is not only changed in a manner that inspires fear and pain, but that it also is "distorted" by the experience of these emotions. That is to say, she is not simply altered physically, but altered in her self-perception. She knows what she was and what she has now become; she watched it and felt it happen. And the pain she felt in the transformation and the fear she felt in the experience of that change were the fears and pains of a mother. They affect her entire being; her emotional and physical states are woven together, and to her they are very real. In fact, they are the central realities of her being. Sin's perception of herself is properly a distorted one—she might even be said to have arrived at her true form only now—but a specifically obstetric fear and pain together constitute the astigmatic lens through which she looks at herself and through which she expresses an odd, but very important, allegorical self-consciousness.

It is through such a distorting lens, or in such a distorting mirror, that Milton here requires us also to gaze. He is, in fact, suggesting—because the perceiver here is *Sin* and Sin is speaking as a mother—that our gaze is always distorted, conditioned as it is by the general sin of postlapsarian existence, of which birth pain is a key manifestation. The naturalistic and dramatic aspects of this allegorical passage function like the ripples or distortions in the glass in which we now see darkly. And the key to the complex working of the allegory is that those ripples and the precise ways in which they distort our view of ourselves come in the shape of the commonplace pains and fears of postlapsarian reproductive life.

It has been traditionally assumed that because Sin is beautiful from the waist up and stinging serpent from the waist down, she signifies the temptation of what Milton calls "individual sin" with a strong emphasis on sexual indiscretion. However, if we take the gender and appearance of Sin as signi-

fying a temptation to immoral, dissolute, and destructive behavior with a
strong emphasis on sexual immorality, the only solid subject position the
allegory provides is one for a man who might be allured by the fair upward
appearance. The gender of Milton's figure in the reading I am suggesting,
however, comes to have a wider significance, providing, as I said before,
subject positions with which both men and women can identify in a complex
figurative tableau with childbirth at its center. Milton's birth imagery here
functions rhetorically to include the reader in the allegory, therefore suggesting that human birth itself must be read allegorically. This forces the
female reader to see herself, when she sees herself as mother, as an allegory
of the consequences of original sin and of her own fear in confronting those
consequences. It no less forcefully functions in this way for the male reader,
though for the male reader it is his mother, lover, wife, or victim whom he
sees transformed into one part of the allegory, while he plays the ultimately
destructive role of Death or the originally responsible role of Satan. Sin,
along with her obstetric content, should be seen, I would suggest, as a
figure for the fallen state itself, one in which birth plays the part of a
complex metonymy for a set of experiences that compromise the free exercise of the will by presenting it with a strong temptation to despair.

   All postlapsarian human life, mired as it is in what Milton calls "the sin
common to all men" (*Christian Doctrine*, 6:382) as opposed to "the sin of
each individual" (382) is in its essence turned away from God unless choice
amends it. The question posed by Milton's allegory, therefore, is how we
are to enact the amending choice. All fallen human life, irrespective of
personal morality or faith, therefore, manifests a process of decay that, as
Milton puts it when he speaks about the "spiritual death" that came with
the Fall, occasions "loss or at least the extensive darkening of that right
reason, whose function it was to discern the chief good" (*Christian Doctrine*, 6:395).[28] Sin signifies the terror that comes between humankind and
God in a universe degraded by an original disobedience from its original
perfection. And here Milton has made the key distorting experiences violent, incestuous sexuality and painful, disfiguring, and dangerous
childbirth.

   In the seventeenth century the childbed was a place where the human
potential for choice was severely tested. The pains and dangers confronted
there were, in themselves, things the human will had no choice about.
Choice, however, did come into play with the contemplation of what to do
in the face of either one's own suffering or that of a loved one. The childbed
should be seen, therefore, as one of the places where Milton (both bio-
graphically and in his imagination) confronted a brute fact about human
experience and was spurred by that confrontation into the action of writing
Paradise Lost. In the decision of Adam and Eve to accept their lot in love
of each other, in submission to God's will, and in hope derived from a

providential narrative whose climax is itself the result of human generation, Milton models for the believing reader a response to the terror signified by the allegory of book 2, a response not easy to make, but necessary to the *regeneration of humankind.

Notes

This work originally appeared as "'Conscious Terrors' and 'The Promised Seed': Seventeenth-Century Obstetrics and the Allegory of Sin and Death in *Paradise Lost*" in *Milton Studies* XXXII, Albert C. Labriola, ed., © 1995 by University of Pittsburgh Press. This version is reprinted by permission of the publisher.

1. See Louis Schwartz, "'Spot of child-bed taint': Seventeenth-Century Obstetrics in Milton's Sonnet 23 and *Paradise Lost* 8.462–78," *Milton Quarterly* (1993): 98–109.

2. Audrey Eccles, *Obstetrics and Gynecology in Tudor and Stuart England* (Kent, Ohio: Kent State University Press, 1982), 125. The figure is a conservative one, excluding women who died undelivered as well as those who died in the event of a stillbirth. It is difficult to account for the numbers in these cases because there are no baptismal records to set against the burial records. The nature of stillbirth, however, as we shall see below, argues for a very high rate of mortality in such cases. Compared with statistics available today for both the industrial West and the Third World, the magnitude of suffering signified by the seventeenth-century figure becomes clear. For example, according to the *United Nations Statistical Yearbook* 38th ed. (New York: United Nations, 1993), 164, 167, in the United Kingdom in 1988 there were only six deaths per 100,000 births (eight per 100,000 in the United States). With a birth rate of 2.5 per woman per lifetime, this number is in aggregate nearly insignificant. If we contrast these numbers with an approximate rate of 400 deaths per 100,000 among the !Kung people of the lower Kalihari (where births are generally unassisted) and a rate of 600 in contemporary Bangladesh, we can see just how appallingly bad things were in seventeenth-century England. See Marjorie Shostak, *Nisa: The Life and Words of a !Kung Woman* (Cambridge: Harvard University Press, 1981), 179, as well as the *Statistical Yearbook* and the World Bank's *World Development Report 1993: Investing in Health* (Oxford: Oxford University Press, 1993), 300–301. As the Kalihari figure suggests, in unassisted birth the mortality rate is about six times lower than that experienced in seventeenth-century London. Therefore, the high rate was due, it seems, not to a lack of intervention, but as we shall see below, to the means of intervention themselves.

3. Roger Finlay, *Population and Metropolis: The Demography of London 1580–1650* (Cambridge: Cambridge University Press, 1981), 133–50.

4. Although many critics have touched on the significance of birth motifs in *Paradise Lost,* the critic who has paid them the greatest and most concentrated attention is Michael Lieb. See *The Dialectics of Creation: Patterns of Birth and Regeneration in "Paradise Lost"* (Amherst: University of Massachusetts Press, 1970). While Lieb says nothing about the relationship of Milton's figures to contemporary conditions, any analysis of the significance of birth in the poem, including my own, owes a great debt to his book. See also Mary Adams, "Fallen Wombs: The Origins of Death in Miltonic Sexuality," *Milton Studies* 29 (1992): 165–79.

5. John Milton, *Christian Doctrine*, in *Complete Prose Works of John Milton*, 8 vols., ed. Don M. Wolfe et al. (New Haven: Yale University Press, 1953–82). All

references to Milton's prose are to this edition and are cited parenthetically in the text.

6. John Milton, *Paradise Lost*, ed. Roy Flannagan (New York: Macmillan, 1993). All references to *Paradise Lost* are to this edition and are cited parenthetically in the text.

7. *The Workes of that famous Chirurgion Ambrose Parey, Translated out of the Latin and compared to the French Tho: Johnson* (London, 1634), 899. Hereafter cited as Paré, *Works*.

8. See, for example, Jane Sharp, *The Midwives Book* (London, 1671), 168, and Jakob Rueff's *The expert midwife....* (London, Printed by E. G. for S. B. and sold by Thomas Alchorn, 1637), book 1, chapter 3. This belief led even the most "advanced" physicians to hold that a fetus was viable should it be born in the seventh month or the ninth, but not in the eighth. Revising an older medieval numerological explanation in the light of protoscientific reasoning, physicians explained that the fetus, which became strong enough to try and effect its birth in the seventh month, usually failed to do so because the womb remained stubbornly closed. The infant was so exhausted by the effort that it needed the whole of the eighth month to recover. If it should by some means be forced out during the eighth month, it was sure to die. See Paré, *Works*, 901–2; Sharp, 173–74; and Reuff, 64–65.

9. "[H]ow great furtherance the *foetus* doth conferre to its own *Birth*, several observations doe clearly evince. A certain *Woman* here amongst us (I speak it knowingly) was, (being dead over night) left alone in her Chamber: but the next morning an Infant was there found between her *Leggs*, which had by its own force wrought his *release*." William Harvey, *Anatomical Exercitations Concerning the Generation of Living Creatures: To which are added Particular Discourses, of Births, and of Conceptions, &c.* (London, 1653), 491.

10. Ibid., 492–93.

11. First published in England in 1540, *The Birth of Mankind* was translated by Richard Jonas from Christian Egenolph's *De partu hominis* (1532), itself a translation of a German original by Eucharius Rosslin called *Der swangen Frauwen und Hebammen Roszgarten* (1513). Rosslin, according to the introduction to the text, was state physician of Worms and Frankfurt am Main. The book was revised and republished in England in 1545 by Thomas Raynald and went into thirteen editions, the last in 1654, when it was superseded. See Eccles, *Obstetrics*, 11–12, and "The Early Use of English for Midwiferies 1500–1700," *Neuphilologische Mitteilungen* 78 (1977): 377–85. Eccles notes, ironically, that because the practices were recommended in *The Birth of Mankind*, it might have been, at least in the earlier period (up to the middle of the seventeenth century), "the better educated and more consciously professional midwife who learned them" (*Obstetrics*, 88).

12. See Eccles, *Obstetrics*, 88–90; Sharp, 170.

13. Willughby seems to have been on a one-man crusade for the use of podalic version, a technique he learned from reading Paré early in his career, but which was not very commonly practiced. See Percival Willughby, *Observations in Midwifery* (1863; reprint, Wakefield: S. R. Publishers, 1972), 54.

14. Ibid.

15. Willughby goes on to relate several more cases, one cited from an authority ("Zactus Lusitanus, *De praxi medic, admirand.*, lib. 3. obs. 141."), *Observations*, 54, 159.

16. Eccles, *Obstetrics*, 106.

17. La Vauguion's *A compleat body of chirurgical operations* (1699), quoted in Eccles, *Obstetrics*, 107.

18. As a poet Milton was no stranger to figures of rape. He chose a rape as the central figure of one of his first efforts ("On the Death of a Fair Infant Dying of a Cough," another poem about infant mortality). It is also, despite all the rhetoric about inviolate chastity, a very real threat to the Lady in *Comus*, mentioned in the exchanges of her brothers and hovering just behind Comus's offer of the cup. In *Paradise Lost*, 2.503–5, Milton alludes to the stories of Sodom (Genesis 19) and Gibeah (Judges 19), both stories in which women are offered to a mob to keep them from raping men.

19. The frequency and difficulty of birth under contemporary circumstances were causes of a great deal of sickness among women, who were sick far more often than men and often chronically so. A fascinating account of the anxieties and ailments suffered by Jane Josselin, who lived into ripe old age having experienced at least fifteen pregnancies, five of which ended in miscarriage and ten in live births, can be found in Lucinda McCray Beier's "In sickness and in health: a seventeenth century family's experience," in Roy Porter, ed. *Patients and Practitioners: Lay Perceptions of Medicine in Pre-Industrial Society* (Cambridge: Cambridge University Press, 1985), 103–7. Jane's husband, Ralph Josselin, recorded 131 instances of illness in his diary during the first twenty-two years of their marriage (her childbearing years). At least seventy-three of these were directly a result of pregnancy or childbirth, and many others were probably indirectly related (106). In the last twenty years, after she stopped giving birth, he recorded only seventeen (107). See also Alan Macfarlane, *The Family Life of Ralph Josselin, A Seventeenth-Century Clergyman: An Essay on Historical Anthropology* (Cambridge: Cambridge University Press, 1970), 81–89. A very moving first-person account of the ailments that followed women through their fertile years can be found in the selections from *The Autobiography of Alice Thornton*, in *English Women's Voices (1570–1700)*, ed. Charlotte Otten (Miami: Florida International University Press, 1992), 232–58.

20. See Michael McDonald, *Mystical Bedlam: Madness, Anxiety, and Healing in Seventeenth-Century England* (Cambridge: Cambridge University Press, 1981), 19–20; 108–9. Napier's patients came from all social strata and from both rural and urban populations, and his notes are an invaluable resource for understanding the nature of medical practice in the period. All told, he recorded 2,039 cases of mental illness in his years of practice. There were 1,267 women over the age of fourteen (nineteen were younger than that and unlikely to have obstetric or gynecological problems). Seven hundred and forty-eight were men, and in five cases the patients had ambiguous names and the details of Napier's accounts do not clearly indicate gender (ibid., 38). In addition to the eighty cases in which mental disturbance in women was caused by difficult birth, another 204 women—or all together 22.4 percent of all the women over fourteen who complained to Napier of mental or emotional disturbance—also suffered from some form of obstetric or gynecological illness (259).

21. Katherine Park and Lorraine F. Daston discuss the development of this literature in detail in "Unnatural Conceptions: The Study of Monsters in Sixteenth- and Seventeenth-Century France and England," *Past and Present* 92 (1981): 20–54. For one of the central statements of the period on monstrosity, see Paré's catalog of causes in the last section of his *Works*, 961–63. For a fascinating collection of broadsides, see Hyder Edward Rollins's collection, *The Pack of Autolycus or Strange and Terrible News. . . .* (Cambridge: Harvard University Press, 1927). A large number of ballads about monstrosity can also be found in William Chappell and J. W. Ebsworth's edition of *The Roxburghe Ballads* (9 vols. [Hertford, 1869–1899]). See also *The Bagford Ballads* (1876–1878; reprint, New York: AMS, 1968); J. Lilly,

ed., *A Collection of 79 Broadside Ballads 1559–97* (London, 1870); and *The Euing Collection of English Broadside Ballads in the Library of the University of Glasgow* (Glasgow: University of Glasgow Publications, 1971).

22. See Sharp, for example: "But there is yet something worse than all this [that is, miscarriage], when a Child comes to be dead in the womb, and is of full age to be born; for then it cannot help the woman because it stirs not, nor can it be turned that it may be brought forth but with great difficulty" (171).

23. The stillborn infant is also described in terrifyingly grotesque terms as bloated, misshapen, and black with discoloration, details that line up with at least some of the descriptive language Milton uses for Death:

> The other shape,
> If shape it might be call'd that shape had none
> Distinguishable in member, joynt, or limb,
> Or substance might be call'd that shadow seem'd,
> For each seem'd either; black it stood as night.
>
> (2.666–70)

There also may be suggestions of molar pregnancy at work in the passage. The products of these "false births" or "half conceptions" often are described in language close to some of Milton's. See, for example, John Sadler, *The Sicke womans private looking-glasse wherein methodically are handled all uterine affects, or diseases arising from the wombe; enabling women to informe the physician about the cause of their griefe* (London: Ane Griffin for Philemon Stephens and Christopher Meridith, 1636), 122–26.

24. For what remains a comprehensive account of possible sources, see John Steadman, "Tradition and Innovation in Milton's 'Sin': The Problem of Literary Indebtedness," *Philological Quarterly* 39 (1960): 93–103. On the connection with St. Basil's *Hexameron*, see Steadman's "Milton and St. Basil: The Genesis of Sin and Death," *Modern Language Notes* 73 (1958): 83.

25. For an extended discussion of Milton's reworking of Spenser in the passage, see Maureen Quilligan, *Milton's Spenser: The Politics of Reading* (Ithaca: Cornell University Press, 1983), 80–98.

26. Highly sympathetic responses to Sin, particularly from female students, have been a feature of my undergraduate class discussions of the passage for years.

27. Milton uses the term in this way in *The Reason of Church Government* and in *Tetrachordon*. Speaking in the former of the revelation of God's power and wisdom in Christ, Milton says, "this is one depth of his wisdome, that he could so plainly reveale so great a measure of it to the grosse *distorted* apprehension of decay'd mankinde" (1:750; emphasis mine). In *Tetrachordon*, speaking against those who would yoke themselves to "the scribe of syllables and rigid letters" in biblical interpretation, Milton argues that rigidity is only appealing to those who "are fain to stretch & *distort* their apprehensions" (2:636; emphasis mine).

28. Milton understands the sin of Adam and Eve (their "personal," but our "common" sin) as consisting of four kinds of "death": "ALL EVILS WHICH TEND TO DEATH" (particularly guiltiness), "SPIRITUAL DEATH," "THE DEATH OF THE BODY" and "ETERNAL DEATH, THE PUNISHMENT OF THE DAMNED" (*Christian Doctrine*, 6:393–414).

Milton and the Winds of Folly

Peter M. McCluskey

Should a wise man utter vain knowledge, and fill his belly with
the east wind?

Job 15.2

In book 7 of *Paradise Lost* Raphael warns Adam that

> Knowledge is as food, and needs no less
> Her Temperance over Appetite, to know
> In measure what the mind may well contain,
> Oppresses else with Surfeit, and soon turns
> Wisdom to Folly, as Nourishment to Wind.
>
> (7.126–30)[1]

The second edition of the *OED* defines this sense of the word *wind* as "'air'
or gas in the stomach or intestines (or, according to early notions, in other
parts of the body); flatus." In support of this definition, the dictionary
quotes *Lycidas:*

> The hungry Sheep look up, and are not fed,
> But swoln with wind, and the rank mist they draw,
> Rot inwardly, and foul contagion spread.
>
> (125–27)

As in Raphael's admonition to Adam, Milton here equates food with knowledge, nourishment with wisdom, and flatulence with folly.

Images of flatulence may seem incongruous in the works of a poet cele-
brated for his adherence to decorum. Milton's use of such imagery is surprising, but not nearly as surprising as the extent to which he uses it; he
consistently emblematizes folly with flatulence in his prose and poetry,
particularly in *Paradise Lost*, where folly and flatulence figure prominently.[2]
In this essay I trace the development of the flatulence-as-folly metaphor
from its earliest appearance in Milton's prose to its most elaborate and most
important articulation in *Paradise Lost*. Although there exists a long literary

227

tradition equating folly with flatulence that may have influenced Milton, his flatulence imagery forms a unified, self-contained system that requires no context other than its own to be intelligible.[3]

Milton first equates folly with flatulence in his sixth *Prolusion*, where he defends the proposition "that sometimes sportive exercises are not prejudicial to philosophic studies" (12:205).[4] He tells his audience that if he sees anyone not laughing, he will say "that he dare not swell out his belly with laughter, lest not his Sphinx, but his sphincter anus, accompany his mouth in its incantations, and against his will babble some riddles, which I pass over to the doctors, not to Oedipus, for interpretation; for I am unwilling that the groan of a posterior by the sound of its cheery voice should make a din in this assembly" (12:229). Suggesting that anyone unamused by his speech needs medical help, Milton cleverly transforms those unmoved by his folly into flatulent fools. Although intended here for sport, Milton's imputation of flatulence to his opponents anticipates a rhetorical strategy frequently employed in his tracts.

In this oration, Milton effectively uses images of flatulence to reveal the folly of others, but here folly means little more than not knowing to laugh at a joke. Elsewhere, however, Milton consistently uses the word *folly* as he defines it in the second book of the *Christian Doctrine:* "To wisdom is opposed folly; which consists, first and chiefly, in an ignorance of the will of God. . . . Secondly, in a false conceit of wisdom. . . . Thirdly, in a prying into hidden things, after the example of our first parents, who sought after the knowledge of good and evil contrary to the command of God. . . . Fourthly, in human or carnal wisdom" (17:31–35). Wisdom he defines as "THAT WHEREBY WE EARNESTLY SEARCH AFTER THE WILL OF GOD, LEARN IT WITH ALL DILIGENCE, AND GOVERN ALL OUR ACTIONS ACCORDING TO ITS RULE" (17:27). To Milton, wisdom means seeking God, and folly means turning away from him.

While Milton does not equate flatulence with Christian folly in *Prolusion* 6, he does in *Lycidas*. In the passage quoted above, the sheep are fed an improper diet, and instead of receiving nourishment, they fill with gas that corrupts them and infects others. That gas symbolizes the corrupt doctrine spread by an intemperate clergy, the "Blind mouths" (119) that "for their bellies' sake . . . scramble at the shearers' feast, / And shove away the worthy bidden guest" (114, 117–18). This image wittily evokes both the carnal and the spiritual intemperance of these uninvited guests, resulting in the flatulence of the sheep, itself symbolic of their ignorance of God's will. Perhaps inspired by the scriptural phrase "wind of doctrine" (Ephesians 4.14), Milton repeatedly uses flatulence as a symbol of corrupt doctrine.

A notable example of this image occurs at the conclusion of *An Apology for Smectymnuus* (1642), where Milton remarks that prelates "have their voice in their bellies, which being well drain'd and taken downe, their great

Oracle, which is only there, will soone be dumbe, and the *Divine right of Episcopacy* forthwith expiring, will put us no more to trouble" (3:366). Developing the riddle-of-the-sphincter image from *Prolusion 6*, he likens the oracular voice of prelates to flatulence and implies that emptying prelatical stomachs by doing away with benefices would effectively silence that voice. Expanding the metaphor, Milton puns upon the word *expiring* to compare the windy doctrine of episcopacy to a gas pain that can only be relieved by farting.

In *The Doctrine and Discipline of Divorce* (1643), Milton uses similar imagery to prove that invoking custom as a justification of existing divorce laws is an act of folly. Custom, he explains, is considered the best instructor because she rolls up "her sudden book of implicit knowledge, for him that will, to take and swallow it down at pleasure; which proving but of bad nourishment in the concoction, as it was heedlesse in the devouring, puffs up unhealthily, a certaine big face of learning . . . that swoln visage of counterfeit knowledge" (3:367). As with the sheep in *Lycidas*, folly causes flatulent swelling, and Milton again shows that if food is knowledge, then bad knowledge causes indigestion.

A similar image occurs in *Colasterion* (1645) but is made more complex by the addition of images of false pregnancy. Milton remarks upon "the ripenes, and the pregnance of his [opponent's] native trechery" (4:256) and observes "to what a pride hee swels" (4:257). As he continues his assault, it becomes clear that this swelling results not from pregnancy but from folly: "[He] leaves the noysome stench of his rude slot behind him. . . . Who could have beleevd so much insolence durst vent it self from out the hide of a varlet?" (4:266). The *OED* suggests that the word *slot* here means "the track or trail of an animal . . . sometimes misapplied to the scent of the animal," but context suggests that Milton refers not to his opponent's trail but his tail. This reading is supported by the word *vent*, which means *fart* in Milton's description of the defeat of the Spanish Armada: "the very maw of Hell ransack't, and made to give up her conceal'd destruction, ere shee could vent it in that horrible and damned blast" (*Of Reformation Touching Church Discipline in England* [1641], 3:77).[5] Milton thus shows his opponent proudly giving birth to a stinking fart.

The images of flatulence culminate in the conclusion of *Colasterion*, where Milton shows the appropriateness of his epigraph: "Answer a Fool according to his folly, lest hee bee wise in his own conceit" (4:233; see Proverbs 26.5). He challenges his unknown adversary, "let him but send mee how hee calls himself, and I may chance not fail to endorse him on the backside of posterity, not a *golden* but a brazen Asse" (4:272). Punning on the words *backside, posterity* (*posterior*), and *Asse* (*arse*), Milton thus answers his opponent's folly with an endorsement of brassy flatulence.

In *Eikonoklastes* (1645), Milton again combines images of flatulence and false pregnancy to expose an opponent's folly. He begins by referring to his opponent's "worst miscarriages" and quotes the phrase "pregnant grounds" from *Eikon Basilike* (5:99) before dryly observing, "all those *pregnancies, and just motives* came to just nothing" (5:100); the metaphor soon reaches its explosive climax: "And thus his pregnant *motives* are at last prov'd nothing but a Tympany" (5:101). Metaphorically referring to a belly swollen with wind, Milton uses the word *tympany* to transform an image of pregnancy to one of flatulency.[6]

In the *Second Defence of the People of England* (1654), Milton again uses the word *tympany* in an image of false pregnancy: "Not the female only, but the male conceived; Pontia a Moreling . . . More this addle and windy egg, from which burst forth that tympany—the *Cry of the Royal Blood*. . . . [N]ow the shell is broken, they turn with loathing from the rotten and offensive contents. As for More, [he is] inflated in no small degree with this birth of his" (8:37). Milton puns upon the notion that the wind engendered barren eggs by describing More's *Cry of the Royal Blood* as an egg produced by the author's flatulence.[7] As in *Eikonoklastes*, Milton uses the metaphor of flatulence as a monstrous birth to ridicule the book of his opponent, showing the author swelling with folly until it explodes from him in a noisy, stinking blast offensive to everyone.

In his conclusion to the *Second Defence*, Milton quotes More's statement "the wonderful Salmasius will blow the terrible trumpet" and then describes horrid harmonies played on another wind instrument: "You prognosticate health, and give us notice of a new kind of musical harmony: for when that terrible trumpet shall be blown, we can think of no fitter accompaniment for it than a reiterated crepitation" (8:53). Milton responds to the terrible trumpet with a volley of farting, once again answering a fool according to his own folly.

It is in *Paradise Lost* that Milton makes his most impressive use of flatulence imagery. Drawing upon Raphael's analogy that wisdom is to nourishment what folly is to flatulence, Milton weaves an intricate pattern of images that expose human and diabolic folly. Such imagery, although perhaps unexpected in Christian epic, does not violate the decorum of the poem because Milton uses it to attack Christian folly. In *Apology for Smectymnuus*, he cites an impressive precedent for this rhetorical strategy: "Christ himself speaking of unsavory traditions, scruples not to name the Dunghill and the Jakes" (3:308; cf. Mark 7.15–20; Matthew 15.17–20). Similarly, Milton scruples not to use unsavory imagery in *Paradise Lost* when speaking of un-savior-ly behavior.

According to the definition of folly in the *Christian Doctrine*, Satan embodies folly because of his ignorance of the will of God and his conceit of false wisdom. Rebuking Satan, Gabriel juxtaposes the word *wise* several times with the word *folly* (4.904–10), predicts that God's wrath will "scourge that wisdom back to Hell" (4.914), and tersely concludes,

> what folly then
> To boast what Arms can do, since thine no more
> Than Heav'n permits.
>
> (4.1007–9)

(Also cf. Raphael's rebuke of Satan's "folly" in 6.139.) After the Fall, God derides the ignorance of Satan and his followers because they "impute / Folly to mee" (10.621–22) when Sin and Death enter the world, seemingly without permission. Sin, Death, Satan, and the other devils fail to realize that however great their power seems to them, they can do nothing without God's knowledge and permission.

Milton reveals his disdain for diabolic folly with a series of windy images in his description of Hell. Following their rebellion, Satan and his followers find themselves imprisoned amid "a fiery Deluge, fed / With ever-burning Sulphur unconsum'd" (1.68–69). Merritt Y. Hughes suggests that "Milton had sulphur mainly in mind as one of the three or four basic minerals of the alchemists, for whom 'sublimation' meant the refining of metals by the hottest possible fires."[8] However, while a sulphurous fire may burn hot, the odor it exudes resembles nothing so much as the fruits of that strange alchemy performed deep within the body.

Milton further develops this pungent image as Satan takes his first steps across the landscape of Hell:

> on dry Land
> He lights, if it were Land that ever burn'd
> With solid, as the Lake with liquid fire
> And such appear'd in hue; as when the force
> Of subterranean wind transports a Hill
> Torn from Pelorus, or the shatter'd side
> Of thund'ring Aetna, whose combustible
> And fuell'd entrails thence conceiving Fire,
> Sublim'd with Mineral fury, aid the Winds,
> And leave a singed bottom all involv'd
> With stench and smoke.
>
> (1.227–37)

Developing the simile with characteristic thoroughness, Milton first describes the flatulent force of subterranean wind being broken, and then the "combustible / and fuell'd entrails" of Aetna, which spew forth sulphurous winds and fire, leaving "a singed bottom all involv'd / with stench and smoke." These thundering, stinking winds represent diabolic folly, for which Milton reveals his utter disdain. Like Dante's *Inferno*, Milton's Hell is the fundament of the firmament, where sinners wallow in excremental filth, and humiliation is part of their punishment.[9]

Leaving Hell for Earth, Satan passes through the first sphere and finds himself "on [a] windy Sea of Land" (3.440) where "other Creature in this place / Living or lifeless to be found was none" (442–43). Continuing the description, Milton provides an unexpected vision of things to come:

> None yet, but store hereafter from the earth
> Up hither like Aereal vapors flew
> Of all things transitory and vain, when Sin
> With vanity had fill'd the works of men:
> Both all things vain, and all who in vain things
> Built thir fond hopes of Glory or lasting fame,
> Or happiness in this or th' other life;
> All who have thir reward on Earth, the fruits
> Of painful Superstition and blind Zeal,
> Naught seeking but the praise of men, here find
> Fit retribution, empty as thir deeds.
>
> (444–54)

Included among this group are the builders of Babel, suicides, and "Eremites and Friars / White, Black and Grey, with all thir trumpery" (474–75). When these and others presume to approach "Heav'n's Wicket" (484),

> A violent cross wind from either Coast
> Blows them transverse ten thousand Leagues awry
> Into the devious Air; then might ye see
> Cowls, Hoods and Habits with thir wearers tost
> And flutter'd into Rags, then Reliques, Beads,
> Indulgences, Dispenses, Pardons, Bulls,
> The sport of Winds: all these upwhirl'd aloft
> Fly o'er the backside of the World far off
> Into a Limbo large and broad, since call'd
> The Paradise of Fools.
>
> (487–96)[10]

The implications of the phrase "backside of the World" have not gone unnoticed. Norma Phillips calls it Milton's "last vulgar joke at the expense of his fools" and finds it consistent with the tone of the passage, while John Wooten refers to "Milton's backside . . . send-up of all those misguided Catholic priests, monks, and lay folk who expect the cluttered paraphernalia of their religion to aid in their salvation."[11] However, neither Phillips nor Wooten identifies the "backside of the World" as the source of the region's violent winds.

When we consider the phrase "Aereal vapors," the numerous references to wind, and the image of the world's backside in conjunction with Raphael's statement that a surfeit of knowledge "turns / Wisdom to Folly, as Nourishment to Wind," Milton's scatological joke becomes clear. He likens the asinine works of these fools to a cosmic fart let out by the "backside of the World." The strongly breaking winds represent not only their foolish behavior but also "fit retribution" for it.

In contrast to Hell, Paradise is originally free of both folly and flatulence. Before the Fall, Adam's sleep is "from pure digestion bred, / And temperate vapors bland" (5.4–5); to maintain this pure digestion, Adam and Eve must temper their intellectual and physical appetites. In book 4, Milton introduces and makes concrete the analogy that knowledge is food with the Tree of Knowledge and further develops it in book 5, devoting hundreds of lines to the subject of human and angelic appetites. Significantly, when man and angel share "These bounties which our Nourisher" (398) has provided, they temper their appetites accordingly: "with meats and drinks they had suffic'd, / Not burd'n'd Nature" (5.451–52).

In book 7 Milton makes explicit his implicit association of folly with flatulence. Agreeing to continue answering Adam's questions, Raphael explains:

> such Commission from above
> I have receiv'd, to answer thy desire
> Of knowledge within bounds; beyond abstain
> To ask, nor let thine own inventions hope
> Things not reveal'd, which th'invisible King,
> Only Omniscient, hath supprest in Night,
> To none communicable in Earth or Heaven:
> Anough is left besides to search and know.
>
> (7.118–25)

Adam's "desire / Of knowledge within bounds" meets the definition of wisdom in the *Christian Doctrine* since such knowledge would better his understanding of the will of God, while his asking or speculating about "Things not reveal'd" would constitute folly.

The words "abstain / To ask" anticipate the elaborate simile that Milton develops in Raphael's next lines:

> But Knowledge is as food, and needs no less
> Her Temperance over Appetite, to know
> In measure what the mind may well contain,
> Oppresses else with Surfeit, and soon turns
> Wisdom to Folly, as Nourishment to Wind.
>
> (7.126–30)

This analogy stands near the center of *Paradise Lost*, both literally and figuratively, invoking God's commandment that Adam and Eve abstain from eating the fruit of the Tree of Knowledge. Indeed, the phrase "Temperance over Appetite" neatly summarizes Milton's epic thesis: Adam and Eve must not only abstain from seeking forbidden knowledge but also temper their appetites for permitted knowledge, the overindulgence of which leads to "Folly."[12]

In book 8 Adam repeats the main ideas of the analogy to Raphael, saying that the mind is apt to rove until

> she learn
> That not to know at large of things remote
> From use, obscure and subtle, but to know
> That which before us lies in daily life,
> Is the prime Wisdom; what is more, is fume.
>
> (8.190–94)

Adam's juxtaposition of the words *Wisdom* and *fume* provides a fragrant reminder of the correlation between folly and flatulence.

Despite appearing to understand the analogy, however, Adam reveals that he sometimes has trouble distinguishing between folly and wisdom, as when he tells Raphael that whatever Eve does or says

> Seems wisest, virtuousest, discreetest, best;
> All higher knowledge in her presence falls
> Degraded, Wisdom in discourse with her
> Loses discount'nanc't, and like folly shows.
>
> (8.550–53)

Throughout the poem, Milton stresses that although diabolic folly underlies the temptation, the Fall ultimately results from human folly; he unambiguously makes this point when the Son asks God whether man should "Fall circumvented thus by fraud, though join'd / With his own folly?" (3.152–53). God created Adam and Eve free to choose whether to embrace wisdom or folly, and for that choice to be meaningful, they were made with the innate capacity for folly that Adam unwittingly reveals to Raphael. The angel's stern response, "be not diffident / Of Wisdom, she deserts thee not, if thou / Dismiss her not" (8.562–64), emphasizes that the choice is Adam's.

Eve, as Adam's inferior, is more vulnerable to folly than her spouse, and her latent folly comes to fruition first. When she fails to temper her appetite for what she terms "This intellectual food" (9.768),

> Earth felt the wound, and Nature from her seat
> Sighing through all her Works gave signs of woe,

That all was lost.

(9.782–84)

As he consistently does throughout the epic, Milton answers an act of folly with a display of flatulence; here he puns upon the word *seat*, creating the intriguing image of an uncomfortable Nature sighing from her seat—that is, gently breaking wind—at Eve's folly.

And when Adam eats the fruit, Milton accordingly rewards his folly with a more forceful display of flatulence. Adam tastes the apple

> Against his better knowledge, not deceiv'd,
> But fondly overcome with Female charm.
> Earth trembl'd from her entrails, as again
> In pangs, and Nature gave a second groan.

(9.998–1001)

In this crucial passage, the word "fondly" means "foolishly" (*OED*), as is emphasized by its juxtaposition with the words "better knowledge," and Milton again uses pathetic flatulency to underscore an act of extreme folly.[13] Combining images of flatulence and labor pains, he ironically celebrates the ill-conceived birth of human folly. While it may be objected that Milton would not introduce laughter, however grim, at the moment of the Fall, he has well prepared us through the analogy that knowledge is as food, as well as through the scornful displays of flatulence in Hell and the Paradise of Fools, to expect the windy consequences of Adam's and Eve's foolish appetites.

In addition to having their acts of folly announced by subterranean flatulence, Adam and Eve are themselves troubled by metaphoric winds of folly. After Adam and Eve make love,

> dewy sleep
> Oppress'd them, wearied with thir amorous play.
> Soon as the force of that fallacious Fruit,
> That with exhilarating vapor bland
> About thir spirits had play'd, and inmost powers
> Made err, was now exhal'd, and grosser sleep
> Bred of unkindly fumes, with conscious dreams
> Encumber'd, now had left them.

(9.1044–51)

Having eaten intemperately, Adam and Eve are plagued by indigestion—"unkindly fumes" that disrupt their sleep. For Milton, flatulence is a physical consequence of the Fall, but these "unkindly fumes," which contrast with the "vapors bland" of their prelapsarian "pure digestion," represent not only flatulence caused by physical intemperance but also spiritual discomfort caused by intellectual intemperance.

When Adam and Eve awaken and begin to weep, Milton further develops the image:

> nor only Tears
> Rain'd at thir Eyes, but high Winds worse within
> Began to rise, high Passions, Anger, Hate,
> Mistrust, Suspicion, Discord, and shook sore
> Thir inward State of Mind.
>
> (9.1121–25)

While the word *winds* metaphorically stands in apposition to the catalog of emotions that follows, it also punningly reminds us that the minds of Adam and Eve have not been nourished by the forbidden fruit; instead, as a consequence of their intemperance, a metaphoric flatulence racks their minds.

In *Animadversions upon the Remonstrant's Defence against Smectymnuus*, Milton explains that any "grim laughter" appearing in that work "cannot be taxt of levity or insolence: for even this veine of laughing (as I could produce out of grave Authors) hath oft-times a strong and sinewy force in teaching and confuting" (3:107). Likewise, any "grim laughter" in *Paradise Lost* elicited by the winds of folly is far from frivolous, for Milton teaches his readers to laugh at folly, and by laughing, to shun it. Although Milton seems to be having fun at the expense of Adam and Eve, he is deadly serious about the consequences of their intemperance. As God makes clear, Sin and Death ravage the world because of "the folly of Man" (10.619).

According to Michael, the broadest path leading to Death's "grim Cave" (11.469) will be diseases caused by intemperance in eating and drinking, fit retribution indeed for the foolish intemperance of Adam and Eve. The angel shows Adam these maladies, including "Colic pangs" (484), to teach him "What misery th' inabstinence of Eve / Shall bring on men" (11.476–77).[14] He then tells Adam he may reach death peacefully by following

> The rule of not too much, by temperance taught,
> In what thou eat'st and drink'st, seeking from thence
> Due nourishment, not gluttonous delight.
>
> (11.531–33)

Upon leaving Paradise, Adam reveals that he has learned another kind of temperance:

> Greatly instructed I shall hence depart,
> Greatly in peace of thought, and have my fill

> Of knowledge, which this Vessel can contain;
> Beyond which was my folly to aspire.
>
> (12.557–60)

Belatedly, Adam now knows to distinguish between wisdom and folly.

Underlying his final speech is Milton's analogy that knowledge is food, for eating the fruit of the Tree of Knowledge paradoxically brings Adam and Eve not wisdom but folly, and both their minds and their bodies have become polluted. By using images of flatulence, Milton shows us that we need temperance in diet and learning to nourish us both in this world and in the next. Without temperance in learning, as the Paradise of Fools warns us, we will inherit the wind.

Notes

All biblical references are to the King James Version and are cited parenthetically in the text.

1. John Milton, *Paradise Lost*, in *John Milton: Complete Poems and Major Prose*, ed. Merritt Y. Hughes (New York: Odyssey, 1957). All references to Milton's poetry are to this edition and are cited parenthetically in the text.

2. For a brief discussion of Milton's poetic use of imagery drawn from the digestive process, see Kester Svendsen, *Milton and Science* (Cambridge: Harvard University Press, 1956), 186–87.

3. For a good introduction to this literary tradition, see the first two chapters of Jae Num Lee's pioneering study, *Swift and Scatological Satire* (Albuquerque: University of New Mexico Press, 1971); also of use is Mikhail Bakhtin, *Rabelais and His World*, trans. Helene Iswolsky (Bloomington: Indiana University Press, 1984); for two earlier and more general studies on scatology, see Norman O. Brown, *Life Against Death: The Psychoanalytic Meaning of History* (Middleton, Conn.: Wesleyan University Press, 1959) and Theodor Rosebury, *Life on Man* (New York: Viking, 1969).

4. John Milton, *Prolusion 6*, in *The Works of John Milton*, 18 vols., ed. Frank Allen Patterson et al. (New York: Columbia University Press, 1931–38). All references to Milton's prose are to this edition and are cited parenthetically in the text.

5. Cf. *OED:* "Vent. . . . Of persons, animals, or their organs: To cast out, expel, or discharge, esp. by evacuation; to evacuate (urine, etc.)"; Milton's description of the defeat of the Spanish Armada is cited in support of this definition.

6. The word is also a medical term; Lazarius Riverius (1589–1655) describes two types of dropsy, "one from wind, which is like that sort of Belly-Dropsie which is termed Tympanites, or the Drum-belly dropsie" (James V. Ricci, *The Genealogy of Gynaecology: History of the Development of Gynaecology Throughout the Ages, 2000 B.C.–1800 A.D.*, 2d ed. [Philadelphia: Blakiston, 1950], 291).

7. Cf. *Colasterion:* "From such a wind-egg definition as this, they who expect any of his other arguments to bee well hatcht, let them enjoy the vertu of thir worthy Champion" (4:237).

8. Merritt Y. Hughes, ed. *John Milton: Complete Poems and Major Prose* (New York: Odyssey, 1957), 217 n. 235.

9. Dante (*The Divine Comedy of Dante Alighieri*, trans. Jefferson Butler

Fletcher [New York: Columbia University Press, 1931]) depicts sinners in Malebolge wallowing in human excrement (18.106–32), and he punningly describes the ninth circle of hell as "the bottom of the universe" (32.8).

10. Milton's image of airborne monks parallels the flying monks of the anonymous fourteenth-century anticlerical satire "The Land of Cokaygne," in *Historical Poems of the XIV and XV Centuries,* ed. Rossell Hope Robbins (New York: Columbia University Press, 1959).

11. Norma Phillips, "Milton's Limbo of Vanity and Dante's Vestibule," *English Language Notes* 3 (1966): 182; John Wooten, "From Purgatory to the Paradise of Fools: Dante, Ariosto, and Milton," *ELH* 49 (1982): 748.

12. For a discussion of related Renaissance "Traditions of Sobriety," see Howard Schultz, *Milton and Forbidden Knowledge* (New York: MLA, 1955), 1–42.

13. Cf. the words "fond hopes" (*Paradise Lost* 3.449).

14. William Riley Parker reports that Milton himself "suffered much from flatulence" (*Milton: A Biography,* 2 vols. [Oxford: Clarendon, 1968], 1 :286); doubtless the poet found solace in the knowledge that his windy condition was a consequence of the Fall and perhaps rationalized it as an unsavory reminder of original sin.

Paradisal Appetite and Cusan Food in *Paradise Lost*

W. Gardner Campbell

1

In *Areopagitica*, Milton describes Adam's freedom in Paradise with these famous, oft-quoted words: "Many there be that complain of divine providence for suffering Adam to transgress. Foolish tongues! when God gave him reason, he gave him freedom to choose, for reason is but choosing; he had else been a mere artificial Adam, such an Adam as he is in the motions" (733).[1] Adam is a reasonable creature; reason makes Adam an *imago Dei*; reason is impossible without freedom, since reason is realized in the choices one makes. Thought and deed exist on a continuum for monist Milton, just as spirit and matter do not differ essentially (as we learn from Raphael in *Paradise Lost* 5.468–93).[2]

Less attention, however, has been paid to the next three sentences in *Areopagitica*:

> We ourselves esteem not of that obedience, or love, or gift, which is of force. God therefore left him [Adam] free, set before him a provoking object, ever almost in his eyes; herein consisted his merit, herein the right of his reward, the praise of his abstinence. Wherefore did he create passions within us, pleasures round about us, but that these rightly tempered are the very ingredients of virtue? (733)

Milton seems to imagine prohibition not only as psychologically provocative (we desire what we can't have) but also as theologically, even ontologically, provocative; the Tree is God's deliberately teasing, testing, trying creation that (note well) continually winks on the threshold of Adam's vision.[3] Indeed, the "ever almost" formula makes the Tree particularly and especially provocative: "ever almost" plays with liminality in a way that evokes the arousal, the frustration, and (implicitly) the consummation of desire—if one desires to remain obediently abstinent in a way that never fails to be meritorious, praiseworthy, and justly rewarded.

But if abstinence is the proper response to *the* provoking object of the

239

paradisal Tree of the Knowledge of Good and Evil, is abstinence the *only* response to provocation, and is the prohibited Tree the only "provoking object" Milton imagines God has supplied, in Paradise or out? The modulation from "abstinence" in the case of the forbidden fruit to "passions within us [and] pleasures round about us . . . rightly tempered" suggests not. As his diction implies, Milton conceives of abundance, like prohibition, as provocative, for God has given us the rule of temperance; the same God, of course, gives us the abundance. If we were meant only to say no, God would be unfair; if we were meant always and only to say yes, we could not be said to be free. In a world where God commands his creatures to temper appetites he created and is himself continually stimulating, desire is largely indeterminate, and gloriously so: life in that world is joyous but not complacent, and neither the Maker's claims on one's obedience nor his provisions for one's freedom can ever be simple or dully certain—except for the single interdiction that binds Adam and Eve and thus releases their own, and Paradise's, abundance.[4]

Such a world, fallen or unfallen (and Milton seems throughout this part of *Areopagitica* to conflate the two states), is very difficult to imagine. To have one's powers of choice, one's very freedom, continually enabled and exercised by intense, specific, and sometimes teasingly indirect divine provocation seems indecorous, willful (on God's part, if not on Milton's), more like Hell, perhaps, than like Paradise—and certainly a far cry from E. M. W. Tillyard's famous description of an Adam and Eve who, "reduced to the ridiculous task of working in a garden which produces of its own accord more than they will ever need, . . . are in the hopeless position of Old Age Pensioners enjoying perpetual youth."[5] Many readers of late have taken on Tillyard's notorious jibe and argued strenuously for a dynamic, even taxing Paradise, one which calls for Adam and Eve to use every nascent ability to its fullest. Nevertheless, the role of *provocation* in Paradise has not been fully examined.[6]

Often the notion of provocation in Paradise is simply denied, as it is in Dennis Burden's *The Logical Epic*, in which Burden argues that Milton's "provoking object" cannot really be what Milton said it was. Burden insists that Milton could not have attributed such tantalizing, provocative behavior to Adam's creator:

> [I]t was necessary [for Milton] to insist that God had not made the forbidden Fruit provocative, thus almost inciting Man to sin. That Milton had himself in *Areopagitica* described it as provocative must not be allowed to influence the way in which *Paradise Lost* needs to be read since Milton's argument in *Areopagitica* is not as innocent as it appears. . . . The Tree is not in reality compelling, but, when judgment is in abeyance, it can be shown to seem and to be thought so.[7]

This argument must ignore a great deal in both works, including Milton's explicit comment that, as Eve stands with the serpent before the Tree, the mere sight of the fruit itself is almost all the temptation she needs: "Fixed on the fruit she gazed, which to behold / Might tempt alone" (9.735–36). Indeed, rereading Milton's description of the "provoking object" God places in the garden, "ever almost in [Adam's] eyes," one cannot but be struck by the fact that the Tree of the Knowledge of Good and Evil *must* be provocative *regardless* of factors such as its beauty or aroma or the time of day in which it is beheld. It is after all the only such tree in all of Paradise; its singularity coincides with very few other singularities in this garden. (Indeed, the only one that springs readily to mind, other than the Tree of Life, is Adam and Eve's "wedded love, mysterious law, true source . . . sole propriety / In Paradise of all things common else" [4.750–52].) Too, this tree is provokingly near the Tree of Life. Finally, the command not to eat of the forbidden fruit is uppermost in Adam's and Eve's minds, as we see nearly from our first glimpse of them (4.411ff.); as we hear iterated by Adam in response to Raphael's warnings (5.520–22); as Raphael repeats at the end of his creation narrative (7.542–47); as Adam relates in his autobiography (8.323–35—Adam says the "rigid interdiction . . . resounds / Yet dreadful in mine ear" [334–35]); as Raphael reiterates in his valediction (8.633–39); and as Eve makes clear both in her quarrel with Adam (9.273–81) and in her encounter with the serpent (9.659–63). Certainly such a prohibition, with its many repetitions throughout Adam and Eve's prelapsarian experience, is a formidable provocation, especially since the punishment for disobeying the prohibition—death—is something Adam is ignorant of, yet curious about (4.425–26).

But Burden is not alone in his denial. Alastair Fowler, using Burden's analysis, also explains away the "provoking object" of *Areopagitica:*

> The forbidden fruit is now for the first time described as specially attractive and tempting to man. . . . It would have been improvident or provoking of God to have allowed it to seem so before; but now Eve's heart is corrupted. . . . Burden . . . has it that the fact that Eve would always be hungry at *noon* contributes to the crisis. The increased appetitive urge is not, of course, evil in itself—even Raphael got hungry at this time . . . ; but [Milton] means to run excitingly close to a tragedy of necessity.[8]

Fowler's distress, and Burden's before his, is typical. Something about the "true warfaring" Paradise (728)—the *frisson* of conflict and opposition, the very "increased appetitive urge" Fowler admits is not "evil in itself" (and thereby damns with faint praise)—presents itself as a provoking object many of Milton's most sympathetic readers seem unable or unwilling to recognize, admit, or name.[9]

I believe this "increased appetitive urge" is the engine that drives Milton's

Paradise. From our first glimpses of it, we see a Paradise whose bounds are being pushed, a creation always spilling over the lips that try to imbibe its heady liquors. The bargainings and ecstasies at the ends of "L'Allegro" and "Il Penseroso" each find their fulfillment here, in Paradise—a fulfillment, ironically, dangerously, blessedly, that includes *hunger* within its great satisfactions.

2

How can hunger be satisfying? Is Milton a theological Cavalier after all, writing a theodicy in which fruitions of all kinds are denied to Adam and Eve, who in turn desire them mainly because of (and in proportion to) their denial? Or can desire and fulfillment, appetite and its satisfactions, be married? A philosophical analogue from the early Renaissance may be helpful. Milton's treatment of the stimulation and satisfaction of appetite in Paradise is strikingly similar to certain aspects of the philosophy of Nicholas of Cusa, the "artist's philosopher," whose words provide a window into Milton's portrayal of paradisal appetite.[10] In his *De Docta Ignorantia*, Nicholas works out the problem of maintaining desire in a Heaven of perfect fulfillment by means of what William Kerrigan and Gordon Braden call "the metaphor of unappeased appetite"; Nicholas imagines a perfect food that satisfies hunger and quickens appetite simultaneously.[11] Nicholas's words admirably prepare us to understand the hunger Adam and Eve enjoy in Paradise and are worth quoting at length:

> If you will reflect upon these indeed deep [matters], with an inner relishing you will scent God's inexpressible goodness. God, passing over to you, will supply you with this goodness; you will be filled with Him when His glory shall appear. You will be filled without surfeit, for this immortal good is life itself. . . . Now, our intellectual desire is to live intellectually—i.e., to enter further and further into life and joy. And since that life is infinite, the blessed, still desirous, are brought further and further into it. And so, they are filled—being, so to speak, thirsty ones drinking from the Fount of life. And because this drinking does not pass away into a past (since it is within eternity), the blessed are ever drinking and ever filled; and yet, they have never drunk and have never been filled. . . . The enjoyment does not pass away into a past, because the appetite does not fade away during the enjoyment. [The situation is] as if—to use an illustration from the body—someone hungry were seated at the table of a great king, where he was supplied with the food he desired, so that he did not seek any other food. The nature of this food would be [such] that in filling him up it would also whet his appetite. If this food were never deplenished, it is obvious that the perpetual consumer would always be filled, would always desire this same food, and would always willingly be brought to the food. And so, he would always be able to

eat; and, after having eaten, he would still be able to be led to the food with whetted appetite.[12]

In this light, Milton's description of the banquet Adam and Eve share with Raphael becomes especially interesting for its emblematic representation of Paradise itself. Since spring and autumn dance hand in hand in this garden, germination and harvest are not antitheses, but, to use a Cusan term, a *coincidentia oppositorum;* pruning and cutting and plucking in Paradise are, in Barbara Lewalski's words, "restrictive actions that at the same time stimulate greater fertility."[13] In other words, to use up Paradise is also to enlarge it. The implications of this union of reaping and growing specifically recall Nicholas when, in the passage Lewalski cites from book 5 where Adam and Eve prepare to welcome Raphael to their noontime meal, Adam notes that moderation itself is a problematic concept when using a resource stimulates not only its replenishment, but also a new abundance:

> well we may afford
> Our givers their own gifts, and large bestow
> From large bestowed, where nature multiplies
> Her fertile growth, and by disburdening grows
> More fruitful, which instructs us not to spare.
>
> (5.316–20)

In such an environment, no principle of frugality is simple, and Milton's idea of paradisal temperance demonstrates its complexity. There is "No fear lest dinner cool" (5.396); there is also no fear lest dinner someday disappear. God himself promised Adam that he should "Of every tree that in the garden grows / Eat freely with glad heart; fear here no dearth" (8.321–22).[14] Milton takes great pains to emphasize the immoderate quantity of food Adam and Eve prepare for themselves and their guest: Eve gathers "fruit of all kinds" (save one, Milton leaves unsaid) in "tribute large, and on the board / *Heaps* with *unsparing* hand" (5.341, 343–44; emphasis mine). And amidst this dizzying array of aromas, liquids, rinds, and fruits, we find hidden more abundance: Eve hears the dizzying promise that her own womb will be far more fruitful than Mother Earth's prodigious capacities displayed here. As Raphael tells Eve,

> [thy] fruitful womb
> Shall fill the world more numerous with thy sons
> Than with these various fruits the trees of God
> Have heaped this table.
>
> (5.388–91)

The profusion of Paradise is the essence of God's goodness, as Adam (our "author" [8.360]) articulates it to Raphael just before they begin their meal:

> Heavenly stranger, please to taste
> These bounties which our nourisher, from whom
> All perfect good *unmeasured* out, descends,
> To us for food and for delight hath caused
> The earth to yield; unsavoury food perhaps
> To spiritual natures; only this I know,
> That one celestial Father gives to all.
>
> (5.397–403; emphasis mine)

Food and delight are one; power and need are perfectly, symbiotically interdependent. Hunger and increase feed on and nourish each other in the perfect ontology of Paradise.[15] As both Adam and Eve tend, reform, pursue, and submit to the wanton sweet multiplicity of their garden home, they will find their labors beget more strength, more labor, more food, and more not unappeased hunger. Nothing will get used up; nothing will languish unused; even the much-too-muchness has its operation to perform. This Paradise produces itself as a perfect food endlessly produced, endlessly eaten, and endlessly desired. In Milton's imagined Paradise, God wills for original humanity just such nourishment as Cusanus, thinking about the blessedly restless intellect, imagines for the Christian redeemed: you can eat all you want, secure in knowing that you'll always be full, and always want more, and always be able to eat more. Raphael knows this, of course, full well. After all, he is the one who tells Adam and Eve about angelic feastings:

> On flowers reposed, and with fresh flowerets crowned,
> They eat, they drink, and in communion sweet
> Quaff immortality and joy, *secure*
> *Of surfeit where full measure only bounds*
> *Excess*, before the all bounteous king, who showered
> With copious hand, rejoicing in their joy.
>
> (5.636–41; emphasis mine)

These suggestive (and difficult) lines represent some of the very few additions Milton made to the 1674 edition of *Paradise Lost;* in his revision Milton goes out of his way to underscore precisely the kind of paradisal appetite Nicholas describes. (The 1667 edition reads simply "They eat, they drink, and with refection sweet / Are filled, before the all bounteous king.") Fowler notes that "the additions . . . draw closer the link with Raphael's meal with Adam and Eve . . . [and] endow the eating with a spiritual value."[16] Yes, and more: these additions go even farther than Fowler suggests. They hint that the concept of immoderation is displaced by a perfect food, since such food has only paradoxical relations to moderation or measure: one cannot eat too much since one cannot eat more than one can eat.

As in Nicholas's philosophy of infinity, when one's *full* capacity is the only boundary between enough and too much, the meaning of *excess* becomes difficult to assess—excess becomes experientially unattainable. In this way, paradoxically, boundedness and boundlessness, full measure and measurelessness, both partake of and provoke the calculus of infinite blessedness.

The perfect Cusan food that Paradise provides is not only the fruit the earth yields, but also the company it continually attracts. Adam's colloquies with Raphael, for example, are fascinating instances of complicated rhetorical intercourse, often nearly as complex and emotionally charged as the separation scene dialogue between Adam and Eve. And as we read these colloquies, we find metaphors of eating and drinking that continually recall Nicholas's perfect food. One such metaphor occurs in book 7, where Adam,

> as one whose drouth
> Yet scarce allayed still eyes the current stream,
> Whose liquid murmur heard new thirst excites,
> Proceeded thus to ask his heavenly guest.
>
> (66–69)

Adam is Tantalus unbound here, for each new thirst will be provoked *and* slaked by his "affable" (7.41) guest Raphael, whose fluent conversation will not flee from him as Eve's watery image fled from her.[17] John Peter Rumrich says that "Adam and Eve can be described through the Tantalus myth, but through an inversion of it, in which moderate desires are perfectly satisfied."[18] Surprisingly, however, *immoderate* desires have their sanction and satisfaction in Paradise as well, for Milton takes pains to build immoderation into his garden paradise, an immoderation that may lead to Heaven itself, if it is rightly used, obediently pruned and stimulated.

Of course Satan—that hater of paradox and lover of parody—has his own version of immoderate appetite and measureless capacity. In *Paradise Lost* 2.843–44, Satan promises his son Death that in the Earth he will conquer, his son "shall be fed and filled / Immeasurably, all things shall be your prey."[19] Death's endless eating will be postlapsarian, of course. Yet we should also note that Death's hunger distorts, not reflects, paradisal appetite. Death's appetite leads not to an enlargement of its being but, ironically, to its annihilation. In book 10 we learn that Death pines, not with an appetite quickened by food, but with *famine*, famine that seeks starvation—that is, itself—as its best meal. As he says to his mother, Sin:

> To me, who with eternal famine pine,
> Alike is hell, or Paradise, or heaven,

> There best, where most with ravine I may meet;
> Which here, though plenteous, all too little seems
> To stuff this maw, this vast unhide-bound corpse.

(10.597–601)

3

One other aspect of paradisal appetite strongly echoes Nicholas's joyful philosophies of infinity—its direction, or more accurately, its potential (and lawful) *lack* of direction, its enticing aimlessness. Once again Milton's provoking Tree and its forbidden fruit—objects at once (and paradoxically) inescapable and utterly liberating—lead to a surprising description of prelapsarian desire. If they choose to obey God, Adam and Eve will find their burden light; they will find that single prohibition to be a "slight" *and* "sole command" (7.47), one law

> So easily obeyed amid the choice
> Of all tastes else to please their appetite,
> Though wandering.

(7.48–50)

John Carey says of *Paradise Lost* that "'[w]ander' is one of its key verbs, and it belongs to the lost, the fallen."[20] As we can see, however, this is not so; indeed, Milton's praise of wandering in *Areopagitica* also underscores its relation to appetite and satisfaction: "This justifies the high providence of God, who, though he command us temperance, justice, continence, yet pours out before us, even to a profuseness, all desirable things, and gives us minds that can wander beyond all limit and satiety" (733). God's ways to man are just. Providence is provocative.

It is easy to see why Carey (and others) miss the variety of wanderings within Milton's works. Milton's praise of wandering intellectual appetite, satiety-proof, does not fall within the mainstream of Puritanism; it stands strongly opposed, for example, to John Calvin's warnings in the *Institutes* about men's wandering, labyrinthine minds and the dangers they enclose.[21] And of course the fallen angels in *Paradise Lost* 2.555–69 spend their spare time "in wandering mazes lost" (561), their high thoughts leading them in a labyrinth of "Vain wisdom . . . and false philosophy" (565). Yet wandering, like appetite, argument, tears, and toil, also finds its place among the good things of creation, its evil, parodic twin cleaving to it, perhaps, but not necessarily perverting it or finally negating it. One needs to look past the fathers of the Reformation to the "artist's philosopher" to find the origins of praise such as Milton's for intellectual and appetitive wandering, as is plain from Dorothy Koenigsberger's description of Cusan mysticism:

Compared with Cusa, almost all other styles of mystical contemplation move quickly inward to a psychic and spiritual territory. One draws in or withdraws in order to ascend and see. But Cusanus used his unusual immanent and transcendent deity to make the concept of knowledge non-directional. Men might descend to God at the essence of things or rise up to him; they could reach out to God and move in to him. For, God is both the essence and end of all things; in the cosmos He is centre and circumference, all in all and all all at once. In this case the knowing process is not just a simple ascent from particulars to conclusions, nor is it an ascent moving away from the particulars of experience to an inner psychic territory of spiritual insight. Instead it runs a curious zig-zag course between the senses and the various capacities of the mind, from particulars to conclusions, from conclusions to desire, from desire to perfected notions, from the multiplicity of these notions to a further desire for simplicity. Knowing men would know more and, seeing the limit men desire the source and origin.[22]

Temperance is commanded and profusion is supplied, along with the capacity for endless wandering eating. Raphael does tell Adam "govern well thy appetite" (7.546), as well as "knowledge is as food, and needs no less / Her temperance over appetite" (7.126–27).[23] Yet this warning effects a curious circle: Adam mustn't try to find out what God hasn't revealed, but by the same token he cannot find out what he should not ask about unless he asks and is rebuffed. Indeed, it is Raphael's hesitation that seems to keep Adam asking. No sooner does Raphael give one answer than the angel solicits another question; the heaven that Raphael tells Adam "is for thee too high" (8.172) comes within Adam's reach as the angel speaks:

> For while I sit with thee, I seem in heaven,
> And sweeter thy discourse is to my ear
> Than fruits of palm-tree pleasantest to thirst
> And hunger both, from labour, at the hour
> Of sweet repast; they satiate, and soon fill,
> Though pleasant, but thy words with grace divine
> Imbued, bring to their sweetness no satiety.
>
> (8.210–16)

Here once again a perfect food appears that brings forth appetite and satisfaction but no satiety. As physical beings, Adam and Eve may eat their fill, temporarily, of Paradise's vegetables and fruits—except one—but, Raphael's "contracted brow" (8.560) notwithstanding, they cannot eat their fill of Paradise itself; they cannot want God's promises too much, as long as they are content to wait upon him to bring them to fruition. John Milton, inheriting what Diane McColley calls the "gust for Paradise,"[24] a desire splendidly and influentially described by Nicholas of Cusa, here imagines that appetite is heavenly and surfeit is impossible when the perfect tension between capacity, hunger (and the new capacity hunger implies and effects), and obedience is unbroken. The ontological provocation of life in the garden of Eden is much too much—and thus just enough. What Milton in a wonderfully disturbing phrase calls the "enormous bliss" (5.297) of Paradise is not unlike Proclus's description in "The Nature of Poetic Art" of the highest kind of poetry, the kind that we might say soars with "no middle flight" (1.14): "This . . . is an apparent madness better than temperance, and is distinguished by a divine quality."[25]

Notes

1. John Milton, *Areopagitica*, in *John Milton: Complete Poems and Major Prose*, ed. Merritt Y. Hughes (New York: Odyssey, 1957). All references to Milton's prose are to this edition and are cited parenthetically in the text.

2. John Milton, *Paradise Lost*, ed. Alastair Fowler (London: Longman, 1971). All references to *Paradise Lost* are to this edition and are cited parenthetically in the text. Fowler's annotations are cited in my notes by page and note numbers.

3. This concept of the "provoking object," as we shall see, has provoked mainly silence or denial from Milton scholars. The concept, however, is not unique to Milton. For example, one may find the cognate notion of an object by which God tempts or tries man—that is, an "object" of "probation"—in Robert Hill's 1613 volume of dialogues entitled *The Pathway to Prayer and Pietie* (facsimile reprint, Norwood, N. J.: Walter J. Johnson, 1975, *The English Experience* no. 744), 79, 81–82. That Milton shares Hill's position on the nature of divine temptation is clear from the *Christian Doctrine* (985–89). And in *Hamlet* 1.1.155–56, Shakespeare has Horatio say of the ghost's disappearance at the cock's crowing, "of the truth herein [i.e., that "erring spirits" vanish at the cock's crow] / This present object [the ghost's vanishing] made probation" (*The Riverside Shakespeare*, ed. G. Blakemore Evans et al. [Boston: Houghton Mifflin, 1974]; all references to Shakespeare are to this edition). Although "probation" and "provoking" are etymologically related, they are not identical; I take "provocation" to be Milton's own intensification of the more common "probation."

I believe that much, perhaps most, of Milton's poetic, philosophical, dramatic, and theological vision finds its essence in this notion of "provocation." "Paradisal Appetite and Cusan Food" is part of a much larger work in progress I am currently undertaking on Milton's poetics of provocation.

4. One may even speculate that Raphael's words regarding Adam's and Eve's being "Improved by tract of time" (5.498) with their teasing prospect of an expanded venue and (implicitly) an enlarged diet, may eventually make even the one prohibition subject to change, if Adam and Eve "be found obedient" (5.501; see 493–506).

5. E. M. W. Tillyard, *Milton*, rev. ed. (New York: Barnes and Noble, 1967), 239. Some reductive readings of Eden persist, however. In 1989 one critic was still calling Milton's Paradise "pristine." (See John Leonard, "Language and Knowledge in *Paradise Lost*," in *The Cambridge Companion to Milton*, ed. Dennis Danielson [Cambridge: Cambridge University Press, 1989], 97–111.)

6. For descriptions of a dynamic Paradise, see Barbara Lewalski, "Innocence and Experience in Milton's Eden," in *New Essays on "Paradise Lost*," ed. Thomas Kranidas (Berkeley: University of California Press, 1969), 86–117; Diane McColley, *Milton's Eve* (Urbana: University of Illinois Press, 1983) and *A Gust for Paradise: Milton's Eden and the Visual Arts* (Urbana: University of Illinois Press, 1993);

Thomas Blackburn, "'Uncloister'd Virtue': Adam and Eve in Milton's Paradise," *Milton Studies* 3 (1971): 119–37; Joan Bennett, *Reviving Liberty: Radical Christian Humanism in Milton's Great Poems* (Cambridge: Harvard University Press, 1989), 109–18; Dennis Danielson, *Milton's Good God: A Study in Literary Theodicy* (Cambridge: Cambridge University Press, 1982), 164–227. For a dissenting (and thus more traditional) voice, see Mary Nyquist, "Reading the Fall: Discourse in Drama in *Paradise Lost*," *English Literary Renaissance* 14 (1984): 199–229. Nyquist distinguishes between the "different kinds of presentations" the epic affords, specifically the "epic recitals" of prelapsarian life versus the "dramatic" dialogue beginning with the separation scene. While the distinction is valuable, Nyquist's thesis leads her to ignore important variations in dialogic context and content in books 4 through 8, as well as to ascribe a "tragic" or "dramatic" character not only to books 9 and 10, but also to the historical pageant of books 11 and 12, simply because tragedy depends on linear progression: "the poem's . . . 'lofty' epic retrospections and temporal discontinuities are succeeded in books 9 through 12 by the straightforward linear progressions we normally associate with tragedy" (202).

7. Dennis Burden, *The Logical Epic* (Cambridge: Harvard University Press, 1967), 125, 132–33. In what sense the Miltonic argument of *Areopagitica* could appear "innocent" (i.e., free of ideological or ethical or personal motive), Burden leaves unclear. Indeed, Burden's argument consistently flattens Milton's poem into a frieze of rationality: e.g., a "frustrated desire would be a satanic thing"; "[m]arriage is rational," etc. (84–85).

8. Alastair Fowler, ed. *Paradise Lost* (London: Longman, 1971), 481–82 n. ix735–43, 482 n. ix739–40.

9. At least Fowler and Burden are not entirely silent before Milton's provocations. By contrast, Dennis Danielson's "The Fall of Man and Milton's Theodicy" (*The Cambridge Companion to Milton*, 113–29), while a lucid and persuasive essay, simply ignores (by means of selective quotation) the "provoking object" in *Areopagitica* (see 118, for example).

10. The description of Nicholas as the "artist's philosopher" is Dorothy Koenigsberger's: see *Renaissance Man and Creative Thinking: A History of Concepts of Harmony, 1400–1700* (Atlantic Highlands, N. J.: Humanities, 1979), 115. Although I have found no direct evidence that Milton read Nicholas's works, it is nevertheless true that Cusan philosophy was a major part of the Platonism of the Florentine and English Renaissances, as Ernst Cassirer demonstrates in *The Platonic Renaissance in England*, 1953, trans. James P. Pettegrove (New York: Gordian, 1970). Milton, powerfully influenced by Renaissance Neoplatonism, would have known this strand well. Aside from the emergence of the Cambridge Platonists during and soon after Milton's stay at the university, witness also Milton's remarks in *The Second Defense of the People of England* regarding Florence: "In the latter city, which I have always more particularly esteemed for the elegance of its dialect, its genius, and its taste, I stopped about two months" (828–29).

11. William Kerrigan and Gordon Braden, *The Idea of the Renaissance* (Baltimore: Johns Hopkins University Press, 1989), 93.

12. *Nicholas of Cusa On Learned Ignorance*, 2d ed., trans. Jasper Hopkins (Minneapolis: Banning, 1985), 155–56. The brackets are in Hopkins's translation of the original.

13. Lewalski, "Innocence and Experience," 92.

14. "Fear here no dearth": fear here—in eating freely with glad heart of every tree that in the garden grows—no death, either; one may eat freely and gladly with no fear of *dearth* only when one does not eat, for fear of *death*, of one tree, the

prohibited one, whose prohibition provokes dietary freedom in abundance—a cluster of puns and reversals grows within this passage.

15. It is worth noting another Shakespearean analogue and, perhaps, another source for Milton: in *Antony and Cleopatra* 2.2.235–37, Enobarbus says of Cleopatra that "Other women cloy / The appetites they feed, but she makes hungry / Where most she satisfies." Cf. also *Hamlet* 1.2.143–45: "Why, she should hang on him / As if increase of appetite had grown / By what it fed on."

16. Fowler, *Paradise Lost*, 298 n. v6336–40.

17. Adam's thirst and satisfaction and thirsting again contrast sharply with the tantalizations the devils endure in 10.550–77. The devils keep falling, into "the same illusion" (10.571), whereas prelapsarian Adam wants only truth. But see also John Carey, *Milton* (New York: Arco, 1970), 85–86: "Raphael's warning to Adam is teasingly inadequate. . . . When he boasts to Adam that he is going to unfold secrets 'perhaps / Not lawful to reveal' (5.569–70), he is hardly assisting the human pair to take divine prohibitions about knowledge very seriously. He heavily underlines the inferiority of their understanding of the universe to his own, and tantalizes them with alternative theories (8.122–6), only to condemn the curiosity he has been arousing." (Actually, only Adam is so "tantalized," since Eve has already excused herself from the table.) This is a perversely exaggerated account, of course, but like William Empson's urgent exaggerations in *Milton's God*, rev. ed. (London: Chatto and Windus, 1965), it tells a truth. Milton does modulate paradisal conversations in a provocative way; dialogue in Paradise is both context and contest.

18. John Peter Rumrich, *Matter Of Glory: A New Preface To "Paradise Lost"* (Pittsburgh: University of Pittsburgh Press, 1987), 100.

19. Louis Schwartz's work in progress on conditions of childbirth in seventeenth-century London interprets this allegory very powerfully and specifically; I am most grateful for his suggestions regarding this part of my argument.

20. Carey, *Milton*, 95.

21. See Ronald Levao, *Renaissance Minds and Their Fictions: Cusanus, Sidney, Shakespeare* (Berkeley: University of California Press, 1985), xvii–xix, xxiii; Levao discusses Cusanus thoroughly in 3–96.

22. Koenigsberger, *Renaissance Man*, 127.

23. Even after the Fall angels are warning Adam about the need for temperance: Michael tells Adam to obey the rule of "not too much" (11.531). As with Raphael, however, Michael's "not too much" falls within a rather intemperate conversation—in Michael's case, the revelation of all human history that drives toward Adam's summary of all knowledge in his acknowledging Christ his "redeemer ever blest" (12.573; see 12.552–73). In other words, the context here, as before the Fall, offers a "thick description" of "temperance": an extreme plenitude of revelation and simplicity of creed are coextensive, "too much" and "just enough" cleave to each other.

24. See McColley, *Gust for Paradise*.

25. Proclus, "The Nature of Poetic Art," trans. Thomas Taylor, rev. trans. Kevin Kerrane, in *Classical and Medieval Literary Criticism: Translations and Interpretations*, ed. Alex Preminger et al. (New York: Felix Ungar, 1974), 314.

Enormous, as Fowler notes (275 n. v294–7), carries with it the etymological suggestion of abnormality, or lawlessness. Although Fowler quickly adds that *enormous* as it appears in *Paradise Lost* 5.297 is "probably influenced also by the modern meaning 'immense,'" it is worth noting that the 1919 edition of the *OED* cites this very passage in *Paradise Lost* as an example of its first, obsolete definition of "enormous": "1. Deviating from an ordinary rule or type; abnormal, unusual, extraordinary, unfettered by rules; hence, mostly in a bad sense, strikingly irregular, monstrous, shocking." I am grateful to Louis Schwartz for alerting me to this crux.

Dalila, Eve, and the "Concept of Woman" in Milton's Radical Christian Humanism

Joan S. Bennett

DALILA's part in Milton's tragedy, *Samson Agonistes,* is much larger than in Milton's biblical sources, as is the role of Eve in his epic, *Paradise Lost;* and the women's roles are pivotal. Given Milton's own major role and pivotal position in Western literary history, readers are, not surprisingly, tempted to seek in Milton's treatment of these two female figures a Miltonic concept or idea of "woman." Milton himself portrays male characters who puzzle over "woman," seeming thus to invite such questioning from readers. However, all the serious questions in Milton's poetry are raised not so much to be "answered" as to be "deepened" or "opened out"; and each resonates with its connections to the many other serious issues that the poet engages. This essay considers one sense of "woman," or perhaps of human "difference" or "otherness," that does seem to me genuinely Miltonic. I find this concept of "woman" opening and deepening within the framework of Milton's radical Christian humanism.

To begin with elements of that frame, we may consider what can be learned about Milton's conception of "woman" from a comparison of *Samson Agonistes* with the biblical treatments of Samson in the Book of Judges and the Epistle to the Hebrews. The Book of Judges in the Hebrew Bible tells the story of Israel's nationhood so as to confirm at the same time (1) Israel's status as a chosen people and (2) Israel's contingent placement within human history, where God's call to a free covenant is a dynamic one to be worked out by the people of this nation generation after generation. Within this memory of a people being formed into a nation, Samson is significant only as he plays out the drama of divine-national engagement. Samson's internal psychological and spiritual experiences are not memorable in themselves because individual protagonists, whether patriarchs, judges, kings, or prophets, vary from story to story from the twelfth century B.C.E. on into the redactors' own time and beyond, as the Hebrew people respond again and again to God's call; the point of these stories is that God will call and that an unending engagement with that call is necessary. Of even less interest, in this context, is the internal state of the third of this judge's sexual liaisons, Delilah from Sorek, the pawn of Philistine kings (Judges 16).[1]

The author of the passage in Hebrews 11 that resounds with the names
of Samson and the other Old Testament heroes of faith seeks, in one sense,
to widen immensely the concept of a nation's relationship to God, to show
Israel as a light to the Gentiles, leading all of humankind into a vast public
covenant. At the same time, the very largeness of the covenanted body
results in certain narrowings of focus; for the new people of God are a vast
collection of single persons, each receiving his or her own call from God.
They are the first Christian individuals and voluntary small communities
of the Hellenistic world. No longer part of a coherent people or nation,
Jewish and Gentile Christians developed a New Testament theology of the
fulfillment of the promises of salvation through Jesus; the range of possible
meanings in each incident of the old stories narrowed, as a result, so as to
drive toward this Christian theological meaning. Thus, in the Epistles, Hebrew history, in all its contingency and contradictoriness, becomes strung
taut as it is shown reaching for the end of time; ultimate ambiguities of
meaning are flattened out as the ultimate answer is now known. As the
narrative flattens out in this way, the epistler's interest in the interior spiritual state of the actor in the ancient story of faith becomes correspondingly
intensified. But speaking in the language of androcentrism, he draws only
actors who are male, and Delilah at this point disappears; she was merely
incidental to the individual great man's trial of faith.

John Milton, Englishman of the seventeenth century, draws deeply upon
both the Old and New Testaments of his Hebrew-and-Christian inheri-
tance. At the end of Milton's drama, Samson is pronounced to be the faith
hero of Hebrews; and we know from the theologizing angels of *Paradise
Lost* and from the *Christian Doctrine*, as well as from many others of his
writings, that Milton did operate from deep within the theological paradigm
initiated in the New Testament epistles. Nevertheless, for most of his life
Milton saw the English nation as a modern Israel, divinely chosen as a
nation to embody the covenant that was in need of renewal from its biblical
roots. When he worked with the Samson story in his political prose, it was
with Samson's public identity—his role in the nation's collective story—
that he dealt. So, too, when he created *Samson Agonistes*, he created a
protagonist whose identity is public first and only secondarily individual
and private. In spite of his obtuseness and his dreadful failure, the Samson
of Milton's drama is aware that he is, as he testifies to Harapha, "no private
but a person rais'd" (1211).[2]

In correlation with Milton's own deep religio-political commitments,
then, this Samson is drawn on a ground where the contingencies and ambiguities of history are overwhelmingly present to be wrestled with as in the
narratives of ancient Israel, and, as in those narratives, the point is that this
story contains meaning of the utmost importance even though a theological
or ecclesiastical formulation of that meaning is denied to us. At the same

time, because *Samson Agonistes* is a Christian drama, the status of the protagonist's individual soul, and the state of being of each reader's soul, is at stake, imbedded in that unformulatable meaning. For this reason, Milton uses the genre of Greek tragedy to give us a generous look into the mental and spiritual state of Samson. By the same token, Milton gives lengthy attention to the mental and spiritual state of other individuals, including Philistines, who very explicitly are not of the chosen nation and yet are held, in some important way, responsible for the historic covenant with the Hebrews' God. Milton's telling explores, not only for Samson but also for Dalila, both an individual psychological and spiritual state of being and a public responsibility and role.

Marriage is what allows Milton to place in Dalila an intense exploration of the public/private self. By portraying Dalila as Samson's wife, Milton creates a closer tie between the Dalila story and the story of the woman of Timnah than is found in the Book of Judges. As in the Bible's telling of the Timnah story, Samson's choosing a significant relationship with Dalila is seen by him (though not by his family or countrymen) as an active, not accidental, part of his religio-political role. Judges says that the Lord was seeking to provide Samson "occasion[s]" (14.4) against the Philistine over-lords, and Milton chooses to work closely with this interpretation.

What concept of matrimony does this decision of Milton's reveal? The same that is familiar to us from Milton's tracts on matrimony (though we refer to them as the "divorce" tracts, he himself called them tracts on matrimony): the purpose of marriage, even of marriage in Eden, was to bind "the maried couple to all society of life, and communion in divine & humane things; and so associated [keep] them" (2:448).[3] Marriage was instituted by God at, and as, the basis of society; and society was instituted from the beginning for the purpose of turning private beings into public selves so that—as Milton exhorted readers of *The Readie & Easie Way*— each individual would place "his privat welfare and happiness in the public peace, libertie, and safetie" (7:443).

In *Samson Agonistes* Milton invents dialogues in which private welfare's relation to public good is examined. He shows Samson reproaching Dalila: if you were going to treat me as an enemy, why did you marry me, "Then, as since then, thy country's foe profest?" (884). You knew, he says, that I was the leader of Israel—all that I did, wore, drank, married was part of that public identity. He was never, he implies, without a public self, a commitment to human collectivity—not even in his most personal decisions and experiences. Samson's public responsibility was clear—when Dalila married Samson, she married it. The integrity with which Samson carried out his mission was seriously flawed, and the arguing and recriminations in this episode are full of problems; but the only basis for untangling them lies in recognizing that there is, in an important sense, no private sphere apart for either person.

We should look, therefore, at what happens to the private relationship when it is seen primarily to exist for the public welfare. Does Milton's placement of marriage within the public sphere allow for a complete and implicit faith between marriage partners? In one sense it does, and in another sense it does not. Just as the definition of "citizen" contains completely and implicitly the understanding that one does not betray a fellow citizen to a deadly enemy, so one absolutely does not betray a marriage partner. However, the "faith" of free citizens in one another, while committed to the good of one another in the collective, is always in the particular instance *in*complete and cannot be left implicit; so, too, must the faith of a wife and husband in one another's good, and in the good of their marriage's contribution to society, work and work at being *ex*plicit. The marriage faith, like the public trust of which it is a part, means working things through in "free and open encounter[s]" (*Areopagitica*, 2:561). This need exists, for Milton, even in Paradise, where the prototype for human interaction is to be sought, as he shows us in the separation scene between Adam and Eve in book 9 of *Paradise Lost*.[4] That task was hard for Adam and Eve, who were perfect; and it is never finished. Samson, the legend informs us, was—like most of us—much less skilled in this endeavor.

The dialogue between Samson and Dalila encourages us to imagine what Samson, when pressured by Dalila to reveal his secret, "should have done." When she asked, we might say, he should have explained, "It would not be wise for me to give to anyone, even you, vital national security information." But if he had said this, what would have happened? The encounter would have turned into a fallen version of the separation scene of *Paradise Lost:* if you won't tell me, that can only mean you don't trust me— "Thoughts, which how found they harbor in thy breast, / . . . misthought of her to thee so dear?" (*Paradise Lost*, 9.288–89). If you don't trust me, then you don't really love me. Samson, like Adam, is worn down by the need to keep the relationship with his wife both open and oriented to the public good.

This need to stay in relationship, I believe, is central to Milton's Christian humanism, where the need is always simultaneously private and public, individual and collective, ethical and political. We may turn to the humanistic side of his heritage for terminology that is helpful here—to the ancient Greek concept of *phronesis*, that virtue of the mind explained by Aristotle that yields an ethical know-how in which a person's being and knowledge are interlaced with one another in a continual becoming; in which what is universal (principles, doctrines, theologies, eternal verities) and what is particular (historical, situational, changing, contingent) are codetermined.[5] This interlacing is a human being's and a human community's only route to truth, to God, who at the same time is universal Providence and is in the "providences"—the contingencies of human existence, which are no accidents but are fraught with divine importance for humankind.

If we recognize that Milton held onto a Hebrew sense of God's call to a people through their political history all the while that he also held a New Testament sense of individual spirituality, and that these were mediated for him through the classical sense of right reason, can we find in this Miltonic framework a picture that reveals a "concept of woman"? This is a different question from one that seeks to describe Dalila or the woman of Timnah or Queen Christina of Sweden or Henrietta Maria or Mary Powell or Katherine Woodcock. To ask about a concept is to ask for a universal. To answer with individuals in particular situations is to pull that question into the partial, contingent "pieces" of history. But in the paradigm within which Milton viewed the human condition, the universal and the particular are codetermined in the continual coming into being of persons and communities. To experience this relational interaction with the greatest fullness, people need "other selves," a foundational concept that Milton sets forth in *Paradise Lost* (8.450).

By particularizing Eve in the way he does, Milton points to the universals he is developing. In his hands, the need for an "other self" is not narcissistic, as we can see if we give equal emphasis to both of these terms in which Milton's Eve first appears to Adam. Eve is Adam's "other self," "a creature so like him," as Milton characterizes woman from a male point of view in *Tetrachordon* (2:589), and yet, as Adam tries to explain to the angel, so different—"Not equal" (4.296) in the sense of not "identical," as their different sex constantly foregrounds.

At his nadir after his fall, an anguished Adam wants to know why God had not found some other way to populate the earth than by creating this "difference":

> O why did God,
> Creator wise, that peopl'd highest Heav'n
> With Spirits Masculine, create at last
> This novelty on Earth, this fair defect
> Of Nature, and not fill the World at once
> With Men as Angels without Feminine?
>
> (10.888–93)

Although Adam's masculine reason, approaching the angels', is still filled with axioms after his fall, these universal truths are lodged with him useless once he is cut off from the right understanding of the *phronimos* (possessor of *phronesis*) who is able to reason in the contingent realm, the realm of human history. The "masculine" Raphael would not be able to help him now, even reasoning, as the angel can, from axiom to axiom at the speed of light. Their Platonic symposium (from which Eve discreetly excuses herself) exercises Adam in reasoning with universals; but the angel is at a loss to help Adam with human *phronesis*. The angel has a theory of human history: "time may come when men / With Angels may participate" (5.493–94); but he cannot enter that history as a human actor; and because he cannot participate in the particulars, he cannot help to construct those universal truths that comprise this human world. While Adam listens to the being from the higher level in the hierarchy, he feels the transports of contemplation; but the man must work out his own mode of living in relationship with an "other" on the same hierarchical level as himself, one "so like him" yet different. The angel cannot lead Adam to *phronesis*, because *phronesis* requires an ongoing dialectic in which the reasoners are in a continually building relationship. Although the angel has great facility with the laws of rational nature, such axioms cannot in any direct way be "applied" to particular situations; in Milton's conception of them, they are not analogous to mathematical laws or even to the positive laws by which humans in a fallen world govern their own behavior. Indeed, Raphael's brief, awkward attempt at such application is easily perceived by Adam, in spite of his reverence for the angel, to be far off the mark (8.595–611).

The ultimate test of the right-reasoning public/private self—of what it means to be human—is drawn by Milton in book 10 of his epic; it takes place after the humans' fall. Adam and Eve succeed in this trial, but only as reasoning beings in dynamic relationship with one another. Here again we see a pattern in which individual, private human souls are at stake, but can only be reached through a dynamic link with the individuals' collective, public identity. Adam has cut himself off from God and his own sense of his public role: "in mee all / Posterity stands curst" (10.817–18). His "reasonings, though through Mazes" (830) are internally consistent, and therefore valid; but they leave him with no way to hope or to live, even though annihilation is denied. He concludes himself "miserable / Beyond all past example and future, / To Satan only like" (839–41); and he echoes the despair of that ultimately alone angel whose brilliance is useless cut off from relationship, the Devil for whom there can be no history, only endless repetition of the stasis he suffers, where "in the lowest deep a lower deep / Still threat'ning to devour me opens wide" (4.76–77)—"out of which," the man echoes, "I find no way, from deep to deeper plung'd!" (10.843–44).

The first fruit of the man's having locked himself into a satanic aloneness is shown by Milton to be misogyny: "Out of my sight, thou Serpent" (10.867). Reflecting his deadly isolation, he attacks the relational "other self." Eve's feminine praxis at this point reveals a part of what I would call Milton's own "concept of woman" or of the feminine. The woman's relentless commitment to their particular relationship—"Immovable till peace obtain'd from fault / Acknowledg'd and deplor'd" (938–39)—pulls the man's reaching for universals back into the contingent realm, the only place where the answers that Adam needs can be found or, rather, created. The universals that genuinely speak to his situation are determined by the particulars that are becoming human history while the events of that history are determined by the universals being constituted. Wisdom, *phronesis*, consists in this dynamic, interpersonal process. The issues are simultaneously private (forgiveness of one another, planning for their personal and domestic future) and public (joint confession before God, planning for the future of the race). Their letting what is universal and what is particular be codetermined, while holding onto the specific bond with each other, leads them to new understandings of "Death" (1050), "pain" (1025), "labor" (1054), and, indeed, of divine judgment itself (1060–61). In this process, it is Adam who can generalize and articulate the resolution, but it is Eve who knows and leads the way to it; together—and only together—they are the right reasoners, the faithful.

Dalila's function in *Samson Agonistes*—looked at in these terms—is similar, although the outcome in her story is a tragic one. It is her coming, her insistence on relationship, that pulls a despairing Samson back into history. In their encounter, we cannot witness a reconciled marriage and a beginning again of human society; we witness instead a divorce and the liberation of an oppressed nation. The reason Milton believed divorce to be a creative, faithful act, however, is the same reason he believed in marriage itself: the function of the man/woman relation is to create the basis for all human/human relation, which is the ground of human history, the only arena in which the universal divine love for human beings can be realized.

At the midpoint of his tragedy, Samson has shown himself to be in the position of Adam in book 10; the burden of his sin is intolerable and "death's benumbing Opium" is his "only cure" (630). Not possessed of Adam's intellect, he nevertheless records for us the essence of Adam's despair, the "sense of Heav'n's desertion" (632) and the end, therefore, of his own engagement with history. The chorus of Danites perform for Samson the reasoning that Adam displayed in his despair; they rack the many "sayings of the wise / In ancient and in modern books" (652–53), looking for those axioms that will account for Samson's experience; but they are aware that such "studied argument" (658) "with th'afflicted in his pangs . . . / Little prevails" (660–61). The Danites with their store of reasonings know that they cannot help Samson "Unless he feel within / Some source of consolation from above" (663–64), and they pray fervently for intervention from God: "Behold him in this state calamitous, and turn / His labors, for thou canst, to peaceful end" (708–9). Their prayer receives an immediate answer, not in the form of the mysterious "Secret refreshings" (665) they had requested, but in the very earthly woman who has been Samson's wife. They are amazed: "But who is this . . . ?" (710).

Like Eve, Dalila is met, in her attempted reconciliation, with misogyny, which we have seen Milton identify as the fallen masculine's attempt to project his share of the sin in the form of a universal onto another: "Out, out Hyaena; these are thy wonted arts. / And arts of every woman false like thee" (748–49). The man wants to label the woman as an animal, beneath him therefore in the hierarchy of being, while in Miltonic fact, man and woman, the "other selves," are "so like" that they are on the same level of the ladder of being, though different enough to enable a dialectical relationship.

Also like Eve, Dalila seeks to renew relationship and, to do so, is ready to explore all avenues, however impossible seeming. Like Samson, however, Dalila is deeply flawed morally. As a result, the particulars she brings and the universals she reaches for cannot be caught; they fail truly to determine each other's meaning by the same process that we witnessed in Eve's and Adam's confessions and their subsequent back-and-forth creative reasoning. At first, Dalila lingers in particulars, reviewing her "weakness[es]" (774–84) and his; they lead her to an attempted universal, "Love's law" (811). Samson is aware that Dalila's unhappiness is not the same thing as repentance, that indeed her commitment to his welfare remains the same as it was when she betrayed him—her goal is to have him safely out of his public role altogether, in "domestic ease, / Exempt from many a care and chance to which / Eyesight exposes daily men abroad" (917–19) and "so supplied" (926) that what by her he has lost he "least shal[l] miss" (927).

Samson throws back at Dalila the falsity of her attempted universal "Love's law." He asserts that "Love seeks to have love" (837). He then counters with other "laws": those of "greed" (831–32) and "lust" (837). Dalila accepts that her attempted link of "weakness" with love does not truthfully characterize her relationship with Samson; but, at the same time, she denies that "greed" and "lust" are true of her. Bringing to bear the particular actions of the Philistine public officials, she recharacterizes these as calls for her own engagement for the public good. This potentially strong universal, a value shared by Samson himself, cannot, however, withstand the internal contradictions of the Philistines' behavior; although they were public officials, Samson says, they urged action that was "Against the law of nature, law of nations" (890). Even the universal "gods," when linked to their imputed particular actions—"ungodly deeds, the contradiction / Of thir own deity" (898–99)—turn out to be false.

At this end point of the attempt at renewed relationship, Dalila herself turns misogynistic, and she does so for the same reason that Adam and Samson did; she is projecting her guilt for her own deep sense of isolation onto her womanhood: "In argument with men a woman ever / Goes by the worse, whatever be her cause" (903–4). She cannot hold onto her wish to preserve the specific bond with the other and abandons her initial effort to let the particular and universal truths of her marriage's public/private relationship work out their codetermined meaning. All of the particulars finally do come genuinely together in the one barren truth that Samson articulates: "thou and I long since are twain" (929). This is the truth of their divorce. Recognizing this truth in its complex particulars releases Samson from his earlier misogyny. Unlike the chorus, who are still seeking simple universal truths that will explain "woman" (1010–60), Samson now reads his encounter contingently. God "sent" (999) Dalila to Samson at this juncture to activate his genuine self-awareness, which is the same as his public identity—his "most sacred trust" (1001), which is the same as his relation to God.

And though Dalila's and Samson's private relationship has necessarily failed, having lost its public/private integrity, their divorce is simultaneously, for Samson, a true and a creative act. In spite of his violent rejection of her, Samson has, in fact, treated Dalila as a moral person and public equal in their dialogue, not allowing her to claim "female" (777) weakness as a reason for resignation of faithful action. As a result, he has necessarily placed the same demand for faithful public action on himself, a demand that he will now begin to answer. From this point on, Samson's drama changes as he reengages with history, not assuming now that he knows either what a particular event's meaning is or what a universal truly means, but having the faith in his relationship with God that allows him to let the particular and universal meanings—actions and laws; performance in the forbidden temple and faithfulness to the law of God—codetermine one another.

Dalila meets a hard end; presumably, her public role as Philistine heroine earned her a place under the roof of the theater that Samson tears down, killing all who stood within. Perhaps, however, Dalila did not have the stomach to watch Samson's humiliation—perhaps in her way she did love him. If so, we may imagine her as not there, but at home, "Wailing [his] absence in [her] widow'd bed" (806) as she had feared, her public identity no longer an issue. Milton lets go of the potential story he has created for Dalila once she has served to pull Samson out of his deadly stasis and back into history. In this sense, Milton's tragedy is androcentric, as is *Paradise Lost*, which, though it very remarkably gives woman the epic's last and deepest word, devotes the bulk of its words and its readers' attention to human experience seen through a masculine coloring.

At the same time, Milton seems to hold a generalizable "concept of woman"—one that, although it does not explain either "woman" or individual women, does characterize an important feature, in the human realm, of the feminine half of those "two great Sexes [that] animate [our] World" (*Paradise Lost*, 8.151). "Woman," by her difference from "man," figures forth the differences that exist among all humans. Her attractiveness and attraction figure the divine pull of humans into relationships with one another, both domestic and political. Her insistence both on being her own "other" self and on holding onto relationship is an insistence on the praxis that requires *phronesis,* or right reason, which is both private and public. If the faithful man inclines to dwell imaginatively with Providence, the faithful woman inclines to live dynamically with the providences. Together they give life to a human history blessed from its beginning and redeemable in the end.

Notes

1. All biblical references are to the King James Version and are cited parenthetically in the text.

2. John Milton, *Samson Agonistes,* in *John Milton: Complete Poems and Major Prose,* ed. Merritt Y. Hughes (New York: Odyssey, 1957). All references to Milton's poetry are to this edition and are cited parenthetically in the text.

3. John Milton, *The Judgement of Martin Bucer,* in *Complete Prose Works of John Milton,* 8 vols., ed. Don M. Wolfe et al. (New Haven: Yale University Press, 1953–82). All references to Milton's prose are to this edition and are cited parenthetically in the text.

4. See Joan S. Bennett, *Reviving Liberty: Radical Christian Humanism in Milton's Great Poems* (Cambridge: Harvard University Press, 1989), chapter 4.

5. The interpretation of *phronesis* presented here is that of Hans-Georg Gadamer, restated by Richard Bernstein in *Beyond Objectivism and Relativism: Science, Hermeneutics, and Praxis* (Philadelphia: University of Pennsylvania Press, 1983), 146–47.

Dalila, Misogyny, and the *De Casibus* Tradition

LEE A. JACOBUS

THE confrontation between Samson and Dalila is not only the most carefully and intensely gendered agon in *Samson Agonistes,* it is also one of the
most distinctively gendered agons in all western literature. Jim Swan has
considered some of the psychological issues attendant on Milton and the
question of gender, reminding us that terms such as masculine and feminine
"are arbitrary, a set of markers to assert a difference."[1] The traditional
difference between Samson and Delilah that interests us most is expressed
in terms that ultimately dispraise women on the basis of one woman's
behavior. As with many gendered agons, Samson's and Delilah's has produced a misogynistic tradition in which Delilah has become the archetype
of the wheedling, subtle betrayer. Milton's treatment of Dalila is one of the
ultimate tests of his attitude toward misogyny. His view is shadowed forth
in his attenuating somewhat the difference between Samson and Dalila in
his allocation of blame for Samson's imprisonment.[2] His skill is demonstrated in his ability to find his way through the tradition of misogyny—
while using all the resources of its imagery. His achievement is that he
avoids condemning Dalila as a woman even though he condemns her as
a person.

Milton inherited the tradition of misogyny relative to Dalila most forcefully from Boccaccio's *De casibus virorum illustrium,* which was popular
in two versions in England, one abbreviated in Chaucer's "Monk's Tale"
(c. 1387), and one more fully developed in John Lydgate's *The Fall of
Princes* (1431–38). Contemporary activity in reviving misogynistic attitudes
may also have affected Milton's portrait of Dalila. The controversy that
developed in regard to the Swetnam tracts (the original and its numerous
responses) began with Joseph Swetnam's *The Arraignment of Lewd, Idle,
Froward, and Unconstant Women* (1615), which, while regarded by some
as the work of a crank, was also welcomed by some as a reminder of the
dangers of trusting women. The reverberations from Swetnam's work did
not end until early in the nineteenth century. Milton's awareness of these
works seems clear from his own use of shared imagery and shared narrative,

but his ability to distinguish himself from the attitudes of these misogynistic authors is also clear.

To begin with, Milton's portrait of Dalila, "bedeckt, ornate, and gay" (712),[3] is rich, complex, and extensive far beyond the description in Judges. Chaucer's *de casibus* rescension in the "Monk's Tale" is surprising in that, while Chaucer begins with Lucifer and Adam, he accords them only one eight-line stanza each. Samson is treated in ten eight-line stanzas. Delilah is not a central figure in the "Monk's Tale," nor does Chaucer make any effort to develop feminine psychology or examine feminine deception in anything like the depth in which Milton develops them. Chaucer's version concentrates almost entirely on Samson's outward actions, describing his victories and defeat in passionate language:

> now is he in prison in a cave
> Where-as they made hym at the queerne grynde.
> O noble Sampsoun, strongest of mankynde,
> O whilom juge, in glorie and in richesse!
> Now maystow wepen with thyne eyen blynde,
> Sith thou fro wele art falle in wrecchednesse.
>
> (2073–78)[4]

Chaucer's "Dalida" is virtually a bit-part character, alluded to only in terms of what she did and what she caused, and with no effort at analysis of motive or concern for the interiority of the character:

> falsly to his foomen she hym solde.
> And slepynge in hir barm, upon a day,
> She made to clippe or shere his heres away,
> And made his foomen al his craft espyen;
> And whan that they hym foond in this array,
> They bounde hym faste and putten out his eyen.
>
> (2065–70)

Judges' verses 6 to 20 are devoted to Delilah's efforts to tease out Samson's secret. In the Geneva Bible we are told that "came the princes of ẏ Philistíms, and said vnto her, Entise him, and se wherein his great strength *lieth,* and by what meane we may overcome him."[5] The quest for Samson's secret appears to come not from Delilah's and feminine curiosity, but from the anxious princes, fearful for their own skins. Whatever other motives she may have had, she complies with their wishes. Chaucer elides even this detail by cutting to the chase and saying simply, "Unto his lemman Dalida he tolde / That in his heeris al his strengthe lay" (2063–64).

Mieke Bal's analysis of the details of the Bible's pattern of temptation emphasizes its sexual nature, reminding us that "Socially, Delilah's concep-

tion of love is traditionally feminine. It is woman who is supposed to surrender to man."[6] Samson, in what may be a blurring of gender expectations,
surrenders his secret to Delilah, although, as Bal demonstrates, his surrender is actually to the Philistine men. In her analysis, Samson not only
matures sexually, but suffers a "rebirth in Delilah's lap [which] is not only
a return to the mother's womb. It is a return that cuts off wrong choices
and enables him to begin anew."[7] Bal's assumptions include the view that
the story as it is told in the Bible is already intensely gendered and that
Delilah's strategy "conforms to stereotypical female behavior."[8]

Milton subtly develops Dalila's psychology and examines her motivation—some of it offered by Dalila's analyzing herself. And while Chaucer's
"Monk's Tale" does not indulge in psychologizing,[9] John Lydgate's version
in *The Fall of Princes* not only examines Delilah's psychology, but also
examines Boccaccio's attitude toward women and reveals his potential misogyny in order to come to terms with some of the troubling aspects of
Delilah's portrayal, blaming them in large part on Boccaccio's unwillingness
to be fair to women. At the same time, Lydgate takes upon himself the
responsibility of resisting an entire tradition of misogyny.

Chaucer moves speedily on from Samson to Hercules, without a pause
for reflection. However, Lydgate usually provides a conventional envoy to
the princes, his supposed audience, followed by a moral of the kind which
normally follows each of his stories:

> Ye noble Pryncis, conceyueth the sentence
> Off this story, remembrid in scripture,
> How that Sampson off wilful necligence
> Was shaue & shorn, diffacid his figure;
> Keep your conceitis vnder couerture,
> Suffre no nyhtwerm withynne your counsail kreepe,
> Thouh Dalida compleyne, crie and weepe!
>
> (1.6504–10)[10]

Quite unlike anything he does earlier, Lydgate precedes his envoy not with
another moral tale of instruction for princes, but with an extensive critique
of Boccaccio's attitude toward women in "A chapitle of Bochas discryuyng
þe malis of wommen." He begins by saying,

> Myn auctour Bochas reioished in his lyue,
> (I dar nat seyn, wher it was comendable)
> Off these women the malice to descryue
> Generali, and writ—it is not fable—
> Off ther nature how thei be variable,

> And how ther malice best be euidence
> Is knowe to hem that haue experience.
>
> (1.6511–17)

In other words, Lydgate's position is supposedly neutral on whether Boccaccio is correct in portraying women as malicious, although he somewhat
coyly defers to those who have experience. His excursion into these matters
lasts for twenty-eight stanzas (as opposed to the twenty-one stanzas devoted
to Samson and Delilah), with many of his stanzas focusing on various instances of feminine deception balanced by examples of feminine stead-
fastness, as in his balancing of meek Hester with murderous Scylla and
steadfast Alceste with the variable Clymestra. Lydgate may or may not be
apologetic for the portrait of Delilah in his previous story. In establishing
what he asserts is a clear moral position on women, he reminds his listeners
that some women have remained virtuous and that men are as likely to be
variable as women:

> And who that euer off malice list accuse
> These celi women touchyng variaunce,
> Lat hem remembre, and in ther wittis muse,
> Men be nat ay stable in ther constaunce.
> In this world heer is no perseueraunce;
> Chaung is ay founde in men & women bothe,
> On outher parti, be thei neuer so wrothe.
>
> (1.6686–92)

The unsettling aspect of this segment is that Lydgate has put so much
imaginative energy into the portrayal of ways in which women can be
deceitful—especially in terms of reshaping their appearance to suit the styles
of the day—that one can only wonder whether Lydgate protests too much
and is perhaps secretly of "Bochas's" party.

Suzanne Woods, in "How Free Are Milton's Women?" says, "Milton's
profound respect for human liberty has the ultimate effect of subverting his
patriarchal assumptions. He is too thoughtful to accept cultural assumptions
without question, yet he has no frame of reference for responding to biblical
authority in this matter."[11] In a sense, Lydgate may have helped provide
the needed frame of reference, since he at least made a move in the direction
that leads to *Samson Agonistes* and Milton's treatment of Dalila. Certainly,
Lydgate's version expands Delilah's role and offers insight into motive and
character while at the same time calling into question the blanket condemnation of women's inconstancy.

However, Lydgate does add a homely analysis of Delilah and her behavior by asserting that she is in some ways a victim of her gender's proclivity
toward gossip:

> But women haue this condicioun,
> Off secre thynges whan thei haue knowlechyng,
> Thei bollyn inward, ther hertis ay fretyng:
> Outher their musten deien or discure,
> So brotil is off custum ther nature.
>
> (1.6352–56)

Milton's Dalila seems to agree with this misogynistic tradition when she tells Samson:

>   it was a weakness
> In me, but incident to all our sex,
> Curiosity, inquisitive, importune
> Of secrets, then with like infirmity
> To publish them, both common female faults.
>
> (773–77)

Not only does Dalila reinforce Lydgate, but Samson alludes to Boccaccio when he says ironically,

> At distance I forgive thee, go with that;
> Bewail thy falsehood, and the pious works
> It hath brought forth to make thee memorable
> Among illustrious women, faithful wives.
>
> (954–57)

Milton writes with not only a clear understanding of texts that have formed the cultural attitude toward Dalila, but also with telling allusions to those texts. As Woods argues, "Milton's women are not as free as his men, but they remain as responsible for their actions. Milton comes to this position not out of misogyny but out of an original indifference to matters of gender, informed and complicated by cultural and biblical attitudes toward women."[12] Perhaps Milton is somehow indifferent to matters of gender, but there can be little question that the meeting of Samson and Dalila is scrupulously gendered. Milton depends not only on the Bible, which is almost attenuated in its attention to Delilah's gender (while obviously marking Samson's gender in terms of the traditional actions of the masculine hero), but on the rescensions of Boccaccio and Lydgate. Their versions are not only gendered, perhaps stereotypically gendered, but, at least in the case of Lydgate, they also analyze presuppositions relative to gender.

Woods points out that Dalila is "a famous villain in the misogynist's canon,"[13] reminding us that the traditions of misogyny had already been at work in Milton's time. Polemical tracts published in the early seventeenth century in England echo Lydgate's descriptions in their denunciation of women. Especially interesting is their consistency of imagery. Joseph Swet-nam's *The Arraignment of Lewd, Idle, Froward, and Unconstant Women* (1615) went through twenty-three reprints up to 1807 and excited a wide range of response, including *A Mouzell for Melastomus* (1617) by Rachel Speght, who seems to have been the first Englishwoman to publish a po-lemic. Barbara Lewalski says, "Speght is then the first self-proclaimed and positively identified female polemicist in England." Ester Sowernam (a pseudonym and pun on Swetnam) published *Ester hath hang'd Haman,* another answer to Swetnam, in 1617. Constantia Munda (another pseud-onym) published *The Worming of a mad Dogge* also in 1617.[14] Obviously, the activity of counterattacking polemicists reflects the interest in Swetnam's work, although it may not reflect its effectiveness or its ultimate force.

Swetnam's sixty-four page diatribe begins with an allusion to Adam's rib: "women are crooked by nature." That there seems to have been a common language of misogyny is apparent in that Swetnam's comparisons and metaphors parallel those of Lydgate and sometimes anticipate Milton himself, as in Swetnam's comment: "if thou chasten her, then she will turn to a Serpent."[15] Swetnam says that women "are also compared unto a painted ship, which seemeth faire outwardly, & yet nothing but ballace within her."[16] And although Samson and Dalila do not figure largely in Swetnam's complaints, he makes one rather telling observation: "Some with sweete words undermine their husbands, as *Dalila* did *Samson.*"[17] His refer-ence to Samson as Dalila's husband is surprisingly Miltonic and reminds us that it was not an immense leap to see Dalila as a wife, nor is it necessary to think of Milton's attribution as autobiographical, nor even, as does Philip Gallagher, as part of "a rehabilitative reconstruction of Judges."[18]

The serpent imagery, a consistent misogynistic descriptor, appears often in Swetnam. When he recites a litany regarding the strengths of various beasts, he cites: "a womans chiefe strength is in her tongue; the Serpent hath not so much venome in his tayle, as she hath in her tongue; and as the Serpent never leaveth hissing and stinging, and seeking to doe mischiefe: even so, some women are never well except they be casting out venome with their tongues, to the hurt of their husbands or of their neighbours; there fore he that will disclose his secrets to a woman, is worthy to have his hayre cut with *Samson.*"[19]

One attack on Swetnam leads us to think that his age might have regarded him as an old-fashioned fuddy-duddy, someone who might be an easy target for humor if only because he was so out-of-date. *Swetnam the Woman-hater, Arraigned by Women,* an anonymous play published in 1620—possi-bly by Thomas Heywood, who wrote a defense of women later in 1624—was first produced in 1618 or 1619, then again later in 1633. In it Swetnam appears under the alias "Mysogenus." Mysogenus is himself arraigned before women in act 5 where he is accused by the queen of "Comparing vs to Serpents, Crocodiles / For Dissimulation, *Hienas* for Subtilties."[20]

Although Milton uses the serpentine imagery of misogyny, he makes Dalila sympathetic to most readers upon initial contact in ways that go far beyond Lydgate, Chaucer, or contemporary misogynists. The Bible's and Chaucer's Delilah have none of our sympathy. Her role, relative to Samson, is negligible in Chaucer and limited to her repeated requests for him to reveal his secret in Judges. Delilah is more sympathetic in Lydgate partly because she is more carefully developed and more thoroughly presented. The opening imagery that Lydgate uses complements Milton's description of a scented and perfumed woman sailing forth with the grandeur of a schooner. Lydgate emphasizes women's use of "fumygaciouns to rectefie the aiere" (2–6557) and other "hoote spices and oynements soote" (2–6540) that make them not only seem more pleasing, but also constitute the use of "crafft countirfete" (2–6541). Lydgate's ultimate description of Delilah points directly at the special insubstantiality of appearances:

> She lich a serpent darying vnder floures,
> Or lik a werm that wrotith on a tre,
> Or lich an addere off manyfold coloures,
> Riht fressh apperyng and fair vpon to see:
> For shrowdid was hir mutabilite
> With lowliheed[e] and a fair pretense
> Off trewe menyng vnder fals apparence.

> (1.6434–40)

In Milton the question of false or uncertain appearance figures immediately in the chorus's questions when Dalila enters: "But who is this, what thing of Sea or Land?" (710). William Kerrigan is right in reminding us of the specific nature of this ambiguity, since it suggests the amphibian serpent Dagon, which was part male, part fish, and associated by John Selden and Abraham Cowley with "Their Goddess Dagon . . . a kind of Mermaid-Deity."[21] When, after her appeal for his forgiveness, Samson shouts "Out, out Hyaena" (748), Milton reinforces Heywood's two mysogynist connections: serpents for dissimulation and the "Hyaena" for subtlety. Samson follows with: "these are thy wonted arts. / And arts of every woman false like thee" (748–49). His statement specifically does not arraign every woman—only those who have behaved as Dalila does toward a husband "Entangl'd with a pois'nous bosom snake" (763). Samson's ironically learning the "Adder's wisdom"(936)—turning a deaf ear—softens the imagery, although a misogynistic tone is detectable in his subsequent statement:

> God sent her to debase me,
> And aggravate my folly who committed

> To such a viper his most sacred trust
> Of secrecy, my safety, and my life.
>
> (999–1002)

Yet the lines are not misogynistic. Dalila is vastly too well-defined and individuated in her extraordinary speeches to be thought of as a type or as a mere representative of the sex. She is not the representation of women, as in Lydgate's version, or in Swetnam's. Rather she is Samson's wife, an individual who has betrayed her trust.

In *Samson Agonistes* it takes more than two hundred lines to move from her appearing to the chorus "with head declin'd / Like a fair flower surcharg'd with dew" (727–28) to the chorus's ultimate moment of recognition: "She's gone, a manifest Serpent by her sting / Discover'd in the end, till now conceal'd" (997–98). However, the imagery of the serpent—what Lydgate calls, in relation to women in general, "vndirnethe the double serpent" (2–6600)—was present in Milton's mind from the first if only because it had been so carefully associated with Delilah and women in the work of Boccaccio and later misogynists.[22] In addition, Milton may be punning on the word "Discover'd" in that he invokes our memory of its having been used to describe the intense drive women have to discover—"discure"— secrets because of their nature—as established by Boccaccio and Lydgate. What is discovered to the chorus is Dalila's true nature, heretofore cleverly concealed by image structures implying a false presentment.

Milton treats Dalila as responsible for her own fate, as one who wills her own actions independent of the misogynist's claims against her, even as his images align themselves with tradition. The misogynist's tradition naturally admits this much antagonism toward Delilah and more. Peter Abelard condemns not only Delilah, but all women when he declaims in his brief rescension, "O woman, always the greatest ruin of the strong! Woman, created only to destroy!"[23] Milton reinforces the tradition that expanded the role of Delilah in the retelling, while at the same time the tradition of misogyny offered much more opportunity than he took advantage of, especially during the scholastic period (eighth through twelfth centuries) for antifeminist expostulation. Most important for us, however, was Milton's emphasis on the story as a piece of domestic treachery. When Milton makes Dalila Samson's wife—which Chaucer and Lydgate avoid—he raises the stakes higher than had Boccaccio. Milton risks even more than his predecessors, with the exception of Swetnam, to the point that we find it difficult to think how he could have avoided misogyny in his treatment of Dalila.

Yet, his portrait virtually forces us to the conclusion that, while Dalila is both an individuated woman and also quintessentially female—as the tradition insists—her crime against Samson is not specifically a woman's crime. It is, instead, an act of betrayal painfully gendered by the circumstances of her being married to Samson. In other words, it is in the same league with Judas's act of betrayal. The allegorical tradition that F. M. Krouse identifies via St. Augustine establishes Samson as a type of Christ.[24] Milton uses that tradition, along with the portraits from Lydgate and Boccaccio, to create a new portrait that redeems Samson without necessarily redeeming his gender. And if he can do that, then at the same time Milton can condemn Dalila without condemning her gender.

Notes

I am indebted both to Professor Joseph Wittreich, who very generously sent me a chapter from his manuscript in progress (see n. 22) regarding Swetnam, and Professor Pamela Benson, who sent me a copy of *A Mouzell for Melastomus*.

1. Jim Swan, "Difference and Silence: John Milton and the Question of Gender," in *The (M)other Tongue: Essays in Feminist Psychoanalytic Interpretation*, ed. Shirley Nelson Garner, Claire Kahane, and Madelon Sprengnether (Ithaca: Cornell University Press, 1985), 162. Western literature is filled with intensely gendered subjects, such as those of Antony and Cleopatra, Romeo and Juliet, and those of the Bible, including Samson and Delilah. Swan's emphasis is on difference and differentiation.

2. See Laurie P. Morrow, "The 'Meet and Happy Conversation': Dalila's Role in *Samson Agonistes*," *Milton Quarterly* 17 (1983): 38–42. Morrow says, "Samson's awareness of the similarities and differences between his own and Dalila's sins and, moreover, between their responses to these sins, serves as his impetus to resume his position as the champion of God" (38).

3. John Milton, *Samson Agonistes*, in *John Milton: Complete Poems and Major Prose*, ed. Merritt Y. Hughes (New York: Odyssey, 1957). All references to Milton's poetry are to this edition and are cited parenthetically in the text.

4. Geoffrey Chaucer, "Monk's Tale," in *The Works of Geoffrey Chaucer*, 2d ed., ed. F. N. Robinson (Boston: Houghton Mifflin, 1957). All references to Chaucer's poetry are to this edition and are cited parenthetically in the text.

5. Judges 16.5.

6. Mieke Bal, *Lethal Love* (Bloomington: Indiana University Press, 1987), 57.

7. Ibid., 61.

8. Ibid., 43.

9. Apart from the women in *The Canterbury Tales*, Chaucer portrays women in several lights, negatively in "Against Women Unconstant," and positively in *The Legend of Fair Women*, a variant of *De Mulierum Illustrium*.

10. *Lydgate's Fall of Princes*, ed. Harry Bergen (1924; reprint, Cambridge: Harvard University Press, 1967). All references to Lydgate's poetry are to this edition and are cited parenthetically in the text.

11. Suzanne Woods, "How Free Are Milton's Women?" in *Milton and the Idea of Woman*, ed. Julia M. Walker (Urbana: University of Illinois Press, 1988), 19.

12. Ibid., 30.

13. Ibid.

14. Barbara Lewalski, *Writing Women in Jacobean England* (Cambridge: Harvard University Press, 1993), 156; see also 153–75.

15. P. 2 in the original text, Joseph Swetnam, *The Arraignment of Lewd, Idle, Froward, and Unconstant Women* (1615). My reference is to the critical edition of

F. W. van Heertum (Nijmegen: Cicero, 1989), and I use a double pagination: first the original edition, then the critical edition. Thus, this quotation is Swetnam, 2, 197.

16. Swetnam, 3, 197.

17. Ibid., 39, 234.

18. Philip J. Gallagher, *Milton, the Bible, and Misogyny*, ed. Eugene R. Cunnar and Gail L. Mortimer (Columbia: University of Missouri Press, 1990), 156. Unfortunately, Gallagher has very little to say about the misogynist tradition in relation to Dalila.

19. Swetnam, 41, 236.

20. See Coryl Crandall, *Swetnam the Woman-hater: The Controversy and the Play* (Lafayette: Purdue University Press, 1969), 130. In the quotation (5.2.280–81), Aurelia, queen of Sicily, is speaking.

21. William Kerrigan, *Prophetic Milton* (Charlottesville: University of Virginia Press, 1974), 202–3. Kerrigan cites Cowley's *Davideis* (1656) and Selden's *De Dis Syris* (1617).

22. This imagery is examined in detail by Joseph Wittreich in his manuscript chapter, "'Inspir'd with Contradiction': Mapping Gender Discourses in *Paradise Lost*." I am indebted to him for generously lending me his chapter. Wittreich makes the point that the only heirs of Mysogenus in Milton are his characters, "fallen Adam and, later, Samson and the Chorus." Milton stands independent of all of them when they condemn women.

23. G. Vecchi, *Pietro Abelardo*, I, "Planctus Israel super Samson," Testo Critico, Trascrizione Musicali (Instituto di filologia romanza della Università di Roma, Testi e Manuali, xxxv, Modena, 1951), lines 54–57. See David Lyle Jeffrey, ed., *A Dictionary of Biblical Tradition in English Literature* (Grand Rapids: William B. Eerdmans, 1992), 678.

24. F. M. Krouse, *Milton's Samson and the Christian Tradition* (Princeton: Princeton University Press, 1949), 119–33.

Milton's Dalila and Eve:
Filling in the Spaces in the Biblical Text

Stella P. Revard

Anyone familiar with the Bible knows that the biblical accounts of Delilah's seduction of Samson and the Serpent's seduction of Eve furnished Milton with only half the story for *Samson Agonistes* and *Paradise Lost*. Delilah in the Bible is the hired tool of the Philistines—neither a Philistine herself nor Samson's wife—a character in fact who disappears from the scriptural account after she has collected her money and delivered Samson to the barbers. It is Milton's contribution to the story to have her reappear and beg forgiveness, a scene in Milton's drama that would seem to have no warrant whatsoever in the Bible. Eve in the Bible is tempted by the Serpent and succumbs, giving the apple to her husband. Milton's Eve also succumbs, but before she meets the Serpent, she has a lengthy debate with her husband—again, something that seems Milton's invention.

At first Milton's interpolated scenes appear only marginally related to the biblical narratives. But on closer examination both Dalila's scene with Samson and Eve's with Adam are intimately linked to the biblical accounts that Milton used, in fact, are even suggested by and patterned on them. What Dalila says to Samson *later* is closely based on what she said to him *before* when she tempted him in Judges—a sequence of scenes that Milton alludes to in *Samson Agonistes* from several vantage points. Moreover, what Milton's Eve says or rather fails to say to the Serpent is closely related to what she has said to her husband earlier that morning. The scenes in the Bible where Delilah tempts Samson prepare us for the second tempting in *Samson Agonistes,* and the scene of Eve's morning's interview with her husband prepares us for Milton's biblically based account of the encounter with the Serpent. Knowing what the biblical Delilah said before or the biblical Eve later affects our view of Milton's dramatic confrontations in his drama and epic.

Milton disliked doing things in ones when he could do them in twos. In *Samson Agonistes* he gives Samson not one but two wives, carefully interrelating how he behaves with each. It is inevitable that Dalila, having tempted her husband and caused, so to speak, his fall, should appear on the scene a

second time to "tempt" him once again. In *Paradise Lost,* one week before
that fatal Friday when Eve offered the unfruitful apple to her husband, she
was offering innocent fruitful apples to Adam and the visiting angel. Similarly, Eve has a demonic nightmare one week and a heaven-sent dream
vision the next. Adam's wooing of Eve is balanced by Satan's seduction of
Sin. So it is perfect Miltonic strategy that Eve would have not one but two
dialogues on the day of the Fall—one with her husband arguing her ability
to withstand temptation, the other with the Serpent consenting to his arguments and succumbing to temptation. It is also logical that the two should
be related. We have dialogue and counter-dialogue, nonbiblical drama directly intersecting with biblical drama.

1

In *Samson Agonistes,* Dalila comes ostensibly to beg forgiveness and to
offer reparation. She initiates the encounter, has the first and last speech,
and so appears to be in the commanding position oratorically. In Delilah's
biblical encounter with Samson, she does control the situation, and her
attempt to seduce Samson and discover his secret is orchestrated in four
movements (Judges 16.4–21).[1]

Judges introduces us to Delilah (the woman in the valley of Sorek whom
Samson loves) in a brief scene with the Philistine lords, who come to ask
her to "entice" Samson and discover "wherein his great strength lieth" so
that they may prevail against him. They promise to give her "every one of
us eleven hundred pieces of silver" (Judges 16.5). Delilah immediately begins the verbal assault. Three times she asks Samson for his secret; three
times he lies to her, evades her, and breaks the chords with which she tries
to bind him; on the fourth attempt she learns Samson's secret, calls for a
man to shave off his hair, and delivers him to the Philistines, having already
collected the silver.

The orchestration of the Samson-Dalila scene in *Samson Agonistes* dupli-
cates the four-part structure of the biblical scene. Three times Dalila attempts to "bind" Samson [once more] with the "chords" of matrimony—
the chords being her three speeches in which she pleads for forgiveness and
offers her excuses—and three times, as in Judges, he "breaks" these
"cords." She first pleads weakness, female weakness:

> incident to all our sex,
> Curiosity, inquisitive, importune
> Of secrets, then with like infirmity
> To publish them, both common female faults.

(774–77)[2]

But then, she suggests, binding him with the first set of "chords," her weakness corresponds to his, for he should not have made those secrets "known / For importunity" and trusted in "woman's frailty" (778–79, 783). He shares the responsibility for what happened and therefore must make allowances:

> Let weakness then with weakness come to parle
> So near related, or the same of kind,
> Thine forgive mine; that men may censure thine
> The gentler.
>
> (785–88)

It is tempting for Samson to buy forgiveness for himself by forgiving the "repentant" betrayer. But these "green chords" are too weak to bind him; he counters, breaking them, that all weakness is wickedness and refuses to forgive wickedness either in himself or in her. Next she pleads patriotism (duty and religion), arguing that the princes, magistrates, and priests of the Philistines besieged and assaulted her, overcoming her with powerful arguments, enjoining virtue, truth, and duty. On the one hand, she is portraying herself as a private woman overcome by pleas for public good, yet on the other she is implying (as she will later directly claim) that her championship of the Philistine cause corresponded to Samson's support of the Israelite cause. What she is doing here, in effect, is attempting to undermine his special sense of vocation and religion by refusing to allow that she did anything more than to serve her people as he had his. Samson's response is an affirmation of his vocation and of his devotion to God, and an assertion that Dalila's "false" patriotism is as false as her gods. By reaffirming himself God's champion against the Philistines, he breaks for a second time the chords with which she tries to bind him.

In her first two tries in the Bible, Delilah had bound Samson with green withes and new ropes that prove useless; on the third try, she weaves his hair into a web or loom and pins him to it. The web or loom is a symbol for female sexuality—the effeminacy that Samson fears in himself and the weakness of his sexual submission to Delilah that makes her the master.[3] As she draws closer to learning the real secret about his hair, she tries to bind him with his hair to that feminine loom.

Dalila's third plea in *Samson Agonistes* is the most sexually explicit. From the first she has declared her love for him; now she urges him to become quite simply her love object, to let her care for him completely, substituting the satisfaction of his other senses for the sight that he has lost. The Bible tells us that Samson had his eyes put out by the Philistines, but of course, implicitly he was "blinded" first by Delilah; the all-consuming sensuality of his passion for her simply "blinded" his reason and his other senses.

Now Dalila's sensual plea urges him to submit once more to that psychological and sexual blindness. But the Samson of *Samson Agonistes* has learned his limitations; he not only refuses her offer, he refuses to come into physical contact with her, even to let her touch his hand. If she approaches, he threatens to tear her joint by joint, warning her of the rage that fierce remembrance would wake. Yet even as he issues that threat, he knows all too well that physical touch might waken remembrance of another sort, that this is an encounter that, even now, he dares not risk.[4] At this point Dalila comes the closest to binding Samson one more time.

Thus repulsed, Milton's Dalila appears to give up her attempt to persuade Samson—to win, to prevail, as she once had. But she is not without resources. And her fourth attempt to bind him—the fourth "chord" to the "tetrachordon"—does not even seem an attempt. She has entered into a different kind of contest. What she tries to establish is equal status with him. If she cannot prevail over him as the repentant wife, she will win equal place as the Philistine champion or as a Philistine Jael, the Kenite woman who saved the Israelites by practicing treachery and killing the warrior that her generals could not conquer (Judges 4.17–22). In sum, Dalila tries, having failed to get what she came for—Samson's submission to her a second time—to validate her previous conquest as a heroic deed and not a reprehensible betrayal. As she boasts of her future fame as the wife who chose service to country over that to "wedlock bands" (986), she herself unties the "chords" that bind her to Samson and attempts to ennoble her cause.

How successful is she? Here the account in Judges fills in a "space" in Dalila's arguments that she attempts to ignore and pass over. The Bible tells us quite simply that Delilah betrayed Samson for the money the Philistines offered. Milton's Dalila admits to every motive but this—weakness, gullibility, curiosity, jealousy, love, national pride, religious devotion—everything but that she did it for the money. Upgrading the biblical silver to gold, Milton has Samson repeatedly accuse Dalila of having taken the Philistines' gold. She forcefully repudiates the charge: "It was not gold, as to my charge thou lay'st" (849). But was it? After the biblical Delilah has learned Samson's secret, she calls the lords of the Philistines to her: "Then the Lords of the Philistines came up unto her, and brought money in their hand" (Judges 16.18). In replicating Delilah's temptation of Samson, in letting her multiple attempts to win his forgiveness closely resemble the repeated attempts in Judges to bring him down, but in having her deny the one motive the Bible assigns her, Milton makes us seriously reexamine the motives of this biblical temptress.

Milton has also filled a space in the biblical story, telling us what part Dalila plays after she delivers Samson to the Philistines and before Samson destroys the temple. In bringing Dalila on the scene a second time, Milton replays the temptation scene with a different ending—Samson "redeems" himself, he resists, turning away the woman who brought him down. At the same time, Milton permits her to argue her own case. The Bible's Delilah is a seductress who does what she is paid to do; the account in Judges does not explore her motives further. Milton gives us a much more complicated woman, makes her a wife, not just a betraying lover. Is Milton contradicting the biblical account or merely elaborating it? He has deliberately made Dalila a character who offers more than one explanation for her behavior, and he leaves it to his readers, moreover, to make up their minds, which, if any, to believe. Judging from the range of critical reception to Dalila—pro and con—the jury is still out.[5] Yet, at the same time, neither Milton nor Milton's Samson lets us forget the biblical "gold," using it, so to speak, to cut down Dalila's protestations of innocence by reminding her that she did indeed take payment for her deed. Samson never tires of taunting her:

> Weakness is thy excuse,
> And I believe it, weakness to resist
> Philistian gold.
>
> (829–31)

Such taunting shows us that Samson emerges from this second encounter unransomed, unbought by the treacherous gold that first undid him. His final words hurl at her once more the accusation that she accepted money in betraying him: "Cherish thy hast'n'd widowhood with the gold / Of Matrimonial treason: so farewell" (958–59). Whether or not "gold" was the ultimate motive for Dalila's betrayal, it is a decisive factor that strengthens Samson to resist her pleas.

2

The way of the Bible with Eve is different. She has one scene with the Serpent, a scene that the Serpent controls at all points. It is he who begins the biblical encounter by asking Eve about the tree: "Yea, hath God said, Ye shall not eat of every tree of the garden?" (Genesis 3.1). She responds by repeating the prohibition (as the Miltonic Eve also does). The Serpent rejoins by telling Eve that she will not die and that the fruit will confer wisdom: "For God doth know that in the day ye eat thereof, then your eyes shall be opened and ye shall be as gods, knowing good and evil" (Genesis 3.5). Eve eats and gives the fruit to Adam.

In *Paradise Lost* Milton elaborates the biblical account but does not change in any essential way the Serpent's line of argument and Eve's response. Milton's Serpent (like the biblical one) controls the encounter and never relinquishes that control. Eve follows his lead—hesitating only once and never seriously questioning or contesting what the Serpent says; she reacts to him, not he to her. Eve seems to be a pushover for the Serpent's arguments. Is this the same Eve we saw disputing with Adam the grounds of obedience and disobedience? The two scenes seem to contradict one another; in the one we have an active disputing participant, in the other a passive follower. Eve's scene with the Serpent—in energy, in format, in structure—is almost directly opposite to Eve's scene in the morning with Adam.

Neither the biblical Eve nor Milton's Eve initiates the scene with the Serpent. But the Eve of the morning colloquy initiates and to some degree controls the scene with her husband. Like Dalila, she has the first and the last word—though to different effect. Hers is the suggestion for separate gardening to which Adam must respond. He counters with a protective gesture—that the wife

> where danger or dishonor lurks,
> Safest and seemliest by her Husband stays,
> Who guards her, or with her the worst endures.
>
> (*Paradise Lost*, 9.267–69)

Eve's response here is instructive, for she reacts not just to what Adam says, but to the implication of his words, telling him first that she knows (as he knows she does) that they have a foe who designs to tempt them. But more important, she brings right out into the open the subtext of Adam's apparently gallant desire to protect her against the foe. Does he doubt her faith? For it is faith only, she reasons, that will be assailed; their Edenic condition will protect them against Satan's violence. This is now what Adam, given Eve's candid counter-reply, must admit, that is, that he fears Satan's fraud. Yet, even now, he does not directly admit it; there is one more evasion. Adam suggests that he is only trying to spare his wife the dishonor of Satan's attempting her virtue: "For hee who tempts, though in vain, at least asperses / The tempted with dishonor foul" (296–97). Only after does he add, far more to the point, that Satan's malice and false guile should not be lightly contemned: "Subtle he needs must be, who could seduce / Angels" (307–8). Then, attempting to salve Eve's wounded self-esteem, he tells her that he himself feels more virtuously inclined in her presence—a statement that given his own admissions to Raphael and his behavior later that afternoon we must seriously call into question.

It is a credit to Eve's debating powers that she brushes aside both Adam's compliments and the verbiage of his reply and goes straight to the issue: whether or not God's creature (male or female) is "endu'd / Single with like defense, wherever met" (9.324–25)? Nor does she leave unchallenged Adam's assertion that the mere act of tempting dishonors the tempted;

rather, she employs an argument Milton had used in *Areopagitica* to suggest that a virtue that is untried is hardly a virtue at all. Critics have generally been uneasy with Eve's use of *Areopagitica*'s argument. Alastair Fowler, for example, asserts that Milton need not approve Eve's argument, since it appears here in an unfallen context and supports in Eve a "dangerous individualism."[6]

Yet the point is that Eve's passionate defense of the liberty of the individual finally provokes Adam to a fully comprehensive answer to the questions she has raised. She does not make it a gender issue as she does later (9.1153). Some readers may believe, however, that even here gender is implicitly involved. (The issue is not whether the husband may separate from the wife and face trial alone, but vice versa.) Ultimately Adam is forced to agree with Eve that Man (male or female) is neither deficient nor imperfect, if left to face trial alone. Yet, he also usefully adds that the danger lies within (although within the individual's power), since against one's will the individual can receive no harm.

> But God left free the Will, for what obeys
> Reason, is free, and Reason he made right,
> But bid her well beware, and still erect,
> Lest by some fair appearing good surpris'd
> She dictate false, and misinform the Will
> To do what God expressly hath forbid.
>
> (9.351–56)

Because reason in Latin is the feminine noun *ratio*, the pronouns that govern the passage are feminine, contrasting with the male pronoun "he" in line 352 that refers to the creator God who gave her ("reason") to man and woman alike. The entire scene of morning colloquy illustrates for us an Eve who is capable of using that feminine noun "reason" to good effect, responding not just to what Adam says, but to the implications that lie hidden beneath the surface. But it is a reason that must be aware and wary— that must beware of the "fair appearing good." These are the qualities that Eve's reason possesses during the morning colloquy. Are they the ones she carries into her interview with the Serpent?

The morning colloquy gives us, like the colloquy in Heaven of book 3, two friendly debaters who appear to take opposite sides of an issue. As the Son in book 3 challenges God's position, Eve challenges Adam's. Both engage in give-and-take, modifying their original stances. God consents that the Son can take Man's place, that Man need not die. Adam consents that Eve, thus forewarned, may go, affirming her freedom to make this choice and, if it comes to it, to face temptation alone. The divine pair and the human pair agree to individual autonomy.

Given the manner in which Eve has stood up to Adam and questioned his arguments, it is amazing that she does not challenge the Serpent's assertions more forcefully. But whereas she is the initiator of the morning colloquy, she is the respondent at noon. Moreover, she does not respond so much to what the Serpent says, but to the fact that he says it in human speech. Instead of fixing her attention and refuting, right at the outset, the Serpent's opening proposition that she should be a "Goddess among Gods" (9.547), served by angels—that her beauty is neglected in being seen by one man only—Eve gives over control of the dialogue by asking, "How cam'st thou speakable of mute?" (563). The narrator tells us, moreover, that even as Eve listens, his "glozing" words make their way into her heart. So attentive earlier to the threat of an Eden diminished by the loss of freedom, Eve, suspending her active reasoning powers, listens to a tale of a tree with magic powers to grant speech and reason, hardly pausing to consider how this story much rearranges the benevolent, God-ordered Eden she has up to now known. But Milton has given us a clue when he describes Eve as "unwary" (614), as having left her reason unguarded. At this point Eve offers her sole skeptical response: "Serpent, thy overpraising leaves in doubt / The virtue of that Fruit, in thee first prov'd" (615–16). "Overpraising," I believe, refers not to the Serpent's overpraising of Eve, but to his overpraising of the fruit itself. Yet, here, once again, Eve fails to follow up, as she had in her earlier dialogue. She is skeptical only about the tree, not about the Serpent who has praised it. Instead of questioning him more rigorously, she asks him the location of the tree. Does Eve—the Eve we saw conversing with Adam—really have to ask "which tree?" Had she been attentive to the hints in the Serpent's story, she would surely have known "which tree" (as perhaps she does) and declined to accompany him there. But the moment she says, "Lead then" (631), she puts herself further in his power, abdicating the rule of reason for the rule of the Serpent. The very process of being led to the tree is the process of being led astray—of being, as Milton tells us, "misled."

Eve's reaction on arriving at the tree is disappointment; the tree is "Fruitless" (9.648) to her. So she tells the Serpent and twice repeats God's command, on the one hand demonstrating that she knows exactly what the prohibition is, yet on the other adding not one word in support of the obedience it enjoins. The mere repetition of the command is the weakest line of defense. Where are the arguments in support of "firm Faith and Love" (286) that only hours before she spoke of? Where is her wariness of the fraud that might shake or seduce that "Faith and Love"? Finding no resistance, the Serpent goes on to mount a full-scale temptation, undermining point by point the words of the command, denying that Eve will die and insisting that she will gain knowledge from the fruit and she and Adam will be as gods.

Though elaborating considerably, Milton does not alter the thrust of the

Serpent's argument in Genesis nor Eve's response there. Like the biblical Eve, Milton's Eve readily assents to the Serpent's words and accepts the tree as "good for food . . . pleasant to the eyes, and a tree to be desired to make one wise" (Genesis 3.6). Then, what is the difference between the Bible's and Milton's account? The Bible does not assure us that Eve was capable of resisting the Serpent's temptation; Milton does. But, at the same time we must ask, what has Milton gained in showing us an Eve capable of reasonable dissent, if she does not in the final test exercise that capability?

Most discussions of Eve's fall focus on her motives in taking the apple and on her failure to respond effectively to the Serpent's temptings. Few insist that she has the ability—even as the Serpent misleads her—to resist, to refuse, to stand. Yet we can point to places in the temptation scene where we have every right to require Eve to make a stronger reply to the Serpent. She could, for instance, have refused to accept the Serpent's description of God as a "Threat'ner" (9.687). (Had God not been consistently a benevolent Father, Creator, and benefactor—no "Threat'ner"?) She could also have questioned the Serpent's argument that breaking God's sole command would be only a petty trespass, praised rather than punished by God. She herself has described the command as the "Sole Daughter of [God's] voice"—their sole Law, apart from which they live a "Law to [themselves]" (653–54). She could have challenged him when he says God is forbidding something "good" for them. (Does a good God forbid a "good"? Does he not rather forbid an "evil"?) These are all objections that Eve's experience and reason make her capable of raising, if her faith and love hold firm. We have witnessed other Miltonic characters in the throes of temptation mount arguments against similar lies—the Lady in *Comus*, Abdiel in book 5 in *Paradise Lost*, Jesus in *Paradise Regained*. Milton's Lady, having at first been taken in by Comus's deceit, refuses his "treasonous offer" (702) on the grounds that only

> good men can give good things,
> And that which is not good, is not delicious
> To a well-govern'd and wise appetite.
>
> (*Comus*, 703–5)

Abdiel challenges Satan, "Shalt thou give Law to God?" (*Paradise Lost*, 5.822) and defends God as provident "of our good and of our dignity . . . how far from thought / To make us less" (828–30). Jesus (ever wary) rebukes a disguised Satan for suggesting distrust of God; he later tells Satan that he will eat, only as he likes the giver (*Paradise Regained*, 2.321–22). Is Eve capable of mounting similar arguments to counter the Serpent's claims about the fruit, his lies about God, and his authority in urging her to eat? Milton has shown us that she is.

Critics have frequently described the separation scene as Eve's mini-fall or pre-fall, as proof that she was doomed from the moment she parted from her husband. Both Adam and Eve fall, but few critics question Adam's ability to have stood against Satan without secondary help, such as the presence and assistance of his wife might have afforded. Yet there is a long tradition that Eve was able to stand only with Adam's help, that, indeed, his presence was necessary to prop her and to make her a fitting contestant and adversary to Satan. Many twentieth-century critics assent to this view and deplore Eve's fatal mistake in separating from her husband.[7] In some respects the narrator's voice also seems to lend support to this view, as he regrets Eve's parting from Adam and laments her fatal weakness apart from her husband: "fairest unsupported Flow'r, / From her best prop so far" (432–33). Yet, when we examine Eve's responses during the morning colloquy with Adam, we need not fear her weakness nor her inability to contest with an opposite. Rather than proving her fatal disposition to fall, her stance during this scene illustrates exactly the opposite, that is, it is proof of her ability to succeed. Milton's whole epic stands on the proposition that Man (female and male human beings) is able to stand, though free to fall. Therefore, it is absolutely necessary for Milton to demonstrate (before Eve meets the Serpent) that Eve is a capable, independent, freely thinking individual, who can counter whatever argument the Serpent offers. Eve is not yet (in a sense) the New Woman, but as she debates with her husband and goes forth to garden alone, she takes the first step toward that status. Her tragedy—and it is a tragedy—is that the first step ends in defeat.

Satan's is an easy victory, but it need not have been. The Bible tells us only that Eve took the fruit at the Serpent's suggestion, never considering whether she could have said no to him. Milton resists giving us an Eve who yields to Satan because she is intellectually and morally unable to reply to him. By adding a scene of dialogue with Adam on the very day that Eve meets the Serpent, Milton fills in the space in the Genesis text, demonstrating that Eve could have used her reason (as she had earlier) to engage in fruitful debate and to carry her own arguments against the Serpent by applying the same skills she had used in debate with her husband. He is telling us that the story could have had a different ending. Eve is not a weak woman bested by a superior adversary, but a capable woman who fails to carry through and defend the reason, faith, and love that she has only newly won the freedom to defend. Both Miltonic Man *and* Miltonic Woman can stand alone. This is perhaps Milton's most important addition to the Genesis text.

Notes

1. All biblical references are to the King James Version and are cited parenthetically in the text.

2. John Milton, *Samson Agonistes*, in *John Milton: Complete Poems and Major Prose*, ed. Merritt Y. Hughes (New York: Odyssey, 1957). All references to Milton's poetry are to this edition and are cited parenthetically in the text.

3. See Jackie DiSalvo, "Intestine Thorn: Samson's Struggle with the Woman Within," in *Milton and the Idea of Woman*, ed. Julia M. Walker (Urbana: University of Illinois Press, 1988), 211–29.

4. Some critics take Samson's threat seriously. Michael Lieb comments that Samson is capable of carrying out such a *sparagmos* against his wife *(Milton and the Culture of Violence* [Ithaca: Cornell University Press, 1994], 252–53).

5. See Stella Revard, "Dalila as Euripidean Heroine," *Papers on Language and Literature* 23 (1987), 291–302. Among other articles that consider Dalila's motivation, see the following: Mary Ann Nevins Radzinowicz, "Eve and Dalila: Renovation and the Hardening of the Heart," in *Reason and Imagination: Studies in the History of Ideas, 1600–1800*, ed. J. A. Mazzeo (New York: Columbia University Press, 1962), 155–81; William Empson, *Milton's God*, rev. ed. (London: Chatto and Windus, 1965); Thomas Kranidas, "Dalila's Role in *Samson Agonistes*," *SEL* 6 (1966), 125–37; Virginia Mollenkott, "Relativism in *Samson Agonistes*," *Studies in Philology* 67 (1970): 89–102; Mary Weinkauf, "Dalila: The Worst of All Possible Wives," *SEL* 18 (1973): 135–47; John Guillory, "Dalila's House: *Samson Agonistes* and the Sexual Division of Labor," in *Rewriting the Renaissance: The Discourses of Sexual Difference in Early Modern Europe*, ed. Margaret W. Ferguson, Maureen Quilligan, and Nancy J. Vickers (Chicago: University of Chicago Press, 1986), 106–22; Joseph Wittreich, *Feminist Milton* (Ithaca: Cornell University Press, 1987); John Ulreich, "'Incident to All Our Sex': The Tragedy of Dalila," in *Milton and the Idea of Woman*, ed. Julia M. Walker (Urbana: University of Illinois Press, 1988), 185–210.

6. Alastair Fowler, ed., *Paradise Lost* (London: Longman, 1971), 456 n.

7. See particularly Fredson Bowers, "Adam, Eve, and the Fall in *Paradise Lost*," *PMLA* 84 (1969): 265; also see Dennis H. Burden, *The Logical Epic* (Cambridge: Harvard University Press, 1967); A. J. A. Waldock, *"Paradise Lost" and Its Critics* (Cambridge: Cambridge University Press, 1947). For articles responding to Bowers, see Stella P. Revard, "Eve and the Doctrine of Responsibility in *Paradise Lost*," *PMLA* 88 (1973): 69–74; John C. Ulreich, "'Sufficient to Have Stood': Adam's Responsibility in Book IX," *Milton Quarterly* 3 (1971): 38–42; Diane Kelsey McColley, "Free Will and Obedience in the Separation Scene of *Paradise Lost*," *SEL* 12 (1972): 103–20. Further discussions of the separation scene include Marilyn R. Farwell, "Eve, the Separation Scene, and the Renaissance Idea of Androgyny," *Milton Studies* 16 (1982): 3–20; Diana Treviño Benet, "Abdiel and the Son in the Separation Scene," *Milton Studies* 18 (1983): 129–43; Joan S. Bennett, "'Go': Milton's Antinomianism and the Separation Scene in *Paradise Lost*, Book 9," *PMLA* 98 (1983): 388–404, reworked in *Reviving Liberty: Radical Christian Humanism in Milton's Great Poems* (Cambridge: Harvard University Press, 1989). Also see Diane McColley's latest comments on the separation scene in *A Gust for Paradise: Milton's Eden and the Visual Arts* (Urbana: University of Illinois Press, 1993), 162–74.

Contributors

JOAN S. BENNETT coordinates the Undergraduate Research Program at the University of Delaware. She is the author of *Reviving Liberty: Radical Christian Humanism in Milton's Great Poems.*

DAVID BOOCKER, Associate Professor of English at Tennessee Technological University, has published essays in *Explorations in Renaissance Culture, Milton Quarterly,* and *Spokesperson Milton: Voices in Contemporary Criticism.* He is currently working on an annotated bibliography, "Milton in American Periodicals: 1800–1850."

W. GARDNER CAMPBELL is an Assistant Professor of English at Mary Washington College. He has been a reviewer for *Perspectives in Religious Studies* and has presented papers at conferences on John Milton and on film and literature. His works in progress include an essay on Milton and the music in "L'Allegro" and "Il Penseroso" and a book entitled *Milton and the "Provoking Object."*

JAY RUSSELL CURLIN, who received his doctorate at the University of Michigan, is an Assistant Professor of English at the University of Central Arkansas and is book-review editor of *Publications of the Arkansas Philological Association.* His recent publications in this journal include "Chaos in the Convent's Narrow Room: Milton and the Sonnet" and "Casual Discourse Lost: The Separation of Adam and Eve."

CHARLES W. DURHAM, Professor of English at Middle Tennessee State University, is codirector of the biennial Conference on John Milton and coeditor of *Spokesperson Milton: Voices in Contemporary Criticism.*

ROBERT THOMAS FALLON is the author of *Captain or Colonel: The Soldier in Milton's Life and Art* and *Milton in Government.* His essay in this volume is condensed from passages in *Divided Empire: Milton's Political Imagery,* a study of the influence of the poet's political experience on his great works, forthcoming from the Pennsylvania State University Press.

JANNA THACHER FARRIS is a candidate for the Master of Arts degree at Middle Tennessee State University, where she is finishing a thesis on the works of Rebecca Harding Davis. She also teaches English at Brentwood High School in Brentwood, Tennessee.

BLAKE GREENWAY, an Instructor of English at the University of Georgia, is completing his doctorate there. His dissertation is entitled *John Milton and the Politics of Warfare.*

WILLIAM B. HUNTER, now retired from teaching, was General Editor of *A Milton Encyclopedia* and for many years Secretary of the Milton Society of America.

STEVEN JABLONSKI received his doctorate from Princeton University, where he is now a Lecturer in English. He has published an essay in *Spokesperson Milton: Voices in Contemporary Criticism* and is working on a book on Milton's providentialism in relation to his changing political and theological views.

LEE A. JACOBUS teaches at the University of Connecticut. Among his books are *Sudden Apprehension: Aspects of Knowledge in "Paradise Lost," John Cleveland,* and *Shakespeare and the Dialectic of Certainty.* His research interests are in Renaissance English, modern Irish Literature, and rhetoric.

PETER M. McCLUSKEY, a doctoral candidate at the University of Arkansas, is working on a dissertation that explores the representation of Flemish immigrants in early modern drama. He has published an article on Hawthorne in *Publications of the Arkansas Philological Association* and one on Milton in *Spokesperson Milton: Voices in Contemporary Criticism.*

KRISTIN PRUITT McCOLGAN is a Professor of English at Christian Brothers University. She codirects the biennial Conference on John Milton, has published several articles on Milton, and is coeditor of *Spokesperson Milton: Voices in Contemporary Criticism.*

CATHERINE GIMELLI MARTIN is Associate Professor of English at the University of Memphis, where she specializes in Milton, seventeenth-century lyric, and literary theory. Her most recent work deals with the influence of the New Science upon seventeenth-century literature. In this field, an article entitled "'Boundless the Deep': Milton, Pascal, and the Theology of Relative Space" recently appeared in *ELH*. She is also working on a book-length study of the allegorical agents of *Paradise Lost.*

ALICE M. MATHEWS is a Lecturer at the University of North Texas and editor of *CCTE Studies,* the journal of the Conference of College Teachers of English. She has published several articles on *Paradise Lost* and on Arthur Clough. Her current research is in technical writing.

ANNA K. NARDO, Professor of English at Louisiana State University, is the author of *Milton's Sonnets and the Ideal of Community* and *The Ludic Self in Seventeenth-Century English Literature*.

MARY F. NORTON, Assistant Professor of English at Western Carolina University, has published on Milton in *Milton Quarterly* and *Milton Studies* and on Edward, Lord Herbert of Cherbury, in *Rhetorical Designs*.

HOPE A. PARISI is Assistant Professor of English at Kingsborough Community College, City University of New York. She has published an essay in *Spokesperson Milton: Voices in Contemporary Criticism* and is working on a book on Milton's women.

STELLA P. REVARD is a professor at Southern Illinois University at Edwardsville, where she teaches English and ancient Greek. Her book, *The War in Heaven*, won the Hanford award in 1981. She is currently completing a book on Milton's 1645 *Poems* and the tradition of Continental Renaissance poetry.

LOUIS SCHWARTZ, Assistant Professor of English Literature at the University of Richmond, is the author of several essays on English Renaissance poetry, including "'Spot of Childbed Taint': Seventeenth-Century Obstetrics in Milton's Sonnet 23 and *Paradise Lost* 8.462–78." He is working on a book-length study of literary representations of catastrophic childbirth in sixteenth- and seventeenth-century England.

JOSEPH WITTREICH is Executive Officer and Distinguished Professor of English at The Graduate School and University Center of the City University of New York and, currently, is bringing to completion a book entitled *Wars of Truth: Milton and the New Criticism*.

Index